Volume 2, Number 3, Autumn 1981

Inventing Psychology's Past: E.G. Boring's Historiography in Relation to the Psychology of His Time. *Barry N. Kelly, University of Winnipeg.*

The Psychodynamics of the Navajo Coyoteway Ceremonial. *Daniel Merkur, York University.*

Hemispheric Asymmetry as Indexed by Differences in Direction of Initial Conjugate Lateral Eye-Movements (CLEMs) in Response to Verbal, Spatial, and Emotional Tasks. *Kenneth Hugdahl and Horst E. Carlgren, University of Uppsala.*

Approaches to Consciousness in North American Academic Psychology. *John Osborne, University of Alberta.*

Memory and Literary Structures. *Eugene F. Timpe, Southern Illinois University, Carbondale.*

Identity Status in Politically Active Pro and Anti ERA Women. *Sandra Prince-Embury, Pennsylvania State University, and Iva E. Deutchman, University of Pennsylvania.*

Role Playing and Personality Changes in House-Tree-Persons Drawings. *Gertrude R. Schmeidler, City College of the City of New York.*

The Reality of Operationism: A Rejoinder. *Howard H. Kendler, University of California, Santa Barbara.*

Operationism Still Isn't Real: A Temporary Reply to Kendler. *Thomas H. Leahey, Virginia Commonwealth University.*

Volume 2, Number 4, Winter 1981

Black Stereotypes of Other Ethnic Groups. *Linda Foley and Peter L. Kranz, University of North Florida.*

Psychology's Progress and the Psychologist's Personal Experience. *Elaine N. Aron and Arthur Aron, Maharishi International University.*

An Epistemological Approach to Psychiatry: On the Psychology/Psychopathology of Knowledge. *Olga Beattie Emery and Mihaly Csikszentmihalyi, The University of Chicago.*

Is Field Work Scientific? *Linn Mo, The University of Trondheim.*

The Rise, Fall and Resurrection of the Study of Personality. *Silvan Tomkins, Emeritus Professor of Psychology, Rutgers University.*

Ego and IQ: What Can We Learn From the Frontal Lobes? *Pauline Young-Eisendrath, Bryn Mawr College.*

Volume 3, Number 1, Winter 1982

Cognitive Therapies: A Comparison of Phenomenological and Mediational Models and their Origins. *Howard Goldstein, Case Western Reserve University.*

After Oedipus: Laius, Medea, and Other Parental Myths. *Nancy Datan, West Virginia University.*

The Myth and Realities of Genital Herpes. *Stanley M. Bierman, University of California at Los Angeles.*

Models in Natural and Social Sciences. *Manfred J. Holler, University of Munich.*

Reconstructing Accounts of Psychology's Past. *Bronwen Hyman, University of Toronto.*

From Coprolalia to Glossolalia: Structural Similarities Between Gilles de la Tourette Syndrome and Speaking in Tongues. *Sheila A. Womack, University City Science Center, Philadelphia.*

Technical Note: Earthworm Behavior in a Modified Running Wheel. *Robert W. Marian and Charles I. Abramson, Boston University.*

Volume 3, Number 2, Spring 1982

Quantitative and Qualitative Aspects of Experienced Freedom. *Malcolm R. Westcott, York University.*

The Story as the Engram; Is It Fundamental To Thinking? *Renée Fuller, Ball-Stick-Bird Publications.*

What Does the Mind's Eye Look At? *John Heil, University of California at Berkeley.*

A Note on the Mythological Character of Categorization Research in Psychology. *Robert Epstein, Harvard University.*

Technical Note: An Olfactory Shuttle Box and Runway for Insects. *Charles I. Abramson, Josef Miler, and Dan W. Mann, Boston University.*

Volume 3, Number 3, Summer 1982

Foreword. *Arthur Efron, SUNY at Buffalo.*
Metaphor in Philosophy (Introduction). *Stephen C. Pepper.* †
Pepper and Recent Metaphilosophy. *Andrew J. Reck, Tulane University.*
What Pepperian Response to Rorty is Possible? *Peter H. Hare, SUNY at Buffalo.*
The Social Basis of Root Metaphor: An Application to *Apocalypse Now* and *The Heart of Darkness*. *Bill J. Harrell, SUNY College of Technology.*
Pepper's Philosophical Approach to Metaphor: The Literal and the Metaphorical. *Earl R. MacCormac, Davidson College.*
Basic Metaphors and the Emergence of Root Metaphors. *Antonio S. Cua, The Catholic University of America.*
The Psychology of David Hartley and the Root Metaphor of Mechanism: A Study in the History of Psychology. *Joan Walls, Appalachian State University.*
Paradigms, Puzzles and Root Metaphors: Georg Christoph Lichtenberg and the Exact Sciences. *Gordon Patterson, Florida Institute of Technology.*
The Concept of Puzzle: Unrecognized Root Metaphor in Analytical Aesthetics. *Arthur Efron, SUNY at Buffalo.*
'Radical Historicity' and Common Sense: On the Poetics of Human Nature. *David B. Downing, Eastern Illinois University.*

Volume 3, Number 4, Autumn 1982

Kenneth Burke's Systemless System: Using Pepper to Pigeonhole an Elusive Thinker. *Richard Y. Duerden, Brigham Young University.*
Notes on Experience and Teaching of Film. *Barry K. Grant, Brock University.*
Root Metaphor and Interdisciplinary Curriculum: Designs for Teaching Literature in Secondary Schools. *James Quina, Wayne State University.*
World Hypotheses and their Relevance to Curriculum. *Brent Kilbourn, The Ontario Institute for Studies in Education.*
Teaching: A Study in Evidence. *Arthur N. Geddis, East York Collegiate Institute.*
Toward Root Metaphor: Pepper's Writings in the *University of California Publications in Philosophy. Elmer H. Duncan, Baylor University.*
Comment on Duncan's Paper: Further Reflections on the Intellectual Biography of Stephen Pepper. *Joan Boyle, Dowling College.*
Construing the Knowledge Situation: Stephen Pepper and a Deweyan Approach to Literary Experience and Inquiry. *Brian G. Caraher, Indiana University.*
Arabella, Jude, or the Pig? Selectivism and a New Definition of Aesthetic Quality. *John Herold, Mohawk Valley Community College.*
Mimesis, Scandal, and the End of History in Mondrian's Aesthetics. *Terrell M. Butler, Brigham Young University.*
The New Faustian Music: Its Mechanistic, Organic, Contextual, and Formist Aspects. *David B. Richardson, Edinboro State College.*

Volume 4, Number 1, Winter 1983

Hypothetical Constructs, Circular Reasoning, and Criteria. *Austen Clark, University of Tulsa.*
Concepts of Consciousness. *Thomas Natsoulas, University of California, Davis.*
Towards a Reinterpretation of Consciousness: A Study in Humanistic Psychological Theory in the Perspective of Oriental Mystic Thought. *Moazziz Ali Beg, Muslim University.*
The Relativity of Psychological Phenomena. *Douglas M. Snyder, The Professional School.*
Operationism and Ideology: Reply to Kendler. *Thomas H. Leahey, Virginia Commonwealth University.*
Operationism: A Recipe for Reducing Confusion and Ambiguity. *Howard H. Kendler, University of California, Santa Barbara.*
Operationism and the Source of Meaning in Bridging the Theory/Method Bifurcation. *Joseph F. Rychlak, Purdue University.*

Volume 4, Number 2, Spring 1983

Deconstructing Psychology's Subject. *Edward E. Sampson, The Wright Institute.*
Heuristic Model of Synthetic Behavior: Rationale, Validation, and Implications. *Sandra L. Tunis and Ralph L. Rosnow, Temple University.*

The Poverty of Paradigmaticism: A Symptom of the Crisis in Sociological Explanation. *Gerard A. Postiglione, University of Hong Kong, and Joseph A. Scimecca, George Mason University.*

Social Change Versus Perceived Villainy. *Albert Lauterbach, Sarah Lawrence College.*

Left and Right in Personality and Ideology: An Attempt at Clarification. *William F. Stone, University of Maine.*

Benefic Autonomy: Thomas More as Exemplar. *Steven E. Salmony, The John Umstead Hospital, and Richard Smoke, Peace and Common Security.*

Toward a Science of Experience. *A. Kukla, University of Toronto.*

Retrospective Phenomenological Assessment: Mapping Consciousness in Reference to Specific Stimulus Conditions. *Ronald J. Pekala, Coatesville V.A. Medical Center, and Cathrine F. Wenger, City College of Detroit.*

Toward Pepitone's Vision of a Normative Social Psychology: What is a Social Norm? *Leigh S. Shaffer, West Chester State College.*

Volume 4, Number 3, Summer 1983

Von Osten's Horse, Hamlet's Question, and the Mechanistic View of Causality: Implications for a Post-Crisis Social Psychology. *Ralph L. Rosnow, Temple University.*

Functionalism and the Definition of Theoretical Terms. *Austen Clark, University of Tulsa.*

The Theory of "Formative Causation" and its Implications for Archetypes, Parallel Inventions, and the "Hundredth Monkey Phenomenon." *Carolin S. Keutzer, University of Oregon.*

Synthesizing the Everyday World. *Andrew R. Fuller, The College of Staten Island, C.U.N.Y.*

On the Nature of Relationships Involving the Observer and the Observed Phenomenon in Psychology and Physics. *Douglas M. Snyder, The Professional School.*

Homeopathy and Psychiatry. *Daphna Slonim, UCLA-Sepulveda, V.A. Medical Center, and Kerrin White, McLean Hospital.*

Volume 4, Number 4, Autumn 1983

The Opening of the Black Box: Is Psychology Prepared? *Uriel G. Foa and David L. Margules, Temple University.*

The Experience of a Conscious Self. *Thomas Natsoulas, University of California, Davis.*

Causal Attributions: Phenomenological and Dialectical Aspects. *Robert E. Lana and Marianthi Georgoudi, Temple University.*

The Implications of Langer's Philosophy of Mind for a Science of Psychology. *Joseph R. Royce, University of Alberta.*

General Contextualism, Ecological Science and Cognitive Research. *Robert R. Hoffman, Adelphi University, and James M. Nead, University of Minnesota.*

Volume 5, Number 1, Winter 1984

Desires Don't Cause Actions. *J. Michael Russell, California State University, Fullerton.*

Natural Science and Human Science Approaches to the Study of Human Freedom. *Malcolm R. Westcott, York University.*

Empirical Structures of Mind: Cognition, Linguistics, and Transformation. *Robert Haskell, University of New England.*

The Pleasures of Thought: A Theory of Cognitive Hedonics. *Colin Martindale, University of Maine, Orono.*

Lucid Dreaming: A Review and Experiential Study of Waking Intrusions during Stage REM Sleep. *Edward Covello, Pacific-Sierra Research Corporation.*

A Critical Look at Castaneda's Critics. *Anton F. Kootte, University of North Florida.*

Volume 5, Number 2, Spring 1984

The Principle of Parsimony and Some Applications in Psychology. *Robert Epstein, Northeastern University and Cambridge Center for Behavioral Studies.*

Affection as a Cognitive Judgmental Process: A Theoretical Assumption Put to Test Through Brain-Lateralization Methodology. *Joseph F. Rychlak, Loyola University of Chicago, and Brent D. Slife, University of Santa Clara.*

A Psycho-Neuro-Endocrine Framework for Depression: A Clinically Eclectic Approach. *Elliot M. Frohman, University of California at San Diego and The Winfield Foundation.*

A Biofunctional Model of Distributed Mental Content, Mental Structures, Awareness, and Attention. *Asghar Iran-Nejad and Andrew Ortony, University of Illinois at Urbana-Champaign.*

The Double Bind and Koan Zen. *Patrick Jichaku, George Y. Fujita, and S.I. Shapiro, University of Hawaii.*

Occultism is not Science: A Reply to Kootte. *Richard de Mille, Santa Barbara, California.*

Volume 5, Number 3, Summer 1984

The Classification of Psychology among the Sciences from Francis Bacon to Boniface Kedrov. *Claude M.J. Braun, University of Quebec at Montreal, and Jacinthe M.C. Baribeau, Concordia University, Montreal.*

What is a Perceptual Mistake? *Aaron Ben-Zeev, University of Haifa.*

Affect: A Functional Perspective. *Asghar Iran-Nejad, Gerald L. Clore, and Richard J. Vondruska, University of Illinois at Urbana-Champaign.*

The Subjective Organization of Personal Consciousness: A Concept of Conscious Personality. *Thomas Natsoulas, University of California, Davis.*

The Effects of Sensation Seeking and Misattribution of Arousal on Dyadic Interactions Between Similar or Dissimilar Strangers. *Sarah Williams and Richard M. Ryckman, University of Maine at Orono.*

Fatalism as an Animistic Attribution Process. *Leigh S. Shaffer, West Chester University.*

Volume 5, Number 4, Autumn 1984

Logical Learning Theory: Kuhnian Anomaly or Medievalism Revisited? *Joseph F. Rychlak, Loyola University of Chicago.*

Mental Activity and Physical Reality. *Douglas M. Snyder, Berkeley, California.*

Unity and Multiplicity in Hypnosis, Commissurotomy, and Multiple Personality Disorder. *David G. Benner, Wheaton College, and C. Stephen Evans, St. Olaf College.*

A Comparison of Three Ways of Knowing: Categorical, Structural, and Affirmative. *Viki McCabe, University of California, Los Angeles.*

Two Alternative Epistemological Frameworks in Psychology: The Typological and Variational Modes of Thinking. *Jaan Valsiner, University of North Carolina at Chapel Hill.*

Background and Change in B.F. Skinner's Metatheory From 1930 to 1938. *S.R. Coleman, Cleveland State University.*

A Critical Look at "A Critical Look": Castaneda Recrudescent. *Jordan Paper, York University.*

Logic is not Occultism. *Anton F. Kootte, University of North Florida.*

Circulation Department
THE JOURNAL OF MIND AND BEHAVIOR
P.O. Box 522, Village Station
New York City, N.Y. 10014

	Students*	Individuals	Institutions
1 year	☐ $20.00	☐ $25.00	☐ $ 45.00
2 years	☐ $35.00	☐ $45.00	☐ $ 85.00
3 years	☐ $45.00	☐ $65.00	☐ $120.00

Name _____

Street _____

City and State _____

Country _____

Please enclose prepayment or purchase order. We accept checks drawn on US accounts only. (Exception: checks drawn on Canadian banks in US-Dollars, add $3.50 service charge.)   *with photocopy of student I.D.

REVIEW COPY

THE SEXUAL BODY: AN INTERDISCIPLINARY PERSPECTIVE.
BY ARTHUR EFRON, PH.D., SUNY-BUFFALO.
1985, 328 PAGES, $15.00 (PAPER). PUBLISHED BY
THE INSTITUTE OF MIND AND BEHAVIOR, INC., PO
BOX 522, VILLAGE STATION, NYC, NY 10014-0522
TEL: (718) 783-1471. PLEASE SEND US TWO COPIES
OF YOUR PUBLISHED REVIEW.

The Journal of Mind and Behavior

an interdisciplinary journal
Vol. 6 No. 1 Winter 1985
Vol. 6 No. 2 Spring 1985

Special Issue
The Sexual Body: An
Interdisciplinary Perspective
Arthur Efron, SUNY-Buffalo

REVIEW COPY

THE SEXUAL BODY: AN INTERDISCIPLINARY PERSPECTIVE.
BY ARTHUR GROSS, PH.D. (PAPER). PUBLISHED BY SURF-BUFFALO.
POST. 228 PAGES. $15.00 INSTITUTE OF MIND AND BEHAVIOR, INC. PO
147 WEST VILLAGE STATION, NYC, NY 10014-0522.
TEL: (718) 783-1471. PLEASE SEND US TWO COPIES
OF YOUR PUBLISHED REVIEW.

The Journal of Mind and Behavior

Winter/Spring 1985 an interdisciplinary journal Vol. 6 No. 1 and 2

CONTENTS

Chapter One.
Introduction: The Perspective of the Sexual Body 1

Chapter Two.
Psychoanalysis as the Key Discipline 17

Chapter Three.
**Analogues of Original Sin: The Postulate of
Innate Destructive Aggression** 41

Chapter Four.
The Reichian Tradition: A View of the Sexual Body 57

Chapter Five.
**Challenges to Psychoanalytic Theory:
Recent Developments** 73

Chapter Six.
**Reinventing the Asexual Infant: On the Recent
"Explosion" in Infant Research** 89

Chapter Seven.
The Adult Sexual Body: A Missing Theory 127

Chapter Eight.
**The Sexual Body, Psychoanalysis and Science:
Bowlby, Peterfreund, and Kohut** 179

Chapter Nine.
**Lichtenstein, Holland, and Lacan: Ambivalence
Toward the Sexual Body, Cooptation, and Defiance** 219

Chapter Ten.
**World Hypotheses and Interdisciplinary
Sciences in Intimate Relation** 243

References 287

ISSN 0271-0137   ISBN 0-930195-01-9

The publishers wish to express their appreciation for a grant in aid from the Julian Park Fund of the State University of New York at Buffalo, which helped to make this issue possible.

Library of Congress Cataloging in Publication Data

The Journal of mind and behavior. — Vol. 1, no. 1 (spring 1980)-
— [New York, N.Y.: Journal of Mind and Behavior, Inc.],
c1980-

    1. Psychology—Periodicals. 2. Social psychology—Periodicals. 3. Philosophy—Periodicals. I. Institute of Mind and Behavior
BF1.J6575   150'.5   82-642121
ISSN 0271-0137   AACR 2 MARC—S

Copyright and Permissions: © 1985 The Institute of Mind and Behavior, Inc., P.O. Box 522, Village Station, New York City, New York 10014. All rights reserved. Written permission must be obtained from The Institute of Mind and Behavior for copying or reprinting text of more than 1,000 words. Permissions are normally granted contingent upon similar permission from the author. Printed in the United States of America.

Acknowledgments

I am indebted to the Center for Dewey Studies, Carbondale, Illinois, for a grant which enabled me to formulate and produce a first draft of this book. For grants in aid of publication, I wish to thank the Julian Park Fund of the State University of New York at Buffalo; and also the Center for the Psychological Study of the Arts at SUNY-Buffalo. Among the scholars, social scientists, and analysts who provided indispensable references, much needed encouragement, and timely comment, I wish especially to thank Bonnie L. Bullough, Mary Calderone, M.D., Mili N. Clark, Paul F. Cranefield, M.D., Victor Doyno, Sidney W. Fox, James Glogowski, Jerome Greenfield, Peter Heller, John Herold, Robert R. Holt, Otto F. Kernberg, M.D., Milton Klein, Martha Manning, Patricia Meyerowitz, Betty Morris, Ronald Potter-Efron, Ellie Ragland-Sullivan, Ruth D. Rice, Robert Rogers, Alice S. Rossi, I.D. Rotkin, Myron Sharaf, Lawton Smith, Michael Steig, William Sylvester, C.W. Truesdale, Sylvan Tomkins, and Richard G. Waite. I have had the benefit of detailed suggestions concerning the entire manuscript from James Bense, Steven Connelly, and especially Ray Russ. Ingeborg Biller, Managing Editor of *The Journal of Mind and Behavior*, has given me much help in seeing the book through the process of publication. Tom Morris gave special attention to the opening chapter, Dennis Hoerner commented on Chapter Four, and Lyle Glazier on Chapter Seven. Presentation of early versions of what became Chapters Three, Six, and Seven, for the Graduate Program in Psychology of the Department of English at SUNY-Buffalo, aroused challenging remarks, particularly from Norman Holland, Claire Kahane, and David Willbern. Paul Diesing raised useful thorny objections concerning the 60 page draft resulting from that presentation.

I am grateful to Donald Efron, editor of the *Journal of Strategic and Systemic Therapies*, for permission to quote the passage by Vincent Moley regarding an anorexic client, in Chapter Seven. For permission to quote passages from "A Masque of Reason," by Robert Frost (see Chapter Nine), we express our appreciation to Holt, Rinehart and Winston, Publishers.

Thanks are certainly due to Rita Keller for her typing of a difficult manuscript.

My greatest debt is to my wife, Ruth G. Kirstein, for her support and encouragement throughout the writing of this book. She also added several weeks to my existence by compiling the Reference list.

Buffalo, New York   *Arthur Efron*
June 1985

CHAPTER ONE:

INTRODUCTION: THE PERSPECTIVE OF THE SEXUAL BODY

The term "the sexual body" is a deliberately chosen one. There may come a day when such a term is in fact a redundancy, when it will be no more than a synonym for "the human body." At present, however, the term is needed. It has been chosen as the title of this study in order to postulate that consideration of human realities must include the body, and that inherently, the body is sexual, in all the range of meanings that the word has. The term is chosen to prevent the elision, pervasive in most disciplines (indeed within most forms of thought) in contemporary culture, of the whole topic of the sexual (Efron, 1975). In the philosophy of science, this bias shows itself in the title of a volume written by Sir Karl R. Popper and Sir John C. Eccles, *The Self and Its Brain* (Popper and Eccles, 1977). The interdisciplinary argument of these two distinguished thinkers indeed supposes that the human self possesses or owns a brain, which in turn is connected to the central nervous system. The possibilities for raising mind over body with such an approach are easy, and sexuality need never be discussed. A reader will discover, in fact, that sexuality is absent throughout the book's 560 pages, even though the authors' object is to discuss "the relation between our bodies and our minds . . ." (p. vii). Popper, in his section of the book, acknowledges that the body is good for some things, but certainly not for understanding human identity. With little difficulty Popper commits himself to a view of human nature which once more values mind over body: "Temporally, the body is there before the mind. The mind is a later achievement; and it is more valuable" (p. 115).

I would rather err on the side of the body and sex, if a value preference must determine my own approach. Given the prevalence of biases such as Popper's, the common sense notions that the living body must not be mistaken for the person, and that human realities include much that is not sexual in any meaningful sense, are to be foresworn for the duration of this study. They will be set aside on the grounds that these notions almost always turn out in practice to be ways of evading the sexual, along with its emotional and cognitive dimensions. Another dimension is lost as well: those implications for social change that emerge from a consideration of human sexuality. Beyond the decision to write *as if* the sexual body is synonymous with human life, however, is a suggestion that the equivalence is warranted. In this regard I find especially valuable Stephen C. Pepper's concept of evidence and its corroboration by means of hypotheses which allow for the formation of large-scale theories (Pepper, 1942, pp. 39-70). If we consider all the available evidence in the spirit of Stephen C. Pepper's concept of "world hypotheses," we may find that there is relatively adequate support for a view of the world in which the sexual body is central. In the concluding chapter, after giving argument and evidence in the light of the approach taken here, I will come back to this possibility.

Seen from a slightly different conceptual angle, the term "sexual body" is of course a designation; it is an act of "naming," as Dewey and Bentley would say (Dewey and Bentley, 1949, pp. 88-91), which segregates certain "subject-matters" for investigation. Namings and that which is named develop together in the process of inquiry. The particular name, "the sexual body," is not intended as a "hard fact" (a concept of which Dewey and Bentley would take the dimmest view), but of a theory in the making. At this stage of inquiry, it is a theoretical perspective, but it is not a formal theory with testable hypotheses, a distinction explained by Gibbs (1966). Gibbs observed that in the social sciences, what purport to be new theories are actually little different than conceptions. "Apart from its tautological character, a conception is too general to constitute a testable idea" (Gibbs, p. 9). In a somewhat similar vein, Searle has argued that what is put forth currently as "cognitive science" is actually a group of research projects which do not add up to a theory at all (Searle, 1982, p. 3). Searle's intention is to unmask the "myth" of the computer, whereas Gibbs' was to avoid the myths of scientism by starting out with a recognition that most of the time when inquiry begins, what we first have to work with is a general theoretical perspective. The sexual body is one such perspective.

Although the perspective is a general one, it obtains some firmness in the following proposition which I offer along with the perspective itself: Any finding in science concerning the human being, even if it concerns "intelligence" or the "cognitive," will turn out upon investigation to have meaningful connections with human sexuality. The reason these connections have not been seen is that researchers are usually not trying to discover them. Often, they may be said to be trying to avoid them, as I shall argue in the coming chapters.

A tempting simplification, which would allow us to avoid the threat of the sexual body, would be to reframe the axiom just given so that it refers to the connection of all scientific findings about people to the human body. But this will not do. In *Messages of the Body* (Spiegel and Machotka, 1974), for example, it is shown that adult perception of the adult body changes drastically when the perceived body is regarded in sexual terms, even though the body delineation is objectively no different than it is when sexuality is not in the foreground of the perceiver's consciousness. The discipline involved in that inquiry has been named "somatotactics." In keeping with the perspective of the sexual body, I am highlighting only the finding that shows the more intense, threatening feelings connected with perception of the body as sexual (in the conditions of that study, which were intergroup and not intimate conditions), as a warrant for the theoretical perspective of the sexual body. There are many such warrants, as the present study will show.

Merely to enclose the sexuality of the human body within the concept of body in general would also avoid certain specifics. Human sexuality is different than any other kind, in some ways. Anderson has summarized the differences recently, in terms of the differences between humans and other primates. We humans, Anderson writes,

> seem to be the only primate in which the female has forsaken the behavioral phenomenon of oestrus, during which she is instinctively attractive and receptive to the male, for a situation in which she is potentially attractive and receptive throughout the menstrual cycle and at any time from adolescence to old age. We also appear to be the only primate in which the female receives added pleasure from sexual intercourse in the form of orgasm. The exploitation of sex for social purposes may have left its mark in the fact that man has the largest penis of all primates but relatively small testes and sperm reserves, so that if ejaculation occurs more frequently than once every two days semen volume and sperm density decline. This suggests that we are adapted for a low level of continuous sexual activity, which, in contrast to all other animal species, normally takes place in private. (Anderson, 1983, pp. 25-26; 6 supporting references omitted)

Although Anderson's interpretations of the phenomena described are arguable, it is most reasonable to assume, from the perspective of the sexual body, that the phenomena are psychologically meaningful. Anderson goes on to describe further human differences from other primates with regard to the female breast. The breast functions erotically, as it does not appear to do in any other mammal,

> and we are the only primate in which full breast development occurs at puberty. In all other species, including the great apes, the breasts only fully develop during the first pregnancy, several years after puberty. (Anderson, 1983, p. 26, references omitted)

These peculiarities of human sexuality are among the factors which continue to puzzle students of human behavior, and to arouse controversy. (See again Anderson, 1983, and the replies to his article.) The recent emergence of research in primatology on the part of women scientists is already providing doubts over some of the assertions Anderson thought to be factual. In particular, it now appears that the oestrus cycle in many species of monkeys and in apes does not limit the female to having intercourse only while ovulating (Eckholm 1984; cf. Small, 1984). There is a complexity here which precludes any simple substantive definition of what the sexual body "is."

In fact, I am not attempting to give a definition of the sexual body. My strategy is to allow a "descriptive definition" (Pepper, 1946) build up in the course of the study itself. In the descriptive definition, the elements of the symbol to be defined, in this case the term "the sexual body," are continually revised in accordance with new observations. In this way definitions can be socially responsible acts of naming, rather than reifications or conceptually empty conventional markers (Pepper, 1946). Dewey and Bentley, in their stringent review of proposals for the construction of definitions, gave Pepper's theory of the descriptive definition an unusually high level of approval (Dewey and Bentley, 1949, pp. 189-195).

The philosophical contributions of John Dewey will play a guiding role in what follows. It was Dewey who provided, in fact, the painful central question: "Why is the attempt to connect the higher and ideal things of experience with basic vital roots so often regarded as betrayal of their nature and denial of their value?" As he went on to say, "A complete answer" to such a question "would involve the writing of a history of morals that would set forth the conditions that have brought about contempt for the body, fear of the senses, and the opposition of flesh to spirit" (Dewey, 1934, p. 20). Nothing like a complete answer can be expected, but at least this will be part of the writing of such a history in fields where it has not been adequately pursued. I hope to convey the idea that there is at present a new set of ways being invented, within some of the disciplines I am discussing, to re-create an opposition between flesh and spirit, although in our day we might call it the opposition between flesh and the cognitive. If this is the case, can we understand the "why" of it, as Dewey's statement suggests? I will refer to this again in the conclusion. It should be understood, however, that Deweyan ways of thought are in the background of this perspective throughout. I refer especially to his book, *The Quest for Certainty*, (Dewey, 1929b), an unnerving exploration of the human penchant to seek certainty and security in knowledge, and hence to have no knowledge at all, but a series of new superstitions, labelled scientific. *The Quest for Certainty* is even more disturbing however, in its positive advice that we step experimentally into the unknown world of modern social values, into the good and the bad values that we ourselves must create. From the perspective of the sexual body, such thinking is still the most appropriate, since we know so little, yet are required to know enough to make our major life decisions.

Dewey's clarification of the human significance of fruitful inquiry I take as fundamental to the topic of the sexual body. As we learn more about this topic, we are not simply building up our knowledge of an area in which we were previously ignorant. Inquiry does not consist of uncovering "antecedent" objects of knowledge: it both creates new objects where previously there had just been an amorphous "something" to be investigated, and it also leads inevitably to new problems of inquiry regarding these objects. As soon as any major aspect of the sexual body is tentatively discovered by scientific investigation, that aspect becomes part of the use of knowledge in ways that could not have been predicted. Recently McIlvenna, a research director for the Institute for Advanced Study of Sexuality, has said, "I'm having difficulty thinking about sex as it relates to marriage" (quoted in Grosskopf, 1983a, p. 110). He was speaking not of his personal problems nor of the eternal questions of sex in marriage, but of the typically Deweyan—and typically human—problem of what to make of new knowledge. McIlvenna had just completed a careful statistical survey of the sexual lives of married American women. The results led him to ask the question of how sex and marriage are related in American life now, and in the likely future, given the new data at hand. As this example indicates, research concerning the sexual body is a prime example of Dewey's theory of inquiry: we uncover not antecedent objects that have just been waiting there for us to find, but objects of knowledge which themselves are part of a process of further changes in the relations of experience and nature (Dewey, 1929a, 1929b). McIlvenna's survey, in other words, had shown something new about the sexual mores of married women in America, but it had not shown anything about what sexuality "is"; nor could its findings be prevented from becoming part of an inquiry leading to further change, which will in its turn call for a new survey, contributing to further change, and so on into the future. New and problematic contexts are inherent to the process of inquiry. This is nowhere more true than in the study of the sexual body.

To understand the bearing of Dewey's experimentalism and contextualism, it is necessary to refer to alternative philosophical positions in a systematic way. For this purpose, Pepper's concept of "world hypothesis," a name for the philosophical framework within which the categories of thought in any discipline have their grounding, is preferable to the nearly synonymous "worldview" or "metaphysics" (Pepper, 1942). The "hypothesis" is part of an empirically oriented and pluralistic approach that Pepper developed over a period of 50 years, and which later researchers in numerous disciplines have increasingly found to be valuable.

The disciplines of the sexual body are potentially limitless. They are by no means confined to sexology. I have chosen to emphasize certain areas, and would expect my understanding to be modified by other writers. I will be discussing the continuing "explosion," since about 1960, of research in the field of infancy; the contributions toward understanding the sexual body made by the Reichian and Bioenergetic traditions; and the surprisingly neglected discipline of the adult sexual body. Anthropological evidence will be considered, in terms developed by Prescott (1979). Most of all, I will attend to psychoanalytic theory: its roots in Freud, the unconsciously sadistic development of Freud's theories in such fashion as to remove them from their grounding in the sexual body, and several more recent psychoanalytic theories. There are a number of serious interdisciplinary challenges at the present time to psychoanalytic theory as it stands, and this set of challenges seems to be producing an opening of theory that is rare in any discipline, let alone in one that has become as professionally organized as has psychoanalysis.

Up until the current crisis, the history of psychoanalytic theory has been another example, in many respects, of a retreat from the whole perspective of the sexual body. There is a great deal of sexual hatred in that history. Five current theories within psychoanalytic thinking seem to be genuinely different than what has gone before. The theories of Bowlby, Peterfreund, Lichtenstein, Kohut, and Lacan are worth examining in detail because there is a chance in at least four of them for a renewal of contact with the perspective of the sexual body, while even in the remaining theory, that of Lacan, there looms the possibility of a confrontation (not evasion) which will give the definitive separation of psychoanalysis from the sexual body at last.

If it is true that sexual hatred finds its way into psychoanalytic theory, and no doubt into other theory as well, that could only be due to the personal factor. To be sure, what is personal occurs within a cultural context, and in thinking about the sexual body, it is important to not lose sight of the long tradition of opposition to sexual expression at virtually all levels. Nonetheless, the personal factor remains. Theorists are human beings, a platitude which has special pertinence in discussion of sexuality. Dewey's realization that the separation of flesh and spirit, fear of the senses, and contempt for the body was the underlying problem behind the various dysjunctions between theory and practice, or thought and action that he had been criticizing for decades, came only in his 7th decade of lived experience; his earlier statements along the same lines, even in *The Quest for Certainty* (Dewey, 1929b), are not focused on the sexual body. In referring to "the" sexual body, I am referring at some level to my own. I assume that such reference is inevitable, and indeed valuable, in the perspective being developed in the present study. There is a theoretical bearing of intimacy upon theory in this perspective which is unusual in the sciences. That relationship will be worth considering in the concluding chapter, when the evidence has been displayed. But reference to one's own sexual body also helps to avoid reification: the reader will remain aware that the term does not refer to a collective entity, such as "the body politic," nor should it suggest that all sexual bodies are precisely the same as one's own. The reader will have some awareness that even his or her own body has not always been the same as it is today. The complexities of a life that is lived in the body, but in a body which had once been an infant, then a child, then an adolescent, and also an adult are much to the point. We can speak of each of these existences as "the sexual body," knowing also that they are all part of one life cycle. I do not wish to suggest that anyone has four (or more) different sexual bodies, but I do want to say that the paucity of serious thinking about the sexual body has much to do with the failure of most common sense talk as well as scientific discourse to give this complexity its due. The central chapters of this study, on the infant sexual body and on the adult sexual body, are intended as a corrective; they are proposed as a way of showing the sexual body has a complexity which is beyond the grasp of any existing theory, and that only a perspective which focuses on the sexual body can hope to develop such a theory.

Inquiry in the Context of a Continuing Sexual Revolution

The entire study is intended to demonstrate the theoretical perspective of the sexual body in operation, and to show its value as an instrument for critical thinking in several disciplines. The special disciplines in their separate activites should not be mistaken as entities remote from social processes. The sexual body has great interdisciplinary possibilities, but these would not merit as much attention as I am asking from readers here, were it not that the performance and application of research regarding the sexual body continues to be badly needed. Without it, a vast range of human decisions will continue to be made unintelligently.

A similar statement could be made wherever human decisions must be based on controversial value judgments and made against a background of empirically grounded, but not very clear, facts. These decisions are the stuff of life, the "genuine options" referred to by William James (1955). In our own period of history, however, the context of decisions concerning sex take place within what has been called, rightly, the "sexual revolution." Just when and how this revolution began is not my concern at this point; the rough dating of "around the turn of the century," offered by Skolnick (1973, pp. 188-192) will serve for my purposes. Wilhelm Reich, whose name is associated with the term "sexual revolution," published a volume entitled *La Crise Sexuelle* (Reich, 1934), revised and enlarged it as *Die Sexualität im Kulturkampf* (Reich, 1936), before he revised it again and brought it out in English under the title *The Sexual Revolution* (Reich, 1945). The term has come into general use. Skolnick does not cite Reich in her discussion, and it is possible to recognize that there was and is a sexual revolution on without knowing anything about Reich. A recent excellent volume on sex education, which bears the subtitle

The Challenge of Healthy Sexual Revolution (Brown, 1980) does not mention Reich anywhere in its 18 chapters, although several of the contributors do mention him in a conference on childhood sexuality in which they also happened to participate (Samson, 1980). Peter Gay, the historian who has offered substantial evidence for dating the sexual revolution back into the middle or late 19th century in Europe and the U.S., seems to avoid the very phrase "sexual revolution"; yet Gay's "principal intellectual obligation," as he points out, "is obviously to Sigmund Freud" (Gay, 1984, p. 463). In other words, Gay's intellectual roots are in the same intellectual discipline as were Reich's.

No work known to me discusses the sexual revolution on a worldwide basis. Yet the revolution goes on, even though it is a long way from being completed, whether it is underway in the Western world, in China, or the Mideast. The revolution is slow moving, partly because it is opposed. My view is that there are very strong cultural forces at work which aim at the fantasy goal of "eliminating" the human body precisely because it is sexual (Efron, 1980, 1981, 1982a, 1982b, 1982c). On the other hand, there is little doubt that a change, not simply in the decline of traditional mores, but toward sexual self-regulation in Wilhelm Reich's sense (Reich, 1945) has been going on for nearly a century, as shown by such varied developments as the creative restructuring of divorce laws in the U.S. since 1969 (Price-Bonham, Wright, and Pittman, 1983), the legalization of contraception and divorce in even so Catholic a country as Italy, and the beginning of opposition to the practice of clitoridectomy and labial excision in certain Mideast cultures (Hosken, 1979; Lightfoot-Klein, 1984).

The extent and the multiple manifestations of the sexual revolution are probably not generally realized. From the perspective of the sexual body, they become noticeable as part of an overall world social change, penetrating into unlikely areas. Iran, even within the context of a highly conservative theocratic revolution, has enacted a law allowing women to initiate divorce proceedings ("Iranian Law," 1983). The Mullahs who put this change into the lawbooks pointed out that while some men might claim it deprived them of their rights, it actually only took from them powers which they should not have been entitled to, under Islamic law. To be sure, the newsclip from which I gathered this information is not enough to overcome my scepticism—and I presume the reader's—of any major movement toward sexual self-regulation within an Islamic theocracy, but there does seem to be some movement toward change even there. A recently published oral history of a Moroccan family includes an account by a woman outraged at the traditional status of women in Islamic society (Munson, 1984), and Fatna A. Sabbah has published a booklength critique of Islamic cultural documents, including marriage manuals for young Muslim men, which inculcate male supremacist attitudes in erotic relationships (Sabbah, 1984).

In the Soviet Union, where ideology would not be disposed to take a favorable view of the individual as the regulator of sexuality, there is a deep commitment to the concept of romantic love within marriage; that is, Soviet citizens are encouraged to believe that they choose their mates for reasons of personal attraction and self-determined values, and not because of social status (Fischer, 1980). Attempts by letter-writers in the Soviet press to criticize this romantic outlook have been vociferously rejected by other letter-writers. Divorce has become a frequent phenomenon or problem (depending on your perspective) in the Soviet Union, and a few experiments in marital therapy have even been permitted in an effort to "save" marriages. Stern (1980) argues that there is ample evidence for saying that the restrictive sexual mores of the Stalin era have begun to dissolve, even in the face of such social backwardness as the relative unavailability, in the U.S.S.R., of contraceptives. Kerblay (1983) points to figures showing that the Soviet government's campaign in recent years to increase average size of family, that is, to have a rise in the birthrate, has been a failure. Under certain conditions, people today just won't have those babies, and they will take advantage of the availability of abortions (Kerblay, 1983, pp. 122-123).

In Spain, a Socialist government that came to power in 1983 offered the peculiar campaign promise of not nationalizing industry on any noticeable scale while helping to consolidate and codify changes toward self-regulation in sexual behavior that had been largely carried out already among the populace. A visit by the most politically influential Pope in recent times was not thought to have any chance of reversing or even slowing the direction of change in Spain. In October, 1983, a few months after the visit, a limited legalization of abortion was approved by the Spanish Parliament (Darnton, 1983). Later, when the Constitutional Tribunal, the highest court in Spain, voided most of the legislation, virtually all political factions including the conservative ones prepared new legislation to enact the changes now desired by most of the populace, as surveys in fact showed (Schumacher, 1985). In February, 1985, the Parliament of Ireland passed legislation allowing for the sale of contraceptives without prescription to anyone 18 years of age or older. This was the first "defeat ever sustained by the Catholic Church in a head-on confrontation with an Irish Government on social legislation (Feder, 1985, p. A11).

In the meantime, the Catholic Church itself slightly loosened one of its sexual prohibitions: in the first revision of the code of canon law since 1917, it was decided in 1983 that priests who marry before being properly relieved of their vows will no longer be subject to automatic excommunication. They will merely be given "just" punishment ("Vatican Eases," 1983). This change apparently formalizes a policy shift set in motion by Pope John XXIII, who is "reliably reported" to have urged special "dispensations from their vows to priests who had married" (Rynne, 1985, p. 9). His successor, Paul VI, continued new policy by granting nearly 30,000 such special dispensations in the late 1960's (Rynne, 1985, p. 9; see also Hebbelthwaite, 1985). The Church has been having difficulty for some time, in fact, in recruiting new priests precisely because its requirement of celibacy is increasingly perceived as unwise; Dean R. Hoge, a sociologist, has cited survey evidence showing that most American Catholics favor permitting priests to marry (cited in Cornell, 1984; see also Simons, 1984). At a recent conference held by the 615 active priests in Brooklyn and Queens, called for the purpose of dealing with a major crisis in attracting an adequate corps of new priests to the Church, it was suggested by one priest, Rev. Charles Kinney of St. Brigid's Church in Brooklyn, that "optional celibacy" might be the solution to the shortage (quoted in Goldman, 1985, p. B3). Some, but not all, Catholic Bishops are now requiring that couples who cohabit prior to marriage separate for a 3-month period before a marriage rite can be performed; this is hardly a blanket refusal to countenance cohabitation ("New Hurdles," 1984). Even the recent refusal of the Archdiocese of New York to accept a requirement by the city that it agree not to discriminate against homosexuals in its employ, was not followed by the nearby Diocese of Brooklyn, which finds no objection to the homosexual job protection provision (Dunlap, 1984). In theological circles, the learned study by the Jesuit Theodore Mackin, arguing that the church should reconsider its ban on divorce (Mackin, 1984), surely will be read. Mackin in fact concludes that "a woman's happiness in sexual intimacy" is one good reason within Church tradition and doctrine to release her from a marriage which has gone bad (Mackin, 1984, p. 546). There is also the openly rebellious work by Greeley and Durkin (1984), entitled *How to Save the Catholic Church*. These authors argue that sexual love is a sacrament which is essential to the understanding Catholics have of God, and that God loves human beings not only "with the tender passion of a mother" but also with "the fierce passion of a sexual lover" (Greeley and Durkin, 1985). They hold that such love is a vital part of the special commitment toward social justice which Catholics may cultivate (*ibid.*).

The outbreak in Brazil of "machismo" murders of wives who were having love affairs and/or leaving their husbands can be seen as evidence of a conservative marriage institution in that country now reacting violently to increased self-regulation in women's sexual behavior that has been going on, perhaps, for about two decades (Hoge, 1983). In Mexico, where research on sexuality has been minimal, recent findings show that birth control is now having a serious impact on the rural areas, altering the status of women, and changing the lived quality of poverty. Among the middle class, which is officially estimated to comprise 18% of the Mexican populace, the taboo of virginity is being openly questioned, even while it is prized by men who want to get married. Rape, which apparently is omnipresent in Mexican society, has at last begun to be opposed by feminist groups, although these are still rather new and few (Ross, 1983). These indications remind us that the sexual revolution is not confined to the middle classes. In England, a study recently completed of some 1000 lower-class families, over a three generation timespan, has shown that the practice of contraception within the poor family slowly frees it from the burden of unwanted children (Madge, 1983).

India and China are also undergoing cultural change which shows evidence of sexual revolution. In India, it is now estimated that one of seven inhabitants may be counted amongst the middle class, a figure that is equivalent to about 100 million people. The rise of the middle class is having its effect on sexual mores, as it has in other cultures. Evidence of incest within the extended family, especially among siblings who must live together as adults and are unable to marry, has begun to draw attention in psychiatric discussion. In an effort to achieve some degree of self-regulation, Indian adults in some instances have started the practice of putting "personal" advertisements in the press (Stevens, 1983).

China, on the other hand, can hardly be said to have undergone a sexual revolution in the Reichian sense. The relevance of such a term for contemporary Chinese society is probably inappropriate. It would be more in keeping with Chinese society since the Revolution to say that a change in sexual mores was imposed through ideological and political pressure, and that the concept of self-regulation did not govern this process. It appears that Communist efforts to forcibly change the sexual, marital, and child-rearing practices of the peasant population have met with serious resistance, but it is also probable that in China's cities, there has been a considerable departure from the old ways (Johnson, 1983, pp. 223-225; see also Andors, 1983). If that is the case, then it might also be true that further changes will come about and sexual self-regulation will begin to come into existence. Press reports hint, in fact, that there now is concern in China over the spread of divorce. A TV report I saw recently depicted the angry concern of Chinese authorities over coddling of children. Some amount of coddling, however, is a result that might have been predicted, given the government's forceful policy of limiting families to one child. The one child, it turns out, is sometimes spoiled to the point of not learning even the rudiments of toilet training. It would seem that such children will not learn to control themselves in the area of sexual behavior, at least not as readily as they are expected to do. The consequences and scope of such a change cannot be predicted. However, perhaps we are seeing the end of reports out of China such as that of Sidel (1972), where the Western observer admiringly noted how all the infants in a collective nursery are placed "on white enamel potties" just after breakfast and "all have their bowel movements together!" (Sidel, 1972, p. 96).

The value of a TV report in an interdisciplinary study may seem questionable. However, formal scholarship concerning the sexual revolution often lags behind informal study and anecdotal reportage, a problem to which I will return in later chapters. An example in the case of China is the book by Croll,

The Politics of Marriage in Contemporary China (Croll, 1981). This is a serious work of scholarship, involving both fieldwork on the part of the author and perusal of the available Chinese language sources such as newspapers and Party documents. From this study, one would conclude that the effort to transform the marriage institution in rural China so that it reflects a "free choice" of mate, rather than an arranged marriage, has been a failure. Croll draws support from many sources for her conclusions, but it may be that she was too intent on gathering all the information on her topic from the time of the success of the Communist Revolution in 1950 to September, 1979, when she wrote her preface to the volume (Croll, 1981, p. xi). Actually the documentation from periods prior to, say, 1975 or even 1978 may be too old to capture the changes going on. I say this on the basis of another somewhat informal source of information, the film "Small Happiness: Women of a Chinese Village," directed by Carma Hinton and Richard Gordon.[1] In the village of Longbow, located about 200 miles southwest of Peking, in Shansi Province, the film supports the conclusion that marital partners are now beginning to be chosen by the couple themselves, and not according to arrangement. In other words, a primary feature of the Chinese marriage institution has begun to change in the direction of self-regulation, after thousands of years. This change does not necessarily mean that other villages in China are also changing—Chinese villages differ strongly from each other—or that such practices as female infanticide have been stopped. In Longbow, in fact, female infanticide is still practiced, and other inequalities, such as the ritual humiliation of brides who must relocate to their husband's village, remain in force. But it would seem reasonable to look for further changes toward self-regulation in this village, given that mate selection has begun to work according to that principle, and it would hardly be surprising if some other villages among China's thousands were undergoing a similar change.

At the same time, large parts of the Western world have been permeated with some of the basic elements of sexual revolution already, particularly the decline of the taboo against masturbation and of cultural support for involuntary monogamy. The virginity fetish and adolescent abstinence are obviously not the great bulwarks of moral rigidity they once were. The social prohibition against unmarried couples living together has lost most of its power. Recent reports from Sweden indicate that nearly all couples now live together before marriage, whereas only about 1 in 5 did so in Sweden in the 1950's (Lofgren, 1983).

These developments, however, do not sustain the widespread belief that the sexual revolution is "over," or that it has "failed," unless the sexual body is regarded in highly simplistic fashion. Various aspects of sexuality are under-

---

[1] Advance showing at SUNY-Buffalo, May 1, 1984.

going change in various societies, as well as within a given society. Popular belief tends to be overly impressed with spectacular changes such as the increase in permitted nudity on screen or stage, or the "free speech" of a few years ago which has brought formerly tabooed words into many levels of public discourse, or the high-profile divorces and mate-changes of celebrities. Mixed with this credulity is a genuine realization that mores are changing, and probably some fear that they may change "too much" or have already "gone too far." This set of prejudices is fed by the popular press whenever it declares that the sexual revolution is over. What is ignored and is not given intelligent consideration are certain critical areas, such as the failure of the sexual revolution even to reach some large minorities in the population, or the disastrous effects of poor sex education, and also certain key concepts, such as the distinction between chaotic sexual permissiveness versus sexual self-regulation. One neglected minority, for example, is that considerable part of the population labelled as "retarded" (Evans, 1983). Recent evidence strongly indicates also that normal American and Canadian adolescents are woefully ignorant of sexual information even though they begin having intercourse at an average age that is lower than that of their peers in Sweden; they lag considerably behind in sexual knowledge, in fact, even compared to teenagers in Australia and England (Goldman and Goldman, 1982). Olds reports that in her recent research using some 250 intimate sexual autobiographies by college students in the U.S., the old themes of childhood terror over masturbation and sex play, negative feelings upon realizing that their parents engage in sexual intercourse, and an embarrassing ignorance upon reaching the age at which sexual relationships are expected, are all very much in evidence (Olds, 1983).

The ignorance evidently begins early, and is by no means a result of the limitations on children's capacities to understand sex. A study which asked second graders in a Swedish and in an American elementary school to draw pictures explaining "where babies come from" revealed startling cultural contrasts. The American children simply did not know the sexual origin of birth, and thus drew body imagery of the birth process that was grotesque and violent. Babies were "cut out" of the mother's stomach. The Swedish children, on the other hand, showed accurate (but not perfect) factual knowledge, combined with a joyous attitude concerning fertilization and birth. One of them even drew a fine representation of sperm recing happily to get to the egg (Barthelow-Koch, 1980; see also Goldman and Goldman, 1982). Yates (1980) has argued that such sex education as we do give children commits the error of attempting to train the child in knowledge before permitting him or her a basic enjoyment of the sexual body. Johnson, speaking at the same conference, argued that most of the colloquial language children have available to them for talking about sex is so loaded with semantic confusion and antisexual bias as to be worse, perhaps, than no language at all (Johnson, 1980). For those who think the American sexual revolution has gone on far too long, it is worth noticing that as late as the 1960's, sex and dating manuals for teenagers in the U.S. were devoted to what is aptly called "Sex Prevention" by Campbell (1979) who has done a fine bibliographic study of this genre of literature. To be sure, Campbell rightly points to a much more positive outlook in the adolescent sex and dating manuals of recent years, but it is also often the case that "television programs, commercial literature, and sometimes school and community programs unwittingly reduce 'adolescent sexuality' to simply 'adolescent intercourse'. . . ." (Carrera, 1983). In other words, teenage sex is still an area of adult over-reaction, fear, and one-dimensional sexual thinking.

Certain legal changes also provide evidence that the sexual revolution has yet to make any great impact in the U.S., in some respects. Thus, while I believe I have been warranted in referring to the creative rewriting of divorce laws in the U.S. (and some other countries), I might also note a regressive revision of laws regarding marital rape. According to a report from the Center for Constitutional Rights (1983), only three states in the U.S. have abolished the legal exemption from rape charges against men who rape their wives, while three others have partially stricken these exemptions.

> In 1980, however, 13 other states broadened their marital rape exemptions to permit unmarried men to rape women with whom they have been cohabiting. Five of these states gave men the right to rape women with whom they have had previous sexual intercourse whether or not they have lived together, and one state, West Virginia, exempts the rapists of "voluntary social companions"—even where there has never been a sexual relationship. (1983, p. 13)

This chilling social development will undoubtedly be one of the future focal points for renewed efforts to continue the sexual revolution, making sex a matter of self-regulation and not one of coercion.

Other findings are widely taken to show that the revolution has ended. But the fact that Americans are not engaging in casual sex as much as they were a few years ago is better interpreted in Quadland's terms (quoted in Lyons, 1983): "there is a new, more careful and caring" sexual revolution going on. As Wilhelm Reich might have put it, people have begun to quit acting out the distorted desires they previously had been forced to control; they are now acting from the deeper layer of energy that is capable of becoming part of a loving relationship (Reich, 1945; Sharaf, 1976). There probably has been a shift from the emphasis on taboo-breaking to that of longterm sexuality, but that hardly indicates that we now need to know less about the sexual body. It is possible that a recently reported drop in premarital sex and in cohabitation without marriage, among college students at Ohio State University (Clatworthy, quoted in Lyons, 1983), represents a reversion to earlier standards. Before reaching such a conclusion, however, it would be necessary to find out if the new restraint is primarily a result of self-regulation by sexually aware young people, or if it is being produced by family pressure and religious dogma, as in earlier decades. If it is the latter, then a retreat from the sexual revolution has taken place, but if the former, it is a more problematical social change. We could be seeing the results of a less affluent economy in which young people simply cannot afford to move out of their parents' homes. A qualitative problem then would be to determine if their enforced continuing habitation with parents is actually bringing their sexual mores into conformity with an older standard of premarital abstinence.

Research on this point would have to account for motivation, not merely tabulate sexual activity and living arrangements. Such research would have to consider the demographic context as well. It has been pointed out that there has been a sharp increase in the proportion of unmarried to married couples in the U.S. since 1970; were that rate of increase to continue, "America would quickly become a nation populated by cohabitors" (Blumstein and Schwartz, 1983, pp. 36-39). In that demographic context, some decline in the rate of unmarried couples cohabiting can be absorbed without making a great dent in the trend. Nor would the U.S. be the only source of data to consider. The Netherlands, for example, has a substantially higher proportion of cohabiting couples among its population than does the U.S., although the proportion is not as high as that of Sweden (Buunk, 1983).

There is no point in denying, however, that the current social climate of the U.S. has a number of features which appear to threaten the continuation of the sexual revolution. Hysteria over AIDS, herpes, sexual child abuse, and abortion might be documented. Possibly the sexual revolution will be more in evidence in other cultures in a few years than it is in the U.S. On the other hand, the very force of the hysteria may signal a belated mass realization that things have gone too far, that the revolution has progressed past the point at which it might really have been turned back.

The social developments I have referred to signify that research on sexuality, even if it originates largely in the Western countries which have relatively well organized research facilities, will become increasingly pertinent with the changes going on worldwide. The great variety of changes and problems, and the different rates of change in various societies and subcultures obviously point to a mass of evidence and potential evidence which requires some organizing perspective. The best perspective will be one that considers sexuality in its many interconnections with the overall fabric of life, and not one that draws limiting demarcations which would set off the biological from the psychological from the social and historical aspects of the sexual body. In this desired perspective, interdisciplinary knowledge will be essential, but one discipline, psychoanalysis, seems to have a key role.

CHAPTER TWO

PSYCHOANALYSIS AS THE KEY DISCIPLINE

In its "classical" period (ca. 1896-1920), and prior to revisions made by Freud and others, psychoanalysis emphasized the sexual etiology of the neuroses, the reality of libido, the omnipresence of sexual thinking in fantasy, dreams and even in cognitive thought, and the failure of civilized morality to understand what sex was about. The theory of Oedipal dynamics entails a potentially strong criticism of the role of the father in culture, inasmuch as it posits an initial gratifying state of contact between the mother and the infant, rudely disrupted by the father with his patriarchal authority at about the time that the infant reaches the age of 3. The father was thus perceived as introducing the first of a long series of adjustments which look suspiciously like denials of the infant's sexual wishes. These adjustments had to be made by the child, in his or her own mind and body, but without effective conscious awareness of what was being denied. Repression was a sexual matter. The whole theory of repression raised a question that continues to prove threatening to normal assumptions about human life in its sociocultural contexts: was sexual denial warranted? Denial *for what*?

A psychological theory which placed that much emphasis on sexuality was fated for misunderstandings. It took some time before the Freudians outlived their early, unwarranted reputation of being in favor of "free" sexuality. Frequently their efforts to avoid the label have caused them to retreat too far. Marthe Robert, in her exposition, *The Psychoanalytic Revolution*, is at pains to attribute the objections about sexuality that Freud has drawn from his critics to a simple mis-reading on their part. She claims that Freud really intended to reserve the word "sexuality" for only the last phase of psychological development, in which the genital organs are important; in infants these organs "play only a relatively minor role . . ." (Robert, 1968, p. 187). Such assurances can hardly be taken seriously. For one thing, Freud's attention to the phenomenon of sexual gratification at the breast, on the part of the human infant (Freud, 1905b, p. 179), is not offered in the spirit of assurance that such activity is only a minor matter. Freud's texts by no means neatly dispose of sexuality the way Robert suggests, nor is the sexuality of the infant, notwithstanding the infantile physiology of the genitals, any the less sexual for all its being infantile. Philip Rieff, a moralist-interpreter of Freud, attempts to de-emphasize the sexuality by claiming that Freud was not interested in it "as such," but in "the contradictory attitudes toward it" (Rieff, 1961, p. 180). Rieff may have felt better with such a division, but it hardly represents Freud's interest in the interconnections of exactly that which Rieff sunders, sexuality and the human mind. Many readers today would see Rieff's distinction as ridiculous, even without any reiteration of Freud. If that is the case, it is due to a widely diffused popular understanding of Freud (Alberoni, 1983, p. 10) that complicates our perception of sexuality. I suspect that few readers with any interest in psychology would place credence in the advice of a recent non-Freudian writer on effective sex-education, namely that children be taught to think of sex as defined solely by anatomy and reproduction (Bem, 1983, p. 612). It was Freud who taught us better than this, even if the lesson is still unacceptable in many ways of thinking.

Freud on the Sexual: 1921, 1916-17, 1909

Three of Freud's statements on what "sexual" means are pertinent here. In 1921, or a year after he had formally introduced the strange concept of a "death instinct" into his theory, and thus jarred the theory off its moorings (Freud, 1920a), Freud nonetheless strongly defended the "sexual" basis of his thinking. He explained that "libido" is "the energy, regarded as a quantitative magnitude (though not at present actually measurable), of those instincts which have to do with all that may be comprised under the word 'love'" (Freud, 1921, p. 90); by "love" psychoanalysts include both the ordinary language term, with its "nucleus" that "naturally consists . . . in sexual love with sexual union as its aim . . . ," but also, and inseparably from this ordinary concept, all other forms of love:

> Our justification lies in the fact that psycho-analytic research has taught us that all these tendencies are an expression of the same instinctual impulses . . . . (Freud, 1921, p. 90)

The reason psychoanalysis "gives these love instincts the name of sexual instincts" is that the whole corpus of its evidence points to such a usage. No doubt, Freud remarks, this will continue to lead to "the reproach of 'pansexualism'," but there is no way to avoid that reproach without dishonestly trying to protect the theory from criticism by presenting a "nomenclature" that might cause less offense (Freud, 1921, p. 91).

A few years earlier, in the *Introductory Lectures on Psycho-analysis* (Freud, 1916-1917), Freud also described sexuality as a topic of multidisciplinary dimensions; it has no clear definition but yet holds a central place in psychoanalytic theory. "You must not forget" he tells his audience at the University of Vienna, "that at the moment we are not in possession of any generally recognized criterion of the sexual nature of a process . . ."(Freud, 1916-1917 p. 320). Freud does not sound in the least bit worried about this fact. It is misleading to say, as Laplanche and Pontalis do in their learned glossary of Freudian terms, that Freud was "forced to acknowledge" a gap here, or that his "thinking seems to have come to a dead end both as regards the essence of sexuality . . . and as regards its genesis . . ." (Laplanche and Pontalis, 1973, p. 420). Freud if anything is more than glad to "acknowledge" these things, since he believes psychoanalysis is bestowing on the term sexuality its true breadth of meaning (1916-1917, p. 319, conclusions of Lecture XX). As for the discomfort that his refusal to demarcate it would cause, Freud regarded this as a challenge to the disciplines, including biology and physiology, as well as psychology. He enjoyed moving back to the gut-level connotation of "sexuality" and out again into its conceptually unsettled aspects. Thus, he says to his Viennese audience, in the midst of discussing the problematic of sex, "On the whole, when we come to think of it, we are not quite at a loss in regard to what it is that people call sexual" (Freud, 1916-1917, p. 304).

This remark is not one that Laplanche and Pontalis quote. Their emphasis is on fantasy, not sexuality; and so wherever Freud warns that sexuality is *more* than biological reproduction, they transform his meaning in their paraphrases, to the proposition that sex is not "solely" or "not only" to be understood biologically, by which they signal their own turning away from biology. But Freud had a more disturbing approach than they allow. By blasting the definition wide open but also putting it in touch with the commonsense "sexual," Freud was allowing for future developments, such as "sexual politics," which would have been unheard of in his time, but which in our day has become a field of inquiry (Brake, 1982; Schwartz, 1984).

In 1909, Freud also explained the sexual in an important series of five lectures given at Clark University, where he came as a guest of the American psychologist, G. Stanley Hall (Ross, 1971). These lectures are not often quoted in present-day psychoanalytic literature, although they contain some of Freud's most sprightly writing (Mahony, 1982, pp. 141-142; Malcolm, 1982, pp. 10-11), and even an innovation in theory (Malcolm, pp. 31-32). They were published in the *American Journal of Psychology* as "The Origin and Development of Psychoanalysis" (Freud, 1910a), a title little reflected by the one chosen later in the *Standard Edition* of Freud where they are called, blandly, "Five Lectures on Psycho-Analysis" (Freud, 1910c). That title corresponds neither to the American translation, nor to the German pamphlet edition, published very shortly afterward: *Über Psychoanalyse* (Freud, 1910b). It is odd that these lectures are not contained in the widely distributed 5-volume set of Freud's *Collected Papers* published by Basic Books. Yet the editors of the *Standard Edition* translation of Freud's works say that "these lectures still provide an admirable preliminary picture which calls for very little correction" (Freud, 1910c, p. 5). I will quote from the historic American journal version (1910a).

In these lectures, Freud was providing the "first extended synthesis" of his work (Hale, 1971, p. 5). He was also doing it somewhat spontaneously: he did not prepare his presentations during the eight-day ocean voyage from Bremen to the United States, as he had intended to do (Clark, 1980, p. 267). Ernest Jones reports that finally Freud prepared each lecture just beforehand in the course of a half hour walk with Sandor Ferenczi (Jones, 1955a, pp. 58-59). They were delivered without notes. They also went off beautifully. I mention these details because they may suggest that Freud, who was more than aware that these lectures were an important chance for him, somehow wanted to let loose, to say what psychoanalysis was, without the care and caution that he usually felt forced upon him in Vienna. As he put it a few years later, "In prudish America it was possible, in academic circles at least, to discuss freely and scientifically everything that in ordinary life is regarded as objectionable" (Freud, 1914, p. 39). The irony about "prudish America" is a feature of Freud's hostility to American culture, but he knew, by the time he stepped to the platform for the first of the lectures, that his reception in the U.S. was one of warm recognition. Hall had assured him that there was "a wide and deep interest in your coming to this country, and you will have the very best experts within a wide radius" (quoted in Clark, 1980, pp. 263-264). G. Stanley Hall, the president of Clark University, had already given a series of lectures there on sex, in 1904, and had mentioned and praised Freud in his key work, *Adolescence* (Clark, pp. 262-263). At Clark University, Freud must have felt he was on safe enough territory to speak on some of the most threatening topics in a straightforward manner.

Aside from the professional significance of the American visit, there was also a personal context for Freud. His own sexual life had been recently renewed, as he indicates in his statement to Jung, in a letter written after the return to Europe, but not published until 1974. This renewal was not to last for very long: "My Indian summer of eroticism that we spoke of on our trip has withered lamentably under the pressure of work" (Freud and Jung, 1974, p. 292, letter dated Feb. 2, 1910; see also discussion by Mahony, 1979, p. 568; Mahony is the first to recognize the importance of the quoted passage). Freud's "Indian summer of eroticism," occurring when he was in his 50's, was thus part of the underlying *ethos* of his lectures in the U.S. It may have disposed him to argue not only the importance of the sexual body, but in support of the positive value of sexual experience as well.

An extraordinary context for these lectures is thus indicated throughout the preparatory moves. The very topic of the lectures was not even selected by Freud until he had arrived in the U.S. and was encouraged by Ernest Jones to deliver a general rather than a limited presentation (Jones, 1955a, pp. 59, 211-214). Although it was not unusual for Freud to speak brilliantly without notes, there is a quality of spontaneousness to his style in these lectures that is unusual. Some of Freud's major rhetorical modes, such as the heavy use of suggestion, and "the dialectical movement of starts, modifications and resumptions," (Mahony, 1982, pp. 42-43) are little in evidence in the 1909 presentation.

Freud organized these lectures to emphasize sexuality as the endpoint in the series. Moreover, it was the damage to human life which results from sexual repression that he deliberately ended on, after leading up to it skillfully. Freud arranged the five lectures to follow an order that would become increasingly challenging to his audience, beginning with the medical origins of psychoanalysis in its early work on hysteria, then taking up dream interpretation in lecture #3, and going on to "his most explosive subject in his fourth lecture, the existence of sexual impulses in the child" (Hale, 1971, p. 9). After giving an exposition of this topic, Freud said:

> You will now perhaps make the objection: "But all that is not sexuality." I have used the word in a very much wider sense than you are accustomed to understand it. This I willingly concede. But it is a question whether you do not use the word in much too narrow a sense when you restrict it to the realm of procreation. You sacrifice to that the understanding of perversion; of the connection between perversion, neurosis, and normal sexual life; and have no means of recognizing, in its true significance, the easily observable beginning of the somatic and mental sexual life of the child. But however you decide about the use of the word, remember that the psychoanalyst understands sexuality in that full sense to which he is led by the evaluation of infantile sexuality. (Freud, 1910a, p. 211)

Ernest Jones, who took notes during Freud's delivery, reports that Freud's answer to the rhetorical question of why it could not be the case that some neurotic symptoms had causes other than sexual, was more personal and playful than the printed text indicates. Freud said "I don't know either. I should have nothing against it. I didn't arrange the whole affair. But the fact remains . . ." (Jones, 1955a, p. 213). Jones in fact supplies Freud's wording in the original German: "Ich weiss es auch nicht. Ich hätte nichts dagegen. Ich habe die ganze Sache nicht gemacht. Aber Tatsache bleibt . . ." (Jones, 1955a, p. 213).

Freud went on to discuss what he variously called the "*Nuclear complex*," or the "incest complex," elaborated by means of the myth of Oedipus and the drama of "Hamlet." He still had not used the term "Oedipus complex" in his work. The term "incest complex," one of the designations with which he confronted his American audience, is probably a more directly threatening one, in terms of the traditional family and conventional sexual thought. At least Oedipus is a character in an ancient play; the name thus provides a slightly "high culture" overtone to what turns out, in Freud, to be a desperately intimate matter. But "incest complex" is a term without any such buffer. Inasmuch as Freud never at any point in his career gave a full, formal exposition of the Oedipus complex (Sheleff, 1981, pp. 73-74), the paragraphs he spends on it in his 1909 lecture, in the context of this first public synthesis of his work, form a notable text.

By 1909, Freud knew that infantile sexuality was central, and that this meant that the "sexual" was now a vastly problematic area. Nor did he imagine that this fact could be disconnected from the need for social change. In the fifth and last of the Clark lectures, he emphasized the harm done by sexual repression and the need to let up on the pressure. Even Freud's less threatening hypothesis of the creative sublimation of sexual instinct is presented in a way that would not be reassuring for those who would want to emphasize conscious controls: "A repression taking place at an early period excludes the sublimation of the repressed impulse; *after the removal of the repression* the way to sublimation is again free" (Freud, 1910a, p. 217, emphasis added). Hale (1971), whose detailed account of Freud's 1909 visit to the U.S. is highly informative, nonetheless overstates the "ambiguity" of this final Freud lecture to his American audience (Hale, 1971, pp. 11-12). Not only did Freud end by saying that we should not "go so far as to fully neglect the original animal part of our nature" and that "The claims of our civilization make life too hard for the greater part of humanity" (statements which Hale quotes); Freud also says that "A certain part of the suppressed libidinous excitation has a right to direct satisfaction *and ought to find it in life*" (Freud, 1910a, pp. 217-218, emphasis added). Hale quotes that statement only in part, omitting the punch line in the last clause. Further, Freud goes on to say that we should waste little effort as builders of culture in trying

> to separate the sexual impulse in its whole extent of energy from its peculiar goal [i.e., sexual intercourse]. This cannot succeed, and if the narrowing of sexuality is pushed too far it will have all the evil effects of a robbery. (1910a, p. 218; this also is *not* quoted by Hale)

Freud is thus taking a problematical yet radical stance in these and his many other statements on sexuality. There is sexual union to consider, the limitations imposed upon it by civilization, the costs of those limits, the ubiquitous psychological meanings of sex in language and symbol, particularly its interplay with maturation and emotional/mental development, and the extension of the category "sexuality" into the areas of childhood and infancy. But the limits of the term's expansion are deliberately not stipulated. A year earlier, Freud had published his famous essay, "'Civilized' Sexual Morality and Modern Nervous Illness" (Freud, 1908), but that essay, justly considered a radical criticism of sexual repression under the rule of "civilized" mores, and noted by Ernest Jones as Freud's first "pronouncement on social problems" (Jones, 1955a, p. 343), is not as far-reaching a statement on the sexual body as are the 1909 lectures in the U.S. The essay clearly protests against repression, and it implies that "revolutionary changes in society" are needed as countermeasures (Jones, 1955a, p. 294), but it does not take Freud's greatest radical step, the expansion of the term sexuality to cover a virtually unlimited psychosocial area of reference. At the same time, the need for radical change in society is still evident in these lectures, just as it had been in the 1908 essay. Hale's comment that Freud showed a clear "devotion to civilization," and that "at Clark he voiced his full acceptance of the 'higher' aims of culture" (Hale, 1971, p. 15) is not born out by anything Freud actually said in the lectures. Nor does Hale attempt to quote from the lectures in support of this claim. The "higher" aims of culture were subordinated in those lectures to the claims of the sexual body.

Popular Freudianism and Research on the Sexual Body

Since Freud, expansions of the meaning of the term sexuality have proven to be enormous. Masters and Johnson, following Kinsey, using an approach to the study of the sexual body that differs in almost every respect from Freud's, brought about one of the largest expansions. Suddenly, as a result of their research the common sense notion that the sexual body was *not* the human body in old age, became very dubious. Such findings extend the common sense meaning of the "sexual body": common knowledge that sexual intercourse is a continuing practice throughout the adult life cycle assures a tacit definition of the body as sexual, rather than functionally nonsexual after age 50, just as it had been considered to be sexual prior to that age. But the findings do not in themselves lead to a theory of the sexual body commensurate with what we also know of infantile sexuality, psychosexuality, and the sexual basis of political movements such as Fascism (Reich, 1933). Within theories such as Kinsey's or Masters and Johnson's, the full psychological and social dimensions of their own findings are not approachable. Masters was not unaware of this problem: as far back as 1969, he said, in an interview, that "there is no such thing as the pure physiology of sexual response, except as a textbook concept. From a functional point of view, the correct terminology is the psychophysiology of sexual response" (Masters, quoted in Hall, 1969, p. 54). But in the same interview, answering a frequent question about the quality of orgasm, he showed that he could not enter into that psychophysiology, given the nature of his work:

I have been challenged by some attractive guy in the audience who says, "But I enjoy orgasmic intercourse more with one woman than another." And I say, "But I am not talking about what you enjoy. I am talking about what you experience in terms of intensity and duration of experience." (quoted in Hall, 1969, p. 54)

Experience without considering what is enjoyed is hardly the full range of experience, sexual or other. Nor would academic empirical psychology be able to claim, after 80 years, that it has taken up the topic of child sexuality and made Freud unnecessary. It has been pointed out by Goldman and Goldman (1982), for example, that a bibliographical survey of some 5000 articles in child psychology based on the work of Piaget contains virtually nothing on childhood sexuality. New disciplines such as sociobiology seem even wider of the mark. It is all very well for the sociobiologist Edward O. Wilson to say that "Sex is central to human biology and a protean phenomenon that permeates every aspect of our existence and takes new forms through each step in the life cycle" (Wilson, 1978, p. 121). But sociobiology, precisely because of its effort to develop a comprehensive theory on the basis of genetic determinist considerations, was in no position to deal with the protean psychological aspects of sexuality. In fact, in response to his critics, Wilson finally had to admit that there is something beyond the genetic dimension, something which he calls "gene-culture coevolution" (Lumsden and Wilson, 1982)—thus opening the Pandora's box of theory he had tried to avoid. Psychoanalysis, on the other hand, chose to open the box at the start. Psychoanalysis is notorious for its "unscientific" forays into speculations going far beyond what the observed facts would justify, but it also has the merit of that defect: it can keep in view the whole range of the sexual.

Nor has this willingness to depart from empirical norms produced a theory without empirical support. Notwithstanding the perpetual debates over whether or not psychoanalysis is scientific, evidence is mounting for many components of Freudian theory. This is shown with great force by Paul Kline in his stringent reviews of the experimental evidence for the numerous theories and behavioral descriptions of psychoanalytic psychology (Kline, 1972, 1981). The second edition of Kline's work (1981) is 500 pages long. He critically evaluates the research on psychoanalytic concepts, rejects many of the experiments (including some of his own) as faulty, acknowledges that some of the metapsychology such as the pleasure principle may be beyond the reach of confirmation, and discredits numerous studies based on tests and measures of doubtful validity such as the TAT and the Rorschach test. He does not accept clinical evidence or diagnoses as empirical evidence. Thus many of the studies claimed as supporting evidence for psychoanalysis by Fisher and Greenberg (1977) are rejected under Kline's standards. Kline is forthright in reporting that some research seems to refute certain aspects of Freudian theory, such as Freud's belief that the function of dreaming is to be "the guardian of sleep" (Kline, 1981, p. 315), and he scrupulously notes other aspects in which evidence fails to support the theory, such as on the doctrine of penis envy (p. 427). Yet with all these cautions, Kline has pointed to an impressive number and variety of carefully controlled studies in which the results, pointing clearly toward the confirmation of psychoanalytic theory *"should be acceptable to unbiased psychologists of whatever persuasion . . ."* (1981, p. ix, emphasis added).

Kline's work seems to have been little noticed. Grünbaum's highly theoretical probing of the validity of psychoanalytic theory (1983) has attracted much more attention. Grünbaum discusses Kline only to dismiss him as another of the psychoanalytic supporters who are unable to see the difference between the mere existence of repression, a psychological mechanism, and repression as the major etiologic force in the development of psychoneuroses (Grünbaum, 1983, pp. 188-189). Although Grünbaum scores a good point here, and even though the problem of the etiology of the neuroses is certainly a key one, his commentary regarding Kline is seriously misleading. Kline, exactly like Grünbaum, has recognized that the verification of psychoanalytic theory cannot depend on clinical evidence because such evidence is contaminated by the huge powers of suggestion inherent to the psychoanalytic process. Hence Kline relies on none of the clinical evidence, but provides a book full of controlled experimental evidence which confirms various parts of psychoanalytic theory. In other words, Kline has already supplied, in large part, the kind of evidence Grünbaum repeatedly calls for: "*extra*clinical evidence" (Grünbaum, p. 189).

As time goes on, in fact, psychoanalytic empirical investigation is becoming more sophisticated and ingenious. The intensive work of Silverman using subliminal tachistoscope projections of key messages, such as "Mommy and me are one," signals a new breakthrough that will be very hard to dismiss (Silverman, 1971; Silverman, Lachman, and Milich, 1982; Kline, 1981, pp. x, 226-228, 347-349). Work going on in Scandinavia on the "percept genetic" approach is also impressive from an empirical standpoint (Kline, 1981, pp. 229-237, 386-388; Kragh and Smith, 1970). Kline's review of all this work tells us that it is time for those psychologists who have rejected psychoanalytic theory on empirical grounds to admit that they may be losing their battle on those very grounds. There is a booklength refutation of Kline's first edition by the anti-psychoanalytic psychologist Eysenck (Eysenck and Wilson, 1973), but it is effectively rebutted by Kline (Kline, 1981, pp. 389-400, 433-434, 441-442; see also Rosenzweig, 1954). The controversy will undoubtedly continue; those who support Eysenck are by no means ready to concede defeat, but it does appear that psychoanalytic empirical research has entered a new era in which outright dismissals are no longer in order.

It is to the point of the present study that in a number of experiments discussed by Kline, while it is feasible to *include* the results within nonpsychoanalytic learning theories, it is not possible to *account* for them, nor to have predicted them, on the basis of such theories. These experimental results typically are in the areas of libido or sexuality (Kline, 1981, pp. 441-446).

To the extent that other approaches to psychology have not dared to depart from the range of the immediately empirically verifiable, they have been forced to pursue inherently unlikely hypotheses. The substantial work of Izard on emotions has been based on facial expression (Izard, 1971), to the detriment of attention to the rest of the affective psychological repertoire, partly because the face can be observed, whereas subjective emotional states, especially in the infant, seem to be out of observational range (Cicchetti and Pogge-Hesse, 1981, p. 250). This choice finally has not saved Izard from constructing highly theoretical models of neural-emotional development, but it has given his theory an implausible cast because of its excessive concentration on the face. In the field of the study of sexuality, let me mention here the volume *Love and Lovesickness*, where an excellent non-Freudian researcher and theorist of sexuality, John Money, once more takes the typical behaviorist pledge:

> There is an emphasis throughout this book on behavior rather than on thoughts or feelings. The reason is pragmatic: if you can't see, hear, touch, smell or taste it, then there is nothing about another human being that you can know, the claims of the occult notwithstanding. (Money, 1980, p. 13)

Actually, Money's book is illuminating precisely because he violates this pledge on almost every page. He does say a lot about behavior, but rather than stopping there, he also gives his thoughts and feelings, some of which are consonant with a philosophy of self-regulation in sexual matters. He reports on how orgasms feel; "They keep getting better and better" (p. 119). Such feelings are "behavior," but are inseparable from subjectivity. This whole subjective side of Money's book would have to be rejected by anyone following his own declaration of emphasis on the "behavior rather than thoughts or feelings," and researchers who abide by the behavioral science pledge normally do not write about how orgasms feel to them. Money is successful in his effort to discuss sexuality comprehensively only because of his idiosyncratic combination of behavioral commitment and personal reportage. But outside of the psychoanalytic tradition, there are no theories which offer a basis for dealing with sexuality in all its dimensions.

Freud and the tradition of therapy he started comprise the first group of professional scientists and/or medical practitioners faced with the set of problems entailed by a multiple and yet unitary approach to sex. In a sense, such problems would be more difficult than those faced by an outright sexual reformer like Havelock Ellis, or even by a later believer in libido (later Orgone) like Wilhelm Reich. For these, there could be no question of intellectual gymnastics or moderation or compromise or revision; sexuality *has* to be central for them. But by concentrating upon it, they may not have felt the same challenge as the psychoanalysts, who have related sexuality to the most remote, apparently asexual, aspects of the mind. Nor would other depth-psychological theories, where sex is not emphasized, be of much use here. Jung, for example, went on record in a key presentation of his analytic psychology at the Tavistock Clinic in London in 1935. He finds the sexual most repellent.

> I never could bring myself to be so frightfully interested in these sex cases. They do exist, there are people with a neurotic sex life and you have to talk sex stuff with them until they get sick of it and you got out of that boredom. Naturally, with my temperamental attitude, I hope to goodness we shall get through with the stuff as quickly as possible. It is neurotic stuff and no reasonable normal person talks about it for any length of time. It is not natural to dwell on such matters. Primitives are very reticent about them. They allude to sexual intercourse by a word that is equivalent to 'hush.' Sexual things are taboo to them, as they really are to us if we are natural. (Jung, 1968, p. 144)

This could hardly be clearer. Discussion of sex, perhaps the very thought of sex, repels Jung. Jung of course is not fairly represented by this one statement, and interesting comments on sexuality may be found in his voluminous works. But neither the openness toward understanding sexuality in all its manifestations, nor the profound interest in it which we find in classical Freud, is present for Jung.

That commitment and interest, however, remains a problem for the theorist who wishes to abide by the essentials of Freud, who realizes that Freudian theory is still developing and changing, always subject to new evidence and theoretical considerations, and who still would like to have psychoanalysis become a respected member of the psychological sciences. Here the problem becomes that of accepting the challenges of the Freudian emphasis on sexuality and revising that theory so that it meets current societal imperatives. By now, sexuality has become excised in some few responses to the challenge (e.g., Schafer, 1976), while in most others, it is brought to subordination within a theoretical system by a number of typical strategies (not always chosen consciously). The psychoanalytic theorist Joseph Lichtenberg, for example, recently has discussed at some length the question of whether psychoanalysis has or implies any special "Weltanschauung," or (as Pepper would phrase it), any world-hypothesis of its own (Lichtenberg, 1983b). But despite a few glancing comments on sexual concepts such as castration (pp. 222, 230), Lichtenberg never mentions sexuality or the sexual body at all, let alone as an inherent concern of psychoanalytic theory. In his book on psychoanalysis and infant research, also published in 1983 (Lichtenberg, 1983a), Lichtenberg discusses such sexual body topics as "genital awareness" (pp. 127-131) and "psychosexual development" (pp. 153-156), but does not treat sexuality itself as an important category or as a topic requiring any theory whatever.

Yet the original sexual emphasis does not seem to be vanquished. The popular idea of psychoanalysis as a preeminently sexual psychology has never died out. Whether there is basis for it in current theory or not, I suggest that this persistence of the myth be taken as an indication that the myth is not groundless. Pepper, writing about psychoanalytic theory in 1958, still took seriously the possibility of gratification (sexual and other) without repression (1958, pp. 237-242); he was one of the few to argue that this could be part of a workable system of civilized values. Pepper would have known, through his inveterate conversations and continuous learning, that by 1958, most psychoanalytic theory had come around to endorsing repression and calling it an inevitability. In fact, only a year later, Norman O. Brown, in *Life Against Death: The Psychoanalytic Meaning of History*, argued for the position taken by Pepper (without making reference to him), but presented this position as a radical overhaul of psychoanalytic theory (Brown, 1959). Brown was correct, but Pepper may have been calling on the strongest line of argument within the theory.

More recently, the sex therapist Avodah K. Offit (1981, p. 14) has told of her early momentous reading of Freud at age 12. From that reading, she was "indoctrinated," as she puts it, to believe that "Sex was not only the province of psychiatry but also the source of all that was good in human achievement. I still believe this." For her, Freud is no longer the ideal figure he once was, but his central meaning is still there. Interestingly, Offit's popular book, which does not have a single footnote, contains invaluable data on female psychosexuality that is seldom mentioned, to my knowledge, in any but the most extremely specialist source. I shall refer to this data below, in a discussion of the adult sexual body.

Culture and Sexual Repression: The Question Resurfaces

A psychological theory capable of suggesting that sex is the source of all good in "human achievement" (Offit, 1981, p. 14) inevitably raised a radical question for the theory of culture: if sex is the source of good, why should there be sexual repression? Could it not be possible to create a society in which sexual repression is absent? And would not such a society be more sane, more humanly gratifying, and less violent, than the actual civilization we now live in? In *Civilization and Its Discontents* (1930), Freud himself answered that question with an ominous "No." But Freud would not even have come to give his answer had the question not emerged from the development of psychoanalytic theory itself. What this means is that some position concerning the cultural necessity of repression is part of the psychoanalytic world hypothesis.

Recent investigation into the cumulative store of anthropological research now indicates that it is possible to envision a different answer to the radical question of whether sexual repression is a necessary component for the "good society"—specifically, for a society not rent with violence, and capable of generating genuinely affectionate relations among its inhabitants, who would exist in a state of social order. Although the question is obviously fraught with complications, there is at least one surprisingly comprehensive study of human cultures which *would* give an unequivocal "No" to the proposition that sexual repression is a necessity for the good society. I refer to the comprehensive cross-cultural study by James W. Prescott (Prescott, 1979); it is based on R.B. Textor's invaluable work, *A Cross-Cultural Summary* (Textor, 1967), which compiles information about 400 cultures and some 20,000 correlations. Prescott found very high correlations between the deprivation of physical affection during infancy and the development of physical violence, in cultures where those two factors could be identified. Prescott also showed that there is a corresponding group of cultures in which we find a strong correlation between high levels of affectionate, somatosensory contact for infants, and very low levels of violence among adults. Prescott's concept of "physical attention" involves overall approval and love for the infant's physical body, including its sexuality. "Physical attention" does mean for Prescott "body touch, contact, and movement . . ." (p. 67).

According to Prescott, somatosensory contact, the one variable that would make the most sense of all anthropological findings on culture and touching, is absent from the social sciences. It is also largely absent from psychoanalytic thought as it exists today, well after Freud and his followers revised the classical theory. Summing up his work on physical affection and its deprivation, Prescott writes:

> This writer is not aware of any other developmental variable that has this high degree of validity and predictability. Nor is he aware of any such variable in the social-behavioral sciences. Clearly not much more needs to be said except to point out that these findings are fully supportive of the position taken and advocated by Wilhelm Reich in *The Function of the Orgasm*. (p. 95)

This statement comprises a strong confirmation of Reich, not from within the circle of acknowledged Reichians, but from a neurophysiologist investigating anthropological research for the National Institute of Child Development and Human Development. From the theoretical perspective of the present study, it is not merely Reich who is confirmed; it is the original classical psychoanalysis of Freud, in its implications concerning sexuality, and now usually dismissed as a merely popular misconception of Freud.

There is however a complication in Prescott's results which is of the greatest import for the sexual body. For a few societies, Prescott found "a failure of the infant physical affection variable to predict characteristics of sexual behavior" (p. 81). That is, some few cultures scored high on both physical affection to infants and on adult physical violence, including sexual violence. But further analysis revealed that those all were cultures in which there are "repressive premarital sexual behaviors" (pp. 82, 84).

Prescott's hypothesis is a major one. It has already shown its potential for the enrichment of research. Blackman (1980) has applied and extended Prescott's "global multi-casual view" (Blackman, p. 193) in an exploratory research project on affectional touching in 60 pre-school children, representing three different ethnic groups: white-American, Afro-American and recent immigrants from the Cape Verde Islands (p. 182). Among the findings is a confirmation that the white American parents touch their children less than the other two groups (p. 187). She also concluded that for some children, parental touching was less significant than parental hitting. Blackman refined Prescott's theory by making use of Jourard's (1966, 1968) method of analyzing parent-child touch dyads, and by taking into account the gender-cultural differences in the meanings of touching. For little girls, for example, being touched by their fathers and not being able to touch back reciprocally is part of the early enculturation of sexist values (Blackman, 1980, pp. 190-191). Blackman (p. 188) is aware that touching cannot be studied in itself, apart from the variables of culture, but she is nonetheless able to perform a valuable exploratory study that puts Prescott's theories to the test. Her work is only an indication of further research that could be carried out on the meaning of Prescott's theory of an affectional sensory contact variable in the social conditions of industrial society.

David Finkelhor, a leading researcher in the field of child sexual victimization, is also aware of Prescott's theory (Finkelhor, 1979, p. 15). Although Finkelhor gave only tentative assent to the theory in his book, he has followed with later comments which bear on the issues Prescott raises. For one thing, fathers who are child sexual abusers are very often products of a deprivation of affectional touching. In the U.S., fathers hug and kiss their children less than do mothers, probably because adult male sexuality is regarded as dangerous. Furthermore, abusive fathers have been

> ... weaned very early from nurturant and dependent physical contact with parents and adults, and ... in early adolescence avenues of physical contact besides sex are regarded as unmanly. (Finkelhor, 1980, p. 645)

The typical mother of the girl who is sexually abused by a father, or other older male, is likely to be one who is sexually repressive. Finkelhor's research shows that "These mothers were the kind who warned, scolded and punished their daughters for asking sex questions, for masturbating and looking at sex pictures" (Finkelhor, 1980, p. 643). Sexual repressiveness is not the only risk factor by which girls might become victims of sexual abuse, but it is an important one in Finkelhor's sample. It appears to be related to Prescott's theory, in that these girls have difficulty forming a realistic sense of danger in sexual encounters with adults because their sexual bodies have been defined for them as very dangerous territory, to be avoided in touch and thought; their natural curiosity for exploration through affectional contact has been put under prohibition. This makes them vulnerable to sexual exploitation. The research of both Blackman and Finkelhor provides corroboration (though obviously not "proof") of Prescott's theory of the importance of somatosensory touching and affection in childhood and in adolescence—and of the incompatibility of such touching and affection with sexual repression. (I will discuss Finkelhor's work further, in the chapter below, on "Challenges to Psychoanalytic Theory: Recent Developments.") Prescott's work has also been incorporated into a broad sociological description of currently changing lifestyles and religious attitudes in the U.S., by Robert T. Francouer. Francouer's interdisciplinary training includes theology, genetics, and experimental embryology (Francouer, 1983).

The recent research on verbal abuse as a form of child abuse would provide a good example of an area where somatosensory affectional contact is missing (Brody, 1983d). The child who is subjected to insulting scoldings or epithets is being assaulted vocally, and in many cases is being rooted to the spot at attention while the parent sermonizes at him or her. The problem is not just the *content* of the abusive verbal taunting—in fact, given a playful or a warm tone, that content might be overlooked—but the affective *quality* of verbal contact. It would also seem clear that such a child is not receiving much—if any—somatic affection from the abusing parent. I speculate on this topic in order to suggest that somatosensory affection is a subtle concept as well as a necessary one. Attempts to explain the effects of verbal abuse without such a concept must miss the way in which the child's sexual body is affected.

There is, however, a pertinent irony in Prescott's work: the general direction of his results had been anticipated in earlier anthropological cross-cultural studies (though these could not be as comprehensive or as statistically sound as the one Prescott offers), and these earlier studies were undertaken from a psychoanalytic perspective (Whiting, 1963; Whiting and Child, 1953). What Whiting and Child were looking at, in their psychoanalytic cross-cultural studies, were such factors as sexual identity confusion. Prescott reanalyzes some of their data and concludes that their restricted hypotheses share "a common ground" in one significant variable, namely, "physical affection . . ." (1979, p. 70).

Prescott concludes his monograph by affirming the "morality of physical pleasure" (p. 128). Such a claim is hardly taken seriously by, and is certainly not central in, psychoanalytic thought today. The problem is that the claim lacks an adequate theoretical basis in any other discipline. Note that Prescott is not aware of any variable like affectionate touching *in the behavioral sciences at all*. We can think of some theories which might well accept the "morality of physical pleasure," and thus technically refute Prescott: Kinsey, for example, or other supporters of human sexuality such as Alex Comfort, or Masters and Johnson. However, their theories do not have adequate scope or precision such as would lead to an in-depth understanding of the variable of "physical affection." Psychoanalysis, on the other hand, has a theoretical investment in the sexual body which permits the reconsideration of physical affection within a range of overlapping inquiries, such as the study of intrapsychic conflict, cultural values, aesthetic experience, and the relations between subjectivity and scientific observation.

The resuscitation of Freud's theory in its original form is not intended in the present critique. The point is that psychoanalysis by virtue of its early breakthroughs became the only psychological approach to promise a theory of human nature in which the sexual elements were fully credited—even if this meant threatening the forces of cultural tradition. As Maguire, a recent Catholic moral theorist has shown once more, changes in sexual mores are the most salient, intractable changes in what Maguire perceives as today's "Muddle in the Moralscape." As he also ruefully recognizes (quoting A. and M. Edel, 1959), "sex is nearly everywhere [in cultures] highly charged morally, for in addition to its high emotional potential, it is part of the most central nexus of human social interrelationships" (Maguire, 1978, p. 5). René Girard, a thinker whose work has had wide acceptance, has reaffirmed the sexual-moral nexus and reinforced the traditional negative evaluation of the sexual:

> Sexuality leads to quarrels, jealous rages, mortal combats. It is a permanent source of disorder even within the most harmonious societies. (Girard, 1977, p. 35)

Girard's statement can hardly be misunderstood. He is generalizing on the basis of very wide reading in the anthropology of religion. He is also quite mistaken, as I have argued elsewhere (Efron, 1980, 1982b). The "youth houses" of the Trobriand Island culture did not produce a ferocious society, despite its encouragement of unsupervised sexual alliances among adolescents (Efron 1982b, pp. 176-177). But the Trobriand Island culture, before the missionaries put an end to the youth houses, was not living within a repressive sexual morality, either. Fears of radical change arising from a freeing up of sexual behavior, from heightened appreciation of the value of sexuality, and from the enlarged meanings of the term "sexual" since Freud, are all grounded in reasonable expectations. Traditional values, such as involuntary monogamy, and traditional beliefs such as the asexuality of the infant and the child, do in fact become threatened. Countless cultural changes occur. One example of a change that probably would not have been predicted has occurred in the high school from which I graduated in St. Paul, Minnesota. The school now has a daycare nursery for the convenience of its teenage mothers who need to finish their degrees. I doubt that adherents of traditional moral codes would find this a welcome institutional adaptation, though it may actually be more moral in practice than moralists would like to admit.

Issues Underlying the Rejection of Libido Theory

Psychoanalysis as a professional institution has become a tradition itself, largely unable to maintain its original critical edge toward culture; nonetheless that criticism, grounded upon its disturbingly amorphous discovery of what "sexuality" means, cannot be persuasively excised. The "nexus" is much too central in the theory. As one of the most respected among psychoanalytic theorists has put it, in a review of the phases of psychoanalytic theory, "*Classical psychoanalytical theory is a moral psychology* . . ." (Guntrip, 1968, p. 123, emphasis in the original). Its problem is "how to direct and control antisocial impulses," by which Guntrip, in accordance with traditional moral thought, means the sexual and the aggressive. How aggression made its entry into the formula is a problem I will take up shortly; here I wish only to point out that Guntrip as much as Girard sees the importance of sexuality in classic psychoanalytic theory, and realizes that the issue, given his own assumptions about "antisocial impulses," has to be a moral one. By 1968, when Guntrip published his statement, theoretical emphasis had shifted to the ego, in a move that Guntrip and many others recognized as a step away from the instinctual or the biological core of the classical theory. The libido had become passé. The move, in other words, was toward the human mind as the root metaphor of psychoanalytic psychology, in a way that de-emphasized the body and with it sexuality.

Today ego psychology itself is out of fashion, but the shift toward mind and away from the sexual body continues. I have heard the distinguished analyst and theorist, Otto Kernberg, declare at the outset of a presentation (Kernberg, 1981) that he could begin his presentation only if it were understood that psychoanalysis as he defines it is within the Cartesian metaphysical framework, the *cogito*. Obviously, the body and sexuality could not be considered central. To my surprise no one objected (although there was a question raised concerning the location of Descartes' *cogito* within psychoanalytic evidence premised on the mind of the infant!). Peterfreund, another theorist whose work I shall take up in a later section, has declared (1971, pp. 83-84) that most current psychoanalytic thought indeed is premised on the Cartesian worldview. This situation is one that Peterfreund, unlike Kernberg, finds intolerable. The historian of science James Blight (1982, p. 21) has pointed out that Cartesian dualism is in fact prevalent in much of current psychoanalytic theory, and notes that one result and intention of such dualism is to take psychoanalysis out of the disciplines of the natural sciences and place it within some other field, such as the humanities or religion. Incredibly enough, these efforts as well as others which are not attempting to be dualistic at all (sometimes the opposite) are often presented as rescue missions—ways of saving the Freudian heritage—in an age of new findings and assumptions.

The most common theoretical strategy of the past several decades is to rescue Freud's theory from what is taken to be its hopelessly unscientific reliance on an energy concept of innate, biological "drive." It is widely believed now that Freud was a product of 19th century natural science, from which he took over a Helmholtzian concept of drive and discharge which is purely mechanical, and inept for the intricacies of the human psyche: it is also without empirical foundation. The "sexuality" he was concerned with, unfortunately, was closely associated with this drive concept. It is widely believed that sexual drive, energized by a force labelled as "libido," was presumed by Freud to operate "hydraulically," that is, as a simple biological force within the sexual body that always strove for immediate discharge. It seldom achieved this discharge, since repression, instigated by culture and internalized into the psyche, either blocked or delayed or re-channeled it.

As I read Freud, however, he was not overly reliant on Helmholtz. He maintained, even after his conservative metapsychology had been formed, a delicate theoretical realization that deliberately distinguished human biology from the concept of "instinctual drive," and still postulated that human biology and human psychology are inherently related. The instincts were postulated as the interfacing of psychological events (which can be inferred through analysis and self-analysis) with the sexual body, but were not thought to be observable directly.

Libido was regarded as the energy of the sexual body and hence of the mind as well. Too much has been made of Freud's abandoned project of 1895, published only in 1950, of a scientific psychology in which he imagined that it might be possible to "represent psychical processes as quantitatively determined states of specifiable particles . . ." (Breuer and Freud, 1957, p. 355). Although mechanistic biology was *one* of Freud's scientific inheritances, the same natural scientists—Helmholtz, Brücke, and later on Breuer—who are credited with being major sources of that heritage for Freud, have been shown to have also had strongly aesthetic, non-mechanistic lines of thought (Cranefield, 1966a, 1966b, 1970). Cranefield has shown that Heinrich von Helmholtz, far from maintaining a narrow mechanistic stance in his psychophysiological investigations, "was at every possible point aware of the psychological implications of his investigations and interested in their aesthetic implications" (1966b, p. 3). Ernst Brücke, Freud's professor of histology, had strong interests in philosophy and aesthetics; in fact, "most of his monographs had something to do with aesthetics or with philosophical questions" (Cranefield, 1966b, p. 5).

Freud's continued interest throughout his career in an eventual unified theory of psychology and physiology simply does not justify a narrowly mechanistic interpretation. I have quoted above his statement (Freud, 1921) that libido is "the energy, *regarded as* a quantitative magnitude (though not at present actually measurable) of those instincts which *have to do with* all that may be comprised under the word 'love'," and that psychoanalytic evidence warrants naming all of these instincts "sexual instincts" (emphasis added). There is no sharp separation to be made, Freud went on, between this terminology and the whole range of loves: "self-love . . . love for parents and children, friendship and love for humanity in general, and also devotion to concrete objects and to abstract ideas" (Freud, 1921, p. 29). These are all called by the name "love" in popular usage, and this is "an entirely justifiable piece of unification . . ." (pp. 29-30). To refer to "love" in this way is quite in line with the tradition of Plato's "Eros," a definition of sexual love in a "wider" sense—but one that remains sexual. This statement illustrates Freud's willingness to be understood, to some extent, at a popular level, and it also shows his finesse in never substituting the physiological names such as "libido" and "sexual instincts" for the enormous range of meanings the sexual body has. In later critiques of Freud's energy concepts, however, (e.g., Peterfreund, 1971), especially those written after the surprise posthumous publication (Freud, 1954) of his 1895 "Project for a Scientific Psychology" (a title placed on the manuscript by the editors, by the way), Freudian libido is first reduced to an impossibility, a purely "mental energy" as Peterfreund (1971), for example, has it. I can only conclude that such a strategy for revision of Freud has been selected unconsciously by those who reformulated Freudian theory; there is an extreme scarcity of awareness, among revisionists who opt for this strategy, that if you eliminate the drive theory and the theory of the libido, then you will thereby lose touch with the sexual body, *unless* you do something to install new concepts that focus on the sexual. The many texts by those who reformulated Freud, such as the writings by the object-relations theorists, show little awareness of this loss. Revisionists were glad to get away from what they regarded as Freud's excessive "biologizing" of the psyche, but what they mean by his "biologizing" usually comes down to one thing: his introduction of an enlarged, problematical sexuality into psychological considerations.

One example of how the well-intentioned revision of Freud's alleged mechanistic thinking leads away from the sexual body, concerns the concept of *homeostasis*. Holt (1965), arguing for revision, rejects it as a "vague analogy," useless within modern physiology. I agree that there is vagueness within the concept, and there is an error—frequently pointed out—in Freud's assumption that the human nervous system is based on the energy principles of "constancy" and "inertia." These principles lead to the notion that the reduction of tension is always the aim of the organism, an untenable position. The energy theories may also be involved in Freud's belief that the human organism is fundamentally hostile to the experience of emotion, since that experience would contradict the constancy and inertia principles. (See Schachtel, 1959.) Despite these defects, there is implied within a postulation of homeostasis in an organism, a possibility of self-regulation. The body—the sexual body—has a capacity for regulating the excitations it experiences in a healthy, sane manner. In this regard, it is significant that Josef Breuer, Freud's collaborator in the discovery of psychoanalysis, was a major scientific contributor to the understanding of self-regulatory "biofeedback" processes in the human organism, in the physiology of respiration (Cranefield, 1970). In the early book co-authored by Breuer and Freud (1957), Breuer's theoretical exposition of homeostasis is by no means limited to the notion of constancy in the sense of tension reduction (pp. 197-200). As Cranefield has pointed out, Holt seriously underestimated the sophistication of the physiological science with which Freud was most familiar, especially in Freud's relation to Breuer (personal communication, April 12, 1972).

But these are historical details. What is finally at stake in the concept of homeostasis is not its vagueness but its implications for a self-regulative capacity of the sexual body. Freud, we may speculate, could have been finding his way toward a homeostatic, self-regulating concept of sexual expression. Had he taken such a direction it would have been consistent with his strong sense, expressed in his 1909 Clark lectures, of the harmfulness of sexual repression, and its dubious social necessity. The self-regulation of sexuality may have been an underlying assumption of Freud's physiological thinking throughout his collaboration with Breuer and beyond. In his 1909 lectures, he shows no sign of being worried that sexual expression will become violent or destructive if repression is greatly reduced. Nor is the possibility of sexual self-regulation a dead issue today. But this possibility is lost sight of in the efforts to "rescue" Freud from the allegedly simplistic and supposedly outmoded physiological science of his early medical career.

In our own day, the rescue of Freud has been completed many times over. There are even some theories of psychoanalysis where revision has been carried beyond the point of no return. One example is the work of Roy Schafer. Schafer is interesting because he shows another aspect of the typical strategy of rescuing Freud from the drive theory: he does not make a clean theoretical break. Were he to deny that there are drives, then there would be a new confrontation in theory and evidence. But Schafer is not like Peterfreund or Lacan, who did in fact make a clean break. Schafer still acknowledges that "Drives appear to be incontrovertible facts of human nature." However, for Schafer, drives are not significant aspects of psychology. If we consider the example of "a man regarding a woman lustfully," and assume that "the physiological correlates are present," we will find that this man regards himself as "passive in relation to a drive," whereas, if he only chose to do so, he would accept instead that he is "a sexual agent, someone who lusts after a specific woman" (Schafer, 1980, p. 41). The man should (Schafer makes it clear) take responsibility for being a human agent. The moral concept of responsibility thus eliminates any consideration of sexual drive. The man should not hide behind the notion that he has been overcome by a "drive." With this sort of re-labelling, Schafer performs a theoretical ostrich-act regarding sexuality; he is pretending that the sexual is no different than any other kind of action that people are responsible for as active subjects. In Schafer's theory, anything in biological or physiological process is unworthy to be ranked among the human events that lead to meaning. This position leaves him with a thoroughly mentalized version of sex; the sexual body is gone from it. As Kovel (1978) notes, Schafer's reformulation of psychoanalytic theory (Schafer, 1976) *in effect* eliminates drive and energy concepts.

Schafer's major work of revisionist theory, *A New Language for Psychoanalysis* (1976), not only subordinates the sexual body to the generalized category of action; it does not so much as discuss sexuality at all, except in passing. The book has several chapters on the redefinition of emotion (where, presumably the problems of sexuality might be serious), but these fall to the level of vigorously asserting that while emotion may appear to almost everyone to be an experience with passive, uncontrollable elements rather than an action taken, it is no more than another kind of action. By thus making sexuality one more part of the supreme metaphor of "action," the same as anything else, and simultaneously maintaining that in healthy functioning, action is what you learn to take responsibility for (with the help of psychoanalytic therapy), Schafer converts psychoanalytic theory into another recycling of traditional moral-didactic thought, untroubled by the sexuality that bothered Freud. And suddenly, psychoanalysis is put into the service of pre-Freudian reason: action, Schafer explains, is "doing things for reasons" (1976, p. 139). Schafer's solution to the challenge of the sexual body is thus to eliminate it, not as a fact, but as a part of psychoanalytic discourse.

It does not appear, however, that Schafer's theory is acceptable to the discipline of psychoanalysis. As Farrell (1983) comments, it simply will not do to "smother" every problem under the category of "action."

Although psychoanalytic theorists have sometimes been tempted to think that they could dissolve the problems of the sexual body by inventing new terminology, there is a rich tradition within psychoanalysis of genuine struggle and confrontation with the challenge of the sexual body. That is why I maintain that psychoanalysis is the key discipline of the sexual body. Its theorists are members of the first discipline ever to have had to face the larger psychological implications of sexuality in a systematic way; possibly they are the only such group. Their attempts to meet and evade the challenge are rich in implications for the rest of us, both as researchers in other areas and as people living our lives.

Even in present day context, the original emphasis is still visible in the work of some psychoanalytic theorists, although these tend to find themselves in a situation reminiscent of the year 1900. Two researcher-theorists engaged in the study of infancy, Herman Roiphe and Eleanor Galenson, put the matter thus, in their volume, *Infantile Origins of Sexual Identity*:

> One may well ask, as we have so often asked ourselves during the many years of our study, why the army of infant observers and researchers have with a few notable exceptions, overlooked these astonishingly protean manifestations of early sexuality. Once again, Freud seemed to have understood the problem when he stressed the ubiquity of repression of infantile sexuality. His observation seems to apply to not only adults in general situations but to adults as they relate to children. (Roiphe and Galenson, 1981, p. x)

Roiphe and Galenson are restating here the original challenge Freud raised. Their immediate contention is directed at "the army of infant observers and researchers," some of whose work I will examine. But ultimately the Freudian challenge as I have represented it is toward authoritarian controls of whatever kind, within culture, over the sexual body, whether it be adult, infant or adolescent.

Of Paradigms and World Hypotheses

Once we begin talking of the whole of culture, it becomes apparent that we are dealing with something larger than a theory of psychology. The expansion of focus is partially a matter of drawing together in some relationship the many disciplines that have something to do with the sexual body and creating an appropriate interdisciplinary field. The theoretical assumptions in such an expansion are not simply additive. It must be said that the claims of psychoanalytic theory are so basic and all encompassing that they amount to a worldview. This is not to suppose that all the claims can be made good. In certain areas the theory probably still falls short of the necessary scope and precision. Validity is not the issue for the moment; the point is that psychoanalytic theory, however much it may emerge from clinical evidence, is far more than a theory of therapy. To use Pepper's distinction, psychoanalysis is not a "restricted" scientific hypothesis; it is a theory striving to be a *world* hypothesis (Pepper, 1982). There is, for example, a series of volumes entitled *The Psychoanalytic Study of Society* (Muensterberger, Boyer, and Grolnick, 1984), the contents of which would be difficult to reconcile with non-psychoanalytic sociology or anthropology. Nor could Norman O. Brown's psychoanalytic theory of history (1959) be reconciled with non-Freudian historiography. The details of Brown's proposal drew numerous objections particularly over Brown's denial of the possibility of genuine gratification through sublimation, and hence his denial of the possibility of happiness in any culture which attempts to first repress and then make social use of sexuality. But no theorist of psychoanalysis and no psychoanalytic reviewer countered by saying that there should *not* be any special psychoanalytic theory of history. In the same volume, Brown's review of the anal irrationality of the "science" of economics points to another feature of the psychoanalytic world view as it invades still another discipline. In theory of science, Kohut has argued that the scientific method of psychoanalysis is fundamentally different than that of other sciences and that other sciences must learn to model themselves, in some respects, on the innovation in method that Kohut believes psychoanalysis to represent (Kohut, 1977). On the other hand, there has been frequent acknowledgement in the psychoanalytic literature, beginning with Freud, that the theory does not contain an adequate account of artistic or scientific creativity. Kris (1952, p. 20) acknowledged that "we do not at present have tools which would permit us to investigate the roots of gift or talent, nor to speak of genius"; his own theory of "regression in the service of the ego" moves away from Freud's emphasis on primary process thinking in the creative process but does not account for its occurence. At least one theorist I discuss below (Holland, 1975b), now proposes that this gap has been closed. But even if psychoanalysis cannot account for creativity, its theorists realize that it somehow, some day, must do so, because it is a world hypothesis rather than a limited theory of only certain areas of mental functioning.

This leads me to two questions: as a world hypothesis, can psychoanalysis accept changes demanded by new evidence in other disciplines, such as the study of infancy? And, is psychoanalysis today essentially the same or a different (not merely revised and refined) world hypothesis than it was when Freud centered it, in his classical period, on the sexual body? In light of the first question, the suggestion of Milton Klein (1981b), namely that the current paradigm (in Kuhn's sense) for understanding the infant be revised to conform to the new facts of infant research, is problematical. The new research would indeed indicate that it would be best if psychoanalytic theory could reverse itself on the question of whether the infant has a rudimentary "self" at birth. As Klein realizes, Kuhn's theory hardly encourages the expectation that change at a basic level can be made peacefully and constructively by practitioners within an established theory. The deeper issue, however, is the nature of psychoanalysis itself. A scientific theory is a *restricted* hypothesis, whereas a world hypothesis is in principle unrestricted (Pepper, 1982). A world hypothesis must accommodate the data of all fields. But such a hypothesis cannot be brought into line with "science" simply by adjusting its components, because some adjustments are contrary to the theory as a whole, or to its root metaphor. The postulation of a self at birth is part of some larger set of categories. It will be evident from arguments to be presented later, that psychoanalytic theory *as it stands* could not possibly absorb the category of a self within its theory of the infant. The theory would be destroyed rather than revised. That the infant has a sexual body would be a particularly un-absorbable fact. There is another possibility to be considered, however: what we have today as psychoanalytic theory has already been transformed drastically, over the years, from the early paradigm of Freud. That earlier paradigm might be part of a world hypothesis quite different from its later, transformed version.

Could a self be posited of an infant, in theory, for classical psychoanalysis? I would suggest that it could and should, given the perspective of the sexual body.

In my concluding chapter I plan to return to the question of what designations should be applied to the current as well as the original psychoanalytic world hypothesis, and what the implications of that naming are. To anticipate, the perspective of the sexual body may lead to a modified version of a world hypothesis favored by Pepper in his later years, which he called Selectivism (Pepper, 1967). But Selectivism would require no small amount of new learning on the part of those working within the many disciplines which make up, or impinge upon, the perspective of the sexual body.

CHAPTER THREE

ANALOGUES OF ORIGINAL SIN: THE POSTULATE OF INNATE DESTRUCTIVE AGGRESSION

In an earlier article, I have given my account of how it came about that Freud, through his deep loyalties to cultural authority, took steps to water down, and finally to reverse, his early emphasis on the sexual body (Efron, 1977). As a theory, psychoanalysis did not come firmly under the influence of this reversal until the 1920's, and at first only uncertainly, through Freud's postulation of a death instinct (Freud, 1920a). The theory of a death instinct is speculative, and it remains in unclear status within psychoanalytic thought today. It is not necessary to discuss it as such, but the issue it raises is important because the postulation of an innately destructive "instinct" of some general description is necessary if the implications pointing toward sexual freedom in Freud's work of the classical period are to be negated. Today, probably the bulk of writers who accept psychoanalytic assumptions believe that there is an "aggressive" instinct, and that Freud assumed so too. However, the derivation within Freud's theorizing of this aggressive instinct is dubious. As the highly perceptive volume on psychoanalytic terms by Laplanche and Pontalis (1973) notes, Freud had explicitly *rejected* the idea of an aggressive instinct during his classic phase; as these authors also point out, even the death instinct theory of 1920 does *not* rest on data that bear a relation to "aggressive behavior" (pp. 17, 19). Freud of course had an awareness of the reality of aggression in all of his work, but Laplanche and Pontalis are not persuasive in their tacit suggestion that this early practice was but an unexplicit formulation of the later theory of aggression, which Freud had had in mind all the while he actually was stressing the libido, a form of life instinct. Stepansky (1977) has offered an elaborate justification of another kind: Freud had plenty of evidence at hand for the aggressive instinct prior to 1920, but he kept refusing to allow it any theoretical resonance, for reasons determined by Freud's own psychological needs. For a long time, according to Stepansky, Freud needed to "celebrate the triumph of the libido theory" (Stepansky, 1977, p. 111), and when Freud did begin to comment on the possibility of aggression as an instinct, he did so in the context of repelling Alfred Adler's attempt to re-center psychoanalysis on a theory of aggression which denied the primacy of sexuality (Stepansky, 1977, pp. 112-142). On the other hand, it could be that Freud knew what he was doing; it may be true, as the distinguished psychoanalyst Gregory Rochlin (past President, Boston Psychoanalytic Society) has claimed, that Freud concentrated on infantile sexual conflicts and "chose to withhold psychoanalytic consideration" of aggression and of anything else that might blur his focus upon "conflicts which were plainly and immediately sexual" (Rochlin, 1973, p. 74). If so, it is a sign that he knew what he wanted to emphasize.

Freud's move toward understanding aggression as an inherent destructive *Aggressionstrieb* is far from clear on theoretical grounds. Indeed there are clearer statements in the later Freud of a need *to propose* such a theory of aggression than there are on what it really is supposed to be (Rochlin, pp. 11-12, 104). By 1930, Freud, in *Civilization and Its Discontents*, was reverting to notions of the "natural wickedness of man" (Laplanche and Pontalis, 1973, p. 20), which were soon to obscure his own originality. Still worse, his innovative suggestions about aggression, when they finally were made, called for a linkage of libido with death and aggression: a portion of the death instinct "is placed directly in the service of the sexual function, where it has an important part to play. This is sadism proper. Another portion . . . with the help of the accompanying sexual excitation . . . becomes libidinally bound" within the human organism, as "erotogenic masochism" (Freud, 1924, pp. 163-164). This passage, cited as the central one on the topic by Laplanche and Pontalis (1973, p. 19), is complicated and full of problems in meaning. These need not be taken up in the present context: the issue I wish to address is that of overall theoretical direction. Freud not only moved his theory significantly close to an endorsement of the reality of an *Aggressionstrieb*: he also blurred the critique of authoritarian controls over sexuality by bonding sex with aggression, in the formulations just quoted. This bond is much regretted by Rochlin (p. 12), who sees no scientific warrant for it. However, later psychoanalytic theory on this issue after Freud is not any better; one must agree with Rochlin's observation that "Nowhere in psychoanalysis have concepts been founded on less clinical study or given over more to polemics than in the area of aggression" (Rochlin, 1973, p. 179).

Recent thinking on aggression from non-psychoanalytic disciplines would seem to leave the issue moot. Mary Midgley (1978) has argued from a sociobiological perspective that the high incidence of intraspecific killing in humans, in other words warfare, makes it absurd to deny the existence of innate destructive aggression. When it comes to evidence not based on this deductive argument, however, Midgley has little to offer, nor does she try to explain how it can be that some societies do not make war. The directors of the Center for Research on Aggression, located at Syracuse University, on the other hand, maintain that there is *no* evidence for the theory of innate destructive aggression. Their recent anthology of studies on aggression in cultures all over the globe is a model for their approach, which is to study aggression in its many specific cultural contexts without adopting any empirically dubious doctrines about instinct (Goldstein and Segall, 1983).

For psychoanalysts of liberal persuasion, such as Rochlin or Milton Klein (1981b, discussed above), the problem is one of an unfortunate discrepancy between psychoanalytic theory and empirical findings. Rochlin discusses at some length, in fact, the dubious status of "aggression" as an instinct in ethology at all (pp. 52-83). The issue however is more loaded emotionally than such a critique would suggest. The attribution of aggression in some innate, destructive form to human nature places psychoanalytic thought within the many cultural traditions of body-denigration and sexual repression that it initially had broken away from. If Freud was still somewhat hesitant about how to resolve the problem as late as 1937 (as Rochlin shows, 1973, p. 12), later major innovators generally have not been. Melanie Klein—who is credited by J. Bowlby (1980c, p. 384) as being the only theorist after Freud to succeed in bringing about major alteration in the psychoanalytic view of anxiety in infancy—is the key figure here.

The actual attribution of destructive innate aggression to infants came mainly from her. Heinz Kohut, tacitly recognizing her importance, states that what Melanie Klein had called the "paranoid position"—a construct that has become one of the most successful theoretical moves toward making aggressive destruction innate from the age of 3 months or so—does not "constitute the emergence of elemental, primary, psychological givens. . ." (Kohut, 1980, p. 121). Kohut, in denying the innate destructive aggression theory of human nature, was articulating a position which had by his time become unorthodox. (We will examine his views and their bearing on the problem of the sexual body in a later chapter.) Klein, however, claimed that the infant's "position" in very early psychological development had to be paranoid (Klein, 1948c) and her claim has been accepted by many psychoanalytic writers since her contributions. For her as for most later theorists, the mother is assumed to be one who will either reflect or threaten the infant's total dependency. Her existence as an autonomous woman separate from the body of the infant must be perceived first of all as a threat to the infant's self. At 6 months or even at 3 months, the infant will realize the danger of being separated, and will immediately fantasize the sadistic destruction of the mother who brings this threat.

The implications of such an approach for an underlying theory of human nature are brought out in a statement by Klein's disciple, John Arnold Lindon. Lindon, who wrote the article on Klein for the volume *Psychoanalytic Pioneers* (Lindon, 1966), was President of the Psychiatric Research Foundation at that time. He got "great help", he said, from Melanie Klein herself, in writing his piece. His assumptions about human nature are clear:

> The superego begins to operate, in Klein's opinion, much earlier than it does according to Freud's views. From babyhood on, the perceived parts of the mother—and soon the perceived parts of other people in the child's surroundings—are taken into the self as part objects, forming the basis for a variety of identifications, favorable and unfavorable. In the fifth or sixth month of life, with the increasing integration of the ego, the infant begins to realize, at first only intermittently, that the gratifying objects he needs and loves are aspects of the frustrating ones he hates and, in fantasy, destroys. He has matured to the point of perceiving whole objects.
>
> With this discovery, he begins to feel concern about these loved objects, for he cannot yet distinguish between his fantasies and their lack of actual effects. He experiences feelings of guilt and the urge to preserve these objects and to make reparation to them for harm done . . . . Feelings of guilt, such as occasionally arise in everyone, have very deep roots in infancy, and the tendency to make reparations plays an important role in one's sublimations and object relations. This leads to a completely new approach to the understanding of Adam and Eve's original sin and guilt. (Lindon, 1966, p. 370)

I should say that this view of the neonate's mind gave not just a new understanding but a new lease on life to Sin and Guilt, as innate primary human qualities.

Klein herself minced no words. The child's sadistic fantasies directed against the inside of the mother's body "constitute the first and basic relation to the outside world and to reality" (Klein, 1948b, p. 238). I would certainly not want to deny that young infants can and do have passionate emotions, and that given the right circumstances, these could be sadistic in quality. But Klein believed that these were the feelings that make up the first and basic relation to the world.

The possibility of certain personal unconscious determinants should not be overlooked for Klein's disposition to arrive at these findings. Her life-history is seldom mentioned in the literature. The recent memorial papers on Klein in the *International Journal of Psychoanalysis* are silent regarding her psychological conflicts, despite some biographical information and laudation (Joseph, 1983). In fact, Klein (1882-1960) had an unusually stressful childhood and adolescence in which two of her siblings died. Both were extremely significant to her emotional development. Her sister Sidonie, who was 4 years older than Melanie, died at the age of 9. "Sidonie was bedridden for a year before her death and spent a great deal of her time teaching Melanie what she knew" (Lindon, 1972, p. 33). Melanie also had a close relationship with her brother, Emmanuel, who was 5 years older than she; he encouraged her to believe in her creative and intellectual capabilities, especially in music and literature, the fields of his interest. However, he had a heart condition and died at 25, when Melanie was 20 (Lindon, 1972, pp. 33-34). At 21, Klein married, perhaps partially in an effort to protect herself from the loss she must have felt. The marriage caused her to give up her ambition to study medicine, a goal she had set at the age of 14, and one which she always regretted not having pursued (Lindon, 1972, p. 34). The marriage ended in 1923 after the period of Klein's first deep immersion in psychoanalytic therapy as both analysand and analyst. She did not remarry. Her further analysis with Karl Abraham ended in 1925, after 14 months, when he suddenly died. Shortly after this further trauma, she moved to England (Lindon, 1972, p. 36; cf. Segal, 1980). This life-history indicates a special vulnerability to the threat of death to loved ones, and suggests a need to defend against such fantasies. It would be no surprise if her theories were a major part of her defense.

At a formal, professional level, Klein derived her theory from the kind of evidence that Kohut takes as essential to psychoanalysis, from prolonged empathetic clinical immersion. But the immersion was in the context of her specialty, child analysis. Without questioning this sort of evidence, we must still question the derivation. Klein could not psychoanalyze anyone 3 months or 6 months of age. Her work was one of hypothetical reconstruction in that respect. How did Klein determine that the environmental setting was not basically the energizing force behind the sadistic fantasies?

In a lecture given to U.C.L.A. students in 1962, D.W. Winnicott (1965, p. 117) admitted that in his opinion Klein's low estimate of environmental factors did not stem from the facts, but from her bias. He said that she formally acknowledged the role of the environment, but she was just not capable, personally, of taking it into account. Winnicott should have added, however, that her writings often show what can only be called a deep hatred of infants, possibly revealing a projected hatred of herself. Consider for example the following assertion: "In the very first months of the baby's existence," Klein wrote in 1934, it wants to destroy the mother's body "by every means which sadism can suggest" (Klein, 1948c, p. 282). Or, to take a statement from 1930, the baby wants "to possess himself of the contents of the mother's body and to destroy her by every weapon which sadism can command . . ." (Klein, 1948b, p. 236). The language chosen here is significant. When we speak of "every weapon which sadism can command" we are evoking everything from whip to torture chamber. It is a way of blurring the small range of weaponry at an infant's disposal, such as biting, into that whole manifold. The image suggested, of a tiny infant imagining and employing sophisticated torture apparatus, is transparently the fantasy of an adult, laid onto a baby. This baby—a theory-maker's artifact—is credited implicitly with an ego capable of the foresight needed to plan a course of elaborate torture. The same artifact however is not credited with the native intelligence to discern that its mother and itself are centered in two separate bodies, and thus to avoid the "paranoid position" entirely.

Such little monsters can not be handled too firmly. In the case history of Erna, a six year old described in Klein's 1926 essay, "The Psychological Principles of Infant Analysis," we learn that the little girl's neurosis dated from her period of toilet training. "This training, which Erna had felt as a most cruel act of coercion, was in reality accomplished without any sort of harshness and so easily that, at the age of one year, she was perfectly clean in her habits" (Klein, 1948a, p. 148). The child was only disturbed because of "the heavy blow" to her narcissism which struck her "when she imagined" that this training "meant the loss of the excessive affection bestowed on her in infancy" (*ibid.*). Needless to say, the "in reality," the "excessive" and the "imagined" are Klein's value judgments. Klein's value terms might have signalled a serious problem in her approach, but the essay on Erna went on to become the basis for the first chapter of Klein's book, *The Psycho-Analysis of Children* (1932).

Practical problem masks theoretical conclusion. It is so hard to know what an infant is fantasizing that the effort to guess at it has a necessarily privileged space, if theory is going to try to know this material at all. The psychoanalytic theorist is characteristically drawn to make such a guess, as her or his assumptions draw the analyst more and more deeply into suppositions on the earliest states of mind in an infant, those states which may underlay all future intrapsychic conflict. Here the analyst is unable to take the safe path of the behavioral psychologist and simply leave the unobservable alone. The result of such guesswork, however, may indicate at least one thing reliably: the kind of thinking the psychoanalyst was doing, when the topic was actually human nature itself, rather than any neutral description of a psychological process.

Melanie Klein encountered opposition in her years in England, but the battles she and her followers fought with classical analysts could not overcome her basic predisposition to credit all pathology to the innate workings of the mind. Ernest Jones, who sponsored her in England and sometimes disagreed with her over the years, was too close to her in his presuppositons to offer a corrective: ". . . there is no danger of any analysts neglecting external reality," he announced in 1935, "whereas it is always possible for them to disregard Freud's doctrine of the importance of psychical reality" (Jones, 1935). What I have been attempting to show in this discussion of Klein, however, is not merely the privileging of internal reality, but its interpretation in accordance with a moral presupposition about human nature, namely that in the infant there can only be immaturity and a raw, selfish primordial ego, which must be broken, controlled, and directed into the standards of adulthood.

Winnicott's admission that Melanie Klein did not have the ability to take the environmental factors in child pathology seriously did not get into print until 1965. By 1975, when the Institute for Psycho-Analysis and Hogarth Press re-issued Klein's *Narrative of a Child Analysis*, re-evaluation was more than due. This case of 10-year old Richard had originally come out posthumously in 1961. Its influence, however, dates back to the actual 93-session analysis that Klein did during a four-month time period during 1941. One reviewer astutely commented: ". . . the amazing closeness with which Klein followed every detail and verbalized her observations with attributions of motive and phantasy ['interpretations'] . . ." would have made little Richard unable to forget for a second that "he was not alone" (Padel, 1975). Padel found plenty of evidence that Klein read Richard's life selectively, in favor of her own preconceptions. As early as the second session, the boy seems to be trying desperately "to get her to let up a bit, to put a little space between them . . . ." She resolutely missed signals. Or so Padel thinks. Klein herself must have sensed something not going right, because in 1946, when *she* brought out the case of Richard, in a shortened version, she "inverted the sequence of material of the whole session and gave the impression of increasing *closeness* throughout it" (Padel, 1975, p. 799).

Melanie Klein was the founder of the British school of object relations, which remains perhaps the most influential of all psychoanalytic theories today. As theory, object relations is far too complex to be described in detail in the present study (cf. Greenberg and Mitchell, 1983, for an excellent descriptive and critical review of object relations theory). The point I want to bring out is a fatal instability in the theory due to the presence of a basic layer of sexual body hatred, deriving from the work of Klein, overlaid now with a language that does not deal with the body at all, except as providing imagery for the mental representations that permit object relations to be formed (Greenberg and Mitchell, 1983, pp. 138-139). The instability is created, on the one hand, by the positive attitude that informs object relations thought with regard to the infant's social growth: "The object-relations theorists are exceptions among the majority of psychoanalysts in this vein. Their recognition of object-seeking bonding takes into account the infant's need for stimulation" (Cicchetti and Pogge-Hesse, 1981, p. 240). This seems to overcome Freud's inaccurate sense of infantile emotional life as a process of tension-reduction. But on the other hand, the object relation theorists follow Freud in emphasizing "the *disorganizing* effect of affect . . ." (*ibid.*, p. 237). The infant is locked within an endopsychic battle of good and bad "part objects" and good and bad mothers. The doctrine of part objects endows the body with the function of providing the imagery for a psyche that is inherently prone to split its emotional perceptions of the objects, that is to say the persons, to whom it relates. That these theories are not subject to practical empirical test is affirmed by Kline, in his careful review of all psychoanalytic evidence that could be accepted by psychologists of all theoretical persuasions (Kline, 1981, pp. 416-418). Not only is the supporting evidence a reconstruction on the part of the therapist rather than an observation which may eventually be confirmed, but there is scant chance of devising a confirmation or disconfirmation of any kind. We have a "body" in theory only: it can never be made palpable, and unlike the sexual body, it cannot give any trouble to theoretical constructs.

The legacy of Klein's highly negative body imagery was recognized by some of the later theorists, who did not want to follow her in that respect. Guntrip for example found that the infant could not in any way achieve a good relation to the mother's body, nor to its own, in Klein's theory: "I cannot see how, on Klein's assumptions, a baby can ever experience a really good breast at all" (Guntrip, 1973, p. 67). By "good breast," he refers to the "part object" that precedes full ego functioning, in Klein's theory, and it is inevitable that this part object, by virtue of its importance in development, and its inherent reference to the human female breast, is a theory of the body—the bad body, as Guntrip realizes. But working in the wake of Klein, Guntrip himself could only struggle to clean up this bad body, despite his best efforts to assert that object relations theory assumes a "psychosomatic whole" in its model of the infant (ibid., p. 94). This infant was considered in such a way as to postulate a newborn wreck, hardly able to function in any way except irrationally, with virtually no cognitive capacities at all. Indeed Guntrip's defensive assertion that he never had meant to deny the psychosomatic whole, the mind-body unity in human infantile existence, is followed closely with another statement that separates the two, in a way that would cripple interdisciplinary research. The object relations theorist Fairbairn, whose theory Guntrip endorses, had a very clear idea of the problem; Fairbairn, says Guntrip,

> clearly saw that just as biology studies somatic processes by methods that throw no direct light on our subjective personal experiences, so psychodynamic science studies the subjective personal experiences of the psychosomatic whole by methods that throw no direct light on biological processes. (Guntrip, 1973, p. 94)

This split in stance, while hedging on any formal rejection of mind-body relations, throws all the emphasis on psychological experience conceived as separated, for all practical intent, from biological knowledge. The various attempts of Fairbairn, Guntrip, and Winnicott to reformulate object relations so that it did not lead to a hatred of the sexual body, as it does in Klein's theories, fail to come to grips with the intractable nature of world hypotheses: Klein's writing could not be revised to make her theory come out on the side of life, without destroying her theory. In fact, the later theorists who have followed her have merely tempered her constructs while preserving their bias against instinct, biology, body, and sexuality. As Guntrip put it (1968, p. 129), the theory is very clear that the infant "*starting life with a primitive and undeveloped psyche, just cannot stand the loss of his object.*" In other words, the infant, nominally a psychosomatic whole, is actually a maladjusted entity, whose imagined symbiotic delusory tie to his/her "object" (usually the mother) is just too terrible to give up, without necessarily incurring dangerously pathological hazards.

Among Klein's more revealing "adultomorphic" attributions (Schachtel's term, 1959) to the infantile mind, is the notion that the infant's destructive impulses and emotions "arouse persecutory anxiety in the infant," since the infant for reasons of perceptual and developmental immaturity must attribute these destructive feelings to others. Anxiety in early childhood she likewise attributes to "the child's fear of his own aggression, which he can only partially control" (Lindon, 1972, pp. 44, 47). As Lindon believingly puts it,

> The child is anxious about damage he does to himself by uncontrolled aggression (for example, in screaming fits) and about the harm he may do to others. (Lindon, 1972, p. 47)

This set of assumptions would do justice to a disturbed adult with a highly active conscience; the notion that screaming fits in children are replete with feelings of concern for the damage they may do to adults, is adultomorphism *par excellence*. Screaming fits can have more in them than aggression in any case—terror, for example. But it would not even be necessary for the object relations theorist to investigate "many apparently odd manifestations, such as inexplicable phobias of infancy" (Lindon, 1972, p. 49); these are conveniently regarded within the theory as part of the process of "working through" the depressive position already posited to account for them. The opportunity for psychological "artifact" here is virtually unlimited.

Melanie Klein's major rival in psychoanalytic thinking about children was Freud's daughter Anna. Anna Freud arrived in England somewhat later than Klein. As early as 1926, however, the same year that Klein came to England with the case of little Erna already completed, Anna Freud, later to be of the greatest importance in the development of English and American child analysis, lectured in Vienna on one of her own cases; that lecture would be reprinted in her book, *The Psycho-Analytical Treatment of Children* (1946). Miss Freud had been treating a six year old girl who eventually confided to her the content of her fantasies. These were of an anal nature. At first Anna Freud welcomed the patient's trust, but when it turned out that the child was going home and offering anal fantasies at the dinner table, and that her family had walked off in righteous disgust (and with dead silence), the analyst quickly reconsidered. Horrified, she reports that the child had gone on to abandon "all restraints in other respects as well. In a few days she had become transformed into a cheerful, over-bold and naughty child, by no means dissatisfied with herself" (A. Freud, 1946, p. 47). The child's guardian came to Anna Freud to complain. It is interesting that this girl's acting-out looked to her analyst like the giving up of "all" controls. Anna Freud now began to try to undo what she terms her analytic "blunder." She put pressure on the girl to stop, and whenever the child lapsed into what Anna Freud calls "naughtiness and perversion," the analyst acted swiftly by deliberately throwing her back into the illness that had begun to be relieved: "there remained nothing for it but for me to bring about the neurosis again . . . ." After several rounds of this, the little girl began acting properly. Such comportment seems to have been what her therapist, obviously frightened by her patient's new freedom, was most committed to uphold (A. Freud, 1946, pp. 46-49; cf. the revised translation, A. Freud, 1974, pp. 61-65).

Anna Freud, though justly honored for her continuation of her father's work, also, in some of her formulations, provides a good example of the body-hating tendency in later psychoanalysis. She carried this hatred not only into her theories on young children, but on into notions of adolescence as well. A remark of hers, not usually quoted, shows this clearly; it is from her most famous book, *The Ego and the Mechanisms of Defense*:

> There is in human nature a disposition to repudiate certain instincts, in particular the sexual instincts, indiscriminately and independently of individual experience. This disposition appears to be a phylogenetic inheritance . . . . (A. Freud, 1966, p. 157)

During puberty, when bodily maturation causes "a sudden accession of instinctual energy," this antagonism is brought to fruition, as "an active defense mechanism." We must pinch ourselves to see if we are awake here, so blatantly anti-sexual is Anna Freud's stance regarding adolescent sexuality. Her authority continued to be enormous in the further development of the psychoanalytic theory of human nature, as we can see from her being cited in 1972 by Albert J. Solnit, President of the American Psychoanalytic Association, as one who had safely settled the fact that there is an innate aggressive, destructive instinct.

The occasion of Dr. Solnit's statement was a survey on aggression by Dr. Leo Stone, published in the *Psychoanalytic Quarterly* (Stone, 1971). This extensive review of the scientific evidence for backing up the theory of innate destructive aggression concluded that *there simply was no such evidence to be had*: "I do not regard as proved, nor as pragmatically useful, the concept of primary or essential aggression." The next year, President Solnit went into action with a rebuttal, arguing politely that pragmatically—that is, in a "heuristic" sense—there was plenty of use for the assumption. With the aid of ridicule, Solnit also argued that Stone's caution, as well as the caution of Charles Brenner (1971) on extrapolating the evidence back into unanalyzable states of earliest infancy, was quite unnecessary. As far as Solnit was concerned Anna Freud had proven the assumption well enough in her comments on young children, over a period of nearly 50 years.

Winnicott's Hatred of Infantile Sexuality

Probably the most influential descendant of Melanie Klein's object relations approach was the British psychoanalyst Donald W. Winnicott (1896-1971). He is widely credited with being a wise and reasonable man, concerned more with the child than with theory. The suggestion that he too carried on the psychoanalytic tendency toward hatred of the sexual body will undoubtedly be greeted with disbelief.

Winnicott did not repeat such giveaway formulations as that of the baby lusting after "every weapon which sadism can command." Winnicott for the most part was engaged in practical hospital work with children; his essays are full of sensitive comment, but little formal theory. It is said that during his 40 years at the Paddington Green Children's Hospital in London, he "had seen some 60,000 mothers and children" (Ramzy, 1977, p. xii). Unlike Klein he was able to say that "we deal with" reality "according to the way we have had reality introduced to us at the beginning" (Winnicott, 1957, pp. 171-172). Where Klein emphasized the "internal object," the mother image that the infant created in its own mind, Winnicott turned to what he called "the transitional object" as the key factor in early development. A "transitional object" such as a security blanket or teddy bear is a possession, but is not merely something "external" for the infant. Because the transitional object is never under "magical" or "omnipotent" control, it is crucial for the part the child can make it play in learning to get away from the world of totally infantile gratifications (Winnicott, 1971, pp. 10-11).

Despite these important differences with Klein, Winnicott worked largely within the same problematic to which Klein herself was drawn. His article of 1935, "The Manic Defence," is regarded as one of the earliest uses of Klein's theories, in fact (Winnicott, 1957). The theory that emerges from Winnicott's work, informally, and by deduction, is not saved from Klein's implications; it is only made unclear by his reluctance to engage in formal theory. Winnicott still assumes that the infant is unfit by birth for the world of reality, and therefore must be helped to reduce his or her wishes to "normal" proportions. Notwithstanding his realization that there must be a "facilitating environment" for the healthy maturation of the child, he took his stand squarely with the psychoanalytic pessimists, regarding the human ability to ever grow up no matter what the environment: in his popular book addressed to mothers and fathers, Winnicott (1964) wrote that "throughout life" there must always be an "essential dilemma" stemming from the fact that "even the best external reality is disappointing because it is not also imaginary, and although perhaps to some extent it can be manipulated, it is not under magical control" (p. 128). Such a statement about "even the best external reality" is loaded with unacknowledged metapsychological and metaphysical presuppositions. Winnicott is declaring that it is impossible to have a reality which is at once external, an "object" such as Virginia Woolf's lighthouse, and also "imaginary," as that lighthouse also is, for the characters in her novel. Woolf assumed that it is not only possible but essential that any mature view of external reality be able to resonate to both the factual and the imaginary dimensions (Woolf, 1927). Why Winnicott thought this was impossible to do is far from clear, but perhaps it finally came down to an unrecognized metaphysical assumption, namely that what is "out there," external, is also inherently unsatisfying to the aggression-driven human nature that he believed in.

Despite his slight interest in formal theory, Winnicott knew that he was finally dealing with a worldview, not merely a psychology. As the process of decathecting the transitional object goes on over the years, the meanings of this object and other "transitional phenomena have become diffused, have become spread out over the whole intermediate territory between 'inner psychic reality' and the 'external world as perceived by two persons in common,' that is to say, *over the whole cultural field*" (1971, p. 5, emphasis added). Prior to such culturalizing, the infant is considered quite incomplete and incapable of experiential depth: "I repeat here," Winnicott wrote in his key essay, "The Location of Cultural Experience" (1971, p. 99), "a human infant must travel some distance from early experiences in order to have the maturity to be deep." Indeed, as Pruyser has argued, the infant postulated by Winnicott will travel all the way into the "public symbol systems" of the arts, literature, science and religion (Pruyser, 1984, p. 60). The infant by learning to play in his transitional space thus "slides out of playing into cultural experience of every kind," as Winnicott (1965, p. 188) put it. But what seems not to occur either to Winnicott or to Pruyser is that this slide may not be altogether a good thing: Not "every kind" of cultured imagination which the infant may develop is necessarily a healthy development. Winnicott could speak confidently of parenting as the process by which is "handed on . . . the whole torch of culture and civilization" (1965, p. 101). But the "whole torch" is exactly the problem: after Freud, after two World Wars, such blanket endorsement of civilized values is highly questionable. This problem is not a serious one for Winnicott or Pruyser, nor for Klein before them, because their implicit assumption remains that the infant, to start with, is so embedded in aggression and in irrational desire that an immersion in the norms of civilized culture is simply a moral necessity. That way alone does the infant eventually "have the maturity to be deep."

In denying that capacity to the newborn, Winnicott did not mean to say that the very early infant is lacking in strong feelings. It is merely that Winnicott rejects the value of these. Winnicott's profound connections with one of the most anti-bodily traditions in Western thought, that of Plato (or at least one major side of Plato) are revealed in another of his statements in his crucial essay on cultural experience. Implicitly, he moves toward his own need, no doubt born of his own upbringing in a culture which has its own "contempt for the body, fear of the senses, and . . . opposition of flesh to spirit" (Dewey, 1934, p. 20) to devalue the sexual body of the child. Consider the implications of this statement in his discussion of childhood play: "It is to be noted that the phenomena that I am describing have no climax. This distinguishes them from phenomena that have instinctual backing, where the orgiastic [sic] element plays an essential part, and where satisfactions are closely linked with climax" (Winnicott, 1971, p. 9). The use of the term "orgiastic" is an interesting "slip" here, hinting at fears looming up. Discussing the role of instinctual gratifications, Winnicott declares it a "fact" that these pleasures are at the first stage of neonatal life "part-functions" (as Klein would have agreed), which would become "*seductions*"—a word italized by Winnicott—unless they occur when the person has "a well-established capacity . . . for total experience . . ." (1971, p. 98). The infant obviously would not have this capacity as far as Winnicott was concerned. Quite as Plato might have put it, "It is the self that must precede the self's use of instinct; the rider must ride the horse and not be run away with" (Winnicott, 1971, pp. 98-99). The metaphor is modelled upon Plato's Charioteer in *The Phaedrus*, where an authoritarian Soul must rein in, and harshly reign over, the dark, wild horse of the body (see Reeves, 1958, pp. 34-37, 198-202). Winnicott's whole notion of the special psychological space in which play occurs and culture is elaborated, is premised on a denigration of the biological factors; he finds these factors hardly worthy of serious attention by psychology: "this potential space is a highly variable factor," whereas the actual world is largely pregiven, and unlike "personal or psychic reality" is "biologically determined . . ." (Winnicott, 1971, p. 103; see also p. 98).

It is in light of this suspicion of the instinctual life—and therefore of infants themselves—that we may understand the function of Winnicott's serious theory of the nature of play. There is no denying that his observations on the meaning of play are very sensitive. But play experiences are given their special value, according to his own words, by virtue of their nonresemblance to orgasm. Freud of course had shocked the world with his insistence that infants not only are sexual but that they have orgasms at the breast. But the "experiences called playing" which Winnicott emphasized, are "nonclimactic"; psychoanalysts, he thought, have "failed" to give these as much importance as they have allotted to "the significance of instinctual experience and of reactions to frustration . . ." (1971, p. 98).

As Winnicott delineates the problem of infancy, both the costs of the frustration of instinct, and psychoanalysis' critical edge toward cultural demands that would call for such frustration, are devalued. Instead we have an emphasis on non-climactic play, which serves as Winnicott's version of the good white horse of obedience in Plato's metaphor. Now it is not especially evident that play has no climaxes; in fact Winnicott's most extensive case history, that of a little girl nicknamed "the piggle" (to be discussed shortly), shows several references to "climax" in his play with this girl, and in the context of sexually loaded psychological contents, at that (Winnicott, 1977, p. 181). In a gross contradiction, Winnicott stipulates that playing has to be *"spontaneous"* in order to be developmentally valuable (1971, p. 51), but rules that it must not on any account involve genital arousal (p. 52).

We can hardly overestimate the importance to psychoanalytic therapy and theory of having one of its most prominent representatives, one who is greatly respected for his humanity and untheoretical practicality, base his major theories on the presumed unimportance of instinctual gratification and orgasm that infants have in their play behavior. So far as I can see, Winnicott never troubled to give evidence for his denial of such crucial bodily facts. It would seem that despite his reputation as an unfanatical, practical, modest man, Winnicott had engaged in a hatred of infantile sexuality every bit as serious as Melanie Klein's.

This hatred does reveal itself, in fairly undisguised form, in the case history of "the piggle." Beginning when the girl was 29 months old, the treatment continued for a total of 16 "on-demand" consultations, ending when she was five years old, in October, 1966. The parents of the girl add an affirming postscript dated 1975 (Winnicott, 1977, pp. 199-201). Nothing is said in this parental note of the adolescent's sexual development. The girl consented to the publication of the case history (p. 201). The care with which the case has been edited and published is much to be praised. The record comprised, however, is not entirely laudable. Things begin to go awry, I think, in the second session, where Winnicott decides to take a "risk" and interpose his own interpretation of a toy truck the girl was involved with: "I said: It's the mother's inside where the baby is born from" (p. 24). The girl agreed, and added a detail that must have fitted Winnicott's Kleinian theories of infant hatred of mothers: "Yes, the black inside" (p. 24). There is no telling whether this is part of the power of suggestion, nor what the girl's attribution might mean aside from the workings of Winnicott's procedure, inasmuch as the inter-play he has with the girl is a mesh of her initiatives and his theoretically conditioned counterplay.

In the 14th session, however, there is a most revealing occurrence. As Winnicott himself notes, it is here that the girl for the first time shows "evidence of potential capacity for genital enjoyment" (p. 184). He is referring to this part of the account:

> She took a train with lots of wheels and enumerated the wheels, giving them colors. She fondled this engine lovingly and mouthed it and rubbed it across her thighs, and then over her head from back to front. This turned into a game, so that the engine came down over her face and fell onto the floor accompanied by a noise which had a climax. (p. 181)

It seems fair enough to say that the girl at this point is making contact with essential dynamic forces in her own sexual life. The moment is a fragile one, and would be valued by anyone who cared about sexuality. The remainder of this "consultation," however, provides just the opposite denouement. Her game-playing evolves toward an acting out of birth, or "the idea of being born," as Winnicott sees it (p. 183). After some transformations in the game, Winnicott reports that it took the following form:

> Then I had to become a house, and she crept inside the house, rapidly becoming bigger until I could not contain her any longer and pushed her out. As the game developed, I said "I hate you," as I pushed her out. (p. 183)

Winnicott's statement of hate toward the child is all his own; nothing in the session warrants it. Hate had not been mentioned. The fact that hatred can be injected by her therapist into the little girl's profound fantasies about birth and the body, and that this injection follows upon the first evidence of genital gratification, is almost beyond comment. Sure enough, the girl's next feelings, immediately following the above sequence, are at once disturbed:

> This game she found exciting. She suddenly got a pain between her legs and soon afterwards went out to pass water. (p. 183-184)

The pain is a genital one, Winnicott's euphemism notwithstanding. Would it have been there without his own "I hate you"? That question is more to the point than his own overlay of interpretation: "The climax of this [game] was getting in touch with the mother's need to be rid of the baby when it is too big. Associated with this is sadness about getting bigger and older, and finding it more difficult to play this game of being inside mother and getting born" (p. 183). These ideas may reflect Winnicott's idea of birth, and his own sadness; nothing of the kind is reported of the girl. The curious attribution of "climax" to an inferred, psychological construct also seems to reflect his own gratification. Winnicott had encountered genital sexuality in this girl and had succeeded in putting it into its rightful, painful and sad place.

In this he is following Melanie Klein, even though he is different enough from her not to be called a Kleinian (Lindon, 1972, p. 50). His negative attitude toward the sexual body is more important, for the present study, than are the various differences. Nor is the connection between Winnicott and Klein simply a problem of influence. As Lindon rightly points out, by the early 1970's, it had become clear that a large number of psychoanalytic theorists who were not Kleinians had come around to "conclusions that are similar to the most controversial ones of Klein," although they often failed to credit her (Lindon, 1972, p. 54). It could be said, in fact, that Margaret Mahler's theories of infantile autism and psychosis are more extreme even than Klein's, since Klein never maintained that infants went through psychosis: they merely suffered from "transient periods of psychotic-like fantasies" (Lindon, 1972, p. 42).

The turn away from the sexual body in psychoanalysis had, by 1970, become one of its most widely shared assumptions. Fortunately there are significant qualifications to be made, in later chapters, of this conclusion. Something in psychoanalytic theory seems finally to reject the many continued efforts of its revisionists to make the sexual body an unimportant or even nonexistent entity.

CHAPTER FOUR

THE REICHIAN TRADITION: A VIEW OF THE SEXUAL BODY

The only branch of psychoanalytic theory that has developed a coherent sense of the sexual body is that descended from Wilhelm Reich (1897-1957). Even though Reich was expelled from the International Psychoanalytical Association in 1934, and despite the decline of his reputation in later years, his work continues to hold interest for thinkers in various disciplines and in several countries. I have already highlighted (in "Psychoanalysis as the Key Discipline") Prescott's cross-cultural analysis of the connection between physical affection and non-violent adult behavior (Prescott, 1979); this connection may be regarded as a major confirmation of Reich's theories. A recent issue of the respected French journal, *l'Arc* (Dadoun, 1983), devoted to Reich is one instance of the live interest in his thought, and one that is by no means confined to his generally acclaimed psychoanalytic work of the period 1919-1934. Without exaggerating the force of the Reichian movement today, it still can be said that his work is attracting far more interest than any of the other dissidents who split off from Freud, such as Adler, Rank, Stekel, Ferenzi, Horney, or Fromm. Jung's work also is being carried on vigorously, but it has the unique advantage of having its roots in an independent early analytic theory shaped by Jung even prior to his association, 1906-1912, with Freud; it also has an easier time in gaining acceptance in many quarters due to its affinities with traditional religious symbolism and, as I have argued in Chapter Two, because of Jung's disposition to avoid detailed considerations of sexual problems.

The survival of Reichian theory and therapy is thus remarkable, given the poor record of other dissident Freudian therapies; it is all but astonishing in view of the near demise of all therapeutic work in Reichian modes for several years after his death in an American prison in 1957, accompanied by the burning of all ten of his published books, in stock at the Orgone Institute Press. The bookburning took place while Reich's case was still on appeal (Greenfield, 1974, pp. 241-254).

It is worth recalling that this humiliating debacle for the Reichians was brought on in part by direct actions of the psychoanalytic mainstream therapists. Thus, an article in a magazine (Brady, 1947) which attacked Reich, and irresponsibly at that (see Greenfield, 1974, pp. 58-59), was given the unusual honor of being reprinted in the *Bulletin of the Menninger Clinic* (Brady, 1948). Later when Reich was convicted of violating a U.S. court injunction in 1956, the Secretary of the American Psychoanalytic Association, Dr. Richard L. Frank, wrote a congratulatory letter to the Food and Drug Administration, noting that the analysts in this official organization had not had any success in controlling Reich (Greenfield, 1974, p. 152). As Greenfield points out, Reich was not even a member of the group that wished to control him. Reich in fact had not been a member of any of the official psychoanalytic associations since 1934, when he was expelled from the International Association (Greenfield, 1974, pp. 32-33).

Dr. Frank's letter is an indication of a felt threat. But what caused the threat? One probable cause is that Reich's Orgone theory claimed to provide an improved and empirically confirmable revision of the theory of the libido, the sexual body energy. Orgone, in other words, is a concept of sexual energy in a unified somatic and mental framework. The theory remains open to disconfirmation to this day, and continues to gain corroborations of its various aspects in research performed over the past several decades. The reader here may consult Boadella (1973) for an overall review, while Seiler (1982) and Blasband (1984) offer examples of recent confirmatory studies. As a careful reviewer of a recent biography of Reich (Sharaf, 1983) has found, there is no apparent ground for dismissing the Orgone theory or any of Reich's other theories in his later years (1934-1957) as "madness" (Kendrick, 1983).

Unfortunately, most present day adherents of psychoanalytic theory would very likely agree with the estimate of Richard Wollheim (1971), who regards the prospect of subsuming "all instinctual energy" under the heading of "libido or sexuality" as a disaster. Wollheim believes that Freud almost did just that, in 1914, but that he averted disaster by postulating "another group of instincts over and against sexuality" (Wollheim, pp. 114-115). It must be said that Reich did indeed take "libido or sexuality" to its full conclusions, refining libido theory and confirming its workings in a range of contexts. But is it necessarily a theoretical disaster to take this path? Wollheim, a professional philosopher, reasons as follows: were all instinctual energy to be regarded as being in some basic sense sexual, then "this would have meant that the pathogenic role of sexuality would be unsubstantiated" (p. 115). It would appear that Wollheim has offered a non-sequitur. Frustrations or blockages of a natural sexual energy development could be postulated in order to account for the pathology of sex, as indeed Reich (and originally Freud) did. A unitary energy approach, in other words, is not necessarily unable to account for conflict. Indeed a unitary energy concept such as libido (and later Orgone) is better able to account for intrapsychic conflict than a theory that would build on presumably opposed dual instincts of libido and aggression, for the latter theoretical choice automatically creates conflict, as a function of its own theoretical premises, and would not enable the researcher to expect anything else but division. It is interesting in this regard to find that Jacques Lacan, whose revision of Freud is the most thoroughly insistent on the inherent conflictive status of the human psyche, allows that sexual, orgasmic pleasure, or "jouissance," is a positive unifying factor (E. Ragland-Sullivan, personal communication, May 28, 1984) when it does occur. But Lacan, whose work I will consider in a later chapter, seems to have no theoretical room for such unification, so unremitting is his distinction between the ostensible self, the "I," and the sub-self, the "moi." Beginning with that distinction, any connections with "jouissance" are necessarily subordinate notions.

On the other hand, the assumption of one instinctual, sexual energy would challenge researchers to a full exploration of the concept of the sexual body. Such an approach would entail the further postulation of a human organism highly susceptible to sexual pathogenic development, and it would also lead to a critique of culture insofar as culture has encouraged or even demanded the development of libido be subjected to repression. Moreover, as I have argued in the last chapter, Freud's eventual recourse to another instinct, the aggressive, has come up against objections that are much more difficult to overcome either in theory or in empirical corroboration than anything suggested by his libido theory, and at the same time has badly occluded his work on the sexual etiology of the neuroses.

The survival of Reichian theory and therapy into the present day is a result in part of its responsiveness to the essential need within the heritage of psychoanalysis (despite such claims as Wollheim's), for a continuously revised vision of the sexual body in Freud's original, multiple sense. Reichian theory and its own branches, such as Alexander Lowen's bioenergetic therapy (Lowen, 1965, 1967, 1970, 1975) probably constitutes the only thinking going on today that regularly considers adult as well as infantile sexuality, both in their connections and in their differences, and with attention to psychological meaning as well as bodily detail.

A relatively simple example is the discussion by the Reichian therapist Elsworth Baker, of feelings of genital anxiety on the part of some mothers, in connection with nursing (Baker, 1952). The topic of genital anxiety is considered, by Baker, in the context of his discussion of uterine contractions during breast feeding. Baker provides an excellent example of thinking that is well-centered on the sexual body: it involves the adult body, it refers to the specific bodily site where the anxiety is felt, and it locates the origin of the disposition toward anxiety in earlier sex-negative experience that has become "anchored" (not merely "introjected") in the adult woman's body. Moreover it raises an unresolved question about adult female enjoyment of sexual feelings concerning an infant, just as it considers the infant's reciprocal but not identical sexual gratification—most notable in the so-called oral orgasm—of this same contact. The unresolved question is, what place does such contact have in human life? Why is it important, or is it? Now the fact of uterine contractions has become fairly known, especially since writers within the feminist movement of the 1970's spoke of it, and the fact of infant's sexual gratification at the breast has been part of the psychological literature since Freud (1905b). It is barely possible to fit the event of a mother's genital anxiety during nursing into a few other theories, such as the Winnicottian concept of the "good enough mother" who facilitates infant development. However, in Winnicott and other non-Reichian theories, the event Baker discussed in 1952 is little mentioned. Nursing is all too likely to be regarded within most psychoanalytic theory today as a function of "nurturance," an abstraction which should have vital bodily referents but which in practice seldom does. Bowlby's approach takes the problem to be one of maternal-infant "attachment," but this metaphor as Bowlby (1984, pp. 34-35) develops it, has little if anything sexual or bodily about it.

For Reichian theory, precisely because it does continue to explore the meanings of the sexual body, the problem of the mother's genital anxiety is both noted and evaluated for treatment; it is not something to be encouraged as part of a generalized incest barrier. Latter-day Freudian theory would tend to concentrate on the infant's relation to "the breast." Since the infant is considered in such theory to be unable to imagine the actual, entire body of the mother as a separate organism, the woman becomes reduced to a body part, a fantasy in the infant's mind of a breast. Reichian theory would lead to the opposite assumption: that there can be genuine contact between infant and mother, not contact controlled by inaccurate fantasies of each others' bodies. Furthermore, because Reichian theory assumes that sexual energy movements are intrinsically present, mother and infant are regarded as two mind-body energy systems in one mode of human superimposition. The energy interchange can be qualitatively changed through anxiety, not merely "blocked" in a quantitative sense. Nursing can be a bad experience. As a recent Reichian therapist, Robert A. Dew has pointed out, "Armored chests cannot take or give pleasure in nursing, nor can armored pelves allow or enjoy the uterine contractions that attend it" (Dew, 1978, p. 230). Similarly, the training therapist, Robert Lewis, M.D., whose work is within one of the major offshoots of Reichian psychology, namely the Bioenergetics movement founded by Alexander Lowen, argues that a parent "out of contact with its own self . . . is out of touch with the infant, *even when the parent is touching and holding it*" (Lewis, 1976, p. 22). A very similar distinction between breast-feeding as such and affectively charged nursing is made by Jean and Paul Ritter (1959, pp. 58, 243), Reichians whose work I shall turn to shortly.

I have introduced the above findings with Reichian origin not in order to assert their empirical validity, but to show the complexity and pertinence of Reichian thought for the perspective of the sexual body. Reich founded an approach that also offers clarification of more simple findings, even some that contain a high valuation of the human body. Where Prescott, for example, must describe the one great variable of physical affection on the basis of empirically reported ethnography concerning skin contact, Reich could have a finer distinction between contact in which affection is actually felt and that in which it is either blocked or even contradicted. The distinction is made in terms of his differentiation between armored and unarmored character. Prescott, suggestive as are his findings based on the Textor compilation of the Human Relations Area Files, has no room for the possibility that a great deal of touching in modern industrial civilization may be significantly more armored than touch has been in many of the preliterate societies represented in those files. Nor could a theory based entirely on the factor of direct, skin-to-skin contact allow for the superimposition of energies in two bodies which are proximate but not necessarily touching.

It is a misfortune for modern psychological theory that Reich, because he took libido and its repression seriously in the context of finding a natural function for the adult orgasm, could be written off (if one did not actually read him) as advocating orgasm on all occasions. In other words, he could be presented as a hapless, naive theoretical victim of the "hydraulic" or "hydrodynamic" theory of sexual drive, in the early Freud, when in fact Reich developed a contextual theory of couples relations, which was a far cry from one-dimensional sexual "freedom." Thus, he argued that in the case of a couple powerfully attracted to each other sexually, but hampered by the woman's containment within her "good family" life, that is, within the authoritarian sexuality of her parental household, it probably would be better not to consummate a relationship at all (Reich, 1968, pp. 154-155). Baker, in expounding this contextual sense of sexual life in Reich's views a decade after Reich's death, states plainly that one of the greatest problems with couples is in getting them to realize that sexual intercourse should be had only when really desired; no unhealthy "stasis" of psychic/bodily orgone energy is going to occur because of a mere delay. Stasis, in the adult, Baker says, probably takes as much as a year of abstinence to develop (Baker, 1967, pp. 84, 104).

With the abusive labelling of the later Reich as a madman, a whole group of research beginnings, research workers, and their later developments into the present day have been lost to interdisciplinary thought. The psychoanalytic profession has been trying to forget Reich, in some cases entirely. A flagrant example is the volume on psychoanalytic approaches to the discipline of "psychosomatics" by the distinguished German psychoanalyst, Günter Ammon (Ammon, 1979). Ammon's book opens with a 120-page exposition of "the" psychoanalytic theory of psychosomatic illnesses, but does not mention Reich, whose work on the relation of mind and body is one of the major origins of "the" theory. In fact Reich is nowhere mentioned in Ammon's book, even though it dips back into earlier psychoanalytic theory to draw on one of Reich's adversaries, Franz Alexander.

It is impossible that Ammon is unaware of the importance of even the early Reich in the psychoanalytic study of mind-body relations. But Ammon is writing within the terms of a legend which has been propagated, namely that Reich worked in isolation, and that with his death interest in his work declined. Actually, Reich had at least 15 M.D. co-workers with him in his work at Rangeley, Maine, in the 1950's, and some of their students and students' students now comprise a working core of about 30 medically qualified psychiatric specialists, affiliated with the College of Orgonomy, an organization that has recently raised two million dollars for a permanent location to be constructed in Princeton, New Jersey. Reichian theory and therapy centering on infancy and on children had made a good beginning by the time of Reich's death. Meyerowitz (1982, pp. 43-48) lists some 70 published items in this field by Reich and co-workers for the period 1942-1956—but that line of interest has by no means dropped out of the Reichian tradition since 1957.

Reich's essays on children, most of which have been unavailable in English either because they had not been translated or because they had been destroyed and not reprinted after his conviction, have now been republished under the title *Children of the Future: On the Prevention of Sexual Pathology* (Reich, 1983). As Crist (1984) points out, Reich not only had a profound sense of the importance of maternal-infant contact; he also realized that the day to day problems of infant health must not be wished away under a new ideal of "perfect" care. The advantage of the relatively unarmored parent is not in avoiding "the many big and small problems which will turn up and must be handled skillfully," Reich claimed; the advantage is that the relatively unarmored parent will "sense the trouble," and in some cases, be able to alleviate it (Reich, 1983, p. 112). However, "In most cases the trouble will remain untouchable due to lack of knowledge" (*ibid.*). We simply do not know enough as yet about healthy "orgonotic" contact to be able to claim more than this, and there is no point in promising mothers that they can avoid the difficulties in caring for their infants which are bound to occur.

Such advice contrasts with that of Winnicott, who wrote a popular book directed largely at mothers of newborn infants, in which he did indeed idealize the mother's role (Winnicott, 1964). Badinter (1981, pp. 273-274) has analyzed Winnicott's description of the "good enough mother," and found that it actually denotes a woman absolutely devoted to her infant. Badinter charges that Winnicott has attempted to brainwash women to believe that the troubles they encounter in caring for their neonates are not real problems at all. This sentence among others by Winnicott, directed to the ideal mother of his theory, is given as evidence: "Enjoy being annoyed with the baby when cries and yells prevent acceptance of the milk that you long to be generous with" (Winnicott, 1964, p. 26). Although Klaus and Kennell (1982, p. 91) credit Winnicott with a good sense of the need for mother-infant contact just after the baby has been born, it should be noted that Winnicott places value not on the development of contact, but on the "person" and on knowledge. Thus Winnicott advised the mother: "I think the most important thing is that you easily feel that your baby is worth getting to know as a person, and worth getting to know at the earliest possible moment" (Winnicott, 1964, p. 20). These traditional emphases of Winnicott's have proven to be more acceptable in the literature of child care than has the language of Reich and the Orgonomists, who tend to be overlooked.

A Reichian Experiment in Family Life

The American Orgonomists are not the only Reichians unknown to current research. In England, independent followers of Reich who had never worked with him have carried therapy and research projects which deserve to be known. One outstanding example is the work of Jean and Paul Ritter, whose book *The Free Family: A Creative Experiment in Self-Regulation for Children*, was published in 1959.

The Ritters set out to raise their seven children in conditions of "self-regulation," from childbirth on through the school years. According to Boadella (1973, p. 220), the Reichian concept of self-regulation was first formulated by Tage Philipson, M.D., a Danish psychiatrist who worked with Reich from 1933 to 1939. It is also a principle implicit in some (but not all) of the teachings of Maria Montessori, as Ritter notes (Ritter and Ritter, 1959, pp. 235-237). Although I am not concerned with the complete "credits" for the concept of self-regulation, what I hope to have indicated in recounting some of the origins of the concept is that there has been a Reichian tradition, rather than a one-person doctrine. Self-regulation, a central Reichian concept, was adopted into Reich's theories subsequent to its formulation by Philipson, and it undoubtedly had sources in intellectual history prior to that formulation.

In Boadella's summary, "self-regulation" involves a commitment to the infant's and then the child's natural sense of what his or her needs are, and a trust that these needs can be fulfilled at the pace and scale that the infant or child determines.

> It was essential that the child's own organic rhythms of functioning were respected and allowed to develop naturally. From this there developed an entire methodology of bringing up babies in such a way that their natural rhythms could best be preserved. In such functions as breast-feeding it was vital to allow the baby to regulate the length and frequency of feeds. Similarly, in such functions as elimination, sleep, play, washing, and dressing the most important aim for the child's education was to preserve and protect the child's own natural sense of bodily pleasure in his own functions, which was the foundation of his ability to give himself to any activity wholeheartedly and with real commitment.... If the child's fundamental needs are gratified he will much more easily accept the inevitable frustrations and accommodations involved in the process of living, than the child who has lost this basic rhythm and has learnt to suppress his natural feelings. (Boadella, 1983, p. 220)

The references in this passage to the value of commitment and the inevitability of frustration in life itself are not only indications of the Ritters' no-nonsense approach to the free family; they also mark the distinction between freedom and license which is often overlooked. Even Nietzsche, it seems, finally did not fully grasp this difference. In *Beyond Good and Evil*, Nietzsche arrives at the position that because any worthwhile freedom requires discipline, there is therefore a "moral imperative of nature" which is "Thou shalt obey someone, and for a long time; else thou wilt perish and lose the last respect for yourself" (Nietzsche, quoted in Kaufmann, 1960, p. 216). This imperative effectively closes the door to self-regulation in children. Obedience to another is substituted for the self-development of adequate discipline to carry out creative work.

The Free Family is the Ritters' account of how they followed self-regulation, and of how its further practical and theoretical components emerged (Ritter and Ritter, 1959, p. 75), as they raised their children in England, 1948-1958. In a later edition, entitled *Free Family & Feedback* (1976), they give a follow up report, describing the maturation (by almost any standards a very healthy one) of their children into young adults. The follow-up material is copious, adding over 100 pages to the original book.

In their extended application of "self-regulation" to their own lives, the Ritters show awareness of the multiple contexts in which self regulation itself is subject to adjustment. They recognize, for example, that the principle cannot be extended ideologically into all the social contacts that their children will have. Nor do they advise parents to force themselves into practicing the method if it goes deeply against their own grain. Yet through all the diversity of *The Free Family*, the Ritters maintain a practical commitment to self-regulation as "the law of energy in the behavior of organisms" (Ritter and Ritter, 1959, p. 264). All in all, *The Free Family* was—and is—an achievement in the sophisticated application of a basic Reichian approach to the sexual body within family life. Although the full book must be read, I will now describe five key aspects of this approach, illustrating its relevance for current issues in research and theory. There seems to be no awareness of the Ritters' work in any of the psychological fields, nor in psychoanalytic literature, although well over 100,000 copies of the book have been sold, in various editions and languages, since 1959 (Ritter and Ritter, 1978, p. 28).

(1) The Ritters give a detailed description of natural childbirth in terms of self-regulation. They arrive at the recommendation, for example, that when contractions during childbirth seem to be pulling the infant back up into the uterus, there should be no hasty recourse to "holding" the infant "tensely where it is"; such contractions are part of a natural rhythm that will resume of its own accord, leading to a healthy birth. "Relaxation is the aim until the next involuntary contraction makes itself felt . . ." (Ritter and Ritter, 1959, p. 56). Relaxation, in fact, is of greater basic importance than exercise, contrary to what most guidebooks advise. In terms of the present study, the value of a non-armored bodily state is affirmed by the Ritters in a complex analogy between the sexual body in childbirth and the sexual body in sex. In both of these bodies, tense holding is taken as deleterious, and in both, the body and the mind are involved as a unified organism. In both, the reality of body organs is considered directly; there is no retreat to an abstract "embodiment" as in phenomenological philosophy (Poole, 1978). Jean Ritter did not have an easy time obtaining good natural childbirth conditions in England in the late 1940's and early 1950's. The failures and shortcomings of her first few births are described in detail, with attention to a number of variables such as the infant's post-delivery state of contentment, its early expressions of insecurity and security, and effects of a particularly unwholesome hospital birth on one of the Ritter girls as much as four years later (Ritter and Ritter, 1959, p. 94). The possibility of such long-term effects is not even considered in a recent "randomised" study of the Leboyer method versus hospital delivery (Nelson et al., 1980).

The Ritters also take childbirth as part of an overall process that is inherently related to the parent's sexual life, a factor which would hardly be regarded as a function of "natural childbirth" even by most of its advocates today. Within Jean Ritter's Reichian framework, however, it is possible for her to observe that one of her pregnancies had "a far more healthy and genital character," than the earlier pregnancies. This genital health "showed itself" [a phrase not to be taken as meaning "was equivalent to"] "in the strong desire for, and enjoyment of, intercourse up to one or two days before birth, with, in contrast to earlier pregnancies, no disturbance to orgasms due to my physical state" (1959, p. 52).

The Ritters provide numerous details of the comparative study of birth and its aftereffects upon one of their children who had to have hospital delivery. This part of their study did not occur by design, but they take intelligent note of an event that allows them to test the hypothesis that the sexual body will be significantly affected, and in a manner that can be characterized as harmful, by certain hospital practices—a hypothesis which has since been made well known by Leboyer as a kind of assault on the newborn.

(2) The Ritters show in practice how to differentiate, at many levels of interaction between parent and child (and between siblings) the notion of "freedom" through self-regulation, as opposed to license, the crippling encouragement of allowing children to walk all over you (1959, pp. 27, 143-149). They show that self-regulation means, in Reichian terms, not the ego-controls of an abstract "self," but the expression of the needs of a sexual body organism under its own control. Obvious applications of the principle are clearly described in the sexual freedom of these children. Such freedom is taken to be crucial while not at all regarded as a self-contained entity nor as the only thing of importance. Play, for example, is a capacity connected with sexuality: its qualities and its meanings would be quite different in a family of authoritarian regulation. (The contrast with Winnicott's concept of play is obvious.) The very capacity for play might be badly diminished in such a family, were it a rigid enough one. But the sexual body is never reduced, in the Ritter's description, to an "animal" entity that is unconnected with the human mind.

The Ritters (Ritter and Ritter, 1959, p. 89) note a significant agreement between their own theory of self-regulation regarding the child's choice of what to eat, with such psychoanalytic writers as Anna Freud and Edith Buxbaum (1951), and with non-psychoanalytic experts such as Gesell (1952). As Ritter points out, this area of agreement had no effect in provoking further thought on the general benefits of the self-regulation principle amongst either the psychoanalytic writers or the others cited. Perhaps self-regulation of food intake is felt to be a relatively innocuous affirmation, but the same cannot be said of sexuality. The psychoanalytic resistance toward allowing sexuality its due is also shown in the Ritters' analysis of the work of Margaret Ribble. In *The Rights of Infants* (Ribble, 1943), Ribble had produced one of the first liberalized psychoanalytic views of infancy and childhood, but in a later work, *The Personality of the Young Child* (Ribble, 1956), the same author advocated authoritarian "guidance" for sexuality as well as for aggression, and actually reinvented the masturbation taboo. Ribble advises parents to gently "distract" the young child from its own genital play, while pretending not to be hostile (Ritter and Ritter, 1959, pp. 102-107). It is an indication of cultural lag regarding the sexual body that Ribble, in her second edition of her volume on infants' rights (Ribble, 1965), showed no awareness of the Ritters' criticisms; one of the few alterations she made was to *increase* her emphasis on alerting parents to recognize the "early erotic impulses in the baby" and to divert these, "when excessive," into "appropriate play activities" (Ribble, 1965, p. v).

(3) While the Ritters base their family life on affection and assume that love is the core of emotional life for their children and themselves, they also deal with hate, recognizing both its easy formation in the frustrated needs to children, and the need to have safe expressions of destructive urges within the

context of the family (such as in childrens' aggressive drawings). The consideration of hate by the Ritters demonstrates their awareness of human complexity within their liberating aim. Their concern for the safe, unrepressed expression of hatred, within an *approving* family context, has great implications for the preventive avoidance of a bodily anchored sadistic or self-destructive sexuality (Ritter and Ritter, 1959, pp. 20, 24, 183-188, 215-216). The Ritters thus offer a living demonstration that the acceptance of the sexual body in family life does not entail the belief that since the human being is basically good (able to handle self-regulation), therefore every emotion is of a benign nature.

(4) The Ritters provide brief, trenchant critiques of alternative approaches to childbearing, citing the available literature of the English psychoanalytic school descending from Melanie Klein, and the work of Piaget. Commenting (p. 164) on Piaget's *The Origins of Intelligence in the Child* (1952), they note that in 400 pages, emotions are not mentioned. In contrast, they argue that the intellectual development of their children is also their emotional development. Emotion, considered in the Reichian sense of energy contact between one's perceptions and feelings, is taken to be essential to the growth of the mind. At the same time, emotion is inherently a bodily process. The Ritters, in anticipation of a great deal of research regarding "infant competency" during the past decade, notice that the pace of development in their children (as well as in children of some like-minded friends of theirs) significantly exceeds that given by Arnold Gesell in his *Infant Development* (1952). They attribute this acceleration not to their own lack of shortcomings and personal problems (these they acknowledge openly), but to the intellectual enablement that comes from unrepressed emotional expression under self-regulation (p. 173). Their approach thus goes contrary to current theories which emphasize the cognitive alone, and is irreconcilable with the position maintained by the anti-psychoanalytic child psychologist Jerome Kagan, that cognitive development is virtually unaffected by most of the negative emotional contexts which infants and children undergo (Kagan, 1984). This is an area in dispute, not to be clarified without further research. It is worth noting, however, that the Ritters were seeking for a quality of cognitive development, a non-authoritarian thought process that avoids the "security" of certainty (Dewey, 1929b). Any testing of cognitive development which fails to distinguish "open" from "closed" mental attitudes (Adorno et al., 1950; Rokeach, 1960) is not a test of what the Ritters reported.

(5) The concept of "rhythm" in self-regulation is given empirical substantiation. Especially noteworthy here is Jean Ritter's careful record of self-regulated feeding patterns determined by her nursing babies, as she fed them according to their demands. Two charts are provided, one showing an hour-by-hour basis, the "self-regulated breast feeds for the first month of Erica's life," while a second chart gives similar information for the "second

month of Penny's life." Each chart shows that such rhythms of feeding are orderly and manageable for a mother without, however, exhibiting uniform "clock" regularities. Certain of the variations are attributed to extraneous variables; thus, the choice of one of the girl infants to nurse continuously for 70 minutes during one session (her usual time was about 10 minutes) is speculatively connected with that infant's experience of particularly inhumane birth in the hospital. Contrast between infants' self-regulated rhythms of nursing and the rigid feeding schedule very popular in the 1950's is shown in graphs (1959, pp. 60-63). These records of breast feeding rhythms have led Dr. Eva Reich, Reich's daughter, to maintain that Jean Ritter is the first person to study self-regulation at the breast (E. Reich, 1980).

The loss, in effect, of the Ritters' data to psychologists, although it is published in an easily available form, is illustrated by the omission of any reference (to my knowledge) to *The Free Family* in the professional literature. There is no mention of the Ritters, for example, in *Psychobiology of the Human Newborn* (Stratton, 1982b). Peter Stratton's collection is one of the finest I have seen in the field of neonatal research, and its editor makes it clear that he does value (not merely study) the newborn. However, there is a total absence in this work of any perspective like that of the sexual body. Even the editor's own richly detailed survey, "Rhythmic Functions in the Newborn" (pp. 116-119), contains no study of rhythms in breast feeding and lacks the concept of self-regulation on the part of the infant, although both crying and sucking are discussed. Stratton takes as one of his main objects the formulation of a precise notion of "rhythm" itself, but the issue of self-regulation versus imposed scheduling of feeding, as a crux in the attitudes taken by culture to the sexual body, is not visible in the forest of research proposals and methodological cautions. So little is known with scientific reliability about how rhythms function in the infant that it is far too early, Stratton feels, to engage in "elaborate speculation about the more esoteric implications" (1982b, p. 142). There is so little "speculation" in his book, in fact, that the issues of the sexual body do not even get raised. The Ritters' "creative experiment" (though it contains some supporting observations based on other families) cannot count as a controlled study, to be sure, but this hardly explains why it is not even consulted for its research suggestions. Although Stratton's interest in the definition of rhythm is well warranted, it is difficult to credit his statement that a lack of such a concept has been a major obstacle to the progress of research thus far (p. 141).

From a Reichian perspective it would seem that the concept of rhythm is too closely associated with the natural biology of the sexual body, and hence would be taken, almost automatically, as an embarrassment to hard-headed laboratory research. In this respect, it is significant that Stratton's own case for the presence of a basic rhythmic pattern in the infant, of periods of relaxation alternating with pendulum swings of steady energy expenditure, is virtually asexual. His article on "Newborn Individuality" has a section on cognitive processes but none on emotional ones; presumably these are incorporated under such headings as "Soothability" and "Irritability" (Stratton, 1982b, pp. 221-261). But such omissions cannot be blamed entirely on Stratton, since most of what he has assembled in this essay summarizes work in the field by all investigators. Stratton's entire edited collection of research reviews on the newborn, in fact, has very few references of any kind to sexuality in any of the 15 contributions.

Thus research moves backwards, away from the sexual body, away from the body itself, and toward some pure, nonexistent mind. Emotions, taken by the Ritters as essential, are not considered by Stratton in the rhythmic functions of the newborn. He assumes that "differential emotional response" is largely "irrelevant" in very early life (pp. 124-125).

The Reichian journal *Energy and Character: The Journal of Bioenergetic Research* in recent years has published much from the Leboyer movement in birth practices. (Leboyer cited Reich as one of his own inspirations, along with Freud and Otto Rank, who gave us the hypothesis of the birth trauma.) Leboyer confirms many of the findings of the Ritters, who in their "creative experiment" in child-rearing had to rely on such earlier pioneers of natural childbirth as Grantley Dick-Read (Dick-Read, 1942, 1947, 1955). Leboyer's findings, especially if considered within a Reichian context, continue to bring out realities of the sexual body that seem to be lost to researchers such as Stratton within the formal laboratory disciplines of experimental psychology. According to Leboyer, it is precisely Stratton's "subject," the "newborn," during the first four or five minutes of life, whose heart structure is changing radically: the heart ventricles alter as the umbilical oxygen supply is phased out, and the lungs begin to function (Leboyer, 1975, pp. 17-18). Stratton, who knows that the heart is quintessentially rhythmic, and who provides precise counts of the heartbeat cycles in the fetal life before birth and in the neonate later (1982b, pp. 126-127) does not pause to consider the possibly traumatic adjustment to air in the first moments; elsewhere he makes light of Leboyer's accomplishment (p. 7). To think in Leboyer's fashion, it is necessary to think of the heart within the body as a whole, rather than as a rhythm in itself, and as part of a feeling human being. Dr. Michel Odent, an obstetrician who has carried on Leboyer's work and developed it further, has promoted the practice of giving birth in a squatting position, partly because such a position encourages emotional expression by the mother. Odent also speaks of the newborn's need to obtain "early expression of the rooting reflex," with explicit denotation of "expression" as an emotional behavior. "The free expression of the emotions," Dr. Odent says, in an excellent Reichian formulation, "is on a par with the freedom of the body" (Odent, 1980, p. 13). Odent, very like the Ritters more than a quarter of a century ago (Ritter and Ritter, 1959, p. 30), and like Reich before them, recognizes and values the profound energy interaction of mother and fetus during the birth process itself.

Few psychologists or psychoanalysts realize that Reich shifted his interests in his last few years to the problems of infancy and childbearing. Most of the articles he wrote about this appeared in journals which were burned on government order. Reich's attention to the adult sexual body is better known; in other parts of this study I make reference to its importance in the light of current theory and research—or the lack of such—on the adult sexual body. In this section, I have deliberately emphasized the 1959 book of the Ritters partly to correct the impression that Reich was concerned only with orgasm and orgone. My broader purpose, however, has been to demonstrate that the Reichian tradition, by virtue of its intelligent adherence to a theory of bodily, sexual energy, contains insights into the vast field of problems that psychoanalysis, as well as the more scientifically "mainstream" disciplines, continues to face concerning the sexual body. The following excerpt is typical of the Ritters' thinking:

> To hold a baby feelingly is to allow a warm flow of love to give pleasure to the infant as well as the adult. This flow of love is not a metaphor but concrete reality. If a child is held in an unrelaxed way, so that neither the soft feelings of love nor the flow are present, the difference in its reactions become, over a long period of time, very obvious. (Ritter and Ritter, 1959, pp. 91-92)

Presumably, this statement is at best nonsense to most of the responsible scientific investigators of infancy. Such terms as "warm flow" and "to hold . . . feelingly" would seem an embarrassment to the designer of experiments in human behavior. The Ritters' reference in this passage to love is also an essential research omission in current non-Reichian thought. For example, the extensive recent study on the lives of "American couples" (Blumstein and Schwartz, 1983) contains practically nothing about love, although love (or the lack of it) would probably have been prominently mentioned as one of the main things in life by every one of the couples studied in depth. But from the perspective of the sexual body, love—not only sexual love but the sexual aspects of any love—would be an essential area for creative investigation. The terms "warm flow," "to hold . . . feelingly," and "love" are neither meaningless nor empirically insignificant.

But the Ritters also refer to other "obvious" results, at the end of the quotation just given; these bring out still further dimensions of the sexual body. One result for the Ritters concerned the inculcation in the infant of a desire for symbiotic union with the mother, such as psychoanalytic theory has come to regard as normal. In contrast, the Ritters' children, much to the surprise of some visitors, frequently "have wriggled to get out of our arms and indicate that they don't want to be carried any more, because they have had enough of it" (p. 92). This is an early indication, in the literature on child research, that the dangers of over-protection or excessive contact are spontaneously kept under control and rendered negligible, *if* self-regulation is practiced. The contemporary distinguished infant/maternal care researcher Terry B. Brazelton seems quite unaware of this possibility (as do most other researchers such as Kagan), when he comments that maternal-neonate contact after birth may interfere with infant autonomy (comment given in Klaus and Kennell, 1976, p. 57).

The overall contribution of the Ritters to human knowledge of self-regulation in a family, with the sexual body assumed throughout as the essential variable, is important. It is as yet unknown in the disciplines. The basic Reichian idea that it takes self-regulated parents who accept their own sexuality and practice it, to make self-regulation in the family work, is invaluable. In recent years, there has been a reasonable call from feminist theorists such as Dinnerstein (1976) and Chodorow (1978) for shared parenting. This proposal has received wide agreement. It took several years of discussion before other feminists began to point out that it would do no good to expose children to the care of fathers if those fathers had a consciousness incompatible with giving loving attention to their children (Breines and Gordon, 1983). T. Berry Brazelton, whose popularity in the area of infant and child care is becoming as marked as that once held by Dr. Spock, has similarly failed to see that his own recommendation for parents to be "empowered" to develop their own expertise in child-rearing (Collins, 1984) is subject to the degree of psychosexual health in those parents. In terms of the Reichian tradition, if the parents are armored, empowering them will only increase their powers of domination over children. The Ritters not only knew that, they showed how self-regulation could be practiced and understood. Their experiment is especially timely now, inasmuch as the "failures" of many of the American experiments in family structure of the 1960's are now popularly regarded as evidence that self-regulation does not work. The Ritters took care to make self-regulation possible.

What the Ritters did could not have been done perhaps by the generation of the 60's in the U.S., where adult sexual mores changed in rapid, confusing fashion, sometimes in the direction of self-regulation and other times in tune with the willful "liberation" of the day; in either event the role of the children was secondary. The Ritters could show how self-regulation worked as well as it did with children because their own marriage was vital, and lucky enough to stay so. Their life experiment stands as a fine example of the Reichian tradition in practice. With their work and the continuing work of others in different disciplines (incidentally, Paul Ritter is an urban planner and industrial designer who has brought his Reichian insights into those fields; see Ritter, 1963, 1966) the potential input of Reich will continue to be available for use among all researchers interested in the problems the Ritters have taken up. While committed Reichians may continue to keep a low profile, as in the

Journal of Orgonomy, there is good reason for anyone who undertakes to deepen knowledge of the sexual body to mine the rich ores of Reich, and of those who have followed in his wake (cf. Boadella, 1976).

CHAPTER FIVE

CHALLENGES TO PSYCHOANALYTIC THEORY: RECENT DEVELOPMENTS

Psychoanalysis has always been challenged, or even held in a state of siege, by its commentators and co-workers in other psychological disciplines. Up to now, however, most of the challenges have missed the point. The charge that the theory was a kind of pan-sexualism bothered Freud, but not as much as it has later theorists; Freud sometimes courted this charge, as I have suggested earlier, while his descendants have successfully negated it. By the time of Freud's visit to the U.S. in 1909, he had emerged from a period of intense theoretical and clinical work during which he had still not credited the reality of sexual instinct in the infant and child (Sulloway, 1979, pp. 111-112, 210-213); the fact that he had felt forced to change his mind on this, and to expand his definition of the sexual body to include the whole of infantile and adult life must have made Freud leary of any temptation to play down the role of the sexual. But of course he did not mean to endorse the later Reichian attitude in which healthy sexuality and health itself were closely correlated. As Sulloway has shown, Freud in fact was gathering heavy opposition in professional circles in Europe at about the time of his visit to the U.S. in 1909, more in fact than in the earlier years when he published his *Three Essays on the Theory of Sexuality* (Freud, 1905b) or his *Interpretation of Dreams* (1900). An awareness was growing that Freud was not merely endorsing the importance of the sexual body. He was showing its connections with too many other areas. There were others in Europe who courageously emphasized the need for attention to sex, but none who both dared to write about it in plain language

73

(instead of Latin euphemisms, such as Kraft-Ebbing used), and who at the same time connected sexuality with neurotic symptom formation (Sulloway, 1979, pp. 205, 457).

The other standard accusation, in addition to that of pan-sexualism, and one which is a veritable stock in trade for objectors to psychoanalysis, concerns a lack of empirical evidence. But this has failed continually, partly because there appears to be considerable empirical support for pschoanalytic theory (Kline, 1981), but also because such criticism has consistently ignored the specifications of the theory and underestimated its complexity (Masling and Schwartz, 1979). To demand, as did Sartre, that there be some direct empirical confirmation of such complicated constructs as sublimation, for example, is a tactic that descends into anti-intellectualism (Efron, 1973). Criticisms of psychoanalytic theory based on contrary assumptions about human nature are not directly refutational of the clinical reports in great abundance which "confirm" again and again that the endopsychic forces postulated by the theory are very much present in the human psyche. Like other theories making use of clinical evidence, confirmation can be found, but no one knows if the evidence is an artifact of the clinical situation. In an atmosphere of hostility and rejection within which psychoanalytic therapy has had to exist, it is only to be expected that the clinical "proof" would be honored and even made sacrosanct by practitioners. Moreover, the origin of criticism among a populace of researchers and other commentators who had not themselves undergone psychoanalysis presented a problem of disparate worldviews. A few years ago, the psychoanalytic theorist Norman N. Holland, then a colleague of mine, declined to consider an article I showed him, which contained a sharp criticism of Freud's famous case-history of a child's neurosis, the case of little Hans (Freud, 1909). Holland remarked that it is perfectly feasible but quite inconclusive to tear the old cases apart with nonanalytic logic; valid criticism could only come from within the field.

Such defense is almost foolproof, and it was reinforced until recently with the firm conviction that the early Freud had indeed set the stage for the later theory through his discovery that nearly all the patients who had led him to believe they had been sexually molested or "seduced" as children, by parents or other older relatives, had actually undergone these seductions only in their own, endopsychically produced fantasy. Ultimately such fantasy is a part of the infantile psyche, and is not susceptible to laboratory experiments; it can only be inferred retroactively through privileged evidence that emerges during adult and child therapy itself.

One theorist, Heinz Kohut, has formally raised the analytic experience itself to the status of a special empirical ground from which psychoanalysis gets its evidence (Kohut, 1977). Kohut was far from intending, by this move, to evade unsettling evidence; on the contrary, he wanted to open the way fully to any data, however distressing these might be to practitioners, but no piece of empirical data can be permitted an automatic veto over evidence that emerges in the only area or "laboratory" that is central to the discipline of psychoanalysis: the analytic process itself. By defining the essence of psychoanalysis to be the prolonged empathetic introspective immersion in the inner life of the human being, as this immersion occurs during an analytic situation and with that situation as the prime source of psychoanalytic evidence, Kohut hoped that he had cleared the way for the reconsideration and if need be the rejection of any specific psychoanalytic notion, no matter how sacred. Thus, while he admitted that he could not imagine getting along without such basic concepts as transference and resistance, he could in theory see how these concepts might some day be superseded, and psychoanalysis still retain its essence. Kohut would have liked his open definition of psychoanalysis to "do away with the *ex cathedra* rejection of findings and thoughts which are at variance with established doctrine . . ." (Kohut, 1977, pp. 308-309). It was Kohut's hope that psychoanalysts would accept his innovation and thus become able to give themselves over to the task of recognizing newly described configurations and processes.

The openness to evidence displayed by Kohut is of dubious merit, however, if it should serve as a further reason for the refusal to consider other *kinds* of evidence, such as the findings of infant research. Through most of psychoanalytic theorizing until recently this problem seemed not to be critical. Not only was it believed that no one would be able to prove what an infant was fantasizing, feeling, dreaming, or thinking; the psychoanalytic community could also point to a certain amount of empirically grounded theory on the infantile psyche, notably that by René Spitz and especially by Margaret S. Mahler, which supported the major theory that had emerged after 1920. This research claimed to show that the infant was poorly equipped during the first months of life, in almost all dimensions—mental, physiological, perceptual and emotional. Spitz found in his psychoanalytic study of the infant that the newborn has no faculty of perception, representation or volition (Spitz, 1965). This amounts to Melanie Klein's assumption again, that the infant's "earliest reality is wholly phantastic" (Klein, 1948b, p. 238), though without supposing the fantasies are destructive. Such an infant could not be expected to differentiate, at first, between its own body and the body of its mother, much less between two different selves. This denial of the capacity for differentiation in the neonate has become axiom, supported by the highly respected controlled observations of Margaret S. Mahler (Mahler, Pine, and Bergman, 1975, p. 44). Mahler tells us that during the second to fifth months, "The infant behaves and functions as though he and his mother were an omnipotent system—a dual unity within one common boundary." This period of "symbiosis" is described in a way that fits well with my characterization of much psychoanalytic theory of the infant as an expression of hatred toward the infant: "The essential feature of symbiosis is hallucinatory or delusional, somatopsychic omnipotent fusion with the representation of the mother" (Mahler, 1968, p. 9, quoted by Milton Klein, 1981b, p. 91). The earlier developmental period, prior to the "symbiotic," is an even more dramatic expression in this light: it is called the "autistic" phase, which is best understood "in physiological terms" (Mahler, Pine, and Bergman, 1975, p. 41, quoted by Klein, 1981b, p. 76). In other words—and it will not do to dodge this conclusion—the neonate is reduced, for all intents and purposes, to a kind of amorphous mass. Eventually, however, the infant learns differentiation, but it does this only by means of a painful process of psychological separation which damages the infant's delusory feeling of omnipotence. Development is premised on the infant's creation of dual images of the mother as part-object: a good mother who obeys the infant's needs totally, and a bad one who hatefully and inexplicably denies these needs. At this juncture, Mahler's theory of infant development and Melanie Klein's were closely joined, with Klein emphasizing the "splitting" of good and bad object-representations and Mahler the "autistic" and "symbiotic" phases.

Criticism of Theory: Three Issues that Cannot Be Dodged

Recent developments have disturbed the complacency, and aroused the defensiveness of psychoanalytic epistemology. These developments have come from several sides. One is the scholarship on Freud, where, for example, Frank Sulloway (1979) has shown decisively that Freud was seriously committed to giving his theory a biological base. Freud, contrary to legend that had grown up around him, never gave this up, even in his old age. He did not consider biology a dimension of theory that could be dispensed with. Sulloway chose to portray Freud as a "biologist of the mind," an act of naming which lost touch with the multidisciplinary force of his "sexuality"—but this simplification cannot erase the sound research in Sulloway's work. Sulloway's proof (and the term may be used here with assurance) that Freud never left biology has the effect of putting the body back into the psychoanalytic world view.

Secondly, Freud's so-called "seduction" theory has been resurrected, partly through increased recognition of the widespread problem of child abuse, and partly through the very recent publication of the complete text of Freud's own letters at the time that he rejected the seduction theory in favor of his own conclusion that the root cause was fantasy, not bodily interaction in the family. This publication came after several researchers had become increasingly dissatisfied with the decision of the Freud Archives to refuse publication of the material (Efron, 1977, p. 254; Sulloway, 1979, p. 188). The psychoanalyst who edited the material for the Archives, Dr. Jeffrey Moussiaeff Masson, was dismissed from his post because of his outspoken insistence that the revelations are sufficient for a reversal to be made in psychoanalytic assumptions. If actual sexual abuse and not fantasies unaided by such abuse were the key factor, analysts, said Masson to the press, "would have to recall every patient since 1901. It would be like the Pinto" (quoted in Blumenthal, 1981a; see also Blumenthal, 1981b and 1984). With this flamboyant declaration, Masson not only got himself dismissed; he also signalled his own tendency to simplify the issues. As he presented it, Freud's decision to de-emphasize the seduction theory became an issue in moral action, in "honesty" and "courage," rather than a matter of science and psychology. To be sure, Masson occasionally qualified his attack on the image of Freud by saying he did not think Freud "ever made a conscious decision to ignore his earlier experiences . . ." (Masson, 1984a, p. 189); but Masson's unexplained anger at Freud regularly overwhelms his writing about the issue. The issue is reduced to one of personalities—Freud's versus Masson's. With Janet Malcolm's somewhat gossipy character portrait of Masson (Malcolm, 1983, 1984)—presented largely in Masson's own words during an extended interview or series of interviews—the stage was set for his discrediting. There has been speculation in fact that Malcolm chose deliberately to concentrate on the personal, journalistic aspects of the controversy; according to Milton Klein (Klein, 1984) who was present (along with others including Masson) at Malcolm's home during some of the discussions leading to Malcolm's book, important theoretical issues were brought up only to be given very little play in the book as it emerged. Instead a portrait of Masson dominated Malcolm's text; he is portrayed, according to Robert Coles, as "a grandiose egotist—mean-spirited, self-serving, full of braggadocio, impossibly arrogant, and, in the end, a self-destructive fool" (Coles, from a review in the *Boston Globe* of May 27, 1984, as quoted by Masson, 1984c, p. 46). Walter Kendrick, reviewing Masson's book, advised readers not to trouble to read Masson at all: anything of value that his book might contain could be found in more readable and reliable form in Malcolm's debunking version of Masson's research (Kendrick, 1984, p. 12). In addition to the obvious problem of urging that interested readers in the disciplines rely on a secondary source and ignore the original, this advice shows an excessive willingness to credit Malcolm's interviewing as an objective account of Masson's sexual body; one of the most florid details she offered was Masson's alleged statement that he had had sex with some 1000 women (Malcolm, 1983, p. 101). Masson has since denied the accuracy of Malcolm's interview reports, and another journal has offered to give an independent, impartial report on the contents of Malcolm's 50 hours of cassette tape interview material with Masson (English, 1984; Masson, 1984c). But the object of diverting discussion of the issues to Masson's personality seems to have been temporarily accomplished.

Masson's book has coincided with a recent public interest in "child abuse," which is often accompanied by a reversion to a pre-Freudian concept of the infant and child as "innocent"—innocent, that is, of having a sexual body at all. There are already glimmerings of a general anti-sexual streak in the concern about the problem of child-abuse. Katz, a psychologist working in this area, reports receiving complaints from frightened people about virtually any sign of adult-child affectionate touching; he warns that excessive concentration on sexual abuse not only serves to take attention from other forms of abuse such as emotional bullying, but that it will interfere seriously with the newly emergent child-rearing patterns in which affectionate touch is an accepted and valued practice (Katz, 1984). The Reichian theory of orgastic gratification at the adult level provides a distinction between touch that is an expression of affection by an adult toward a child, and touch which expresses adult impotence and is thus potentially a form of foreplay with sexual intent. But this is a difficult concept to get across to a public not generally well versed in the differences between touching with affection and touching with sexual aim.

Nonetheless, intelligent discussion of child-abuse is increasing. The recent flyer I received from the National Committee for the Prevention of Child Abuse features emotional abuse where touch is not involved at all as one of the important forms of child abuse, in addition to sexual abuse (Cohn, 1984). Research into "emotional deprivation" as a form of child abuse is well under way (Brody, 1983d). And in psychoanalytic circles, the seduction theory controversy does not seem to be dying out. Nor, as Milton Klein has explained (Klein, 1984), is the seduction theory a simple one involving purely external (nonpsychological) assaults on the child. In fact, the theory emerged within the context of Freud's development of his theory of repression, and it hinged on a subtle hypothesis of the igniting of repressed memories of early childhood seduction during a later phase of development (Klein, 1984). The theory is critically explosive, however, in the way that Freud's investigations of the sexual body tend to be, because it connects traditional family practices in child-rearing with sexual practices which are to all intents violations of the sexual body of the child, as well as being expressions (in Reichian terms) of the orgastic impotence of adults whose own sexual bodies are in a pregenital, that is, psychobiologically infantile, stage of development. And in some of the cases, it would appear that these adults are the parents themselves. The possibility of parental involvement had already been raised by a number of reseachers prior to Masson's highly-publicized comments, although earlier inquiry had to proceed without benefit of the unpublished materials to which he had access. Milton Klein and David Tribich, both of whom are psychoanalytic therapists, have published sharply critical articles on Freud's virtual blindness to the damage caused by parents to children, which is the overall issue of the seduction theory as they see it (Klein and Tribich, 1979; Klein and Tribich, 1982). Klein and Tribich in fact have reasons for seriously questioning all five of Freud's major case histories on precisely the grounds that he was blind to the ways in which these patients had been damaged by parental and other adult hostility, always in relation to their sexual bodies. Unlike Masson, who has tended to make flamboyant statements which play into the hands of those who would like to forget about the seduction theory and its problems, Klein and Tribich have presented a formidable critique which will be difficult to refute in detail. An additional powerful critique of Freud's dismissal of the seduction theory has been launched in three books by the Swiss-trained psychoanalyst, Alice Miller (Miller, 1981a, 1981b, 1983). Miller has developed her argument beyond the level of merely criticizing Freud; she connects the seduction theory issue with larger problems of child-rearing in society, and takes a position regarding the value of somatosensory affection that is similar to that taken by Prescott (Prescott, 1979; see Loewenstein's review of Miller: Loewenstein, 1984b, p. 325). Like Klein and Tribich, Miller reinterprets all of Freud's case histories to show how he mistakenly de-emphasized the factor of adult hostility and aggression toward the child, often in matters of sexuality (Miller, 1981b).

A very late addition to the research on one of these five case histories tends to add weight to the criticisms now being raised. Freud's famous patient, the so-called Wolf-Man, came to the conclusion that Freud had been quite wrong in finding a primal scene fantasy through interpretation of a dream. The Wolf-Man did not deny that Freud had been insightful, but in this crucial point, the very one which has been used for 70 years to support the doctrine that images of sexual violation are endopsychic productions of children's thinking about sex, regardless of life-situation or environment, the Wolf-Man has to firmly disagree with the analyst (Obholzer, 1982). The Wolf-Man points out that unlike other Freudian dream interpretation, the key elements in Freud's derivation of the primal scene from his dream remain pure interpretation, related in no discernable way to the dream material (Obholzer, 1982, pp. 35-36). The parts of the dream which should eventually have made emotional sense to the patient never came to do so, even after 60 years. As Loewenstein (1984a) has argued, Obholzer's evidence of Freud's longterm ineffectiveness with the Wolf-Man must be taken as a serious indication of an over-emphasis on the highly speculative primal scene material at the expense of much stronger evidence that the Wolf-Man had been "sexually and emotionally exploited as a child" (Loewenstein, 1984a, p. 9).

The sociologist and legal expert Sheleff (1981, pp. 70-87) has also provided a devastating critique of Freud's handling of the "seduction" and child abuse issues. David Finkelhor (1979), in one of the most widely respected recent empirical studies of sexually victimized children, has found evidence to show that the Freudian theory is wrong, not only with regard to the rate of occurrences of such victimization, but in its concept of the resultant trauma. Freud was led to believe that the trauma comes from the child's guilt feelings, because the sexual contact with the adult would have amounted to an acting-out of prohibited incest wishes on the part of the child. The child would have been in complicity with its own sexual victimization. Finkelhor found instead that the short-term, coerced violations of the child were far more productive of trauma than the long-term ones involving consent and complicity (Finkelhor, 1979, pp. 104-115). Finkelhor's conclusions are supported by Constantine's comprehensive review-analysis of some 30 studies of the impact of childhood incest and sexual encounters with adults, comprising some 2500 subjects (Constantine, 1980).

Once again, however, there is the problem of how the new insights into child-adult sexual contact, and the issues they raise, can be integrated into a theory that seems to have no place for certain propositions. By now, the position that psychopathology is primarily a matter of endopsychic processes has become entrenched in psychoanalytic theory. Even where it is modified by an emphasis on the need for good mothering—or the "good enough" mother as in Winnicott—the cognitively helpless infant lacking a capacity to differentiate itself from the mother, and overwhelmed with imperatives of its own emotional and physical constitution, leaves little expectation that it will become a credible witness of its own child abuse. Yet it would seem that the impact must be felt; perhaps the change in theory will first go on underneath the denial that it is being made. That is, the supposition that the patient has fantasized his or her account of being sexually abused as a child will now become the *last* rather than the *first* assumption to operate within the therapist's mind. I suspect that some shift in the direction of giving credence to the patient's reports already is taking place in therapy, despite Bruno Bettleheim's dismissive prediction that the dispute over the seduction theory "won't change the way anyone does anything" (quoted in Goleman, 1984a).

The question of how an infant or young child could have the cognitive competence to carry such a memory of early sexual abuse, and have that memory be an accurate narrative of something that actually occurred, may no longer be pushed out of sight. It is here that a third and probably most serious challenge to psychoanalytic epistemology has been brought to bear, because there is now an immense amount of research on the neonate, the implications of which are a reversal of psychoanalytic theory of the infant in early development. The "explosion" of knowledge in infant studies over the past two decades has produced a complicated series of findings and new questions, but there is little doubt that these findings call into very serious question what psychoanalytic theorists have taken to be true. Infant "competence" is now a well-supported notion, and it goes ill with psychoanalytic assumptions. The fact that infants under two months old can "habituate to a novelty stimulus" has only become clear since 1972 (Haith, 1980, p. 7); it implies that doubts about a memory capacity of infants under two months, based on a belief that they could *not* so habituate, lose most of their force with this finding. Similarly, it becomes increasingly implausible to suppose (as psychoanalytic theory now does) that a young infant cannot discriminate the boundary between its own body and that of its mother when new research shows, for example, that the newborn infant has three-dimensional vision and displays some hand coordination with this vision, apparently for purposes of orientation (von Hofsten, 1982).

In psychoanalysis, the impact of neonate findings has been felt especially with regard to the widely accepted psychoanalytic theories of Margaret Mahler. Both Emmanual Peterfreund (1978) and Milton Klein (1981b) have argued in detail, and within the pages of psychoanalytic journals, that Mahler's findings on the infantile psyche are thoroughly, radically wrong, in the light of new research and with a re-examination of Mahler's own methodology. Klein refutes her work on its merits in light of the evidence now available, and also finds that she has been a great deal less than responsive to this evidence than a responsible investigator might have been (Klein, 1981b, pp. 82-83; see also Bowlby, 1984, p. 43). Inasmuch as Mahler's theory offers the most prominent and the most detailed synthesis of research on infancy that psychoanalysts have been able to point to, this is a serious confrontation. Peterfreund and Klein are both active within the field of psychoanalytic training, a fact that will make them difficult to ignore.

The threat posed by new evidence is in fact greater than even Peterfreund and Milton Klein indicate; so fast is the field of neonate research developing that they did not take into account one of the most directly challenging developments to date, namely the discovery of very early capacities on the parts of infants to imitate expressions of adults. These have been proposed mainly by Meltzoff and co-workers, in several presentations from 1977 and continuing. Although most accounts in the press concerning Meltzoff's work have concentrated solely on his finding of facial imitation (e.g., "Newborns Found," 1982), it should be noted that one of his original experimental findings was that infants as young as 12 days old were able to imitate "sequential finger movement (opening and closing the hand by serially moving the fingers)" (Meltzoff and Moore, 1977, p. 76); moreover, other research has now been reported which shows "early imitation of additional non-oral behaviors" (Meltzoff, 1981, p. 101). Potentially, this is a finding concerning bodily functions in the process of imitation; it involves fine-tuned self-corrective behavior on the part of the infant as it attempts to approximate the expression it is imitating, in a sequence *not* at all like that of the animal "releaser mechanism" (1981, p. 101). The "major claim" Meltzoff makes about early imitation is that it "involves active intermodal matching" (e.g., visual perception and tactile imitation)

> in which infants recognize an equivalence between the act seen and their own act which is done at a later time.... Our corollary hypothesis is that this imitation is mediated by a representational system that unifies different modalities. (1981, p. 102)

The significance of these findings for psychoanalytic theory is even greater than for Piagetian psychology. As Meltzoff argues, Piaget would have been forced to admit that infants have a capacity for forming accurate representations of stimuli which they imitate, at a much younger age than Piaget had supposed. The empirical findings lead Meltzoff to formulate a conclusion which jars not only the Piagetian edifice of psychology, but rocks the psychoanalytic theory of the infant right off its stand:

> The ability to act on the basis of abstract representations or descriptions of perceptually absent events needs to be considered as the starting point of infant development, not its culmination. (Meltzoff, 1981, p. 109)

Precisely where this starting point would be located in developmental time is still open to question. Many of the findings apply to infants 12 to 30 days old, but newer experimentation has applied to increasingly younger subjects. By 1977, some of the subjects were newborns, one of them only an hour old, and quite able to engage in facial imitations (Meltzoff and Moore, 1977, p. 78). Meltzoff and Moore's findings will require careful interpretation; their meaning is too far-reaching to be clear at this point. Nonetheless, such findings can not be read as a favorable indication for a psychoanalytic theory of infantile cognitive fusion—and thus confusion—of representations of the infant's own body with that of its caretaker, mother, or general environment.

So far, most of the response to these challenges on the part of those who wish to defend psychoanalytic theory in its present forms, has been by way of avoidance. An influential training analyst and theoretician in England, Dr. M. Masud R. Khan, reviewed Sulloway's *Freud, Biologist of the Mind* contemptuously. Khan's reasoning was at this level: "*Mind* is a concept, hence there can be no biology of it" (Khan, 1981, p. 125). Khan similarly denied the value of new research into the circumstances of Freud's early psychoanalytic theorizing, the period in which the seduction theory was devalued. Instead of welcoming the new data, as Kohut might have hoped, Khan has bemoaned the release of certain of Freud's letters written to Dr. Wilhelm Fliess, even on the limited basis that had been taking place prior to their recent publication in full. He has let it be known that any attempts to analyze Freud's psychological processes at the time of the rejection of the seduction theory, even if the methods of analysis are psychoanalytical, must be considered foolish and impertinent (Khan, 1982). Khan's response to the recent challenges to psychoanalytic theory thus is one of dogmatic defensiveness. His objections to the publications of new material pertaining to Freud's famous dream of "Irma's injection" (Freud, 1900, pp. 106-121, 292-295), which were brought out as early as 1966 by Freud's personal physician, the psychoanalytic theorist Max Schur (Schur, 1966), shows a desire to turn back the clock, a wish to erase almost twenty years of research. It was exactly Schur's new evidence which I stressed in my own reopening of the seduction theory controversy

(Efron, 1977, pp. 258-260), and which Masson rightly takes up again. But the very fact that Khan has been led to make such bald, hostile statements can be a sign of recognition that the threats are serious. Khan usually writes with sophistication.

The Seduction Theory: Denials and Issues

More authoritative is the denial by the late Anna Freud, in one of her last letters, that the seduction theory could be incorporated into psychoanalytic thought in any way. Writing to Masson, Anna Freud says:

> Keeping up the seduction theory would mean to abandon the Oedipus complex, and with it the whole importance of fantasy life, conscious or unconscious fantasy. In fact, I think there would have been no psychoanalysis afterwards. (quoted in Malcolm, 1983, p. 125)

Anna Freud of course is defending her father's decision to reject the seduction theory, insofar as she means to say that Freud could not have gone on to his own greatest discoveries without taking this step. I am inclined to agree with her, and in fact have taken that very position (Efron, 1977). However, to say that Freud's abandonment of the seduction theory is warranted by "the whole of the analytic theory altogether" (as she does, in the same letter), and to link this issue to an all-or-nothing position regarding the Oedipus complex and "the whole importance of fantasy life" is merely a revelation of her own immersion in the theory as it exists today rather than of any necessity in psychological theory. It would seem obvious enough that any psychoanalytic theory or for that matter any general psychological theory of the sexual body in infants and children must come to grips *both* with fantasy life and with the actual occurrences of childhood sexual victimization (Finkelhor, 1979). Anna Freud thought that was too much to ask, but I doubt that future psychoanalytic theorists will be able to hold the line, as she urges in her letter to Masson. Some may not even want to.

Masson's accusations in *The Assault on Truth* (Masson, 1984a) have met with a virtual stonewalling, as in the prominent review of his book by Anthony Storr (Storr, 1984). Certainly Storr brought out the weaknesses of Masson's book, but his efforts to serve these up as a pretext for rejecting the seduction theory all over again, seem to have had the effects of overkill. Knight and Herik (1984) rightly label Storr's review one of these "nonresponsive condemnations" that do no one any credit. And even Storr had to acknowledge, in the midst of his attack on Masson's book, that Freud indeed may have badly underestimated the frequency of childhood seduction (Storr, 1984, p. 3). In another effort to stonewall the issue, Norman Holland claimed that, contrary to Masson's account of the matter, Freud points out cases of sexual abuse of children "in most of his later case histories" (Holland, 1984).

But to this Masson was able to reply that after 1905, the *significance* of such abuse of the child's sexual body is not discussed in the remaining 35 years of Freud's writing career (Masson, 1984b). Holland augmented his charges during a session on the seduction theory controversy at the annual conference of the Center for the Psychological Study of the Arts, SUNY-Buffalo, May 12, 1984: Freud's position was not that "all hysterics' recollections of sexual abuse are lies," but neither are all adult hysterias the result of childhood sexual events. Holland's evidence, however, was a Freud passage (Freud, 1925a, p. 34) which contains a bit too much finesse; it sounds suspiciously like rationalization:

> When . . . I was at last obliged to recognize that these scenes of seduction had never taken place, and that they were only phantasies which my patients had made up or which I myself had perhaps forced upon them, I was for some time completely at a loss . . . . When I had pulled myself together, I was able to draw the right conclusions from my discovery: namely, that the neurotic symptoms were not directly related to actual events but to wishful phantasies, and that as far as the neurosis was concerned psychical reality was of more importance than material reality. I do not believe even now that I forced the seduction-phantasies on my patients, that I "suggested" them. I had in fact stumbled for the first time upon the Oedipus complex . . . but which I did not recognize as yet in its disguise of phantasy. Moreover, seduction during childhood retained a certain share, though a humbler one, in the aetiology of neuroses. But the seducers turned out as a rule to have been older children. (Freud, 1925a, pp. 34-35)

For Holland, this quotation from Freud was proof positive that Masson had no case, that the issue was "simply hype." But I cannot agree with Holland's reading of the passage. It contains a repetition of an unequivocal denial that the seductions had ever taken place at all, combined with an admission that some of them did, but that even if they did, they were not very important psychologically, and besides, only non-adults took part in them "as a rule." The whole passage resembles the old story of the man who explained why he had not returned the pot he had borrowed: first, I did so return it, second, I never borrowed it, and third, it had a hole in it anyway. The restriction of the seducers to the actions of other (older) children is especially suspect, in light of Masson's report that Freud had declined to reveal that in several of his cases, the violator was actually the father (Masson, 1984a, p. 93). As Masson pointed out in August, 1984, none of the hostile reviewers of his book have quoted the relevant passages in Freud, previously unpublished, in which Freud showed that he knew of a two-year-old girl who had been "brutally deflowered" by her father (Masson, 1984d; see Masson, 1984a, p. 116).

There is also some question concerning the way we are to read Freud's qualified and incomplete denials of the value of the seduction theory. In another note, this one written in 1924, and attached to a new edition of his essay "Further Remarks on the Psycho-Neuroses of Defence" (Freud, 1896), Freud explained why he no longer accepted his early theory of childhood seductions, but noted that "we need not reject everything written in the text above," and went on to say that he still thought that the seduction theory "retains a certain aetiological importance . . ." (1896, p. 168). These guarded remarks, however, are probably as close as Freud could have come, within the terms of his own theory of mental functioning, to issue a denial. After all, Freud is the psychologist who alerted us to the manner in which outright denials or "negations" tend to mask the unconscious affirmation of that which is denied (Freud, 1925b). The essay "Negation" (Freud, 1925b) in fact came out one year after the two belated passages concerning the seduction theory were published. Then, one year later, Freud issued the text which would dispose of the seduction theory for good, to all intents and purposes, insofar as psychoanalytic thinking was to follow Freud. In *Inhibitions, Symptoms, and Anxiety* (Freud, 1926a), he made the theoretically fateful leap of proposing that it really made no difference whether a patient's anxiety had an environmental cause or not; anxiety, and by implication sexual hysteria as well, now became a result of endopsychic factors (Efron, 1977, p. 267).

Nor is the problem of the seduction theory important primarily within the framework of Freud's original theory of sexual hysteria. Hunter has shown that some women patients Freud found to be suffering from hysteria might be better regarded as valuable reformers whose hysteria served a successful social purpose (Hunter, 1983, pp. 485-486; following Israël, 1980). In the problem of the seduction theory, we are talking about the tendency or bias of a theory of the sexual body: will it face clearly the facts of family sexual violence, and of incestuous relations in fact as well as fantasy, or will it place all its emphasis on what, as Freud put it, "my patients had made up . . ." (Efron, 1977)? For Judith Herman, whose powerful study of father-daughter incest should be considered part of the evidence in dealing with this problem of theory, it is more than plain that the psychoanalytic tradition has lent itself to denying the sexual violence of the family and reports by victims of actual incest, through its determination to deny the seduction theory. She points out, for example, that "Helene Deutsch's massive *Psychology of Women*, published in 1944, makes no mention of it whatsoever" (Herman, 1981, pp. 10-11).

In the seduction theory controversy lies an indication of Freud's personal allegiance to traditional patriarchal values, that same social order which his emphasis on the sexual body threatened to undermine. The new scholarship on Freud's early decision to drastically de-emphasize this theory will have an impact for a long time to come on how psychoanalysis is understood in therapy and even, thanks to Masson's simplifications, at the popular level. The seduction theory controversy seems to have struck a nerve. When I pointed out that Holland's dismissal of the whole issue leaves psychoanalysis in the position of expressing a theoretical indifference to the extent of child abuse—the theory would remain the same whether there were 2% or 80% of children involved in sexual victimization—and that such a theory could not be good for children's health, Holland replied that he was inclined to agree:

psychoanalysis *is* primarily an endopsychic theory, and it probably is *not* the best theory to use if you are concerned with children's health. Holland then went on to reassert the integrity of the theory as an entity in itself which gives us our best understanding of the human mind (Holland, remarks during session of annual conference, Center for the Psychological Study of the Arts, SUNY-Buffalo, May 12, 1984). But it is exactly the adequacy of the present day psychoanalytic psychology which is at issue.

Where the Challenges Can Lead

The last of the three current challenges, however, is perhaps even more interesting for its threat to the psychoanalytic sense of the sexual body. Again, the infant research findings have often met with denial or with dismissal. One analyst writing on this topic in the *Psychoanalytic Quarterly* (Dowling, 1982) first noted further evidence of the surprising perceptual and learning capacity of neonates, only to go on to declare hastily that this can make no difference to the theory. Dowling found that infants as young as 16 to 21 days can observe and imitate tongue and mouth movements in an adult, and that 29-day-olds can recognize which of two perceived shapes (pacifiers) they had already tactually explored (by sucking). There is nothing in these or other findings to make Dowling even consider that the infant might be able to produce mental representations of self and of the object, nor does he see any relevance to the psychoanalytic assumption that the infant's ego is nondifferentiated, that is, the baby makes no distinction between itself and its mother because it does not yet have a self. Therefore, no change in psychoanalytic theory is called for. Similar dismissive reasoning on infant research findings by Kaplan (1978, p. 256) has been noted by Klein (1981b, p. 84), who refutes Kaplan's denial convincingly. It would appear that denials and dismissals of this kind can only be a form of whistling in the dark; eventually the findings will have to be faced, or the credibility of psychoanalytic theory will be damaged for all but the most willing true believers.

The three challenges to psychoanalytic theory discussed in this chapter all bear upon the sexual body. The first, the biological underpinning recovered by Sulloway, in what has been called the most influential book on psychoanalysis in the past decade (Prawer, 1983), makes it more difficult for future psychoanalytic theory to attempt to bypass the body and sexuality; the second, the seduction theory controversy, will encourage a greater interest in psychoanalysis as a radical critique of traditional family structure, with all of that structure's powers over the sexual body of the child; and the third, the research findings on infancy, will open more minds to the possibility that the newborn infant is a living sexual body rather than a still-to-be-born helpless dependency lacking a self, and teeming with aggressive desire. All three of these challenges coming at once may bring an overall change, or willingness to change, or recognition that change is necessary.

Because psychoanalytic theory has built so grandly on its own image of the infant, the infant research material may be the most serious of the new challenges. I will now examine it in some detail, not only to permit a better grasp of what it involves, but to show why psychoanalytic theory—because it is the only theory that takes infantile sexuality seriously—is still necessary for understanding the human infant; indeed, such understanding is more necessary now than it was during the years 1920-1930, when a cruder but not necessarily inaccurate Freudianism was still drawing attention to the multiple meanings of the sexual body in human life.

CHAPTER SIX

REINVENTING THE ASEXUAL INFANT: ON THE RECENT "EXPLOSION" IN INFANT RESEARCH

The recent revolution in the study of the infant involves a massive theoretical shift from considering the infant as "a passive organism who was the object of forces which determined development," a view taken in very different ways by Freud, Watson, and Gesell, to the mapping out of the competencies that infants have and of the limits to those capabilities. In the years after 1960, "there has been an explosion of infant research of all kinds, and our knowledge continues to expand at a rapid rate" (Appleton, Clifton, and Goldberg, 1975, pp. 102-103). The term "explosion" has occurred repeatedly in the research literature (Klein, 1981b, p. 7; Stern, 1977, p. 144; Stone, Smith and Murphy, 1973, p. vii; Stratton, 1982a, p. 1), and by now things have simmered down. Some have urged that the revolution is over and it is time to get on with other, more important things. But it would be hard to deny that there has been a great access of new and surprising findings in the study of the infant, with results that are confusing.

Research results are still flying in every direction, from numerous disciplines and with few attempts to bring the fragments together. A great deal of confusion is inevitable so long as the underlying theoretical problem of conflicting world hypotheses (Pepper, 1942) is not faced. Stone, Smith and Murphy preferred to edit some 202 articles within their compendium on "the competent infant" (1973), but apologized for slighting the purely theoretical level (p. 5). From the perspective of the sexual body, the theory of infant development remains undeveloped still.

One basic issue lacking resolution is whether early traumatic experience, such as separation from the mother during key periods (e.g., shortly after birth) has any long-term deleterious effects on a child, whether these effects are seen at the time, somewhat later, or even in old age. Psychoanalytic theory is committed to a hearty "yes" in reply to this question, and the arguments of Leboyer and the whole "natural childbirth" school concur, but there are good researchers who deny that any such thing is known at all (Chess, 1978; Chess and Thomas, 1981; Clarke and Clarke, 1976; Goleman, 1984b; Kagan, 1976, 1980; Vaillant, 1977). The controversies, problems, and disputed issues put before us basic questions about infant life which are still unanswered, although they perhaps are not quite as unanswerable as they once were thought to be. One huge, persistently confusing factor underlying much of the difficulty in all such research is the evident bias in favor of cognitive rather than emotional knowledge, showing little consideration of the body or sexuality.

In their survey of psychological research on the emotional development of infants, Cicchetti and Pogge-Hesse (1981) report that the topic had been sadly neglected; in fact, the psychoanalytic literature on "attachment" was practically alone in the field (pp. 215-216). This neglect goes hand in hand with a 40-year lack of interest in human emotions by psychology under the influence of behaviorism (p. 218). Piaget's developmental model virtually excluded sexual development, as Goldman and Goldman argue (1982, pp. 10-12). Nor did Piaget's followers do any better. Goldman and Goldman report on a survey of 1,500 Piagetian studies, none of which have much to say about sexuality (Modgil, 1974). To their credit, Goldman and Goldman do try to right the balance; they are Piagetians themselves in large part. They find that Piaget's stages of cognitive development apply, but only with considerable adjustment, to the development of children's sexual thinking (pp. 375-377).

As for research into childhood sexuality by academic psychologists in general, I offer this comment by Goldman and Goldman (1982):

> ... Recently the *American Psychologist* published a special issue (1979) entitled "Psychology and Children—Current Research and Practice" to commemorate the International Year of the Child. Although intended as a survey of Child Psychology and Child Development, a thorough reading reveals nothing on the normal sexual development of children and no mention of sexual thinking, despite several informative sections on children's cognition. One would at least expect in the section headed "Identifying the Problems and Needs of our Children" there would be some recognition of the area of sexuality. The nearest reference is in the article on "Child Abuse" which mentions the sexual abuse of children in defining the terms used, but concentrates the discussion entirely on physical violence. An examination of the bibliography confirms this tunnel vision. The only other allusion to children's sexual development is in the article on "Divorce".... (pp. 2-3)

Thus it appears that Freud's early challenge to psychology, the challenge of childhood sexuality, has never been confronted by "respectable" scientific psychology. There is no rival in this field to contest the status of psychoanalysis as the key discipline in the study of the sexual body.

Even behaviorism, when it occasionally did have something to suggest regarding the sexual body, was ignored during the long period of its own dominance. In 1928, J.B. Watson, no less, reported "rage" as a reaction to the prevention of movement of the child's limbs, but there was very little research interest in his observation (Watson, 1928, cited in Jackson and Jackson, 1978, p. 178). Yet the linkage between restriction and rage is culturally significant in a civilization which has depended on rage as motivation for its wars of righteousness (Efron, 1981).

One reason behaviorism would not study the development of affect in the infant is given by Campos and Stenberg (1981, pp. 306-307): how could we find the primary reinforcers in a neonate? Besides, as they also point out, it would be a bit silly to suppose that direct reinforcement is the major mode of learning for the infant, since rather early in a young child's life, it becomes important to understand warnings about various dangers (such as electrical sockets in the home) which cannot be confronted through reality testing. But long before the current research "explosion," some psychologists had proposed theory and pointed to evidence which would have allowed for the investigation of infantile emotional development. Charlotte Bühler suggested in 1930 some of the findings of today's research concerning neonate responsiveness to face and voice during the fifth through ninth months of life; she based these suggestions on exploratory but careful experiments (Bühler, 1930, cited in Campos and Stenberg, 1981, p. 305). K.M. Bridges, in several articles on infantile emotional development published in the early 1930's, maintained that in the first three weeks of life an infant learns through experience to differentiate what was initially a state of generalized "excitement" into the discrete emotions of distress and delight (Bridges, 1930, 1932, cited by Ciccheti and Pogge-Hesse, 1981, pp. 240-241). The precise theories and assumptions of Bridges need not be described here for the point to be underscored: as early as 1932, we had observations pointing strongly to the development of different emotions in the infant. In fact, Charles Darwin, in his "Biographical Sketch of an Infant," offered a whole set of interesting, subtle observations on emotional expression, especially facial, in babies (Darwin, 1877). But little was done with this line of research until quite recently. If the infant's emotional life could not interest researchers, how much less would the sexual life, with which emotion is intertwined, attract their interest.

The common explanation for the long delay in learning that the neonate is competent, active, and equipped with very considerable sensory-motor capacities has been the sheer difficulty of studying a human being prior to the development of most motor abilities and all language. This explanation rings hollow, however. There is no reason why it should have taken until 1966 to learn that a "quiet, alert state" is what the infant demonstrates during most, if not all, of the first hour after its birth (Desmond et al., 1966, cited in Klaus and Kennell, 1976, p. 66). During this state, the eyes are wide open and the newborn is able to respond to the surrounding environment. All one would have had to do would have been to look at the infants and notice, although that kind of looking might not have shown the alertness if obstetric drugs had been used in the birth. Actually, just learning to *look* at the infant was what enabled the most startling breakthroughs in the field of infant study to occur. In the study of infant visual behavior, says M.M. Haith, one of today's leading research workers in that area, "an adequate methodology was lacking until Fantz (1958, 1961) popularized an easily implemented technique which opened new vistas in infant visual research" (Haith, 1980, p. 1). The number of studies since 1960 that have followed Fantz's easily implemented method has numbered into the hundreds. The technique, as Haith puts it, was "very straight-forward . . ." (*ibid.*). "A person can determine what a baby attends by watching the baby's eyes! The reflection of the stimulus the baby fixates appears on the cornea near the center of the black pupillary opening of the eye" (Haith, 1980, pp. 1-2). You give an infant a chance to look at two different visual stimuli while you watch its eyes to see which one it looks at most. Or, you present stimuli in sequence and see which one gets the most attention from the infant. This methodology is so simple that it could hardly have been sought for within the programmatic scientific ambitions of academic psychology, but once found, it "has been unmatched for utility and applicability to a wide range of issues and problems in infancy including: attention, habituation, learning, cognition, preference, detection, discrimination, recognition, identification, intermodal and space perception, motivation and affect" (Haith, p. 2).

What has been learned about all these issues and problems is that the infant is far more competent than had been believed. But the issues and problems have been studied singly, or in small clusters of groups, with the highly complementary results brought together periodically in surveys. Theories are either lacking or one-sidedly cognitive. Peter Stratton, editor of the recent Wiley text, *Psychobiology of the Human Newborn* (1982b), repeatedly urges the most circumspect doubt and caution concerning the meaning of neonatal findings. The series editor, K. Connolly, seems to suggest that now, after thousands of careful experiments over the past two decades, it is time to begin thinking: ". . . we now have in outline form a framework within which to analyse and consider the newborn's behavior" (Stratton, 1982b, p. xiv). An example of a one-sided cognitive approach is found in G. Butterworth's, *Infancy and Epistemology: An Evaluation of Piaget's Theory* (1981). The book makes no mention of such matters as feeling or emotion, much less sexuality; it concentrates on memory, imitation, and representation, overlaid on a concept of the infant body as a desexualized sensorimotor apparatus. Nor would one gather that the infants described in the Butterworth collection ever went through the process of childbirth. Yet the type of childbirth—whether "natural" or, as Leboyer might put it, "assaultive"—would have to be taken into account if we are really to "analyse and consider" the infant. As one of the writers in Stratton's collection acknowledges, we now have excellent evidence that obstetric drugs do have harmful effects on the newborn:

> Medication during the labour is associated with degradations of a variety of behaviors in the newborn, including sleep, arousal attention, motor competence, and sucking and feeding. (Barrett, 1982, p. 275)

As the work of Brackbill (1975) and Muller et al. (1971) has shown, some of the most common drugs in obstetric use have been shown to affect IQ at age nine! But while Barrett cites all this information and Stratton includes the comments in his anthology, no one seems to realize that (with very rare exceptions) the findings surveyed throughout the same anthology are not considered with regard to the simple distinction: drugged or not. Stratton's own attitude may be inferred from his demonstration that neonate individuality shows up strongly even in a baby born under difficult conditions, with induced labor and 22 hours administration to the mother of the drug synoctin (Stratton, 1982a, p. 4; see also his Fig. 1, showing photos of this infant on the first successive 28 days of his life). It may be argued that the demonstration of individuality here occurs *in spite of* the drugging; without drugging, the quality would have been otherwise, as the Brackbill and Muller studies indicate.

The sexual body somehow got left out of the research explosion, and now the infant is moving toward being understood once again as asexual. Jerome Bruner, in a major review article on the study of the infant (1983a), currently supports the idea that infants are not as intelligent as their parents—or their researchers—have come to assume. He opts for a purely social theory of the formation of the self, in the tradition of George Herbert Mead. But the emphasis is not even on Mead's great theory of the child's active acquisiton of a self through "taking the role of the other," but on the infant's being guided toward the development of a social self through the influence of parental teaching. For this theory, Bruner relies on the work of Kenneth Kaye (1982), which is aptly subtitled, *How Parents Create Persons*. Now the theory of the self, the "person," is not what I would wish to focus upon in this study of the sexual body, but somewhere it is unavoidable as part of my topic. It is enough to say at this point that in Kaye's theory of how a baby should progress to becoming a person, there is very little room for the sexual life of the infant. You would never know, for example, that an infant has genitals and touches them. There is practically nothing on sex nor the sexual body anywhere in Kaye's book. Given that absence, and given Kaye's belief that the parent—not the infant—must very carefully engage in "the management of the infant's level of arousal" (Kaye, 1982, p. 230), the possibility for sexual self-regulation on the part of the child is nil.

Reviewed along with Kaye's book in Bruner's article is Howard Gardner's book on the theory of "multiple intelligences" (Gardner, 1983). The "frames of mind," which appear to be related to the differential faculty psychologies of the past, go well with the parental "frames" in which Kaye sees the infant benignly contained. They also are asexual. Even the chapter on "Bodily-Kinesthetic Intelligence" (Gardner, 1983, pp. 205-236) is asexual. There is no sexual body to be investigated in these powerful, sophisticated new theories. The slate has been wiped pure. True, the fact that both Kaye and Gardner are former star graduate students of Bruner at Harvard (as Bruner mentions in his autobiography, 1983b), may have something to do with the way the review is written. But that would not explain the paucity of sexual focus in Michael Lewis' new edition *Origins of Intelligence: Infancy and Early Childhood* (Lewis, 1983). The 15 large survey essays in this book contain very scant mention of sex, the body, infantile penile erection, vaginal lubrication, or even REM dreaming. A small amount of data on emotions is tucked under "affect." That is as close as these all-intellect infant artifacts are allowed to get to the sexual body. There is now a veritable army of infant researchers; neglect of the sexual body in this research can only be due to the aggregate of choices made by this group. Bruner reports:

> . . . infant psychology and even infant psychiatry are now both flourishing professions, their respective world conferences in the last couple of years each drawing more than a thousand participants. The study of development, and particularly of development during infancy, has become a major growth industry. (1983a, p. 84)

Only a few of these workers in the professions of infant development and a few of their predecessors have fought for the issues of the sexual body. Among the few are those who have raised the question of what happens to the infant when it goes through the process of birth.

The Leboyer Challenge to the Disciplines and to Cultural "Assaultive" Birth

In the background of the dispute over childbirth and evidence lies some 40 years of "natural childbirth" advocacy, by Grantley Dick-Read, Reich, Ritter and Ritter, Lamaze, Bradley (see Sheleff, 1981, p. 238), and finally Leboyer and his associate, Dr. Michel Odent. In the literature on natural childbirth, the effects of drugs have been repeatedly noted. There is good evidence that the "home birth" movement in the United States, Canada, and Europe, has led to birth practices in which there is significantly less use of drugs, and with no loss (in fact probably with some gain) in overall health safety for mother and baby (Hahn and Paige, 1980). There is thus both a cultural option (people may choose natural childbirth or conventional obstetric delivery), and an interdisciplinary research issue (effects of drugs used in childbirth procedures). The dual option of research and cultural change is often the case with the sexual body.

Both possibilities might have been in view for Ann Oakley, who makes a nervous comment on Leboyer in the Stratton volume—virtually the only one in all of the articles, except for a gibe by the editor (Stratton, 1982b, p. 7). After surveying obstetric practices cross-culturally, Oakley (1982) writes:

> The pleas made by Frederick Leboyer (1975) on behalf of the newborn hark back to some of the neonatal practices I have described in this chapter, but the only randomized controlled trial of Leboyer delivery so far conducted came up with the interesting conclusion that the only difference between the Leboyer delivery group and the control group of women undergoing normal "humane" childbirth was that the first group had a shorter first stage—presumably in anticipation of the delights of the Leboyer delivery in store for them .... (Oakley, 1982, p. 311)

Oakley is bemused, I suppose, and perhaps also is a bit smug or enthnocentric: we in the West, she implies, can not be expected to "hark back" to preliterate societies (Oakley, 1982, p. 311). Yet the anthropologist Stanley Diamond has given a reasoned theoretical case for the crucial need of the West to "hark back," which does not mean to copy or simply imitate, the so-called primitive world before it disappears entirely (Diamond, 1974).[1] Oakley is partly scoffing at the subjective judgment of the mothers, whose concerns are reduced to the immaturity of anticipatory "delights." She is also reflecting her own world hypothesis, which is grounded in class struggle and in feminism. As she argues in her book, *The Captured Womb* (Oakley, 1984), the modern hospital has not come to grips with the actual problems of poverty and class inequality which millions of women have, and variations in childbirth care such as the Leboyer method do not fundamentally change this inequity. Nor does Leboyer directly attack the domination of childbirth procedures by the male medical doctor, a problem which also concerns Oakley very deeply.

The randomized study (Nelson et al., 1980) to which Oakley refers is not any real test of Leboyer's theory. Anyone who takes note of how *Birth Without Violence* is written will realize that Leboyer was quite sincere when he said, in an address I heard at SUNY-Buffalo (November 10, 1978), that he does not actually have a "technique," a series of steps to be followed in childbirth, but an attitude of love and of living respect for what the infant must be going through at birth. It is with reason that Dr. Leboyer has refused all his life to publish his work on childbirth in any medical journals: his own sense of the sociology of medicine makes him hold that change would not occur through

---

[1]Morris (1980) has explained Diamond's "project of understanding the primitive . . . as one primary means of disclosing the 'nature of human nature' or 'human possibilites' denied in civilization. Diamond posits a radical transformation of civilized life informed by a critical knowledge of the primitive" (Morris, 1980, pp. 99-100).

those journals in any case; moreover, how could he talk about "love" in a medical journal? Yet love, and as I will show, love in a way that is quite bound up with the sexual body, is the basis for what Leboyer has to say. The *New England Journal of Medicine* study is not investigating love, nor does it mention it; instead the investigators wanted to find out if Leboyer delivery is "better" than conventional, humane birth, in these terms:

> The outcomes that we examined were the safety of the mother and the infant, infant irritability and responsiveness in the neonatal period, maternal experience and perception of her labor and delivery, and maternal perception of the infant. (Nelson et al., 1980, p. 655)

The first of these "outcomes," on the safety of the Leboyer delivery, did in fact show that it was safe, contrary to the experimenters' expectations (p. 659). It is doubtful, however, that anything is accomplished by having the fathers give their newborn babies a warm bath, under the conditions of this experiment, since this ignores Leboyer's idea that the newborn is somehow sensitive to hostility anywhere in the room (including the research assistants engaged in observing reactions). In a hospital in which the Leboyer delivery was being put on trial, it is not surprising that the 19 infant baths worked in just the opposite way from what Leboyer had found in the thousands he and his co-workers had supervised: the newborns either stayed "alert," unrelaxed, or they "reacted with irritable crying" (p. 657). The experimenters present this finding as if it were definitive, not pausing to wonder at the implication that Leboyer would have had to have been extraordinarily lucky in his hundreds of deliveries using the same bath "technique" to have found that almost always the result was profound relaxation for the newborn. They do not have a word to say about the one statistically significant positive result they did obtain: "at eight months, the mothers in the Leboyer group were more likely to say that the delivery experience had influenced the child's behavior ($p = 0.05$)" (Nelson et al., p. 659).

This study, which ends with the relieved assurance that prospective parents need have no qualms about the wisdom of well-conducted conventional childbirth procedures, strikes me as an artifact created by the experimental design and the experimenters' biases (Rosenthal, 1966). In any case, Oakley's reference to this study as "the only randomized controlled trial of Leboyer deliveries so far conducted" is misleading even if true to the canons of research. There exists some follow-up research in France which supports Leboyer's claims. Some 120 "Leboyer" babies, at various ages up to three years old, show better than average psychomotor functioning, are very largely free of digestive, sleeping, toilet training, and self-feeding problems, and also "from the paroxysmic crying associated with the neonate." Important too, considering the recent interest in right and left brain hemisphere functioning, is that these babies commonly remain ambidextrous (Kliot and Silverstein,

1980; Rapaport, 1976). The *New England Journal of Medicine* study dismisses the French follow-up as "uncontrolled," and does not inform its readers of this result, nor in fact of any of the specifics of the follow-up. The infants were given the Brunet and Lezine test for psychomotor functioning, and scored a good deal higher than the average comparable French baby; a control group is hardly necessary for this to attract notice. But it got none in New England, nor from Oakley, who also omits any reference to the writings of Dr. Leboyer's co-worker, Dr. Michel Odent (Odent, 1976, 1979; see also his books in English, Odent, 1984a, 1984b). Odent's work at the childbirth clinic in Pithviers, France, had drawn the attention of *The Lancet* (Gillett, 1979), well before the publication of Oakley's article in 1982. Oakley also chose not to comment on (or simply did not know of) the favorable reports on Leboyer's "gentle birth" by Oliver and Oliver (1978), or of Salter (1978). A review of the research on Leboyer by two authors who support his work, the obstetrician David Kliot and the psychiatrist Louise Silverstein, provides controlled data showing a lesser degree of internal physiological tension and a greater alertness in the Leboyer newborn than in the controls:

> Salter observed the state of six "Leboyer" and six control group infants during three 15-minute observation periods within the first 24 hours postpartum. Although she did not analyze her data statistically, she reports that the "Leboyer" infants spend more time in the quiet-alert state than did control group infants in all three observation periods. Oliver and Oliver, observing spontaneous behaviors occurring in the delivery room during the first 15 minutes postpartum in "Leboyer" and control group infants (N=17 in each group), found that the "Leboyer" babies spend significantly ($p < .01$) more time with eyes open and hand muscles relaxed than did control group babies. (Kliot and Silverstein, 1980, pp. 283-284)

But I realize that such "significant" results could easily appear unimportant: after all, what are 15 minutes? Without an appreciation of what Leboyer was trying to achieve and the assumptions behind that effort, such research can be written off.

Let me turn to Leboyer's own descriptions of his project. These must have provided a shock for any respectable, conventional scientific psychologist who happened to read them. The love that Leboyer wants in the delivery room is not only a term that is simply awkward for the experimenter; it is also sexual. Arguing that since we can use neither language nor, very well, gesture, to communicate with the newborn, we must use "love," Leboyer imagines himself asked if he really means that we must "speak of love" to a newborn baby.

> Yes, speak of love. Speak the language of lovers.
> And what is the essential language of lovers?
> Not speech. Touch.
> Lovers are shy, modest. When they want to embrace, they seek the darkness; they turn

> out the light. Or simply close their eyes.
> And in this darkness, they quiver, caress each other, lightly stroke each other.
> Put their arms around each other. (Leboyer, 1975, p. 36)

It is not a matter, as the conventional experimenters thought, of having the baby receive a "massage" from its mother and a warm bath from its father. Without the involvement of the adult sexual body in this contact, the "techniques" are meaningless. Lest there be any doubt that Leboyer intends a close link between loving the newborn and adult sexual love, note the following:

> But, people will say, you're making love to the child:
> Yes, almost.
> To make love is to return to paradise, it is to plunge again into the world before birth, before the great separation. It is to find again the primordial slowness, the blind and all-powerful rhythm of the internal world, of the great ocean. Making love is the great regression. (Leboyer, 1975, p. 62)

These statements would have been worse than incomprehensible to the research worker unfamiliar with a positive sense of the sexual body. They would have produced hatred, even, the same hatred of the sexual that I have shown as a broad cultural substrate in many of the writings of psychoanalysts such as Melanie Klein and D.W. Winnicott. Leboyer, as did Freud before him, strikes something deep in any reader, when he makes the sexual body his underlying focus. His disciple, Odent (1984a) continues to deepen the sexual body focus of natural childbirth; photographs from Odent's *Birth Reborn* (1984b) of women giving birth in an upright, supported position, show strong indications of orgasmic gratification on the part of the woman at the moment of birth (Kahn, 1984). Sheila Kitzinger has discussed this phenomenon under the term "birth passion" (Kitzinger, 1983, p. 109).

Leboyer's reason for allowing the umbilical cord to stay after birth until it stops pulsating is not only that it is "gentle" to allow the infant a slower leave-taking from the womb, but that the early minutes of life allow for immediate practice of self-regulation on the infant's part: the newborn is not forced to start breathing at once, but can, and in Leboyer's observation, does, experiment at her or his own pace with letting go of the oxygen supply from the cord and changing over to that from the air in the room. This issue of self-regulation (a Reichian consideration, as I have shown in discussion of Ritter and Ritter, above), is matched by the issue of aggression: the sudden clamping of the cord confronts the infant with aggression, hitting the infant at the vital level of its breathing, almost at the instant of birth. This is the beginning of a habituation to fear which will be very hard to overcome later on in development (Leboyer, 1975, p. 51). Leboyer is making a value judgment: he prefers a world where not aggression, but the sexual body, is the center of value.

The Natural: A Category or Not for World Hypotheses?

From another discipline, psychohistory, evidence seems to be emerging that would connect mass social outbursts of violent aggression in war with fantasies of painful, strangulating birth experiences. Lloyd DeMause, editor of the *Journal of Psychohistory*, has collected examples from political rhetoric and press commentary during periods preceding the outbreak of war and found them loaded with

> figures of speech and images related to biological birth. These involve strangulation, choking, being crushed, dark caves, craving for the light on the other side of the tunnel, descent into the abyss, life and death struggle for breathing space, drowning, hanging, and feeling small or helpless. (Grof, 1977, p. 303)

The very fact that DeMause is working in a controversial new discipline (and making upsetting generalizations as well as daring speculations) makes it unlikely that respectable psychological research workers will take up his hypothesis for experimental investigation. This would be all right if the issues he raises did not matter, but unfortunately they matter all too much for social survival.

The problem thus is not merely methodological (can we trust Leboyer's account, based on the 1,000 births he has worked on, and those of the follow-up studies?), but world-hypothetical: can anything having to do with the natural connection of infant body and mother's body be taken seriously in scientific research today? And, if the answer should be *yes*, can sexuality be included and considered seriously in theory, to be followed by appropriate social practices? If your world hypothesis contains no major category for the natural, then you will be tempted to exert your efforts or lack of effort toward a negative reply to the question I have posed.

Thus Hahn and Paige, psychologists who have an excellent understanding of the success and the limitations of the "home birth" movement, qualify the term "natural childbirth" by saying—correctly—that in many respects it is still a "medical birth." Their interest, much like that of Oakley's cited earlier, finally lies in the power relations between the medical profession and women of all social classes who give birth. The natural childbirth movement is not of prime importance in this struggle, they believe, partly because it is a middle-class movement (Hahn and Paige, 1980, p. 169). They are missing something: although it is true that a contemporary natural childbirth cannot be natural in the same sense the word would have were it applied to birth practices prior to the rise of modern medicine, there is still far less interference with the biological childbirth process in "natural childbirth" than there is in alternative obstetric practice. There seems little chance of avoiding the term "natural" here, however much we may attempt to avoid its implications in order to think instead in terms of such social ideals as egalitarianism.

Three major controversies in infant research which demonstrate the shadow-boxing of alternative world-hypotheses behind the portrait of psychologists engaged in a collaborative scientific enterprise are the problem of neonate visual preference for the human face, neonate synchrony of body movements with the human voice (especially female), and the theory of maternal-infant bonding. In the context of an examination of these issues, I will also comment on a number of additional research breakthroughs in which the sexual body does not exist: it has been erased by the investigators. In the background of these problems hovers the issue of the category, "natural."

Faces, Body Conversations, Vision and The Sexual Body, Mothering without Touching

Despite decades of research, pioneered again by Fantz, which has led many observers to conclude that "there is an innate bias in human newborns to attend visually to human faces," the highly respected Hanus Papoušek and Mechtild Papoušek calmly report that the latest surveys of all the research tell us "that there is only very little evidence" for this finding, "and that the perception of faces seems to follow the general course of form and pattern perception" (Papoušek and Papoušek, 1982, p. 375). That the Papoušeks can write this in the context of their comprehensive survey of research on the infant's "Integration into the Social World," and that this essay makes no reference to infantile sexuality of any kind (psychoanalytic or other) is ominous. In fact, the only discussion the Papoušeks offer of emotional factors in the social integration of the infant occurs in a preliminary paragraph of a section aptly entitled "Early Integrative Capacities: To Know Means Almost Everything" (pp. 369-374). The experiments discrediting the theory that infants visually prefer the face consist primarily of a methodology of confusing the neonates with two dimensional patterns, some of them schematically facial and some with various facial elements skewed or omitted. These experiments lead to the conclusion that it is not until the age of 5 months that "facial communication patterns" are "available to the infant," and that up until that time "the use of patterned visual information involving the whole face is not likely to occur . . ." (Campos and Stenberg, 1981, pp. 296-297). With such language we are now referring to information processing, in which indeed the slogan may be applied: "To Know Means Almost Everything" (see discussion below, Chapter Eight). But let me speculate that a live face may emit affect, in some ways, which the infant can receive (and may be especially equipped to receive), and hence that the infant's inability to know whether the cardboard pattern before it looks like a face or not is irrelevant to the understanding of infancy.

What is at stake in this de-emphasis on the possibility of the newborn's preference for the human face is not merely that set of findings, but a whole view of the human being: does the baby need warm human contact for its "integration," as Prescott's arguments strongly suggest, or is development mainly a cognitive matter having to do with such abstract matters as "form and pattern perception"? By presenting the findings only within discrete fields, such as form and pattern perception in the infant, the researcher can avoid the larger implications of an infant who not only seems to prefer the face, but also the human voice, the human skin, and the human body, rather than neutral or non-human stimuli.

Findings of conversational synchrony between adult voice and neonate body movement (Condon, 1977; Condon, 1979; Condon and Sander, 1974a, 1974b) have led to a research impasse discussed at length by Rosenfeld (1981). Once again, it appears that the impasse is due to differences in world hypotheses, not to the demands of scientific research. The findings show that as early as the first day of life the infant "moves in precise and sustained segments of movement that are synchronous with the articulated structure of adult speech" (Condon and Sander, 1974a, p. 99). These rhythmic movements had not been observed prior to the Condon-Sander research design because of their short duration (a small fraction of a second) and their complexity of location and coordination in the neonate's body. But as a result of that research design, coordinated movements in synchronization with adult speech patterns (regardless of which language is spoken, e.g., English or Chinese) can be seen. They show up, to take a typical example, in the neonate's head, left elbow, right shoulder, left shoulder, right hip, and toe of left foot (*ibid.*, p. 100). As Rosenfeld points out, these discoveries have immense implications for the study of language, communication, the nature of the infant, and social interaction: "Surely these discoveries must rate among the most significant of any science" (Rosenfeld, 1981, p. 73).

The research impasse comes about because no one outside of researchers connected with Condon and Sander have even *attempted* to replicate the experiments, despite their importance, and despite the heated state of research in human infant studies. Stratton (1982a, pp. 140-141), who cites only the 1974 study by Condon and Sander, sees the matter as one more instance in his "chronicle of loose ends" (Stratton, 1982a, pp. 140-141).

Rosenfeld has serious doubts about the findings of Condon and Sander, on logical and methodological grounds, and expresses the hope that his own call for independent replications will be heard (Rosenfeld, 1981, p. 74). The disinterest in replication of these widely publicized experiments considerably puzzles Rosenfeld. In terms of the present study, the importance of the human body as a function of intelligent social interaction in the infant-adult relationship is probably what turns most researchers away. At the same time (as Rosenfeld suggests, p. 74), those who welcome the results are also afraid that replication might not validate them, and hence do not attempt it.

An analogous research development (though one that has not resulted in a controversy) is the finding by Stechler, Bradford, and Levy (1966) that neonates of two to six days old show body behavior correlated with their giving visual attention to anything they are looking at. The conclusion is reached by measuring skin potential, which is inherently tied to the autonomic nervous system. Infants do not have to be *moving* in order for their bodies to be very active: "It is clear that electrodermal reactivity is enhanced during the state of target fixation" (p. 1248). But while some of Stechler's other research is incorporated in the comprehensive volume by the distinguished researcher M.M. Haith (1980) on the organization of newborn visual activity, the findings on skin potential and visual focussing are not even mentioned. By narrowing his own focus, Haith produces a hypothesis that is purely neurological: neonates engage in "visual activity" in order to "keep the firing rate of visual cortical neurons at a high level." Such a level is judged to be adaptively essential for later development, and is not explicable as a stimulus-response situation (Haith, 1980, pp. 106-118). Haith thus emphasizes brain neurology, to the exclusion of all else whether it be affect, emotional value for the infant of visual activity, or the body activity shown by Stechler. Brain is here taken as synonymous with the human being, while the rest of the body is ignored. In other words: a choice of brain over body. Had Condon and Sander come up with results showing that the infant *brain* is coordinated with adult speech but not that the body is intimately involved, Rosenfeld's puzzlement over the lack of interest in replications might not have been necessary.

This supposition is born out by Daniel Stern's well-known "microanalysis" of mother-infant interaction (Stern, 1971, 1977). Stern's findings give good empirical support for showing that the infant (age 3½ months) takes an active role in regulating its own contact with his or her mother through eye contact and its avoidance, thus countering earlier widespread assumptions of infantile passivity and helplessness, as well as psychoanalytic expectations that regard neonatal functioning as a matter of symbiotic fusion with the mother, a situation that does not allow for a perceptual differentiation on the infant's part of the two different bodies. Indeed, Chodorow has argued from psychoanalytic evidence that the infant could not even be aware of the good care it is getting from its mother (!) because, as Winnicott had put it, the infant exists as "almost a continuity of the physiological provisions of the prenatal state" (Chodorow, 1978, p. 84, quoting Winnicott, 1960, p. 592). Stern reports that the infant's active turning away of his head to break contact occurs as early as the second week of life (Stern, 1971, p. 503; following Stechler and Carpenter, 1967; Stechler and Latz, 1966). However, Stern, like Haith, does not mention Stechler's results regarding skin potential in the neonate, even though he cites other research of Stechler (Stern, 1971, p. 516). This is consonant with Stern's own decision that his study of mother-infant interaction should not include body contact: "all periods when the mother is touching the infants and conceivably restricting or causing infant motion were excluded from this analysis" (Stern, 1971, p. 511). Stern does not realize that this exclusion, far from purifying his study, has rendered it a fiction of the human body, in which eye communication is all and body contact is nothing, during interaction.

The research approach of Campos and Stenberg (1981) is superior to that of Stern, if considered from the perspective of the sexual body. Although immersed in the vocabulary of information processing, Campos and Stenberg are clear at least in their realization that within infant cognition, there is nonverbal communication. Contrary to the tradition of Piaget (which was adopted uncritically by some psychoanalytic theorists), they present excellent evidence from recent research on infants and in conjunction with knowledge of animal behavior, to show that "object constancy" is *not* a prerequisite for certain emotional reactions, such as fear of strangers, that infants show sometime after the fifth month (Campos and Stenberg, 1981, pp. 282-284). In fact, what they are using the information processing vocabulary *for* is to study infantile development of affect rather than knowledge as such. Pursuing neither the criterion of semantic comprehension on the part of this infant, nor the high-precision "systems" synchrony proposed by Condon and Sander, Campos and Stenberg still have made important investigations into the ways that "patterned information in the *voice* can . . . specify affective information" (p. 301). But congruent with their conclusion that the neonate does not evince visual preference for faces until the age of five months, they seem to assume that vocal information—which can convey such affects as anger, fear, sadness, boredom, and joy, and can convey these through variations in pitch and vocal rhythm—also only starts to become important to the infant at five months.

At least, that is where Campos and Stenberg were when they reported their findings in 1981. In only the few years since, there has been much more interest in the emotional life of the neonate and infant. Perhaps the complaints of Cicchetti and Pogge-Hesse (1981), mentioned at the beginning of this chapter, concerning the neglect of the emotions in research on infants, signaled the beginning of the end of the wave of cognitive concentrations. By June 1984, Campos was able to comment on a new study of neonates (Gaensbauer and Hiatt, 1984) which showed that an *abused* infant as young as three months old could look sad:

> Psychoanalytic theory held that an infant could not feel true sadness until he had formed a strong attachment to his mother or some other caretaker—by about eight months. Then he would feel sad when he was separated from that special caretaker. (Campos, quoted in Goleman, 1984d)

The new findings indicate an earlier arrival for sadness, in some infants—and not one that has to do with separation anxiety.

It appears that the infant research "explosion" continues to explode, giving us new and surprising findings, with a general direction that tends to refute more and more the psychoanalytic theory of the neonate. A year before Campos and Stenberg published their excellent survey on infantile emotional development and their own theory of "social referencing," DeCasper and Fifer published new experimental findings in *Science* which showed that infants of three *days* old (or less) show a preference for their own mother's voices (DeCasper and Fifer, 1980). That a newborn would be capable of altering its sucking patterns in order to hear its mother's voice and to tune out other voices and sounds is an indication of the bodily immediacy of voice, a mother's voice, for the sexual body at the earliest age. It would be interesting to know what impact this finding would have on the theories of Campos and Stenberg, who do not cite the work of DeCasper and Fifer, probably because it simply was unavailable to them when they went to press.

Other recent evidence corroborates the findings on infant's and mother's voices by showing that mothers learn to recognize their own infant's cry, distinguishing that cry from others in the neonatal nursery, within three to eight days after giving birth (Morsbach and Bunting, 1979). The tendency of research to concentrate on visual interactions in the mother-infant dyad (Stern, 1971, 1977) might have obscured this reciprocal recognition of voice within the maternal-infant dyad. Similarly, visual relations as an emphasis of research would have tended to overlook olfactory processes; but there now is evidence that shortly after birth, infants are drawn to the odor of their own mother (and not to the odor of another mother), just as mothers are able to recognize their own infant's odor three or four days after giving birth (Schaal et al., 1980). The evidence concerning mothers' recognition of their own infant's cries and of the reciprocal olfactory recognition of infant and mother is cited in support of the maternal-infant bonding theory (Klaus and Kennell, 1982), to which I will now turn.

The Maternal-Infant Bonding Controversy

Maternal-infant bonding is the theory that there is a "sensitive period" in the first few hours (or days) following birth in which valuable emotional ties are created through somatosensory and visual contact between mother and infant. As a theory, it is distinguished from the notion of bonding as a generalized process of attachment taking place over weeks, months and years, such as is described by Sluckin, Herbert, and Sluckin (1984). The maternal-infant bonding theory was developed by Marshall H. Klaus and John H. Kennell, both professors of pediatrics, who presented evidence for it in the 1970's, in professional articles (Kennell, Trause, and Klaus, 1975; Klaus et al., 1972) and in a modified, popular format in their book, *Maternal-Infant Bonding* (Klaus and Kennell, 1976). A variety of replication and parallel studies in the U.S., Germany, Guatemala, Brazil, and Sweden have provided confirmation, while other studies fail to replicate the results. In 1982, the concept was given a negative scientific evaluation in a comprehensive review by the psychologists Michael E. Lamb and Carl-Philip Hwang (Lamb and Hwang, 1982). The review by Lamb and Hwang is likely to be regarded as persuasive. For example, Alice Rossi, who at first had thought highly of the concept, now refers to their study as a definitive cause for rejecting the maternal-infant bonding theory (personal communication, August 8, 1983; Rossi, 1984). The issues concerning the sexual body in this controversy will be approached through my own critical comment on Lamb and Hwang's review.

That review is so detailed and inclusive that the reader is likely to lose sight of which studies might apply to Klaus and Kennell's claims and which do not. For example, a study in which *clothed* "newborn" babies were handed to their mothers is included by Lamb and Hwang as "another failure to replicate." Another "large and careful study" with insignificant results is described even though the infants were not given to the mothers until seven or more hours after birth (Lamb and Hwang, 1982, p. 23)—clearly not in time for the critical period as set forth by Klaus and Kennell. When the dust finally clears, it seems to me that Lamb and Hwang have exactly *one* strong failure to replicate to report. This is by Svejda, Campos, and Emde (1980). These researchers entitle their article "Mother-Infant 'Bondings': Failure to Generalize."

Stella Chess and Alexander Thomas have promptly reprinted this report of failure in their *Annual Progress in Child Psychiatry and Child Development* (1981), where it underscores their own research emphasis: a longitudinal study following the infant into adult life, under the rubric of such variables as "activity level," "attention span," "persistence," "quality of mood," "distractibility," "threshold of responsiveness," "approach or withdrawal," and "intensity of reaction." (See discussion in Jackson and Jackson, 1978, pp. 191-195; also Goleman, 1984d.) These—and even the characteristic of "rhythmicity" which Chess and Thomas study—are defined too abstractly to admit of anything sexual. It is not surprising that they welcome a study, begun while their own massive project is still in progress, which assures us that nothing important really happens during the critical period. That period occurs too early to figure in their own work, or to have been investigated in their project. They are probably apprehensive, as well, over their own reliance on interviews with the parents for the first three years of their project, for what they term "the obvious reason that no one else is in a position to supply as detailed and comprehensive picture of the child as they can" (Chess, Thomas, and Birch, 1965, p. 24). Besides, they had concluded on the basis of preliminary study that "the newborn infant's behavior varied significantly . . . even hour from hour, and that data collection and analysis would be an exceedingly demanding and complex process" (Thomas and Chess, 1977, p.

20). They also believe that not until the child is between the ages of six and ten years can reliable predictions concerning personality be made (Thomas and Chess, 1980, p. 114). With all this distaste for the study of the neonate, it is little wonder that Chess and Thomas welcome a "failure to generalize" concerning the early bonding theory.

But this "failure" concerns observations made over the first 36 hours after the infants' birth. Lamb and Hwang emphasize that it is a very well-designed study; they credit it as a failure to replicate within their category of "short-term" consequences of early bonding. In fact, the Klaus and Kennell theory extends to findings and speculations well beyond this short term, and several other studies *confirm* the short-term benefits to some degree. There is hardly a clear-cut "failure" involved.

What else is in Lamb and Hwang's critical review? Aside from further irrelevant studies of clothed infants (1982, pp. 15-16), there is a large amount of positive confirmation, which they attempt to discredit. In a study of "104 lower income primaparae and their newborns," it was found that mother-infant dyads in which early contact had occurred, had several notable indications of emotional bonding: the mothers were less easily distracted from the infants, the mothers and infants both seemed more calm and relaxed than were the control dyads, and the mothers more frequently took the initiative in "stimulating the infant with facial communicative behavior" (Lamb and Hwang, 1982, pp. 14-15). The Brazelton scales showed that the early contact infants "showed fewer stress responses" (p. 15). These confirmations are eagerly disparaged by Lamb and Hwang: ". . . these findings may simply have occurred because the early contact infants were more sleepy" (p. 15). While there is a report in the experiment that they were harder to arouse from sleep, the objection seems more exaggerated than the claims. Similarly, in one of the Swedish studies of short-term effects, the research findings included a report that the babies in the control group cried "a great deal more" during the observation period at 36 hours. Lamb and Hwang suggest that this discredits the positive results of the study: it leads "one to wonder whether the group differences were attributable to differences in the infants' behavior" (p. 14). That 20 babies just happen to behave differently in a control group from 22 other babies in an early-contact group is not a glowingly persuasive scientific argument! On the face of it, the difference in crying is another indication of the effects of early contact or its lack, even if the experimenters were not *measuring* crying. In a follow-up study of long-term effects for this same group, Lamb and Hwang similarly try to explain away the confirmation of the value of maternal-infant early contact with an *ad hoc* hypothesis that perhaps "the control group was temperamentally more irritable (remember that they cried at both 36 hours and 3 months)" (p. 21).

A number of experimental observations in Guatemala concerning early contact and breastfeeding are described *en bloc* by Lamb and Hwang, who give the impression that these studies have no confirmatory value. In one of these studies, however, "it was found that the early contact mothers breastfed significantly longer than mothers in the control group. In addition, these infants gained more weight over the first 6 and 12 months" (p. 25). Lamb and Hwang distract from this finding by first reporting two other Guatemalan studies, performed under different conditions, where the evidence is not favorable to the theory. They comment: "Only in one of three studies, therefore, was there evidence that early contact affected the duration of breastfeeding" (p. 14). To be sure, the evidence of these three studies is difficult to evaluate, and it does seem to conflict. Yet the study of breastfeeding duration, at a hospital that served mothers from lower middle and middle class families, is hardly negligible. Lamb and Hwang comment further that in any case the mothers in that sample did not nurse their babies as long as Guatemalans are usually reported to do, but they fail to mention the influence of infant formula giveaways on nursing habits in the third world, which are widely reported to have discouraged breastfeeding.

The Guatemalan confirmation might have been considered in conjunction with another study from Sweden. This is a careful study, and it showed that "mothers who experienced early contact showed more contact and fewer noncontact behaviors" during two different observation periods (p. 17). According to Lamb and Hwang, another careful study in Germany reported in 1981 that mothers who had had early contact with their newborns showed more tender touching and cuddling on the second and third days than did the control mothers (Lamb and Hwang, p. 17). These differences were not observed on the fourth through ninth days. Lamb and Hwang are again led to suggest that the short term effects simply disappear: there may be "a short-lived beneficial effect for some mothers" (p. 17). Interpreted in the light of Klaus and Kennell's original theory, however, this decreasing difference would be evidence of a critical period in the first three days, and the suggestion that the benefits are gone once the additional cuddling and touching is not repeated is a myopic reading of a complex biopsychological situation. Benefits are not measured solely by whether the same behavior continues, but by what difference the somatosensory affection will make later on. Some of the long term results are in other modes than touching.

Thus, as part of their supporting data, Klaus and Kennell (1976, pp. 58-59) cite the interesting ongoing work by Ringler (see Ringler, Kennell, Jarvella, Navojosky, and Klaus, 1975; Ringler, Trause, Klaus, and Kennell, 1978), which indicates in a controlled study that some of the same infants who had received the additional early contact showed a number of surprising differences at age two, and then at age five, with comparable infants who had not had that contact. Lamb and Hwang seize upon the finding that in four different tests given to the five year olds, "there were no group differences in any test" (Lamb and Hwang, p. 20). Despite this, they do acknowledge a major series of findings in these studies: there was a positive correlation between mothers' IQ in the early contact group and their children's linguistic and intellectual development on some specific measures. What the findings mean was summarized by the researchers themselves thus:

> ... the present summary suggests that how mothers speak to their 2-year-olds is associated with the children's speech and language comprehension at 5, but only among pairs who experienced extra postpartum contact.... Much detailed research is still needed to document the steps through which this occurs. (Ringler et al., 1978, p. 865)

The fact that these correlations did *not* occur in the control group is a difficult matter for Lamb and Hwang to explain. They admit that they cannot (p. 14). But they also express no support for the further detailed research that Ringler et al. call for.

A study of infant-mother interaction when the early contact infants had reached the age of two (Ringler et al., 1975) has bearing on the issue of self-regulation, since it was found that the early contact mothers "issued fewer commands to their children but asked more questions" (Marano, 1981, p. 66). Lamb and Hwang make no comment on this issue, nor would their adherence to value-free science permit them to have commented. From their point of view, the linguistic development advances on the part of the early contact infants are merely one more "measure," and are probably insignificant given that on many other measures no significant results were discovered. From the perspective of the sexual body, however, the enhancement of self-regulation in children's language interactions with their mothers could be hypothetically linked to an enhancement of sexual self-regulation. Such a relationship could be investigated with suitable research design.

In another study by Kennell, Trause and Klaus (1975), interesting differences were found at the child's age of 42 months in a group of babies who had been born preterm but had received considerably more early maternal contact than had a control group. In the words of Money, who takes a favorable view of the approach, here is what the study showed:

> At 42 months, the early-contact and the late-contact babies had average IQs of 99 and 85, respectively, and there was a correlation ($r = 0.71$) between IQ and the amount of time the mothers had spent looking at their babies during a filmed feeding at age one month. (Money, 1980, pp. 168-169)

But as Lamb and Hwang describe the same findings, they come out thus:

> ... the mothers who had been allowed into the nursery looked at their infants more while feeding them than did the mothers who had been separated. No other behavioral differences were reported, and there is no conceptual reason to interpret a difference in looking as an indication of closer bonding.... At 42 months, the children in the early

contact group reportedly had higher IQs but again the lack of information about the sample and about the statistical procedures makes this finding hard to evaluate. (Lamb and Hwang, 1982, pp. 11-12)

In this instance, Lamb and Hwang have methodological reservations which I take very seriously. For one thing, the group of infants that had been separated from their mothers were *separated for three weeks*; so that what the experiment investigated was much more than the effects of early contact. By three weeks, the early-contact pairs were much more familiar with one another. And the statistical information given in the report was indeed too sketchy. To say that the IQ differences are "hard to evaluate" is an understatement; actually, in their 1982 edition, Klaus and Kennell retract that finding entirely: the IQ differences were the result of a statistical error (Klaus and Kennell, 1982, p. 46). On the other hand, to maintain that there is no "conceptual reason" to think that eye contact has anything to do with closer bonding sounds like cultivation of the traditional blind spot that cognitively oriented researchers have toward the body. Their review is simply not a responsive attitude toward results that are still most suggestive about the effects of early somatosensory contact and interaction, and which come out of a new research strategy which after all was only about five years old itself at the time of the report.

Others have made much of the fact that Klaus and Kennell's sample of mothers came from a special social group: poor and black. Kaye (1982, pp. 254-255) and Leiderman (1980) believe that the Hawthorne effect was decisive. But some of the Swedish, German, and even Guatemalan positive evidence cited by Klaus and Kennell is based on middle class mothering.

It is useless to claim that the Lamb and Hwang review is biased; it merely reflects the psychological assumptions of the authors. At the surface these are methodological, but inevitably underlying assumptions regarding human nature and "what is good for people" are also involved. Without trying to further resolve the issue of the correctness of the review article, I would at least add this: it suffers from a lack of scientific commonsense, if I may use such a term. Klaus and Kennell pointed out that their original study involved hospitalized women who had had some anesthetics and drugs during childbirth, and who did not have their babies placed in contact with them until one or two hours after birth. This would not have been the situation in home-birth delivery (Klaus and Kennell, 1976, p. 59). The authors may have been hinting that an inquiry into maternal-infant bonding should be directed at a situation involving immediate post-birth contact between mother and infant. In fact, some of the Swedish studies in which positive results were obtained did have this condition. By 1982, Klaus and Kennell were much clearer on this point, because they now had new research findings (Emde and Robinson, in press) from another area, showing that in the first hour of life the newborn is likely to experience a quiet, alert state with a capacity for viewing the environment with wide-open eyes. In the second through fourth hours, on the other hand, the newborn is likely to go into a deep sleep. The first hour seems all the more crucial in this light.

The further challenge to research is to study maternal-infant contact at its optimum, in natural childbirth delivery. This is a challenge to perform a delicate but valuable investigation without disturbing the contact. Lamb and Hwang were interested not in the inquiry but in dampening it. They end their study with warnings that the whole idea of maternal-infant bonding could be socially dangerous. It could make some parents feel guilty for not having provided this kind of birth experience; it could encourage a simplistic panacea for all the needs of the mother who comes from lower socioeconomic classes; and worst of all, it could be highly embarrassing to the professionals in the field of behavioral pediatrics (Lamb and Hwang, pp. 31-33). This theory may bring that field into "long-term disrepute." But in my reading, what is in "disrepute" is the sterile scepticism which prematurely denigrates the pioneering work of Klaus and Kennell. The other dangers referred to by Lamb and Hwang are real, but they could be avoided without throwing out the bonding theory, a theory which raises basic questions about the sexual body.

World Hypotheses Behind the Bonding Controversy

The maternal-infant bonding controversy obviously is not a purely academic one. The issue is a threatening one in itself to those whose world hypotheses have little use for a category of natural, biological value in which body contact is essential.

Some feminist scholars see the interest in bonding as evidence of a reversion to sexism (Breines and Gordon, 1983, pp. 496-499). This is part of a larger dispute within feminist thought regarding the importance of biological factors in the quality of women's lives. Alice Rossi (1977, 1981) is among those who hold that parenting is a biosocial affair, and that women have a bodily relation to mothering that cannot be swept away by changes in ideology. On the other side are Nancy Chodorow (1978), who relies primarily on the psychoanalytic theory of object relations, and many other feminist thinkers. In empirical psychological studies, bonding tends to be dismissed as an unconfirmed "emotional" theory. Eva Reich has emphasized maternal-infant bonding in her past several years of lecturing in several parts of the world, even though she is not referred to by other discussants (e.g., Sheleff, 1981, p. 230) who wish to emphasize the mother-infant relationship without considering sexuality. The bonding advocates sometimes speak as if the infant and mother will provide a revival of the pre-Freudian "innocence" that denied infantile sexuality altogether. The loss of Eva Reich's contribution to most academic and therapeutic research is especially unfortunate because she has specialized in brief therapy techniques for "re-bonding," given to mothers who voluntarily present themselves as lacking a sense of emotional contact with their very young infants (E. Reich, 1980). The potential value of such work is too basic to be ignored.

Opponents of the bonding theory may not have heard of Eva Reich, but it is harder to understand why they would often fail to cite the most comprehensive statement of the theory which they oppose. The indispensible text, available since 1976, is the book edited by Klaus and Kennell, containing within it critical comments by (among others) the pediatrics specialist, T. Berry Brazelton, an anthropologist, B. Lozoff, and one ex-president of the American Psychoanalytical Association, Albert J. Solnit. The key chapter, "Human Maternal and Paternal Behavior," is written by the two editors, but includes numerous critical comments from this panel (Klaus and Kennell, 1976, pp. 38-98). Another recent survey of the maternal-infant bonding in *Journal of Child Psychology and Psychiatry* mentions neither Prescott's overall studies of the value of affectional touching in infancy nor this key work by Klaus and Kennell in the very field being surveyed (Sluckin, Sluckin, and Sluckin, 1982). (This negative report on bonding is *also* promptly reprinted by the wife-husband research team of Chess and Thomas in their *Annual Progress* series. They never seem to find any favorable article worth inclusion; see Chess and Thomas, 1984a.) The Klaus and Kennell main volume is cited neither by Breines and Gordon, in their recent feminist rejection of bonding, nor by any of the writers in Stratton's *Psychobiology of the Newborn* (1982b), although both of these sources cite more restricted publications by Klaus and Kennell. But the book-length presentation is uniquely important for several reasons. For one, it allows scope for employment of multidisciplinary approaches to suggest an overall theory. Second, as Diesing has pointed out, a theory in the social sciences depends on "contextual validation" in which a convergence of evidence from many sides is brought to bear; some of it is "weak" evidence *if* considered in isolation from the theory (Diesing, 1971). Third, two of the strongest points raised in the feminist scholars' objections would have to be considerably modified were the more comprehensive statement taken up. In their central chapter Klaus and Kennell (1976) do *not* base their work on mammalian studies, as Breines and Gordon (1983, p. 496) have charged; the facts of "Maternal Behavior in Mammals" are treated as a separate chapter and are not referred to in the main one. Neither is the complaint that bonding is limited to the mother's role in parenting, and is hence a sexist investigation, born out by the Klaus and Kennell chapter, plainly entitled "Human Maternal and Paternal Behavior." The authors in fact define the concerns of their book as "the bond a mother or father forms with his or her newborn infant" (p. 1). As if to underscore the point, Klaus and Kennell titled the second edition of their book (1982), *Parent-Infant Bonding*. One of the reports cited by Klaus and Kennell (1976, p. 69) is by an anthropologist, J. Schreuber, who told them of *extended* bonding patterns in a small farming community in Italy: "Within 5 minutes of the birth, the parents, grandparents, and, on the average, five other relatives, will have kissed the baby" (Klaus and Kennell, 1976, p. 39). Eva Reich, whom I have heard lecture on the topic of bonding, has also made it clear that bonding is not limited to the mother (E. Reich, 1980).

All of which is not to pretend that a father is as central to the early life of the neonate as the mother. On this opinions differ. Lamb and Goldberg (1982), in a comprehensive review of research on the father-child relationship, strongly suggest that no differences are to be found between the responses of fathers and mothers to neonates. They cite two extensive and careful studies in which parental response to the baby's crying was investigated; these showed "no sex differences on measures of physiological responses *although the mothers reported more extreme emotions*" (Lamb and Goldberg, 1982, p. 65, emphasis added). The clause I have emphasized seems to me to render the intended conclusion dubious, inasmuch as emotions are tied to physiological functions: if they are "more extreme" in mothers, that *is* a difference in physiological response. Klaus and Kennell, while they do discuss the father's role in bonding, may be fundamentally correct in assuming that the bonding relationships they are investigating occur more readily between mother and infant. (In my discussion of Lichtenstein, Chapter Nine, I will come back to this topic.)

It should be evident that when I describe Klaus and Kennell in their own language their theory can be imagined as a plausible one, whereas the largely truncated descriptions of their theory in the writings of their critics makes it seem misconceived, naive, falsified, malicious, and not even worth knowing. This has ever been the case with the study of the sexual body. The issue can be stated as a struggle between those who take biology as an essential part of the human psyche and those who want biology to be out of the picture. When biology goes, the body goes, and the sexual body need never be considered. There probably is some simplification in the assumptions of those who defend the theory of maternal-infant bonding. As Rossi points out (personal communication, August 8, 1983), no one should suggest that human *survival* mechanisms are dependent upon the experience of mother-infant contact during the first hours after birth. Evolutionary process would not have fixed upon one lone normative event, so easily violated. But until researchers become more generally disposed to attend to the "natural" bodily connections in birth and infancy, the cycle of exaggerated claims and misconceived disconfirmations will go on indefinitely.

"Bonding" would seem to be a concept especially easy for its critics to dismiss as naive, because it is so obviously a metaphor, and its proponents seldom speak of it as such. So for that matter is "attachment" a metaphor, but probably it does not raise any ungainly images in the mind: we know that the baby is not literally "attached" to the mother, whereas we are not so sure that something *purely* metaphorical is being implied with the term "bonding." And indeed it is not: maternal-infant bonding is a metaphor implying connections between two bodies which are established through contact and through energy exchanges, including particularly an exchange of the emotion, love. This may account for some of the animosity of those who would like to discuss it as if it were not a metaphor at all, but a literal fact of some sort. There is a whole additional type of curiously linear argument which I will now take up. Behind the literalness, I suggest, is another instance of that "contempt for the body" which Dewey located in the history of morals (Dewey, 1934, p. 20). The assumption seems to be, if it is a body-to-body contact, it must be a simple matter. Hence, Arney (1980), Sluckin, Sluckin, and Sluckin (1982), and Chess and Thomas (1984b) continually tend to speak of bonding as if it involved nothing more complicated than putting one body next to another for a few hours. They have no difficulty "refuting" this ghost of the sexual body.

Biology, the Sexual Body, and Feminist Psychoanalytic Thinking

As support for their arguments, Gordon and Breines cite a more comprehensive treatment of the maternal-bonding issue by Arney (1980), a man. Arney has a reasonable methodological skepticism concerning the study by Ringler et al., (1975); how can we be sure that the children who had higher IQs and a higher degree of self-regulation at age five actually got those qualities from the early extra contact with their mothers during the first hours of postnatal life? Any group over a five year period would show numerous changes in other areas, such as perhaps improved relations between the parents, or special input of learning from unidentified sources. Arney also makes two more general claims, however, which display the underlying issues in a glaring light. In his world hypothesis, human beings are defined as human because they create their meanings for themselves out of their experiences; bonding, he declares, is a concept that denies human meanings because any meaning it creates is biological rather than human in nature. This division of the subject on ideological grounds rules out interest in bonding or in any other aspect of the sexual body. The very realization that maternal-infant bonding creates (or might create) meanings (relational, affective, experiential) would be exactly what is unacceptable, to this point of view, since it would make it all too evident that we do not step outside of nature to live our lives; instead we are part of nature (cf. Dewey, 1929b, p. 307).

The other major claim by Arney is even balder: that research showing the existence of maternal-infant bonding in humans not only is flawed, it must always be invalid no matter how well it is done!: "It would be impossible to conduct research that could conceivably lead to the conclusions of bonding research . . ." (Arney, 1980, p. 551). By this, he appears to mean that it would be impossible to take a group of mothers and infants, plus a control group, and follow them under conditions of airtight control, subtracting all other causes of good maternal-infant interaction, and thus replicate the benefits of bonding. You might be able to observe infants in their cribs for a few hours after birth, in other words, under conditions of stringent control, but never a live relationship between infant and mother over a five year period in normal social conditions.

The problem here, finally, is one of intelligence, in Dewey's sense. If people are ever to make intelligent decisions, such as what sort of childbirth practices to adopt, they cannot be expected to ignore all indications that appear to give weight to the metaphor of the maternal-infant "bond" simply because there could never be fully conclusive evidence for it. The actual choice would be made not in terms of conclusive/inconclusive evidence, but in respect to what alternatives available for child-rearing appear to be the most sane and healthy: the value judgments of such terms cannot be avoided. Arney's approach to the problem of maternal-infant bonding is thus to obstruct rather than face it.

The proponents of the "sensitive period" that occurs shortly after birth may eventually come to be discredited; if such reviewers as Lamb and Hwang, Sluckin, Sluckin, and Sluckin, and Gordon and Breines, are to be taken seriously, the idea of such bonding already has been discredited. Nonetheless there is still no reply to Prescott's simple formulation of the issue:

> No other mammal except the human mammal separates its newborn from its mother at birth which prevents immediate sucking at the breast. These departures from mammalian universal behavior can only be considered abnormal. (Prescott, 1979, p. 100)

In Freud's original classic period, there would have been no reason to deny this. Today, however, the sexual body is usually kept out of sight in psychoanalytic thought.

Nancy Chodorow's work, and her controversy with the non-psychoanalytic feminist sociologist, Alice Rossi, forms a significant confrontation between an approach which denies the significance of biological considerations and one which takes the sexual body seriously. Chodorow's book, *The Reproduction of Mothering: Psychoanalysis and the Sociology of Gender* (1978), is a major feminist reinterpretation of psychoanalytic thought. This also contains no reference to the work of Klaus and Kennell, although it takes a strongly negative view of the alleged evidence for maternal instinctive behavior. The author argues, in the context of a detailed reconsideration of psychoanalytic object relations theory, that this theory provides convincing support for the position that "motherhood" is not instinctual, but a sociologically induced gender-role combination brought about by society. Nor is the mothering role a neutral one: the very preponderance of women in the role of mothers assures that both men and women will have developed as infants much stronger early "object relations" with mothers, not fathers. They will create incurably ambivalent hate-love objects in their mothers; indeed it is likely that there will be more hate than love, given the denial of the value of woman that is built into the mothering role. The cycle will reproduce itself indefinitely, unless the one basic change that could break the cycle is introduced: the equal sharing of "primary," i.e., close, early, nurturing, parenting (mothering), by men and women.

When confronted with objections from Alice Rossi that there are very likely biological considerations that make the mothering role primarily that of the natural mother, Chodorow gave skeptical replies. Thus to Rossi's data showing that the infant's cry produces an increase of oxytocin in the mother, which stimulates nursing, uterine healing and erotic contractions after childbirth, Chodorow countered that Rossi had not shown that oxytocin stimulation had to do with anything more than lactation itself; who could say that it had any connection with bonding? Besides, was it not possible that nonlactating women produce oxytocin too? It might be supposed that this is an irrelevant answer, since Rossi's point concerned the psychophysiological interaction of a nursing mother with the voice of her infant, and then with a nipple/mouth contact, whereas other women who were not nursing, although they might produce the chemical, could not experience the nursing cycle. And, Chodorow advises, do not forget men: maybe they have an oxytocin level comparable to that of a nursing mother, for all we know (Chodorow, 1978, p. 18-19). Actually, there is some reason to believe that oxytocin is produced in the male body as part of the orgasmic cycle (Davidson, 1980, pp. 308-309), but again, the mere production of the substance is not the issue so far as the sexual body interaction of caretaker and child is concerned. Chodorow is trying to reduce the bonding metaphor to a set of literal components.

On the basis of such reasoning Chodorow urged that Rossi's arguments be dismissed. However, in an exchange with Rossi a few years later, Chodorow began to change her outlook toward the relevance of biological and evolutionary evidence:

> I have been convinced by Rossi's argument that I and other feminists must be open to the investigation of biological variables and that those who argued or implied that such investigation is illegitimate were wrong. We are embodied creatures, and our experience as people of either sex includes this embodiment. There is certainly some biological basis, or influence, to some sex- and gender-linked experiences, though this biology does not dichotomize the human population perfectly, nor do all men and women have the same reproductive or sexual experiences. (Chodorow, 1981, p. 507)

It is to Chodorow's credit that she could make this shift. Not surprisingly, her work continues to be known and praised for its refusal to regard biological factors as important in mothering (Breines and Gordon, 1983, p. 498). The reconsideration just quoted may turn out to have no effect, particularly since it was followed at once with Chodorow's reindorsement of psychoanalytic object relations theory, for "its rich account of how we come to make something psychologically" of our embodiment, "which includes our sexuality, creating in the process important parts of our personality and our emotional life" (Chodorow, 1981, p. 507). Now I maintain that this praise for object relations is both misplaced and misconceived. It is misplaced because the body hatred of Melanie Klein and even of Winnicott infused their theories with a negative evaluation of the sexual body; it is misconceived because of the mind-over-body bias built into the formulation. What could be implied, after all, by the phrase "how we come to make something psychologically" of our sexuality, but another disparagement of the sexual, except as it may serve to furnish material for "higher" things? The steps up Plato's ladder toward the ideal await any such formulation as Chodorow's. From an interdisciplinary standpoint, and from the perspective of the present study, it appears that Chodorow has acknowledged that in her book she was only able to argue the noninstinctual, nonbiological nature of mothering by avoiding rather than confronting the relevant disciplines. She was enabled to do this by virtue of her reliance on the very psychoanalytic thought which she continues to regard as the discipline of choice for understanding the sexual subordination of women. On the basis of that theory, she believes, for example, that the young infant has an "absolute physiological and psychological dependence, and . . . total lack of development of its adaptive ego functions . . ." (Chodorow, 1978, p. 83). From this position it would not be possible for her to adapt to the findings of recent infant research which indicate in many ways that the belief is false.

The Survival of Maternal-Infant Bonding and the Sexual Body

It bears repeating that mother-infant interactions are sexual interactions, if psychoanalytic theory is accepted at all. What the dimensions of this sexuality might be is a question permanently occluded by avoiding the problems of contact, uterine contractions, hormonal changes in pregnancy, body energy considerations, infantile sexuality and the woman's sexual life as an adult. One major impetus of the upsurge in interest in maternal-infant bonding has been to begin to refocus on all these considerations within the earliest hours and days of neonatal life. The eye-contact between newborn and mother, as observed by students of bonding,

> is not very different from what happens when a man and woman fall in love: mutual gazing, touching, fondling, nuzzling, kissing. (Marano, 1981, p. 65)

One can simply declare such observations a "category mistake." But, as Pepper used to ask, "on whose categories?" If that shortcut is not taken, we are left with an overlap of the languages of adult-adult and adult-infant love, comparable to the original creative confusion caused by Freud's use of the term "sexuality." The sex therapist Offit (1977) is the only writer, to my knowledge, to report that sexual stimulation of mothers by their babies is a serious *problem* for adult relationships in some contexts:

> Caring for babies is at once a source of immense maternal satisfaction, a huge erotic stimulus, and a tedious drudgery. . . . It becomes routine to shut off the sexual arousal afforded by intimate body contact all day long. Many mothers masturbate regularly at their children's naptime to relieve the sexual tension generated, although they are not aware of their children's role in nourishing it. This leaves them less interested at night. (Offit, 1977, p. 155)

Offit lacks the Reichian distinction, here, of adult genital gratification which would make a great difference in defusing such arousal, and in preventing sexual energy from becoming directed toward incestuous fantasy. Nonetheless, she has described a little-known problem about the adult sexual body in its relations with infants. It sheds a startling light, I think, on reports that men are "jealous" of their own babies, for the attention that mothers give those babies. It would appear that in some instances there would be a sexual body reason for this, and not a mere disturbance through the common male fantasy, in our society, of possessing the woman. To know that maternal-infant contact could produce such a pattern of arousal and discharge may throw light on Chodorow's discomfort with the uncritical adulation of the "intensity" of mothering the young infant, expressed by male psychoanalytic theorists (Chodorow, 1978, p. 87).

Although the psychobiology of the dynamic maternal-infant interaction is a matter of obvious, overriding interest in infant research, the "army of observers and researchers" (Roiphe and Galenson, 1981, p. x) has been far from responsive to some of the most basic and obvious needs for knowledge in this field. The following comment, from a review of research on the nutrition and feeding of the newborn is fairly astonishing:

> Apart from a few workers such as Richards and Bernal, there has been little interest in the study of the naturally occuring infant and mother feeding behaviours. . . . Perhaps even more surprisingly, rarely has a comparison been made between breast and bottle feeding beyond the first week of the infant's life, and certainly not to explore the potential precursors of obesity. This is particularly surprising since breast and bottle feeding are so different and could provide very different (learning) experiences according to technique. (Wright and Crow, 1982, p. 341)

Wright and Crow go on to report a most interesting comparative longitudinal study of their own on breast and bottle feeding, with infants from four days up to six months of age. The results show a startling contrast in feeding patterns for the two groups. As the authors point out, "Interpretation of such data is not easy" (p. 352). It would be much more feasible to evaluate it if the infant research disciplines had not already created an asexual theoretical and experimental context for such studies. It remains to be seen if the fine research start and brilliant initiative of these two researchers will find any echo in the discipline. Unfortunately, Wright and Crow do not cite (and probably are unaware of) Jean Ritter's much earlier study of self-regulation in breastfeeding, discussed above (Chapter Four). Their study, excellent as it is, is narrowly focused on nutrition and feeding, with little psychological inquiry except toward the cognitive dimension, that is, to learning. The sexual body, so near at hand, is not considered.

Nor is it considered in Kaye's excellent research into the social significance of biological mother-infant feeding interactions. Kaye (1982), whose book received such a warm review from Bruner, deserves much praise for his discovery that the human infant feeds in a rhythmic pattern of "bursts" of sucking, followed by a pause, and that during the pause, the mother intuitively jiggles the infant, causing a delay in the onset of the next "burst" of sucks. This pattern is not found in other primates. Nor is the jiggling apparently a culturally determined behavior. Kaye reasonably speculates that the mothers intuitively convert the biologically given burst-pause cycle into a precursor of mother-infant taking of turns, and thus into an early social interchange. Kaye did not recognize the sexual dimensions of sucking (possibly he would deny these exist); he also did not consider the variable *quality* (not just the fact) of body-to-body contact between mother and infant, as a factor in creating the variable quality of social interchange. The jiggling can convey disruption, character stiffening, a tone of hurrying-up, or it can suggest affectionate contact and ways of dealing with people.

On the Sexual Body of Neonates

Infantile genitality, unlike the problems discussed in the past several sections, is not a research area producing vital controversies. However, this is primarily because of avoidance, not because there is no pioneering experimental observation which might have had the effect on this field that Fantz' methodology had on the study of neonatal visual perception. Here I would like to refer to some of the findings of Peter H. Wolff. Wolff, like Fantz, is credited with a key role in originating the great infant research "explosion" (Stone, Smith, and Murphy, 1973, p. 6), and like Fantz, his methodology was surprisingly commonsensical: he spent long hours, sometimes as many as 18 consecutive hours (Stone et al., p. 239) in careful observation of the infant's "state," such as whether the infant was awake or asleep, agitated or quietly alert. Wolff found that infant boys of as young as four days have cycles of penile erections while they sleep; these cycles coincide with their Rapid Eye Movement during sleep, which are known to be a major time of dreaming in children and adults (Wolff, 1966). Wolff's observations were accompanied by suggestions of a theoretical nature that indicate the ease with which complicated bio-psychic rhythms may be disrupted, and how substitute behavior may be overlaid on top of the same neurobiological channels:

> Fourth day, 25 minutes of regular sleep. The record begins immediately after the infant has voided. During the first 12 minutes he has seven erections, each lasting about one minute, and separated on the average by about 30-second intervals. On three occasions while the penis is erect a jar to the crib elicits a vigorous extensor startle followed by an immediate complete detumescence that persists for one and a half minutes (in contrast to the usual interval between erections, which never exceeds 39 seconds). When the crib is no longer jarred, erections resume; now each erection lasts about two minutes, and sequential erections are separated by approximately 20-second intervals . . . . This record indicates that spontaneous erections may occur immediately after urination and therefore independent of bladder distention; that erections, mouthing movements, and spontaneous startles can substitute for each other; that elicited startles can inhibit spontaneous discharges; and that mouthing movements and erections have their own specific rhythms. (Wolff, 1966, pp. 22-23)

It is entirely likely that most psychoanalytic observations on the infant have been made without awareness of this material, or at least without any consideration of what it may mean, although the raw fact that baby boys get erections was certainly known and referred to in the early Vienna years. Not surprisingly, given the cultural predisposition I have alluded to, it then dropped out of theoretical and indeed clinical or even experimental notice for a very long time.

The psychoanalyst Phyllis Greenacre (1952), however, did deal with the topic, in 1952. She even cited studies of infantile erection in the psychological literature dating back to 1917 (Martinson, 1981b, p. 59, has unearthed a French study published in 1883!). Greenacre's major source for her own psychoanalytic considerations was a large, careful study by H.M. Halverson, a Yale psychologist (Halverson, 1938, 1940). For Greenacre, Halverson provided evidence of the infant's innate tendency toward anxiety. Unfortunately Halverson's study was an almost perfect instance of the experimental artifact. As Martinson (1981b) has argued, Halverson's finding that penile erection did not occur while the neonatal boy was sucking at the breast could have come out of the experimental set-up itself, which

> served to deter from a full pleasurable response—apparently no caressing or fondling by the mother, no eye-to-eye contact, no opportunity for the infant to touch the mother's face, or to place its fingers in her mouth existed. The question left unanswered is how many of those infant boys would have responded with penile erections under normal nursing and cuddling conditions. (Martinson, 1981b, p. 65)

In other words the crucial missing variable once again is Prescott's somatosensory affectional contact. Martinson, whose critique of the Yale experiment I have just cited, is one of the handful of social scientists who realizes Prescott's importance (Martinson, 1981b, p. 72). Greenacre, writing in 1952, could not have known either Prescott or the findings of Wolff. Nonetheless, it is significant for the fate of the sexual body, in theory and research, that Halverson's anxious, upset neonatal boys with penile erections could figure in the psychoanalytic literature, whereas the later article (Wolff, 1966, where the boys are functioning in accordance with a natural rhythm of the sexual body) never seemed to have had an impact. With Wolff's much respected work, however, the topic has been set forth indelibly for further investigation.

Yet interest in it has been slight. Anneliese Korner's study published in 1969 is the only notable exception, to my knowledge. Her sample consisted of 32 infants, 17 of them male, at 45 to 88 hours after birth, all of them bottle-fed Caucasians. The study called for observations not only of erections, but of neonatal startles, smiles and "reflex sucks." Some of Korner's conclusions are of great interest for anyone maintaining (as I am) that sexuality is especially problematical and not yet understood: "The data . . . suggest that erections are spontaneous behaviors which occur over and above other discharge behaviors" (Korner, 1969, p. 1048). Observer agreement as to whether an infant did or did not have an erection was 100% (p. 1044). There was "a highly significant [statistical] relation between the occurrence of erections and the infant's state." As in Wolff's study, the erections "most commonly occurred during irregular sleep, and during that state the large majority are seen while the infant is having rapid eye movement" (p. 1047). However, "Erections were also noted during waking states, particularly during crying. These were brief and in a sense not entirely spontaneous, since the proprioceptive feedback from the diffuse activity associated with crying undoubtedly served as a stimulus" (p. 1047). Unlike evidence for adult males, Korner's data did not indicate anything like a 95% correlation of REM sleep periods and erections, but as she pointed out, the findings "nevertheless demonstrate the beginnings of such an association" (p. 1047). The observations suggest possibilities for further research, and the distinctions Korner employed, such as between spontaneous and non-spontaneous discharge, were most interesting ones. Yet little happened: no research boom followed on infant genitality, although Korner herself suggested one of the most obvious questions: could it be that females as well as males have "an additional discharge channel" that complements the erections of the neonatal boys? (p. 1048). Korner continued to do extensive research herself on newborns, but by 1977, she was emphasizing the female's greater cutaneous receptivity and oral behavior, such as reflex smiles and rhythmical mouthing as a differentiation from the male, who tended toward more total body movement (Korner, 1977). She found that "the overall rate of spontaneous discharge behaviors was almost identical for males and females *when erections were excluded*. . ." (p. 13, emphasis added), but said nothing about what role these erections could have.

The first hint I found of a positive answer to Korner's initial question—as to whether little girls might have "an additional discharge channel" to match the male infantile erection—appeared in a book by Mary Calderone and Eric

Johnson, *The Family Book About Sexuality* (1981). What they say is that "a girl baby every few hours shows sign of fluid in her vagina, similar to the lubricating fluid that will be produced later when she is sexually aroused." This rhythmic occurrence begins "soon after birth . . ." (p. 18). This still does not tell us whether the cycles are correlated with anything else, such as REM dreaming.

Let me acknowledge that in this instance I am giving the perspective of the sexual body the benefit of a doubt. In fact, the *evidence* for Calderone's assertions regarding the girl neonate's rhythmic vaginal lubrication is far from persuasive. It stems from a report given by a Norwegian researcher at the Montreal conference on childhood sexuality in 1979, and that report is quite lacking in experimental details (Langfeldt, 1980). Langfeldt has given further details in another article, but his findings must be considered preliminary, rather than conclusive (Langfeldt, in press). The perspective of the sexual body, however, would impel research to continue on this finding, and even to presume that a basis for it will emerge. The fact that only an informal report at a specialized conference on child sexuality is the source of the data thus far is a problem, but it is also a reflection of the low priority given to the sexual body by researchers. As for the human neonatal male erection, Calderone and Dr. James W. Ramey now report that there is good evidence that it begins during prenatal life (Calderone and Ramey, 1983).

Unfortunately we are in no position to begin to understand our data concerning infantile genital sexuality because we have developed a culture of science dedicated for the most part to investigating a nonexistent organism, the asexual infant. When research threatens to bring results that are not evidence for asexuality, little is heard of it. A study of newborn behavior during the first two days after birth (Phillips, King, and DuBois, 1978) came up with the results that newborn boys are indeed a good deal more active than girls. Judged by two observers who did not know the sex of any of the infants, the boys had a higher "total activity score," that is, the boys had higher levels of wakefulness, facial grimacing, and various kinds of body movements such as movement of hands and feet than did girls. The study was carefully controlled, and did not include any boys who had been circumcised. The presence of "experimenter effect" here is made very dubious, especially in view of Phillips'—the chief investigator's—own statement that she expected *not* to find these sex differences (Phillips, quoted in "Researcher Finds," 1978). The two graduate students in psychology who did the rating of the infants were women: this was not a case of men finding what they wanted to see. Phillips' report appears to conflict with the interpretation of Korner, based on earlier extensive observations of newborns, in which no differences in activity levels were found between boys and girls (Korner, 1977). Although the authors call for further research into sex differences at birth, I am unaware of any follow-up. Clearly, some would find the results not pleasing for ideological reasons, although, as the authors point out, a high level of spontaneous bodily activity is not necessarily an advantage in life; it may in fact be associated with the high incidence of "hyperactivity" in males (Werry, 1968). And no one seems to be very interested in evidence by Friedman, Bruno, and Vietze (1974), showing that two week old girls are better learners in some respects than are boys of the same age: they respond better to "discrepancy" (novelty). To further such investigations would be to compromise the asexual portrait of infancy now being created in many research efforts.

Similarly, there seems to be no interest in following up Brackbill's finding that circumcision of the neonatal boy (average age, 37 hours) has an effect on the boy's response to *auditory stimulation*. Recently circumcised boys showed a statistically significant difference in heartrate from that of the uncircumcised boys or from that of the girls (Brackbill, 1975). Such a finding could be a clue, however minor, to the little understood psychophysiology of the infantile sexual body. The article is not so much as mentioned in Stratton's comprehensive review volume of the *Psychobiology of the Human Newborn*, although several other items by Brackbill are cited. Circumcision—a matter if there ever was one, of the sexual body—is not worth discussing for those who see the study of the newborn as ultimately the study of how the newborn acquires knowledge, rather than of how the sexual body lives through the early months of life.

If we consult the psychoanalytic literature even of the present day, however, we find the sexual body at least some of the time. Roiphe and Galenson (1981) argue unabashedly on the basis of much clinical evidence for the presence in girls of (not culturally caused) penis envy. They make the by-now-rare observation that "Very early genital zone experiences during the first 16 months of life contribute to a vague sense of genital awareness and undoubtedly exert an influence over many ego functions" (p. 284). This, as they point out, is a position consistent with the early Freud. Somewhere in the nonpsychoanalytic literature there must be—or should be—a consideration of this genital awareness in the very youngest humans. Somewhere there is a researcher or theorist who will discuss it for us without involving us in the doctrine of penis envy. But where?

Infancy and Mind-Body Unity

There remains the possibility that the two models, one of a cognitively competent infant and the other of an emotionally intact, sexual infant (stemming respectively from recent infant research and from the Reichian branch of psychoanalytic thought), will be combined into a single "object of knowledge" (Dewey, 1929b). Within psychoanalytic tradition there has been the related concept of the "undifferentiated" infantile psyche, a term referring to the alleged inability of the neonate to have thoughts in any sense recognizable by the civilized adult. Indeed the neonate is not even credited with being able to know that its mother is not an extension of its own body. That aspect of undifferentiation may be set aside, at some point in the future, under the weight of findings which indicate that the neonate indeed knows that difference. A strict reading of empirical evidence about babies would not support the notion of an undifferentiated state, and Peterfreund, one of the theorists seeking a reform in psychoanalytic thought, has thrown the idea on the trash-heap (Peterfreund, 1978). I myself have reconsidered doing the same, in the years since I strongly endorsed the undifferentiated state concept (Efron, 1973), not foreseeing at the time that a great deal of evidence would soon make it doubtful. There may be something not only salvageable but vital in the concept of undifferentiation, however, which would make simply discarding it unwise. Viewing the infant as one whose feeling and thinking capacities include the sexual and the cognitive, without the benefit or burden of having verbal levels to distinguish one from the other, is at least one way for us to *imagine* that in human life, mind and body are not split. I think that is what the unorthodox analyst, Ernst Schachtel was telling us in his great book, *Metamorphosis* (1959). Perhaps that is why the book was never reviewed, so far as I can determine, in any of the psychoanalytic journals. If there is a period in the development of each baby in which mind-body unity is a fact rather than a wish, that would be a major qualifier for my own speculative theory of a "residual asymmetrical dualism" as the human condition (Efron, 1980). It would also, more importantly, be part of the life history of each of us, which we could then wonder about and use to reconsider our experiences.

Research orientations in this matter of the neonate's sexual body are beset by an either/or proposition that seems to be implicit in our thinking as civilized adults. We tend either to suppose that the neonate is born with a complete set of emotions and cognitions as Reich finally thought (Placzek, 1981, p. 118)—*or* that lacking this complete set, the neonate is not a complete human being. Karl Popper has seriously urged on us the consideration that a baby cannot measure up to Immanuel Kant's criteria of a person:

> "A person is a subject that is responsible for his actions," and "A person is something that is conscious, at different times, of the numerical identity of its self." (quoted by Popper, in Popper and Eccles, 1977, p. 115)

I suspect it is in reaction to this strong cultural tradition of defining the person in this way that Carroll Izard has theorized that a very young infant has the whole set of emotions of the adult, including those of guilt and shame (as discussed in Cicchetti and Pogge-Hesse, 1981, pp. 249-258). We are trapped so long as we imagine that the newborn must either be completely equipped with emotions and cognition, or else no person exists. As long as the neonate has enough sense to know pleasure, pain, and what Izard was finally constrained to postulate as "a bodily sense of me" (quoted by Cicchetti and

Pogge-Hesse, 1981, p. 254), then he or she is a person, and that implies being born into selfhood. What we are learning about the infantile sexual body makes this a reasonable position to take.

But that position would not be accepted by the one psychoanalyst who has attempted to integrate the research findings on neonates over the past 20 years with psychoanalytic theory (Lichtenberg, 1983a). In *Psychoanalysis and Infant Research* (1983a), Joseph Lichtenberg concedes that there must now be modifications in psychoanalytic theory, but ends by avoiding the issues, insofar as the issues are of the sexual body. His theory of affects, for example, endorses a greater positive role for affect in infant development than psychoanalytic theory had been inclined to allow, but dismisses the possibility that there is any sexual energy, in Freud's sense of libido, involved in such development (p. 170). Again, my point is not to deny that there are difficulties with the libido theory, but to underscore the tendency to "revise" psychoanalytic theory so that it becomes asexual. Lichtenberg's general orientation is toward a psychology of the self, in which affects contribute to cognitive integration and self-esteem, but it is difficult to see why the "erotogenic zones and early libidinal phases" of classical theory must therefore "give way" to an "undifferentiated," that is, nonsexual, ego functioning (Lichtenberg, 1983a, p. 182). Lichtenberg avoids crediting the research "explosions" with fundamentally altering the psychoanalytic model of infantile life by means of a simple defense mechanism: although the infant can do all sorts of things we had not realized before 1960, when we were still in the days of the passive imperceptive infant, all of those things are done on a basis of "preprogrammed" response (p. 162). Only the infant who has advanced to the age of about 18 months can be credited with genuinely *human* abilities, as Lichtenberg in effect defines them, for only then do we find an organism capable of mental "representation and symbolic formation" (p. 165). Needless to say, this conclusion is Lichtenberg's own interpretation of a mass of evidence regarding the competence of neonates and younger infants, and could surely be disputed. However, the real issue is whether the infant can be said to *know* pleasure and pain, through a bodily sense of itself. Lichtenberg obviously does not think so: because of the "nonsymbolic nature of the infant's mind" (p. 173), it can hardly be said to know anything. It merely performs according to preprogrammed "action patterns," even when it interacts with its mother or other caretaker. "For the infant, affects are felt; for the parents, affects are both felt and labelled" (p. 173). The flatness of this distinction hardly requires rebuttal; taken as it is phrased, it implies that the neonate cannot identify a pleasurable experience with sufficient clarity (that is, with a "label") to attempt to repeat it, nor could the neonate learn to locate any thing or person that is causing it pain.

Lichtenberg in fact is aware that there is ample evidence showing a capacity in the neonate for distinguishing pleasure from pain, but insists that this "differentiation" has nothing in common with any "symbolic process" (p.

58); for him, such a process would imply "a level of organization definitively different from that of the biological-neurophysiological-behavioral level found in the first year" (p. 58). Establishing the allegedly "definitively different" level of the second half of the second year, however, proves to be a taxing exercise in semantics, leading Lichtenberg into further hyphenized neologisms. Thus, the infant has a "sense of the self-as-a-whole," which "emerges" in the second year, but it already has a "self-in-action" prior to that point in the developmental timetable (p. 114). The "unity of the sense of self" is built up during first-year experiences of pleasure and "unpleasure" (pp. 124-125), but this unity of self does not count, somehow, as evidence for the existence of "the person as a total entity" (p. 146). In fact, the "sense of self" comes later than the neonatal stage, as Lichtenberg proposes in another place in his text (p. 30). The reason for these unclear distinctions is probably to be found in Lichtenberg's world hypothesis, which I infer requires a category of pure mind in order to qualify any human sexual body as a human being: if experience can be "manipulated intracerebrally and interpersonally" (p. 109), then it would qualify as evidence for the self as a "whole" and would reflect the "total entity of the person" (p. 109). On the other hand, whenever an infant seems to be responding to its own situation in an immediate, feelingful manner, without the distancing effect of a cerebral "objective" sense of itself viewed as if by an "outsider" (p. 145), then the infant's perceptual system has "collapsed" into the earlier developmental form of organization. The term "collapse" (or "collapsing," "collapses") is used repeatedly, and with no apparent awareness of its negative connotation, to describe the psychological processes which go on in the neonate's mind (pp. 54, 134, 135, 137).

Despite expressing admiration for the research of the past 20 years which has shown that the neonate is far from the passive, imperceptive artifact manufactured by earlier theories, Lichtenberg plainly does not think the neonate should be credited with having much of a mind. He believes that it will take the infant "several years" *after* reaching the threshold of symbolic representation to learn to "differentiate genital sensations from bowel, bladder, and perineal sensations" (p. 144). Once again, psychoanalytic theory is reverting, in this formulation by Lichtenberg, to the construct of a baby unable to perceive its own body accurately.

Obviously an infant so handicapped by its very state could not be trusted to provide any standard for its own self-regulation. Lichtenberg in fact discusses the need for "human interrelatedness and self-regulation" (p. 205), but when referring to the neonate, he can only imagine "regulation" through the caretaker's provision of "a background of successful overall regulatory effects" (p. 178). It does not seem to occur to Lichtenberg that the "preprogrammed" capacities he dismisses as unimportant for the consideration of the notion of self, are precisely the sexual body aspects of the neonate's existence, and are the potential basis for a genuine self-regulation based on the sexual body. Unwittingly, Lichtenberg has recreated the mind-body split, with the body consigned to the dumb world of the "nonsymbolic," and the mind once again raised to the level of that which is truly human. The early stage of neonatal behavior, which he labels as "preadaptedness," can only become respectable and human when it is transformed into "a form of adaptedness that is psychoanalytically meaningful" (p. 44). Although he concedes that psychoanalytic theory has perhaps overestimated the mind's freedom from "our animate and inanimate surround" (p. 35), Lichtenberg is intent on building his model of the infant on the "intrapsychic representational world" (p. 35) of the mind. In that mentalized world, the psyche is largely independent of bodily functioning; the psyche governs somatic experience but is not based upon it, nor is it obliged to allow any gratification of sexuality. The absence in Lichtenberg's model of a theory of sexuality assists in eliminating the Freudian challenge of the sexual body.

Lichtenberg's book avoids the necessary confrontation between psychoanalysis and infant research which it purports to bring about. By soft-pedalling the issue (e.g., calling the demise of the validity of the helpless, symbiotically dependent model of the neonate a "new twist to our view of object relations," p. 17), Lichtenberg perhaps has hoped not to alarm the psychoanalytic establishment. But a real confrontation may occur in the future, and it may cause the kind of shift in psychoanalytic theory which would once again bring it back to a functioning awareness of the sexual body. At this point, it also remains to be seen whether the new wave of research that has begun to emphasize rather than avoid the emotional life of infants (Goleman, 1984c) will be capable of encountering the sexual body in the object of knowledge which it will create, and in the "self" or "person" it will construct. If one asks *why* bother with a definition for the infant of the self, or of the person, the answer might be that not to attempt such an act of "naming" (Dewey and Bentley, 1949, pp. 154-167) is socially harmful. As Pepper pointed out long ago in his argument about the nature of definitions (Pepper, 1946), definitions can have pernicious social consequences when they conceal certain value judgments. The judgment that a newborn is without a self or is not yet a person has helped to reinforce all those authoritarian assumptions regarding child-rearing which come into play when a human being is considered radically incomplete until he or she acquires a central core of personal identity that only the family can supply. There is no longer any reason to suppose that psychological science supports such a judgment. Probably there never was. Kant's specification that a self must take responsibility for its actions tells us that Kant thought very highly of the ideal of responsibility, but that ideal should not be imposed upon human infants as they are perceived by adults.

CHAPTER SEVEN

THE ADULT SEXUAL BODY: A MISSING THEORY

In adult sexuality, there has been no research explosion underway, at least not since the heyday of Masters and Johnson. It might be more correct to refer to an "explosion hangover," a period of relative complacency during which it was assumed that the major facts about adult sex had become "known." Masters and Johnson initially were too little concerned with emotions, with relationships, and with adult psychology in general, to prevent their extraordinary empirical findings from being taken as a script for the oversimplification of sexuality. There was one earlier, more limited, but potentially explosive breakthrough, however, which promised to give a new and profound sense of the mind-body, sexuality and dream relationships. That breakthrough in sleep research was reported (among other places) in a book widely distributed within the psychoanalytic community. I refer to Charles Fisher's "Dreaming and Sexuality" (1966), first presented as the A.A. Brill Memorial Lecture for the New York Psychoanalytic Society in November, 1965, and then printed in a memorial volume dedicated to Heinz Hartmann. Fisher offered to his psychoanalytic audience and readers some excellent empirical evidence showing a strong correlation between the occurrence of adult male erections in sleep, and the occurrence of REM dreaming. The correlation was shown to continue into advanced age, even into the years during which the male dreamers no longer engaged in sexual intercourse. Fisher expressed the modest enough hope that his work might be "a contribution to the psychobiological investigation of the id," and that it would help to fulfill Freud's goal "for a future meeting of psychoanalysis and physiology . . ." (p. 567). The hypotheses Fisher drew from his research were that some daytime perceptions and feelings are processed within the dream work, and that the genital area of the body is indispensible in the neurophysiological event. Sexuality thus acquires an additional and little understood dimension. The erections of REM dreamers were *not* related to recent sexual gratification. Attempts to correlate dream affect with degree of erection were not successful while correlations with dream content were found. Fisher found that when the content was erotic, rapid erection accompanied the REM dream, but if the content was anxiety-provoking (castration anxiety, in the psychoanalytic terminology), detumescence set in promptly. Similar findings were reported independently by Karacen, Goodenough, Shapiro, and Witkin (1965). Such a set of findings would appear to be definite support for Freud's classical psychoanalytic position which postulates sexual body connections for an enormous range of mental functions. His masterwork, *The Interpretation of Dreams* (Freud, 1900), connects dreaming with sexuality in innumerable ways. Speaking even more generally, Freud wrote in 1905:

> . . . I can only repeat over and over again—for I never find it otherwise—that sexuality is the key to the problem of the psychoneuroses and of the neuroses in general. No one who disdains the key will ever be able to unlock the door. (1905a, p. 115)

Freud realized that "the chemical changes" in the human organism which must provide an "organic basis" for the neuroses were not available to the scientific world of 1905; but he held that "we should expect to find" such changes, given a more powerful method of inquiry (Freud, 1905a, p. 113). The correlations of REM dreaming and penile erection might well be taken as an indication of an essential link between sexuality and the human mind. The meanings of the correlation are still unclear; they could be regarded as an "index of limbic activity" in the brain during REM dreaming, as Kline (1981, p. 319) points out. This still would be a facet of the sexual body, and one more such aspect that would cause us to expand and revise our overall theory of sexuality.

At present, it has been established that dreaming does not occur only during REM sleep; it also happens during non-REM sleep, although not as frequently, and without the full-fledged "dreamwork" that Freud (1900) had described (Arkin, Antrobus, and Eldman, 1978). From the perspective of the sexual body, it would be valuable to attempt to determine if this kind of dreaming has connections with sexuality, beyond the obvious fact that even such dreaming goes on in the sexual body. Moreover, the content of even such dreams occurs in a human mind which we would assume to be pervasively sexual in some way, or ways, if we are to take the perspective of the sexual body at all seriously.

But so far, even the REM-dream findings on erections have made little impact on psychoanalytic theory. Palombo (1978), in a major new psychoanalytic theory of dreaming, makes little of the erections. Disdain for the sexual has now become so entrenched in psychoanalysis that there seems to have been virtually no further interest in Fisher's suggestions. An obvious next question, for example, would have been: do women have any genital engorgement during REM sleep? The topic has not been the subject of much discussion; I myself heard nothing further about it until I encountered an affirmative answer in a popularly written book by Offit (1981), a sex therapist. She states: "Women also have REM patterns of altered vaginal blood flow, pulse pressure, and possible clitoral enlargement" (p. 19). Ironically, although I have kept some contact with specialists in psychoanalytic theory and read much of the literature, my first encounter with this statement by Offit was in a part of her book reprinted in *Cosmopolitan* in 1982 (Offit, 1982). This is not to claim that nothing was being done all these years; Korner had, I noticed, cited an abstract on this topic by Shapiro, Cohen, DiBianco, and Rosen (1968); that abstract reported a simple experiment involving one subject. But the lack of prominent mention, or any serious discussion, is one indication of the low priority that psychosexuality has held in the disciplines. The comprehensive college textbook, *The Question of Sex Differences: Psychological, Cultural, and Biological Issues* (Hoyenga and Hoyenga, 1979), does not so much as mention dreaming at all, much less the penile erections of males and the vaginal blood flow of females. Neither does the popular college text for courses on sexuality, *Our Sexuality* (Crooks and Baur, 1983), nor even the more interesting text of the same kind, *Becoming a Sexual Person* (Francoeur, 1982). Perhaps one can dream without becoming a sexual person, since one already is one, but the dreaming/erection cycle is a part of "our" sexuality. Any additional knowledge of erection cycles and REM sleep must be culled from the more generalized work on sleep and dreams, and then placed within a theory of sexuality. One example is the finding already mentioned that aggression as thematic content of dreams tends very strongly to inhibit or cause detumescence of the erection (Schwartz, Weinstein, and Arkin, 1978, pp. 197-201). This indicates that the later, post-classical Freudian connection between sexuality and aggression is *dis*confirmed at a deeply significant sexual body level.

Avoidance of the sexual adult body has much to do with the recognized lack in current psychoanalytic theory of a unitary theory of adult life (Altman, 1981). The volume *Adulthood*, edited by Erik Erikson (1978), consists of a miscellany of cultural approaches. These consider adulthood from such varied perspectives as the spiritualism of Japan, the Islamic tradition of maturity, the Confucian perception of adulthood, and various aspects of life in the United States. Russian adulthood is considered as it is "refracted" in the writings of Leo Tolstoy. Two years later, Erikson and the sociologist Neil Smelser edited another volume on *Themes of Work and Love in Adulthood*. This miscellaneous collection displays an overall preference for the ideal of "maturity" in the traditional humanistic sense of an ever-evolving unified personality development throughout the adult years, clearly transcending the perplexities of sexual experience (Smelser and Erikson, 1980). In his recent work, Erikson (1982) has been moving toward reifying the stages of his life-cycle theory, so that the stage of young adulthood is largely identified with the motif of "love," while the next stage, "adulthood," is centered on "care." These classifications tend toward the dogmatic, as Sedgwick (1983) points out; they also badly simplify the sexual body.

Erikson had actually begun to play down the continuity of sexual expression in the life cycle in his landmark volume, *Childhood and Society* (1963), where he remarks that genital sexuality in small children (providing we did not overreact to it) would amount to little or nothing: it "is apt to lead to no more than a series of fascinating experiences which are frightening and pointless enough to be repressed" during latency (p. 86). This is a nervous and unconvincing combination of terms. Something that fascinates cannot have been considered pointless and anything scary enough to be repressed is not pointless, psychoanalytically speaking. What we have here is a personal discomfort with, or serious ambivalence toward, the sexual body.

Erikson had at least been able to discuss much childhood sexuality in that volume, and he offered a reasoned defense of the concept of infantile sexuality (1963, pp. 48-108). He also recounted a significant anecdote (p. 71) about Gesell, whose historic *Atlas of Infant Behavior* (1934) includes a series of photographs of a naked one-year-old boy looking at his image in a mirror. Gesell confided that he had deleted certain photos showing the erect penis of the boy. Unfortunately, Erikson himself omits the value of genital play among children who are no longer infants; he had less to say about it than did the Reichian parents J. and P. Ritter (1959, pp. 101-107). The Ritters were among those who concluded what now seems to be the consensus of research: children generally do not have a "latency" period, during which their interest in sexuality goes away, to reappear only in puberty. Goldman and Goldman, who are probably the leading empirical researchers on children's sexual thinking, advise that latency may be safely called a myth (Goldman and Goldman, 1982, p. 391; see also Janus and Bess, 1981; and Martinson, 1981a). The sexual body changes in many ways during the life cycle, but there is more and more evidence for Mary Calderone's contention that we are sexual (genitally sexually active) throughout the life span, including prenatally (Calderone and Johnson, 1981).

Psychoanalytic theory since the classical period (i.e., since about 1920), has not been able to come to terms with this. Even a direct attack on the problem during the latter part of the 1960's, by a fine psychoanalytic theorist who attempted to reconsider Freud's theory of sexuality in order to restore it to its central position, fell afoul of the author's deeper moralistic bent. Here I refer to the late George S. Klein, noted as a brave prober and revisor of Freudian theory. In his now famous article, "Freud's Two Theories of Sexuality," Klein (1976), under the guise of discussing the "plasticity" of human sexuality, turns out to mean quite clearly that sex is a totally insatiable appetite unless checked by social controls. He recognizes without a qualm that this makes it "inevitable" that society is always going to be organized so as to deflect and inhibit sexual arousal and choice. Klein also has a long footnote in his essay "Peremptory Ideation" (1967), rationalizing that the adult sexual orgasm is not an important consideration for a psychoanalytic theory of the erotic (p. 97). Klein thus simultaneously opened and stifled one major chance for psychoanalytic theory in recent years to return to a strong interest in the adult sexual body.

The burgeoning field of adult "stages of life" (Erikson, 1982) probably owes more to Jung than to Freud. Study of these stages can tell us a great deal about the patterns of professional careers (Levinson, Darrow, Klein, Levinson, and McKee, 1978; Vaillant, 1977) but nothing about the continuities of neonatal and early childhood sexuality with adult living. We would hardly gather, from the excellent Levinson et al. study, *The Seasons of a Man's Life* (1977), that the *quality* of sexual relationships has any importance in the lives of male novelists, workers, biologists, and executives (the four occupational groups studied). We learn only about marital status and the symbolic quality of certain women (the "special" ones) for these men. The discipline of life-span developmental psychology with emphasis on "normative life crises" would seem to be an asexual one, judging by the papers in the 1975 volume edited by Datan and Ginsburg (1975). Except for a few comments on sex roles, the sexual body is not considered. A few years later, the same conference on life-span developmental psychology was devoted to "dialectical perspectives on experimental research" (Datan and Reese, 1977), but the sexual body again did not prove to be a part of these adult dialectics. Yet Datan, the major editor of this series, has argued for the importance of sexuality in later life, and has cautioned against the destructive myths which link impotence and aging (Datan and Rodeheaver, 1983). But her more specialized essay may not carry as much weight in the field of psychology as the life-span developmental series itself, where sexuality is largely omitted.

A partial exception to the general neglect of the adult sexual body as a problem in psychological theory is the work of Otto Kernberg, a psychoanalyst (Kernberg, 1974a, 1974b, 1980a, 1980b). Kernberg offers a variety of insights and new conceptual tools for understanding adult and adolescent sexuality as well as couples relationships in these articles, but with considerable underlying doubts about the value of the sexual body and of sexual experience, which he tends to balance off too neatly against social demands.

Kernberg is startlingly alone among recent psychoanalysts in raising the question of whether professional success in America is even worth having, given what it might cost in the development of the capacity to love (1975, pp. 332-333). Success can mean pathological narcissism. This radical insight, however, is not a major theme in Kernberg's work; he merely uses it in the course of arguing for the importance of mature "object relations," a theory to which he himself has contributed great confusion (Klein and Tribich, 1981). What none of the research on adults addresses is the problem of a "civilized" equivalent for Prescott's findings (1979) of a high correlation between sexually approving, affectionate, child-rearing and adolescence in "primitive" cultures, and an adult personality that is low in violence and other "asocial behaviors" (Prescott, 1979, p. 69). It is as if no one wants to know about this sort of correlation, even though there is every chance of its occurrence *in some form* within recent generations raised during the "sexual revolution" beginning about 1900 in the Western world.

The Sexual Infant and the Adult Body

As I have argued, Prescott's conclusions are highly significant and still fairly difficult to translate into practice within modern industrial culture, where touch does not necessarily have an affectional quality. Touch may be purely mechanical, in which case it probably has no beneficial effects, or is even a method for the transmission of hostile feelings. Moreover, the developmental connection between infant and adult will become more complex as new research findings are considered from the perspective of the sexual body. One kind of finding points to a reconsideration of adult functioning in terms of the seemingly ever more competent, active, self-activating infant. A recent example concerns motor development, an area generally not favored by researchers of the great "explosion," who have tended to accept that cognitive capacities are the ones to investigate. The usual assumption is that surely the newborn's motor coordination must be strictly infantile. Yet one recent study of kicking behavior in relation to learning (activating a mobile by leg movement) in 3 month old infants shows that the babies used neuro-muscular mechanisms very like those we adults would use in adjusting our pace and respiratory equipment during some learning task requiring movement. The neonates could vary the amplitude and frequency of their kicking, and do so with enhancing, supportive bodily adjustments that are biophysically quite like those "of mature humans" (Thelan and Fisher, 1983).

Because of the relative absence of directly sexual overtones, this kind of study will receive more attention, I suggest, than the observations reported 20 years ago by W.C. Lewis (1965) on infants of 8 to 10 months, who showed "coital movements." Bowlby (1980a, p. 158) could incorporate Lewis' findings into his ethological revision of psychoanalytic theory by treating babies' coital movements as discreet, psychologically meaningless premonitions of part-functions of adult sexual intercourse. For Bowlby, they are merely additional evidence for "instinctive behavior," such as the mounting behavior shared by many species. What W.C. Lewis reported, however, is not so easily understood, especially from the perspective of the sexual body. The "coital movements" consist of "pelvic thrusting," and one of the most interesting aspects is that thrusts occur only when the infant feels very, very secure in its affectional touching relationship with its mother. From a psychoanalytic perspective, it could be said that repressive child-rearing practices or attitudes could easily extinguish such thrusting. Further, both male and female babies show this thrusting. While it is not associated with orgasm (or in boys, with erection), it has interesting rhythmic qualities: there are "rapid rotating pelvic thrusts" toward the direction of the mother, accompanied by delighted holding on to her abdomen and nuzzling her chin. The thrusts occur "at a frequency of about 2 per second," and for no more than approximately 10 to 15 seconds. Reich might have welcomed this evidence that both sexes engage in pelvic thrusting; in his theoretical framework, it would be not only a datum of ethology but a suggestion for another aspect of energy discharge. To my knowledge, no one has taken up this information about pelvic thrusting in babies and attempted to connect it hypothetically with the child's development into an adult with a sexual body.

Drawing even less attention are the more specifically psycho-sexual observations regarding the young boy, by Anita Bell (Bell, 1961, 1965). Bell noted that the psychoanalytic and psychological literature in general has very little to say about the significance of the scrotal sac and testicles in male development. All psychoanalytic attention has been focused on the penis (or on the phallus) but the boy's sexual body has other genitalia that may be equally important psychologically. Her observations lead her to hypothesize that in the boy, the scrotal sac is highly sensitive to the surrounding environment; that the sac changes its shape and size more or less continuously during waking life, depending on what the boy is feeling. As the boy grows through prepubescence, his ability to register such changes becomes automatic, and for the most part goes unnoticed in his conscious thinking. This ability is still present as a vital form of perception.

Bell also noted the psychological problem of the changing male body, as it matures, particulaly in relation to the testicles. Not only are the adult testes much heavier than those of the boy's; they cannot be retracted into the inguinal canal. Most boys, it seems, can retract at least one teste. In other words the boy has an experience of variable genital interiority which the man cannot continue to have (Bell, 1961, pp. 262-263; 1965, pp. 183-184.). Bell developed her ideas within a psychoanalytic framework, but proposed certain revisions, such as the great importance of an equivalency, in male fantasy, between the male testes and the female breasts, and somewhat less emphasis on the role of the penis in symbolic mental activity. Bell's pleas for an integration of this most interesting and psychoanalytically relevant theory have led to nothing in the years since she made them. As a somewhat displeased psychoanalyst noted in 1970 (Ehrlich, 1970), the human body no longer seems to play much part in psychoanalytic therapy. Recently, a similar plea has been made by a therapist who found that the human skin is a most useful indicator of unconscious processes, but that this aspect of the sexual body has not been given admission either to psychoanalytic theory or therapy (Biven, 1982).

The Transitional Sexual Body: Adolescence

An interesting fact about the last four writers, Lewis, Bell, Ehrlich, and Biven, is that their comments on the importance of the sexual body and its neglect in theory all are printed in standard psychoanalytic journals. This may represent editorial tokenism in the journals, but it is also an indication of how undisplaced the sexual body is, in psychoanalytic theory, despite all efforts to get it out of the way. To readmit the sexual body to the workings of the theory today, however, would require coming to grips with the increased complexity it has accrued since Freud's time. We would not only have to trace developmental continuities and stages, but also acknowledge fully the differences between infantile, adolescent and adult sexual bodies. REM sleep and genital engorgement are steady correlations throughout life, but their functions must differ for the neonate and for the adult dreamer if for no other reason than the vast differences in experience. The neonate will not have dream input coming from its adult relationships, since it does not have these, although it has relations with adults. And the adult, no matter how infantile he or she may be in the unconscious or in conscious fantasy, does not live within an arithmetically enlarged infant body. Adolescence is a great body change event. This change includes the brain: "There is much to suggest that during puberty . . . a reorganization of hypothalamic function and the hypothalamic pituitary axis occurs" (Wiener, 1980, p. 230).

Whether or not our culture is attuned to the magnitude of these changes is an important question. More could be done to facilitate the adolescent transitions than we as a culture do. The anthropological theorist Stanley Diamond has noted that "primitive" societies place their greatest ritual emphasis on this transition (Diamond, 1974). Such rituals involve direct physical attention to the individual body. In our own culture, it is instructive that Erikson tried to make adolescence, the time of life where the shift in body reality occurs, into a basic category of psychoanalytic thought. In today's psychoanalytic literature his contribution in that area still has had very little impact, by comparison with the interest in the infantile. Adolescence, to be sure, is written about, but it has become a semi-separate field. Generally the talk remains far more that of infantile sadistic or omnipotent wishes, based on an utterly helpless baby body. Margaret Mahler, who has done much to promote such talk, has been quoted lately to the effect that there is one other time of life that is as crucial for psychological change as infancy: adolescence ("Analyst Focuses," 1984). But it will take some time for this view to have an impact on the theory.

Peter Blos continues the virtual omission of sexuality in his distinguished psychoanalytic summing up, *The Adolescent Passage: Developmental Issues* (1979). Blos, who was trained by the psychoanalytic pioneeer of child psychology, August Aichorn, and who also worked with Anna Freud, writes about adolescent Americans precisely as if they do not have any active sex life (1970, 1979). A more up-to-date volume on the topic of adolescent problems, also within a psychoanalytic approach, similarly keeps sexuality out of sight, discussing it discreetly within the general context of "mood disturbance" (Golombek and Garfinkel, 1983). One of the contributions to that volume argues that empirically, there is little reason to believe that normal adolescence is characterized by moodiness or mood swings (Offer and Franzen, 1983). This is a curious position to take in view of the "falling in love" experiences which are widely known to parents for the virtually uncontrolled moodiness and elations which they see in their adolescent offspring—but falling in love (see Alberoni, 1983) is not discussed. A psychoanalytic book on the psychiatric treatment of adolescents which is more concerned with sexuality, is edited by Aaron Esman (1983). Esman differs with Anna Freud, and believes that there has been a sexual revolution in young people's lives which must be taken into account. However, the book is a collection of practical essays designed to guide other therapists, and contains nothing on the theory of adolescent sexuality. Among the contributors, Harley (1983) shows good awareness of sexuality in adolescent patients, and Laufer (1983) has an unusual awareness of the meaning of adolescent body changes for the boy. Williams (1983), also in Esman's volume, describes a case of a girl whose anorexia can be understood as part of her general running away from her own sexual body, but the reasons behind this drastic avoidance are not dwelt upon.

Yet if psychoanalytic theorists do not explore the anorexic-sexual avoidance connections, who will? In another source, a non-psychoanalytic treatment of a 28 year old woman suffering from bulimia (binge and purge) indicates that sexual pathology is at the core of the disorder. The patient's words show this, as she describes a breakthrough in her struggle:

> I don't know what started me. I started getting angry. I was in town and I decided: OK. I'm going to binge, I started trying to concentrate on what was going on, and I got madder and madder and I got really mad. So I went to the store and got all the stuff: pizza and cheese cake, lots of cookies and some soda and I started eating on the way home. I was just furious and I had more anger than I could imagine. And it was at men mostly. I went over to my son's father's house and I felt I really wanted to get even with him. I felt like

going to his house and just going to bed with him, just out of anger. If I thought he wouldn't have expected that continually I'd have done it. I was just so mad and then I started getting mad at John [current boyfriend]. I really focused it on him. It wasn't so much that he'd done something; it was more that he represented something and I really was into it; I felt that he had violated my free agency. And I was really mad and I started eating.... I really ate... and all of a sudden I got this panic to get rid of it. I ran to the bathroom and tried to throw up and just couldn't. I was so frustrated and just started getting hostile and realized that a whole lot of that turned into sexual hostility, so I started to masturbate and I got into this whole fantasy thing on how I wanted to call John and tell him I wanted to go to bed with him, and then I thought he wouldn't do it... I was going to rape him at gun point. I was getting into it [laughs]....

... I know I had lots of these feelings before and I was trying to focus it on to my son's dad but I couldn't pin it on to him. And I feel like there must be something that happened way back. And this somehow triggered me into that anger that has to do with sex.

... What'd have made me associate anger with sex, with men? A lot of these things are so way back and I can't think of anything particular that would have started it. (Moley, 1983, pp. 24-25)

The therapist here is not particularly interested in the insight; as a "strategic systems" therapist his focus is on breaking the cycle of binging and purging in such a way as to enable the patient to get out of it. As it turns out, his instructions to her, to eat more than she wanted even in this binge, which was a *planned* binge coming after a period of desisting, has the correct combination of a paradoxical command to enable that cycle to get derailed. But the sexual core of the problem cannot be pursued: "While this fascinating soliloquy provides a fertile ground for interpretation," Moley acknowledges, "such a course of action would prolong treatment." And so, with quite the opposite interest of a psychoanalytic therapist, he directs her to concentrate on describing what she did, and not on "what she thought or felt about the meaning" (Moley, 1983, p. 25). I suggest that here again is evidence for the importance of the sexual body, this time in a combination of sexual denial-and-longing and eating disturbance—but only in the psychoanalytic tradition could this be explored fully. Most of the time the sexual body of adolescents is ignored by this very tradition. Yet it is among adolescents that the incidence of anorexia is especially increasing ("Teens Show," 1984); similarly, the "vast majority" of bulimics are "in their teens and 20's" (Brody, 1983a; see also Boskind-White and White, 1983; and Cauwels, 1983).

A basic challenge to the psychoanalytic avoidance of adolescent sexuality was sounded by Alice Rossi (1981), again in her critique of the feminist psychoanalytic theory of mothering developed by Chodorow (1978). Rossi suggests that contrary to psychoanalytic theories of development, "hormonal events and physical changes in puberty can extinguish all but minor traces of early experiences and substitute a whole new set of characteristics predictive of adult personality" (Rossi, 1981, p. 496n). Kagan (1980) summarizes research projects, some of them by himself, which show that early childhood experience does not provide good predictions of later behavioral patterns.

Unfortunately, Kagan, in his opposition to psychoanalytic theory and to the whole Western assumption of continuity in development, does not focus upon the study of sexuality in his numerous research efforts. In his recent book, *The Nature of the Child*, Kagan offers dismissive comments about the alleged subjectivity of all those who believe that continuity is crucial, but fails to cite or to discuss the works of Leboyer (1975) or Klaus and Kennell (1976, 1982), who are among the major adversaries with whom he is contending (Kagan, 1984).

The disparity of approaches points up what is lacking: an inquiry into the sexual body of both infant and adolescent in some organized framework. What we have, however, are competitive research efforts vying for the superior importance of one or the other of these developmental spans, using quite different theoretical approaches, and largely ignoring the implications of each other's findings.

The social issues at stake in the study of adolescence are by no means remote. Reich was one of the first to conclude that adolescents are entitled to a genital love life, and to recommend sincere social implementation of this right through provision of a suitable private place, such as an apartment, in which "to have coitus" (Reich, 1972, p. 114). The issue is being hard fought still. Currently, the U.S. government, through its Adolescent Family Life Program, is spending large amounts ($13.5 million spent in 1983; $16.3 million was scheduled for 1984; and 1985?) to discourage teenage sex (Isikoff, 1983).

As is often the case, the sexual body leads directly to questions of sexual politics. The legal scholar and advocate of children's rights, Leon Sheleff, provides an example of excellent critical research and theory that aims to help "youth," but is largely silent on sex (Sheleff, 1981). Sheleff refers (p. 232) with approval to such works as Richard Farson's *Birthrights* (1974), but neglects to mention that author's chapter on "The Right to Sexual Freedom" (Farson, pp. 129-153); Sheleff also describes John Holt's *Escape From Childhood* (1974), but neglects the penultimate chapter in that book, entitled "The Law, the Young, and Sex" (Holt, 1974, pp. 270-276). A new book published by Columbia University Press, *The Sexual Rights of Adolescents* (Rodman, Lewis, and Griffith, 1984), is all the more timely, given the current political context of adolescent sexuality in the United States, and the pervasive avoidance of the sexual body by researchers in many disciplines. Not surprisingly, this careful new examination of the social and legal issues of American adolescent sexual bodies leads to a policy recommendation opposite to that which the government is trying to implement: "Legislation should be passed by the states giving minors the right to consent to reproductive health services at age 15" (Rodman, Lewis, and Griffith, 1984, p. 133).

The need for new research efforts into adolescence as it occurs in a society that has been undergoing the sexual revolution, a drug revolution, and a crisis of belief in its own future, is dramatically indicated in statistics (cited by

Cohn, 1982) showing a huge increase in the rate of homicide in the U.S. among the younger cohorts of the population (not counting those under age 12, for whom no national figures are compiled!). Suicide rates among adolescents and young adults have risen sharply over the past quarter century. Youthful murderers tend to be in the age range of 13 to 15, thus exactly during adolescent development (Nelson, 1983). It is significant that research by Zenoff and Zients (1979) shows that youthful murderers (boys under age 16) either tend to have spent their first year of life in an institution where they received very poor affectional contact, or came from families with dominating mothers and absent or passive fathers. In addition, the boys in this second category were often taunted about their masculinity. These categories would both be related to Prescott's theories of the connection between inadequate somatosensory contact and violence. The first category shows an obvious lack of such contact. In the second category, the finding was that boys had been subtly encouraged by their parent to commit a murder (pp. Zenoff and Zients, 1979, 540-541)—a learning experience that would have to be based on an expectation that their value as boys would be confirmed not by their sexual bodies but by their violent obedience. Terrible as the facts of the second category are, boys in that group are still somewhat susceptible to therapy, whereas those whose affectional responses had been deadened during the first year of life are considered at present to be untreatable (Zenoff and Zients, 1979, p. 548).

As for the suicide rate, it is increasing most rapidly in the age group of 15 to 19 (Cohn, 1982, p. 621). Given the widespread skittish avoidance of theory and data concerning adolescent sexuality, it is to be expected that new research will neglect the sexual body in its attempts to understand these disheartening problems. To treat the adolescent for "depression" and neglect the high level of hormonal production, sexual drive, and feelings of sexual despair, is a likely but futile strategy, a reinvention of the sexual teenager worthy of pre-Freudian times. The lack of a perspective of the sexual body has prevented the formation of an adequate inquiry on the relationships between sexuality and teenage suicide. A hypothesis which might be suggested by such a perspective, for example, would be that teen suicides occur least seldom among those who are engaged in a sexual relationship, and do not occur among teenagers who have a gratifying relationship in progress. Moreover, in those suicides by teenagers who were involved in sexual activity, culturally-induced guilt may be predicted as a major disposing factor. A further problem for investigation would be the possible heightening of self-awareness among adolescents regarding their "failure" to become sexually active. The judgment of peers might label as "failure" the already lonely teenage person, whose despair and suicidal tendency might be exacerbated. The latter problem would be one more function of the sexual revolution as it moves through its numerous social phases.

While there is no simple "sexual answer" to teen suicides, I would interpret the angry, almost hysterical comments by high school teenagers interviewed on National Public Radio (June 26, 1984) on the topic of teen suicide, as an indication of where the problem begins. What they emphasize is the sheer *pressure* on adolescent youth to make it in school, to succeed, to live for their future job. Adolescence, as a period in which sexuality and sexual relationships are given the time and the affirmation of value that Reich would have advised, is not being permitted to occur. Permission to go to bed is not the same as affirmation of the sexual body. The relationship between teen suicide and social pressure to perform—specifically to excel in schooling, which means grades—is indicated dramatically in reports from West Germany. "Schulangst" is estimated to seriously afflict about one third of German students aged 16 or under, and the high rate of teenage suicide in that country is widely thought to be linked to the inflexible educational system ("Suicide Among," 1978). The Bavarian teacher Wilhelm Ebert, who was then the president of the World Teachers Association, has put the matter in succinctly bodily terms: "Only the grades count. At the center is naked fear" (quoted in *ibid.*).

From a classical psychoanalytic viewpoint, such fear would occur in the context of the intense dynamism of libidinal energy movement during adolescence (Haim, 1974, p. 254). As late as 1969, André Haim was attempting to develop a psychoanalytic theory of adolescent suicide along these lines. His pioneering work was translated into English in 1974, at a time when the statement in his preface, that "there are relatively few adolescent suicides" (Haim, 1974, p. xiii) would arouse little notice. Haim argued that whatever impedes the intense libidinal dynamism of adolescence, and whatever interferes with the adolescent's need to re-structure the earlier Oedipal relationship, and thus denies "the triumph of Eros," must be considered "suicidogenic" (p. 254). Most of Haim's book is doctrinal psychoanalysis of the classical period, with some additional development in its theory of adolescence provided by Anna Freud. It is a book that does not attempt to go very far, and it shows little sense of any specific adolescent lives. But the fact that no further major inquiry of a psychoanalytic nature on adolescent suicide has followed Haim's, is another indication of how the earlier breakthroughs, grounded in a sense of the sexual body, have not been followed up.

Yet the early breakthroughs do not lack confirmations in current research. It now appears that some of the suicides reported for young American males (and perhaps for a few females as well) are not suicides at all, but "autoerotic deaths." This chilling new category is applied to those who accidentally asphyxiate themselves while attempting to heighten masturbatory pleasure usually by hanging with a rope around the neck. Of the 132 cases studied by Hazelwood and his associates, 127 were male (Brody, 1984; Hazelwood, Dietz, and Burgess, 1984). Here again reticence proves humanly expensive. Not a few parents are ashamed that their sons died in this way, and would prefer to let the death be attributed to suicide. Less excusable is the high school administration which did not warn its students, even after the parents of one boy who had died of autoerotic asphyxiation begged them to. Soon another boy died of the same cause (Brody, 1984). Research into this form of death might ask the Reichian question: had this victim really had an opportunity to develop a live sexual relationship? Or did he come into adolescence already psychologically crippled by an environment which (subtly or grossly) showed a detestation of his sexual body—and at the same time demanded that he come to terms somehow with the peer pressure that makes sex a competitive hurdle for every young person to get across?

Sol Gordon, of Syracuse University, a sex counselor and researcher on American adolescents, is the only writer I have encountered who has emphasized the sexual difficulties of adolescent girls as a cause of their distressed behavior: ". . . as many as 40% of the girls who run away" from home each year in the U.S. "do so because they are pregnant." Moreover, according to Gordon, pregnancy "is reliably reported to be the most prevalent reason for suicide among teenage girls" (Gordon, 1981, p. 96). Among the runaways, however, "many end up the victims of pimps, who immediately make them into prostitutes" (p. 96). Runaway, pregnant girls make statements in interviews which indicate that the sexual revolution has yet to hit home; the following are quoted by Gordon:

> "My father said that if I ever became pregnant, he'd kill me." "My mother said that if I ever became pregnant, I shouldn't come home." (Gordon, 1981, p. 96)

Such threats undoubtedly put an end to any discussion of the sexual body in the context of the family, making it in effect as unmentionable as it must have been in the homes of the young autoerotic males who died in their attempts at masturbation. But the sexual body is not always denied effective verbal recognition. For example, therapy with adolescents who have undergone sexual abuse is one field in which the sexual body is an unavoidable topic. Joan Riebel (1980) found that discussing sexuality openly, particularly the pleasurable aspects of incestuous sex, was very helpful to a group of girls in therapy.

> I was once working with a group of girls who were incest victims. . . . Near the end of one session one of the girls began to talk about the sexual pleasure she had had during sexual encounters with her father. Other girls too began to talk about the positive aspects of their experiences. In subsequent sessions we spent more time on those parts of the incest the girls felt they had provoked, enabled, or enjoyed, either physically, emotionally, or situationally. . . . It was a delight to watch the girls, embarrassed and shameful at what they saw as their roles in the abusive situations, openly acknowledge and begin to accept themselves as full human beings. (Riebel, 1980, p. 690-691)

Riebel—identified as On-Site Coordinator for Region V Child Abuse and Neglect Resource Center at the University of Minnesota Medical School,

Program in Human Sexuality—is calling attention to the importance of the "positive aspects" at a time when the popular press is trying to simplify perception of the adolescent troubled with a history of child abuse to one of pure asexual victimhood. If her insight is correct, it will not be possible to help such girls unless their sexual body experiences are talked about frankly, acknowledging pleasure when there was pleasure. But of course, sexuality is not usually openly discussed between adults and children or teenagers, as Riebel points out (p. 691; see also Burgess, Groth, and Sgroi, 1978). Some 80 years after Freud's advent in "the public mind," it is still difficult to talk intelligently of the sexual body, especially where such talk is most needed.

The Two Major Human Sexual Bodies in Human Development

Given the importance of the adolescent sexual body, it is not always wise to simply contrast the infant and the adult sexual bodies, as I often do in this study. My purpose is to highlight some important differences in adult and infant because the issue for psychoanalytic theory is located along the lines of that contrast, not to suggest there are two and only two sexual bodies in every adult's life history. The differences, however, are real enough, and they do warrant making distinctions. They may even be marked enough in common-sense experience to appear to warrant the psychoanalytic fiction of the helpless undifferentiated infant. There may be some reason, given these differences, for the psychoanalytic emphasis on infantile fantasy, if we may speculate that many fantasies are "felt" to be spinning around in our brains; they are not felt as direct impulses or as "gut" feelings so much as they are "in the head," as D.H. Lawrence wrote concerning adult sexual fantasies (Lawrence, 1960, pp. 121, 128, 157-158). In the infant, there may be a special vulnerability, because the baby has a head which is very large in proportion to its body; the adult does not. Robert Lewis has pointed this out in his article, "Infancy and the Head: The Psychosomatic Basis of Premature Ego Development." The head, which will reach 54 centimeters average circumference at adulthood, is already 35 centimeters around at birth, and is up to 46 centimeters by the end of the first year (Lewis, 1976, p. 21). During the first two years, brain weight, already large porportionately, increases 350 percent (Appleton, Clifton, and Goldberg, 1975, p. 144). Moreover, the infant's head is one major scene of her or his physical action: "The first gross motordevelopmental milestone is the infant's ability to lift its head" (Lewis, 1976, p. 21).

A review of infantile competence notes that "Development proceeds from head to foot . . . . Control of the head precedes control of arms which precedes control of the trunk" (Appleton, Clifton, and Goldberg, 1975, p. 130). This outlook provides a rationale for Lewis' sub-heading: *Heads Up: A Matter of the Utmost Gravity*. The adult body, however, is differently made. Obviously it is not mostly head. Linden reminds us that a lot of the adult bodily life is still in the head: "The brain consumes 20 percent of the total body oxygen consumption despite the fact that it is only 2 percent of the material substance of the body" (Linden, 1978, p. 68). But in the body of the adult, unlike that of the infant, there is a large system of blood-filled veins below the level of the heart. Choisnel points out that at birth, 50% of the blood stream "is in transit in the brain" (1981, p. 55), but this ratio is not only reduced in the course of child development, the blood becomes subject to gravitational pulls that make for a difference, for example, in the ratio of air to blood flow "between the upper part of the thorax and the lower" (*ibid.*). In the adult body gravity is felt differently than in the infant body, especially since, as Linden points out, there is continual movement from periods of standing to periods of reclining (Linden, 1978, p. 67). Yet in current psychoanalytic thinking, I find virtually no awareness of this idea. It is true that Erik Erikson once proposed that differences in "postural modalities" between infantile and adult phases of the life cycle are psychodynamically significant, but he himself acknowledges that psychoanalytic theory has made little of this revision (Erikson, 1982, p. 40). Nor is it a part of academic psychology. In psychoanalytic thinking about the infant—which dominates thinking about the adult—the assumption is that what comes first is the infant's illusion of having no boundary between its own body and that of its mother. This assumption prejudices any consideration of later fusion of two adult bodies, such as in the orgasm; it is an assumption which focusses on infantile psychology. As the Reichian analysis of orgasm suggests, two adults may also communicate through a kind of permeable energy boundary between them, but this is not the same as claiming that therefore they are functioning in accordance with states of mind learned during early infancy.

The difference might be expressed, in part, through this distinction: the large proportion of blood flowing through veins located below the heart, in the adult, must also be part of an adult's intimate empathic contact with another adult, if contact is to be considered from a sexual body perspective. But the nature of such contact cannot be extrapolated from the infantile model, where the vein system of the lower body is far less prominent, and the body rhythm of standing upright and lying down is not there. Furthermore, adult contact, no matter how permeable its boundary, may be radically affected by a variation in patterns of breathing which is not available to the infant body: "Abdominal respiration," according to Gerda Boyesen, a bioenergetic therapist, "helps emotions well up and find release, in contrast to 'chest cage breathing' which is more restrictive and limits emotional experience" (Boyeson, quoted in Liss, 1976, p. 243). Adults may well have learned how to limit their breathing and their experience, but babies can hardly be considered capable of such a feat, at least not before some sort of socially-induced fear or threat makes them start to learn how to do it.

To go still further, we usually find in the psychoanalytic model of interpersonal space, or intersubjective contact, no mention of adult genitals. Such genitals are just not to be found in the infant, and in any case, it is presupposed in theory, that "infantile sexuality does not start within the genital sphere..." (Smirnoff, 1971, p. 57). Considering the evidence of infantile erections, this thought is not especially compelling, nor is "the genital sphere" a simple continuing factor from infantile to adult body. Bioenergetic thinking (indebted to Reich) distinguishes between the "birth reflex"—in which the baby makes an "extensor thrust" out from the foetal position—and the adult orgasm, in which the ends of the body tend to pull *toward* each other; in the first, movement is from a feeling of floating to one of landing and of consciousness; in the second, the move is from a feeling of everyday consciousness to a dimming, toward what Freud called "oceanic" feeling (Freud, 1930, pp. 64-73; Smith, 1980, pp. 24-25). A Reichian description of the oral orgasm that the infant may have, often after feeding at the breast, involves a distinct direction of energy movement in the body:

> At the end of nursing one frequently observes a quivering of the lips in the infant. These quiverings spread to the face, finally ending in trembling and soft convulsive movements of the head and throat, sometimes of the whole body. (Baker, 1967, p. 312)

Early Freudian theory on the distinction between genital and pregenital sexuality could have made something of such differences, but today this distinction is referred to, if at all, in the abstract, with no concrete bodily awareness. Kinsey in fact insisted that infantile orgasm "is a striking duplicate of orgasm in an older adult," except for the lack of ejaculation in the male (Kinsey, Pomeroy, and Martin, 1948, p. 177). Kinsey did report that orgasm has been observed in a 4-month-old girl, and in a number of infant boys who were between five and eleven months old (*ibid.*). His relative lack of interest in the differences in energy movement between adult and infant orgasm is largely a function of his disinterest in energy theories at all, and partly a function of his primary insistence in showing that the sexual body did indeed exist, even in infancy. That was in 1948; surely it is now time to look into the differences.

Optimal Adult Sexual Body Feeling

The adult body, regardless of variations in infant-mother dynamics, is different enough to call for a place in any theory of human psychology. To draw out the contrast and difference that I would like to convey, I will go on, not merely to look at the grown up body but at the sexual body in a state of health, enjoying a mood of optimal function. This is not a suggestion that psychology or psychoanalysis ought to turn toward "the healthy," whoever they may be. I feel assured that adults too have their psychopathologies, regardless of the issue of the infantile body as a model. Nonetheless, how does it feel to feel really good? The question is worth asking at last. A few academic psychologists have approached the topic of "wellbeing," but the bodily aspects and the qualities of feeling, let alone anything about sexual feeling, play virtually no role in their descriptions (Cohler and Boxer, 1984; Lawton, 1984). By way of contrast, here is Millicent Linden, a bioenergetic dance therapist, giving *her* description of what it's like: for one thing, the brain, still quite important in the adult body, gets its "dynamic oxygen satisfaction" and the head seems "extra clear and 'bright'." More than that, however, is the sense of the whole person, who "feels like a NEW almost 'different'," almost "another being." The whole is not just the sum of body parts, and as a function of its wholeness, "the body feels less of its weight." This however is no duplicate of the old fantasy of infantile flying: ". . . paradoxically, the greater the sense of weightlessness, the greater the sense of feeling within the body's sensibilities" (Linden, 1978, p. 69). Specifically,

> The head seems to "fall upward," the shoulders are loose, free and just resting where they go of themselves, the "separation" in the chest is specific, the expansiveness feels "right," as though it should always have been there, light and gossamer-like, but always present, the pelvis is independently tilted forward and up, drawing the abdomen along with the new smooth curve of the spine, the thighs are relaxed and move more with involuntary reflexes, sort of "just themselves," and the feet feel the surface of the earth from the heels to the toes but without feeling the usual, hard, impact of the solid surface, rather more like a solid bounce. And, of course, the sensitive areas of the face, lips, ears, delicate membranes within the nostrils, etc., experience a sense of glow and warmth. (Linden, 1978, pp. 69-70)

If we wish, we can defend against this description by using psychoanalytic tools. My point is, as I have said, that from within current psychoanalytic theory one can do *nothing but defend* against such reports. The theory has ammunition available for the ready reduction of what Linden says we all may feel. The reductive line should be familiar: what she describes is merely the re-creation of an infantile state, the head "falling upward" is moving into that fused space of the boundaryless mother-child dyad. Or, Linden is just giving her own privileged perception, generalizing irresponsibly, and offensively. And so on. These reactive moves do not convince me. If human life includes bodily experiences such as these, then psychoanalytic theory and psychology in general have yet to come into contact with them. I specify *contact*, in order to brush away affectless acknowledgements, attempts to accommodate the information or to agglutinize it within the infantile. The telltale specifics finally mount up: the head "falling upward" *might* be the infantile body, with its mostly head physiognomy, but not the tilted pelvis, nor the feet feeling the earth with a solid bounce. And given those specifics and all the others, even a fantasized infantile head, if that is what we have here, becomes different than it was during infancy. The head is in a new configuration of adult experience.

I have been suggesting a manifold dilemma between psychoanalytic theoretical requirement and responsiveness to evidence concerning the sexual body.

Given the direction the theory has taken since about 1926, psychoanalysis has no choice but to take the infantile body and its vicissitudes as a model for the human body, in all its psychic significations, which means taking the infantile body also as a basis for the self and the adult. Moreover, the model is biased toward *distrust* of the body. Crews, for one instance among many I could cite, summed up the life implications of the theory this way: "Our common plight is to be forever seeking acquittal from the fantasy-charges we have internalized as the price of ceasing to be infants" (Crews, 1970, p. 22). This prospect may have been one factor in Crews' later renunciation of the psychoanalytic world hypothesis (Crews, 1975). If so, he could hardly be reproached.

Sex Research and the Adult Sexual Body

The adult sexual body in the complexity of its many dimensions has gone begging, not only because of the absence of serious psychoanalytic thought about it, but because of a general neglect of comprehensive discussion in any of the disciplines. Many of the non-psychoanalytic approaches are deliberately limited in scope. Alex Comfort's two best-selling books, *The Joy of Sex* (1972) and *More Joy of Sex* (1974), were deliberately cast by their author in a mode of mildly euphoric fantasy; adult sex could be presented, Comfort realized, in the mode of a gourmet cookbook, for those who felt they already knew enough to cook the plainer dishes. Comfort's aim, as he has since explained (1978) was to advance both the affectionate practice of sexuality and respect for it as a formative core of self-regulative behavior, without suggesting to the reader any anxiety. Hence the "joy of" presentation, for which Comfort is often held in contempt. Offit's two books (1977, 1981) present the adult sexual body from the point of view of a sex therapist with a fine penchant for making interesting, feelingful comments, but with little interest in the broader social issues or implications. She is indebted to Masters and Johnson (1966), but not to the extent of accepting everything they say, nor of adopting their clinical, abstract tone.

It is to the researchers that Comfort and Offit are really indebted. Research on adult human sexual behavior has taken place because courageous interdisciplinary researchers were willing to work at it, going against the grain of professional opinion and risking fund deprivations. Albert Kinsey was a zoologist. William Masters was a gynecologist who had distinguished himself in the field of reproductive biology, and his coworker Virginia Masters (who gave up her career as a singer to work with him) never got a formal degree in psychology. Masters has worked at his research and therapy every day without a day off for 17 years (Hacker, 1983). Despite their success, basic research on sexuality is again threatened with a severe shortage of funds (Haberle, quoted in Boffey, 1983). According to Money (1980, p. xv) there is still no Department of Sexology or anything of the sort at any hospital or medical school, anywhere in the world.

To some extent, the contribution of Masters and Johnson, courageous as it has been, has also been formed by their quest for scientific certainty, in Dewey's sense (Dewey, 1929b): they claimed, for example, to have discovered at last the "anatomic baseline" of the female sexual response cycle and of orgasm (Masters and Johnson, 1963). Here was a case of science delivering the promised goods of objectivity. But such goods are bogus, in Dewey's world hypothesis; they are merely additional incidents of the belief that "certainty is attained by attachment to fixed objects with fixed characters" (Dewey, 1929b, p. 129).

As time went on, however, the certainty of these findings came to look dubious. Several problems were involved. For one, the writing style of Masters and Johnson seemed to occlude clear understanding of what they were saying, and led at once to popular semi-authorized restatements of what they meant (Lehrman, 1970). Tavris and Sadd (1977, p. 69) suggest that Masters and Johnson "had to write up their physiological research . . . in impenetrable jargon so that no one would accuse them of writing pornography . . . ." Within a few years, the frequent objection that the sex performed under laboratory conditions with various equipment for measurement of effects attached to the body could hardly give a representative outline, was put to the test by the married physiologists, C.A. and B. Fox. Also using measurement equipment, but in their own home, they promptly discovered serious discrepancies between their sexual experiences and the Masters and Johnson findings (Fox and Fox, 1971; cited and discussed more fully in Singer, 1973, pp. 174-176; see also Davidson, 1980, p. 296). A survey of women's own accounts of their orgasms (published originally in MS) showed that the distinction between vaginal and clitoral was not being relinquished even by women researchers, some with strong feminist commitment (Seaman, 1972).

On re-reading Masters and Johnson in the 1980's, I am struck with the internal contradictions between their confident, famous claim that the female orgasm shows no differentiation between clitoral and vaginal response (Masters and Johnson, 1966, p. 66), and the actual data they give. They acknowledge early on that they had a "lack of information" concerning the clitoris in its orgasmic phase (1966, p. 49). When their chart is formally offered, detailing the "Sexual Response Cycle of the Human Female—Genital Reactions" (pp. 288-289), this lack of information is striking. During the four phases of the cycle, clitoral arousal is noted for the first, clitoral retraction for the second, and, during the third, or orgasmic phase, the authors simply write: "No observed changes." Rhythmic contractions of the vagina and uterus, however, *are* noted in considerable detail during the orgasmic phase, and *only* during that phase. Thus Masters and Johnson's great refutation of the myth of the vaginal orgasm turns out (as Offit, 1981, pp. 29-31 says) to amount only to the claim that some clitoral sensitivity does go on throughout the cycle. The physiological "baseline" only tells us the lowest physiological common denominator (Boadella, 1973, p. 28).

More recently, some research has suggested that women "ejaculate" during orgasm, or rather that a small percentage of women probably do ejaculate a fluid from the periurethral or "Skene's" glands (Sevely and Bennett, 1978; Whipple and Perry, 1981). The trigger for this emission is not the clitoris, "despite what we have been taught for thirty years" (Francoeur, 1982, pp. 156-157). "It turns out that Freud was partly correct in suggesting a vaginal versus clitoral orgasm" (Francoeur, 1982, p. 157). Some female orgasms are set off by stimulation of the so-called "Grafenberg spot," according to these findings, which is "located in the front wall of the vagina" (Francoeur, p. 158). Francoeur hypothesizes that the reason so few women report this ejaculatory response is that when it is first felt, subjectively, it is easy to confuse with urination. "The initial response of wanting to urinate, or the fact that they once ejaculated and thought they had urinated, may be the reason many women hold back their sexual responses" (Francoeur, p. 159; see also Davidson, 1980, p. 310). The "anatomic baseline" which Masters and Johnson had located in the clitoris is not refuted by the additional factor of the Skene's gland function, but it becomes more problematic.

Some of the more interesting aspects of Masters and Johnson's research tended to be overlooked since these afforded no certainty; these were surprising relationships between sexual response as it is graphed and as it is subjectively felt. We might understand the sexual body better, for example, were we able to take seriously their finding that during female orgasm, women frequently reported feeling their heart beat "vaginally." Could heart pulsation possibly be felt in an expanded form, to include the vagina? The medical books do not say so, but the authors of such books were not thinking along these lines. Masters and Johnson brush such puzzling reports aside, attributing them (without evidence) to the capacity of women to tailor their sexual responses to the dictates of "social influence" (Masters and Johnson, 1966, p. 134). From the perspective of the sexual body, however, it might be suggested that reports of heartbeat felt vaginally refer to bodily events which are still not fully understood.

The part played by the Masters and Johnson findings in sexual politics has been discussed exhaustively. Less known is the seismic wave effect among educators and research workers. The textbook *Fundamentals of Human Sexuality* (Khatchadourian and Lunde, 1972), a product of a course on sexuality at Stanford University that drew literally thousands of students, and a book club selection, illustrates some of the fallacies concerning the sexual body brought about by a basically physiological approach within American academic psychology. The book confines its description of orgasm to a chapter on "Physiology of Human Functions," classed arbitrarily within the area of "biology" rather than "behavior" or "culture." The description given of orgasm is heavily indebted to Masters and Johnson, who are cited, but elaborations of the original neutral language suggest that an orgasm is a tightening up, not a letting go:

> In intense orgasm the whole body becomes rigid . . . the abdomen becomes hard and spastic, the stiffened neck is thrust forward, the shoulders and arms are rigid and grasping . . . . (pp. 58-59)

As if to cover all possibilities, the authors report that during such "intense" orgasm "the toes curl in or flare out"; also "the eyes bulge and stare vacantly or shut tightly. The whole body convulses in synchrony with the genital throbs or twitches uncontrollably" (*ibid.*). These equivocations perhaps reveal the problem faced much earlier by Reich, though not by these psychiatrists, who have "broad backgrounds in the behavioral and biological sciences" (Hamburg, 1972, p. vi). The problem is a qualititative one, in which it is necessary to evaluate, not construct a merely verbal parallel: there is an orgasm that is a whole body rhythmical convulsion in synchrony with genital functions, as opposed to one where energy is controlled by rigid grasping and rhythmic twitching.

That textbook, however, is not so much in use in the mid 1980's; and some of the newer college texts for courses in sexuality, such as Francoeur's, phrase their descriptions of orgasm in more plausible terms. Moreover, there is a move in current research to reconsider the nature of human orgasm from a more qualitative side. Julian M. Davidson, of the Department of Physiology at Stanford, has offered a reexamination of the psychobiology of sexual *experience*, in which he takes seriously the resemblance of orgasmic experience to Altered States of Consciousness, and in which he also credits Lowen, whom he calls a "neo-Reichian authority" (Davidson, 1980, p. 308). Another researcher at last has raised the possibility of connecting sexual response with depth of involvement (Mosher, 1980). These surely are developments to be welcomed.

I am less impressed however with the fetish of "comprehensive model" building in current academic psychology, when it submerges the "burgeoning research area" of sexual "responding" (Kelley and Byrne, 1983, pp. 484-485). For Kelley and Byrne, Mosher's new effort to understand orgasm is merely an "atheoretical" approach to one of the "limited segments" of sexuality (*ibid.*). There is something about the crudity, the felt immediacy, of the sexual body, which rapidly gets lost in such flow-chart styled models as their own. I would think that Mosher's new breath of air on the topic of orgasm would be valued in itself, considered carefully, and if considered valid, given priority for any models that might be built regarding adult sexuality. Kelley and Byrne's chapter is part of a huge new "sourcebook" on social psychophysiology (Cacioppo and Petty, 1983), where sophisticated models are reviewed and further developed. Yet some of the goals seem ill-conceived. For example, there is an emphasis on measuring physiological responses and their affective correlates with great empirical accuracy, in the field of sexual fantasy (Kelley and Byrne, pp. 468-472). This is unobjectionable, except that it seems to lump all "erotic stimili" into one category, whether it happens to be a sexy photograph or a human being with a live sexual body—and usually the study concentrates on the photograph or other "stimuli," and not on the way people respond to each other in sexual body terms.

Certain non-laboratory investigations of the past decade I would rate more highly for their value in understanding the sexual body, as the body develops as an "object of knowledge" (Dewey, 1929b) in continuing relation to the sexual revolution. One of these, a book called *Breasts: Women Speak About Their Breasts and Their Lives* (Ayala and Weinstock, 1979), came about when the authors saw the need to expand their initial plan for a book of unretouched photographs showing a variety of adult female breasts, to include extensive verbal reports by nearly 40 women volunteers who posed for the photographs. The theory is that of the sexual body: as one of the women explained, "I can't talk about my breasts without talking about being a woman." The authors include a 95-item questionnaire, and ask that other women who read the book also send in their answers to these questions in the interests of further research. The author's own commentary places the discourse of the women within the context of American "titillated" culture. It is a critical, not simply a descriptive, account. The sexual bodies depicted form a selection in no way dictated by the popular culture of the ideal breast. The subjects even included a woman, for example, who has undergone unreconstructed mastectomy. *Breasts* introduces an essential aspect of the sexual body to educated discussion. It marks an obvious contrast in approach to the work of Masters and Johnson in that it emphasizes the subjective perceptions of the women, whose feelings about their own breasts are often shown to have changed, with increased experience, and partly through the acquisition of knowledge about their own bodies. The self that these women talk about is inherently sexual, not abstract or neuter. To the extent that breasts are integral to the woman's self, a man could not have such a self. Moreover, the reader of the book can not only observe a series of breasts in an unprecedented setting, but can analyze his or her own feelings about the sexual body. These feelings are bound to be intimate, wide-ranging, and erotic. Ultimately, if such thinking continues, it will call out for theory to organize the various observations. In this respect, much useful work has been offered very recently by the anthropologist Peter Anderson, who recognized that an understanding of the human breast requires special consideration. The adult female breast is not like anything in animal life, even in primate life. Anderson's account of the "reproductive role" of the breast necessarily crosses over into the erotic functions of the breast. The several commentators on his article could by no means agree that we know enough about the breast—nor even that Anderson himself had selected the most pertinent research findings in his survey of the literature (Anderson, 1983). The lack of consensus should not inhibit investigation nor theoretical effort, but it does signal that in the perspective of the sexual body the time is not at hand for confident comprehensive model building.

The New Menstrual Cycle

That is also the assumption of Doreen Asso, in her excellent study of research on the menstrual cycle (Asso, 1983). In the course of critically analyzing some 400 scientific studies of changes associated with the menstrual cycle, the causes and effects of these changes, and the nature of the menopause, Asso notes a large number of gaps in the research (Asso, 1983, pp. 6, 15, 36, 41, 60, 78, 107, 114, 123, 174). When so much of the basic physiological knowledge is still sketchy, it is especially difficult to deal with the psychological affects. Nor is it feasible to present detailed psychophysiological models. Nonetheless, Asso gives a persuasive argument to show that despite imprecision in the state of knowledge, the mood changes and other psychological effects reported by women are not based on "maladaptive attitudes" on the part of these women. At least not for most women. In fact, the often heard suggestion that it is all in the head is unmasked as another way of denying the sexual body.

> The implication is often that the multitude of women, of all types of personality, and at all levels of articulateness and intelligence, have only to "think differently," and fight off social pressures, in order to deal with substantial changes in their own bodies, their physiological processes and their feelings. This is unrealistic and reminiscent of a "pull-yourself-together" morality. (Asso, 1983, p. 169)

Asso might have added that the women in the various studies also come from all types of cultures; she does present substantial cross-cultural evidence which shows some unexplained cultural differences (Mexican women report a shorter period of menstruation, for example, than British women; p. 14) amidst a great deal of highly congruent information about the menstrual cycle in different cultures (pp. 87-88). Moreover, it is the cycle in its entirety that must be studied if there is going to be an understanding of the adult woman's sexual body; most of the research thus far has studied only the premenstrual and menstrual phases, leaving the other two thirds of the cycle virtually unexplored (pp. 15, 78). The research pattern has thus created an artifact: the sexual body of woman consists of a biologically invisible level of functioning over most of the cycle, followed by two phases (premenstrual and menstruation) in which biology rears its ugly head.

Conspicuously ignored are the *positive* mood effects (p. 60) and general good feelings found during the other parts of the cycle. There are indications that at about the time of ovulation there "is an increase in self-confidence, assertiveness, and dominance," along with such feelings as well-being, pleasantness, cheerfulness, elation, vigor, excitement, and affection. As these terms imply, there is also a high energy level (Asso, 1983, pp. 62-63). Even with the small amount of research devoted to these positive aspects, there is good evidence for saying that at the time of ovulation there are "real changes in sensitivity" which cannot be explained away as "judgmental" (p. 33). "Sight, hearing, smell, touch, and taste all reach a peak of sensitivity at ovulation time" (p. 32). At that time also, "response to cutaneous pain actually decreases . . ." (p. 33). Among the odors to which ovulating women are more sensitive than are men or non-ovulating women is that of exaltolide, "a musky smelling substance found in male urine" (p. 34). The menstrual cycle is "a pervasive and continual influence" in the life of the adult women (p. 166), and it provides women with an "internal environment" very different from that of men (p. 166). Despite some variation in moods, there seem to be no comparable cyclical changes in men, judging from the many comparison studies cited by Asso (pp. 74-78, 100, 107, 108, 121-124, 127, 135, 166, 172).

Probably one reason for ignoring the overall influence of the cycle is the evidence showing that women's performance of cognitive tasks does not undergo cyclical variation (pp. 71-73). From a sexual body perspective the problem would not be whether the tasks are performed as well, but the contextual differences of affect within the performance of cognitive functioning (cf. Martindale, 1984)—at different points in the cycle. Unfortunately, academic psychology has been prone to assume that there is no mind to explore unless there is a cognitive difference which can be shown in test scores.

Asso introduces the menstrual cycle within the context of cyclical behavior in general. Cycles such as the circadian day would seem to be an inherent feature of the sexual body. But the circadian is one cycle among many rhythms which are now attracting research interest (Asso, p. 13). Possibly this interest will extend to inquiry into the significance of the infantile penile erection cycles discussed in the previous chapter. One of the most interesting features of cycles is their capacity for coming into synchrony, or "entrainment." The 18th century scientist Huygens noted that the ticking of two clocks became synchronized after they had been hung on a single board (Asso, p. 6). In the remarkable experiment on the menstrual cycle by Russell, Switz, and Thompson (1980, discussed by Asso, pp. 7-8), there was also evidence of entrainment:

> Perspiration was taken from one donor woman and rubbed on the upper lip of a group of five women. Six control subjects were rubbed with plain alcohol. The group which

received the perspiration showed a shift toward the donor's monthly cycle; the control group showed no such shift in menstrual timing. (Asso, 1983, p. 7)

This "menstrual convergence" may have been communicated through a pheromone, but the chemistry is still unknown. Research on the menstrual cycle thus promises to shed light on how individual sexual bodies live in coordinated biosocial patterns.

Although her book is primarily descriptive and non-ideological, Asso does not hesitate to speculate about the significance of the findings for women's lives in contemporary culture. She has a theory of the sexual body, with regard to the menstrual cycle, even though she offers nothing like the sophisticated "models" of psychophysiology. In one of her comments, she astutely criticizes certain studies of women's variations in sexual feeling during the menstrual cycle on the same grounds as my own in objecting to the study of sexual fantasy by Kelley and Byrne (1983): the investigations were "carefully planned and conducted," but they were out of touch with the sexual body. That is, they investigated women's sexual feeling while these women "were without a sexual partner" (Asso, p. 56). Asso's own theory is that women always live with the cycle, but that the quality of women's life will be enhanced greatly if they are fully informed about the effects of the cycle. She points to "attribution" studies which show that feelings of competence are increased if the person is able to interpret a feeling, such as stress, in terms of its source (Asso, 1983, pp. 159-163). There is every reason to think that attribution of menstrual effects will also provide a secure feeling of being like other women, rather than being abnormal in some way. More generally, knowing about the cycle makes it more feasible to live with it intelligently, taking advantage of its positive affects and not being baffled by the negative ones (pp. 169-170). On the other hand, any attempt to deny the mood swings and other psychological effects is a futile, unintelligent attitude to take toward one's own body. Asso is highly aware that contemporary research results concerning the menstrual cycle function within the new "object of knowledge" (Dewey's term), the adult female sexual body in an era of greater sexual enjoyment, extended life-span, and a changing definition of womanhood (pp. 59-60; 121-122). Thus while women would be extremely ill-advised to attempt not to live with the cycle, or to deny its effects, there is every reason for them to choose to live with it, not as an isolated factor in their lives but in the context of a sexual revolution in which they are already participating by virtue of the times in which they live. According to Delaney, Lupton, and Toth (1976) direct references to the menstrual cycle did not even appear in imaginative literature until around 1880, although it is now evident that writers of both sexes did allude to it; Charlotte Bronte in *Jane Eyre* (1847/1960) and George Eliot in *The Mill on the Floss* (1860/1979) seem to have made profound use of menstruation imagery (Davis, 1978). These creative works form a part of the cultural context in which menstruation may be thought of as something other than a "curse." In earlier ages, knowledge of the cycle might have been used to maximize (or minimize) conception, but at present such information will more likely become part of a woman's general sexual awareness. From the perspective of the sexual body, cyclical variations in sexual desire (Asso, 1983, pp. 55-60) are especially pertinent. But as Asso points out, sexual activity itself may have an effect on certain aspects of the cycle, such as endocrine patterns or levels (p. 146). Not a great deal is known about that effect in humans, but it is one of the many potential areas of investigation which Asso's book highlights.

The Real Menstrual Cycle is one of the finest fully professional presentations of research on the sexual body I have encountered. In addition to the topics I have taken up from it, I would note that Asso also discusses more complex interrelations of the autonomic and central nervous systems with the menstrual cycle, citing among other sources some of her own research (pp. 46-51), and the relations of hormonal changes in the cycle to brain physiology (pp. 139-140). She also mentions the hormonal stimulation of REM dreaming (p. 139). Surprisingly, she makes no mention of the recent pharmacological advances such as Ibuprofen (marketed in the U.S. as Motrin) which have greatly reduced menstrual cramps for many women. Discussion of these drugs is easily found in the popular book *Freedom from Menstrual Cramps* (Schrotenboer and Subak-Sharpe, 1981). In fact, few of the 43 references cited in that book are cited in Asso's specialized bibliography, which is ten times the size. The perspective of the sexual body not only continues to provide challenging insights, it is also one which is nourished by information from disparate disciplines. The level at which a discipline is presented quite often is a popular one, where the sexual body is concerned, a factor which leads to special problems in evaluation.

Surveying the Changing Sexual Body

Surveys in questionnaire form are subject to statistical and methodological criticism, but this form of research appears to be indispensible in learning approximately just what sexual behavior among adults is actually practiced during a given decade. The problem is complicated by prevalence in this field of unofficial science, such as the surveys sponsored by *Redbook* and lately by *Playgirl*, and Shere Hite's "reports." As Taylor (1977) has shown, Hite's inadequacies in her report on women's sexual behavior were not so much due to the statistical skewing of her sample (although this was serious), but to her own systematic distortion of the questionnaire results in her discussion. Hite, for example, tried to make the evidence show that clitoral orgasm was all, and vaginal stimulation nothing. But she could do this only by taking great liberties with her evidence. Although I do not advise taking Hite's work seriously, the *Redbook, Playgirl*, and the recent large-scale survey of couples by Blumstein and Schwartz (1983) are much more adequate in their discussion of the information gathered, while the latest survey [Blumstein and Schwartz] is far more responsible to a scientific ideal in its gathering of information through questionnaires, and in the exposition of in-depth interview materials. In Pepper's terminology, survey material is "unrefined" empirical evidence, but should not be thrown out. It should be recognized for both its limitations and value, and further refined if need be (Pepper, 1942, pp. 39-70).

The *Redbook* survey came from the magazine's readership in 1974. Tavris and Sadd (1977) describe the survey and discuss its implications. A notable finding emerged when using data from married women only. Of these married women, 29% had had extra-marital affairs, but there was little evidence that such activity was pursued to the point that it became a threat to their marriage (pp. 161-168). The recent survey sponsored by *Playgirl* was conducted for the magazine by the Institute for the Advanced Study of Human Sexuality. Questionnaires were distributed to women by health care professionals in Ohio, California, North Carolina, and Washington, D.C. It also shows occurrence of extra-marital sex among women (43%) that would have been thought surprising somewhat earlier. Of related interest is Offit's report (Offit, 1981, p. 43) that some 60% of married couples in sex therapy have extra-marital affairs in progress, and that the woman in the couple is quite as likely as the man to be the one so engaged (p. 43). In the Institute for Advanced Study of Sexuality survey, results indicate a mixed psychodynamic picture: although more than half of these reported guilt feelings, the *overall* survey of women's marital sexual activity seemed to show that the sexual body was not proving to be so great a problem as some dire predictions concerning modern sexuality would have led us to believe. Ted McIllvenna, president of the Institute, comments: "These women seem to feel all right about it. I was amazed at how much better they were handling sex. We could see the good fruits of the sexual revolution" (quoted in Barclay, 1983; see Grosskopf, 1983a). Although both the *Redbook* and the Institute studies are scientifically limited, there is too little reliable information about the sexual body in its recent cultural configurations to permit the thoughtful research worker to simply forget about such efforts. For example, Francoeur (1982, p. 157) had guessed that only about 10% of women "ejaculate," but in *Sex and the Married Woman*, more than half of the women were capable of saying that when they have an orgasm, they ejaculate. The question, "Do you ejaculate during orgasm (expel fluid that is *not* vaginal lubrication or urine?)," was answered by 1200 women, or 99% of those who participated in the study. Of these, 13.5% answered Rarely, 22.5% answered Sometimes, 17.15% said it occurred Frequently, and 5.25% said they ejaculated Always (Grosskopf, 1983b, p. 47). Yet having gathered these figures, the editor fails to comment upon them.

If I may refer to my own field, the study of literature, then I must somehow take account of the survey results which indicate that women are much more often than not gaining substantial satisfaction in many ways from their marriages, because this flatly contradicts several hundred years of criticism by "literary" writers of the marriage institution (De Rougement, 1939/1956). It is quite at odds with much feminist thought as well. Some of the disparities in the evaluation of marriage may be artifacts of the methods used to understand it. Nor are all methods equally revealing. A survey of the *Playgirl* type is not even attempting the inner depth of a work of literature, nor does it raise the radical issues which concern feminist thought. But it is also possible that the institution of marriage is undergoing a change in its quality of life. What especially interests me is the indication which several surveys give of a continuing move away from older cultural patterns of involuntary monogamy; indeed the figures for extra-marital sex continue a trend reported in earlier studies, as Tavris and Sadd have noted (1977, p. 163). If such is the case, it would appear that declarations that the sexual revolution is over (now that the more public rebelliousness in lifestyle of the late 1960's and early 1970's has ended in American culture) are incorrect. Such pronouncements are often expressions of fear of what "unbridled" sex may do. For example, Kernberg has suggested that cultural changes toward increased freedom of sexual expression are essentially cyclical and are of little psychological import. His evidence for this, however, consists of rather few historical studies which apply to such aristocratic behavior as that of the French monarchy, or to indiscriminate sexual license during certain historical periods (Kernberg, 1980b, pp. 104-105). This type of evidence lacks the scope or precision needed for confronting a worldwide change in sexual mores that is affecting all classes, and in which there is a better grasp of self-regulation, rather than a concern with licentiousness, extreme privilege, or rebellion for its own sake. The sexual body is more complicated than Kernberg allows, when he compares recent changes to a time in 18th century France when women "were expected to have a lover in order to be socially up to date" (1980b, p. 104-105).

Kernberg is an interesting example of the psychoanalytic discipline's confrontation with the adult sexual body. Several of his articles mentioned earlier contain serious, feelingful, and nonmoralistic observations concerning the sexual life of the heterosexual couple, as well as a beginning of a theory of the inter-relations of the human couple and the human social group. In terms of the present study of the sexual body, Kernberg can be said to be carrying on the psychoanalytic tradition in the highest, most intelligent way; that tradition inherently calls for psychological consideration of adult sexual life. No matter how many revisions of the theory are made, that aspect remains central to it. At the same time, Kernberg's recognition that the couple, involved in its own sexual intensity, may draw apart from the group, leads him to insist that sexuality once more must be balanced against other social needs, which is to say, that the sexual body must be judged as a part of social life before it is allowed to change our sense of what social life should be.

I found it revealing that Kernberg, at the end of a brilliant presentation at SUNY-Buffalo (Kernberg, 1981) suddenly let his guard down to say that he regards a film by the Japanese director Oshima, *In the Realm of the Senses* (1977), a parable of what would happen if the adult sexual body were allowed full expression. The obvious moral that this film shows, according to Kernberg, is that sexual freedom leads to sadistic violence. In the film, the couple draws obsessively together in increasingly sadomasochistic sexuality, ending with the woman *literally* castrating the man. But that Kernberg could imagine that Oshima's film is about the nature of sexuality in its essence is astounding. In this film, the married man falls in love with a prostitute. The woman must still occasionally go out and earn money by practicing her trade even during the course of the relationship with the hero. It is hardly surprising that the woman, starting out as the submissive sex-object, a function of her being the prostitute, eventually reverses roles and becomes the all-powerful dominator, using sex itself as the medium for annihilation. Underneath this dynamic are glimmerings of genuine love. Kernberg's choice of this fictional couple, set in the social environment of Japan in 1930, as a parable of what self-regulated adult sexual life would be like if lived out to the full, tells much about his psychoanalytic attitude toward the sexual body, but nothing of the sexual body.

The distinction I am drawing here, between sexual revolution with longterm self-regulation as its guiding motif, and sexual revolution in the abstract, might be explored through analysis of the result of the large, careful survey (12,000 questionnaires, followed by intensive interviews with 300 of the couples in the sample) by Blumstein and Schwartz (1983). In some ways, the survey results justify the skeptical interpretation which holds that behavior between the sexes is not really changing. This interpretation could be based on the preservation among these contemporary American couples of the traditional sex roles: she does most or nearly all of the housework and he does very little of it. Moreover, in a finding that pertains directly to the sexual body, it was found that women in heterosexual couples regarded genital intercourse (not oral sex) as more important to their happiness than did men. Superficially these are signs that the old ways continue. The meanings of the findings, however, are not easy to assign with confidence. Rossi (1984) has pointed to a number of studies which also show that sex-role behavior with regard to housework, cooking, and childcare of the young infant continue to be performed largely by the women in the house, even in the households where it would seem that untraditional values would take hold, such as the communal living group. Rossi maintains that these findings are tentative evidence of a biological basis for the sex roles. According to Rossi, it is useless to expect much change in these role areas, except under deliberate, persistent effort toward change which would have to work against the biological grain.

The real change reported in Blumstein and Schwartz' survey, and one that would be pertinent to the perspective of the sexual body, concerns the emphasis couples put on the couple relationship rather than on their jobs or careers. Does the man or the woman fall into conventional role here? The figures show that one quarter of the married couples in the sample reported that both of the partners were centered upon their relationship more than upon work, and that a total of 39% of the husbands in the sample said that they focused more attention on their relationship than on work. This I interpret as a departure from tradition: it is a move toward mutual self-regulation of the adult sexual body couple, and a move away from the traditional male-female role dichotomy in which the man worried about work and treated the relationship as secondary. The other finding referred to above—that women tend to find genital intercourse rather than oral sex important—is a refutation of Hite's claims in her "report" (1977) of the primacy of oral and manual sex, but those claims represented her distortions of the evidence rather than any sexual revolution that was actually going on. On the basis of the couples in the Blumstein and Schwartz study, it could be said that in a contemporary American social context, with the sexual revolution well under way, heterosexual married women have found that the sexual body was a crucial source of happiness in genital intercourse. This may not be very surprising, but it is also inaccurate to dismiss this finding as only what married women have always said. In the first place, they probably would not have said so in Victorian England, and in any case, the current American social context provides a different setting for the sexual body than earlier and other contexts might have given. Tavris, who was one of the writers of the *Redbook* report (Tavris and Sadd, 1977), has reviewed the new survey in a spirit of dismissal, saying that there is not much that is new in it (Tavris, 1983). I would advise being more receptive. As Brody noted,

> the findings indicate that married couples engage in sexual activity more often and more regularly than the researchers expected on the basis of previous studies. (Brody, 1983b)

We may not know exactly what this means, but it is new. From a Reichian perspective it might mean that sexuality remains central to couples even after the earlier stages of the sexual revolution, when sex might have been engaged in more because it was prohibited than for the inherent gratification it offers.

I detect a related conclusion in findings on the post-divorce lives of couples, reported by the psychologist E. Mavis Hetherington of the University of Virginia. Divorced people tend to recover within a few years from their stress, but this process is greatly aided if they form a new intimate relationship. If they do not, they are likely to develop serious illnesses, become accident victims, and suffer from increased inability to cope with everyday social reality, all at a greater rate than those who do form such relationships. This holds especially for the men (cited in Brody, 1983c). Although there certainly is no simple equation of "relationships formed" to "happiness and stability," extensive research into the multiple crises of separation and divorce leads Jacobson (1983, p. 253) to conclude that "involvement with new partners mitigates the trauma" of these crises. It would appear that the intimate sexual relationship is positively connected with general well being in a society now characterized by a high rate of divorce and remarriage.

In suggesting this perspective, I admit I am guided by my own interest in the continuing sexual revolution. To some extent, the surveys for *Redbook*, *Playgirl*, and the Schwartz-Blumstein survey, are all artifacts of an approach which chooses to elicit the possibly favorable developments in adult sexuality, especially in couples relationships, such as mutual decision making and sexual self-regulation. I acknowledge that had I chosen to focus instead on, say, the prevalence of teenage pregnancy, or on the alleged increasing rate of rape in the United States (Russell and Howell, 1983),[1] I would have given quite a different account. I must say that it is incredible how little mention of rape is made in any of the three surveys I have discussed. Given the prevalence of rape it would seem that some, at least, of the 6,000 couples in the most recent survey would have mentioned it as a problem. This can partially be explained by the wording of the questionnaire, but not entirely since the open-ended interviewing techniques and the inquiry into "power," or the question of which partner decides when to initiate sexual intercourse, should have brought out something about marital rape (see Finkelhor and Yllo, 1983), rape in the previous experience of the women, and fear of rape. But virtually nothing is said on the topic. I mention this not to denigrate the survey, but to point out the need for a research design which could incorporate the disparate "worlds" of improved couples relationships *and* the high level of rape.

But I also wish to acknowledge and give my justification for the bias I have chosen in emphasizing the couple relationships in a somewhat benign light. As a large, complicated historical movement, the sexual revolution can be expected to have beneficial or "progressive" results in certain areas but not in others, at given periods and in varying populations. The important consideration is that it is still going on, even if unevenly. Those who wish to emphasize the failures of the sexual revolution or its irrelevance to many problems, will hardly choose the emphasis of the discussion just given. For them the sexual body is not a major interest.

---

[1] Russell and Howell (1983) rely largely on Diana Russell's study of 930 women in San Francisco (Russell, 1984). Russell argues for an increasing rate of rape in the United States, based on inferences from her data and on figures gathered prior to 1982; but FBI statistics regarding the incidence of rape for the period 1979-1983 show a decrease during the years 1981, 1982, and 1983 (Zimring, 1984). Obviously there are many unresolved questions and special problems in the compilation of rape statistics.

With regard to the problem of rape, a significant shift in research attitudes seems to have been taking place over the past few years. The trendy belief that rape is a crime of violence, not one of sex, has begun to lose support. Such a distinction is in any case another curious category division of the sexual body. But several recent researchers into the motivations of rapists are coming to the conclusion that rape is indeed a crime in which sexual contact was the aim (Burgess and Holmstrom, 1979; Sanders, 1980; Symons, 1979). This shift in research perspective is a good example of how socially responsible research will come to terms, eventually, with the sexual body, even when it first attempts to avoid obvious sexual dimensions.

I have been guided thus far, in discussing the adult sexual body, by materials bearing on adult male-female interaction. In the next section, I will comment on the adult sexual body in male-male, female-female, and bisexual interactions. However, it is worth noting that living arrangements in the United States point toward a very large percentage of households in which the inhabitants are indeed an adult man and an adult woman, with no other dwellers. By 1975, married couples without children made up nearly 25% of American households. In 1960, only about 18% of United States households were in that category (Mesnick and Bane, 1980, p. 6). The large percentages do not include unmarried couples without children; these probably amount to at least 2% of all households (Blumstein and Schwartz, 1983, pp. 36-38; Macklin, 1983). Male-female couples alone in a household, with about 27% of the total, form a slightly higher portion than households in which a child of dependent age is present (see Rossi, 1984, p. 12) The married couples with no children in the household are the largest single type of household in the U.S. Projections to 1990 show the trends continuing (Mesnick and Bane, 1980). A further diminution of the child-rearing household is coming about through a shorter span of time actively spent in the "childbearing years." For women born between 1935 and 1939, 82% of those who had had children had completed their childbearing by the age of 35. The Census Bureau now reports that in comparison,

> The median time interval from first to last child for women in this age group was 7.4 years . . . down from 8.3 years for women born from 1920 to 1929. ("More Children," 1984)

Research which throws light on adult sexuality among couples in the U.S. is thus likely to have application to an increasing proportion of the populace. It is also reported in a Consumers' Union study of sexual life for American couples over 50 that sexual relations often improve and become more gratifying after the children grow up and leave the household (Brecher, 1984). Voluntary childlessness is an increasing choice among women, and child rearing in general is gradually becoming dissociated from marriage (Rossi, 1984; Veever, 1983). Such trends will augment the predominance of the couple, although they are also associated closely with singlehood (Staples, 1982, Stein, 1983). But the percentage of singles in the U.S. does not appear to be increasing, according to the study by Cargan and Melko (1982); it has merely reverted to the level at which it had been recorded from about 1900 to 1960 (pp. 37-44).

The increased rate of singlehood among black males (Staples, 1982) is a special phenomenon. There are far more black men than women in the U.S. (Peters and McAdoo, 1983). Would we not assume that marriage, given its culturally favored status, would have absorbed these men? But such is not the case. Marriage might be a culturally disadvantageous arrangement for women who must accept an unemployed man, and a man would hesitate to enter an arrangement calling for the possible raising of a family. Research in fact shows that black men are "more satisfied with their marriages than women, because they hold the balance in social exchanges, and thus are apt to have more control over their marital circumstances" (Guttentag and Secord, 1983, p. 200). Other factors contributing to the high rate of singlehood among black males in the United States include the over-representation of blacks in the armed forces, which means that many eligible black males are serving overseas where they are not readily available for marriage (Guttentag and Secord, pp. 207-208); and an initial slight racial difference in birthrate: males are "three percent less likely to be born to blacks than whites" (*ibid.*, p. 208). For these reasons and others, fewer black males are available for the marriage pool. The effect of the disparate sex-ratio on marriage patterns is hardly to be doubted, especially in view of Guttentag and Secord's finding that in areas where the black male-female ratio favors women, such as in North Dakota, there are very few female-headed black households (p. 221). Unfortunately such areas are rare. According to the thesis advanced by Guttentag and Secord, wherever adult females seriously outnumber males—throughout the history of Western civilization, so far as is known—there will be a devaluation of women, and a decline in their social status. Marriages therefore will not be based on mutual control, nor will women be able to participate freely in the process of sexual self-regulation (Guttentag and Secord, pp. 20-21; 227-230).

In the United States at present, sex-ratios are "low"; that is, women outnumber men, although not to the extreme degree of the black minority. A recent Phil Donahue television program featured women in their 50's and 60's who practiced "husband-sharing," so few were the available men. The emergence of such a pattern probably owes something to adults who experimented with "open marriages" and "multilateral relationships" in the 1960's and 1970's; as Weis has argued, these experiments have led to the wider diffusion of "nonexclusive models" of sex in marriage, even if relatively few couples in the total population actually adopt such models (Weis, 1983).

It will remain for further research to attempt a better understanding of the effect of sex-ratios on a whole range of behaviors. Guttentag and Secord

(1983) have made a start, but as the example of the single black male indicates, the sex-ratio factor would have to be considered along with—among others—the social and economic status of single versus married adults. Probably the influence of ethological thought, and its emphasis on bonding (Duyckaerts, 1970) has had an effect in the selective process for research on the adult sexual body. In the initial stages of sex research in the United States, pair bonding was ignored, as Money points out (1980, p. xiii-xiv). Most researchers came out of medical disciplines such as psychiatry and obstetrics in which the individual patient was the focus. The pendulum now has swung: our best studies are of couples. Unfortunately, this leaves a gap with regard to the sexuality of the single adult not in a stable relationship. A study of single life in Dayton, Ohio, made in the late 70's, suggested that the sexual life of singles differed in many respects from that of married couples (Cargan and Melko, 1982, p. 99). But this study did not attempt to examine the number of subjects nor the details of relationships explored by Blumstein and Schwartz in their massive couples survey.

One piece of recent research regarding the sexual lives of single women is an indication of how much may have been missed in the tendency to concentrate on couples. The survey carried out by the Alan Guttmacher Institute studying single American women in their twenties concludes that some 40% of the women who had been sexually active (and over 80% had been) had become pregnant. The surprisingly high rate of pregnancy is connected with the inconsistent use of contraception: "On average, the women did not start using contraception until 8 months after they first began having intercourse" ("Sexual Activity," 1985). It is a question for research to determine why women delay in taking contraceptive measures. The survey showed that 78% of the single women who had been sexually active did use contraception "in their last sexual encounter" (*ibid.*). There may be a relationship between this inconsistency in sexual practice and the current widely diffused perception that abortion has become a "convenience" (McCarthy, 1985). Ehrenreich (1985) has in fact stated that she is among those women who did not always choose the most effective method of birth control because of the health risks involved; for her, the right to abortion is in part a back-up system for the process of contraception.

Changing social perception may bring about a de-legalization of abortion in the United States (McCarthy, 1985); but if that should occur, one result would probably be a sharp decline in the inconsistent use of contraceptive measures among couples not desiring to have a child. It would also lead to a demand for distribution of the newly developed "contragestion" pill, named RU-486. The pill terminates a pregnancy by flushing the embryo during the early weeks of pregnancy; the pill has been tested and is considered safe, without major side effects, for women up to at least the seventh week of pregnancy (Isbell, 1985). The new pill is scheduled for use in France, India and

China in 1986 (*ibid.*), but could also be pressed into use in the event of a successful campaign by "pro-life" forces in the United States. No "abortion clinics" would be needed by women using this method of birth control, which is described by the research-team leader, Dr. Etienne-Emile Beaulieu, as "halfway between contraception and abortion" (quoted in Isbell, 1985). The interaction of the sexual revolution, social pressures regarding abortion, and research in the field of sexual medicine is unusually close in this instance. It is also interesting that a new sexual body category is created in this new "object of knowledge" (Dewey, 1929b): a device that is "halfway between" two other categories of birth control which previously were thought to be exclusive and distinct.

We cannot understand the adult sexual body, however, by studying reproductive behavior, either in singles or within couples, as long as our focus is heterosexual only.

The Male Homosexual, Lesbian, and Bisexual Adult Sexual Body

Implicit from the first in Freud's theorizing of the sexual body was the possibility that the adult body is not necessarily or normally heterosexual. This is true even if Freud did not intend for his insights into psychological bisexuality to be taken radically. His letter to the mother of a homosexual man, written late in Freud's life, is finally ambiguous: it by no means states that the son is to be considered a normal man, but on the other hand holds out encouragement that the son could live a rich, creative life (Freud, 1951). In his last case history, Freud discusses a young woman whose parents had sent her to him for therapy because she had stated she wished to be a lesbian. Freud told her that she was *not* neurotic, but that if she wanted to have effective therapy, she should go to a female therapist (Freud, 1920b). Freud also had a theory of bisexuality. It is not an easy theory to describe; indeed Freud noted in 1930 that "the theory of bisexuality is still surrounded by many obscurities . . ." (Freud, 1930, p. 105), but he had no doubt that "Man is an animal organism with (like others) an unmistakably bisexual disposition" (1930, p. 105).

Laplanche and Pontalis, in their exposition of Freudian terms (1973, pp. 52-53), are again too eager to reduce Freud's meanings of "bisexuality" to a matter of fantasy, rather than of adult sexual behavior. As Lawton Smith (personal communication, August 1983) has pointed out, Laplanche and Pontalis leave out of their entry a key statement by Freud (1923, p. 33). In this statement, Freud maintains that bisexuality, which is "originally present in children," is an important variable throughout the "vicissitudes" of the Oedipus complex. This would not suggest that it conveniently disappears in adult life.

Freud felt so strongly about the importance of bisexuality that he uttered one of his very few denials of the desirability of a correlation between psychoanalysis and the science of biology in order to protect the distinctiveness of the theory of bisexuality. In a little-known letter written in 1935, Freud noted that many psychoanalytic authors had failed "to come to grips with the bisexuality of women," and hence had misunderstood their sexual development (Freud, 1971). Writing to one such author, the now-forgotten Carl Müller-Braunschweig, Freud declared:

> I object to all of you to the extent that you do not distinguish more clearly and cleanly between what is psychic and what is biological . . . . In addition, I would only like to emphasize that we must keep psychoanalysis separate from biology just as we have kept it separate from anatomy and physiology; at the present, sexual biology seems to lead us to two substances which attract each other. (Freud, 1971)

Inasmuch as Sulloway (1979) has assembled a mass of evidence to show that Freud, throughout his career, hoped for a very close connection between biology and psychoanalytic theory, this letter must be considered extraordinary. What apparently troubled Freud most in his objections to "sexual biology" was its hormonal symmetry of two "substances" such as testosterone and estrogen to identify the male and female sexual bodies respectively. Freud had a good intimation here of how "sexual biology" would come to change in later years, when this symmetry would be disturbed. (See the concluding chapter of the present study for a consideration of this issue.) In his last book, *An Outline of Psychoanalysis* (Freud, 1940), Freud pointed to biology as the discipline in which a break had developed between the psychological understanding of bisexuality and biological understanding, or lack of it, for the same phenomena: "It is not in psychology but in biology that there is a gap here" (Freud, 1940, p. 186).

Bisexuality in Freud's theory is a function of his recognition that in the human sexual body, the sexual "object," that is, one's sexual orientation, is not a biological given (Freud, 1910a, p. 210). Nonetheless, in a famous passage in his study of Leonardo da Vinci (Freud, 1910d), Freud explicitly refused to accept that male homosexuality might be a normal variation. In this passage he formally launched the psychoanalytic theory that regards adult male homosexuality as a developmental outcome of a boy's excessive erotic attachment to his mother combined with the absence of the father during the boy's childhood (Freud, 1910d, pp. 98-100). This theory later produced faithful confirmations—or artifacts—in such works as *Homosexuality: A Psychoanalytic Study* (Bieber et al., 1962). But at the same time as the Leonardo study, Freud privately acknowledged the role of "homosexual cathexis" in his own adult relationship with Wilhelm Fliess, his intimate friend and *de facto* analyst during his period of self-analysis (Letter to Ferenczi, Oct. 6, 1910, printed in Jones, 1955a, pp. 83-84). This letter has been in print since Ernest Jones included it in his authorized biography of Freud in 1955. Moreover, Spector (1972, p. 58) has shown that Freud's description of Leonardo's early childhood family constellation was seriously in error: in fact, Leonardo did *not* remain with his mother during childhood (cf. Efron, 1977, p. 266).

Despite Freud's profound sense of the undemarcated limits of bisexuality, and his emphasis on its importance, the psychoanalytic profession has never entertained the hypothesis that homosexuality might be a developmental pathway that is substantially as normal or healthy as that of the heterosexual. Otto Kernberg, one of the most distinguished of current analysts, was asked at his address given at SUNY-Buffalo (Kernberg, 1981) if he really meant to imply—as he does in *Borderline Conditions and Pathological Narcissism* (1975, p. 326)—that homosexuality is a kind of pathology. His reply was a quiet but assured "Yes," based on the patients he has treated as well as the homosexuals he has known. This is hardly persuasive evidence.

There also would seem to be a gap between the major progressive social attitude to the adult homosexual or lesbian and the projects of such scientists as John Money. The progressive idea, as best stated perhaps by Tripp, is obviously that homosexuality is as much a form of health as heterosexuality (Tripp, 1975; see also Weinberg, 1972). In fact, a founder of the Association of Gay Psychologists contributed an article to *Psychology Today* entitled "Homosexuals May Be Healthier Than Straights" (Freedom, 1975). Again, however, these approaches do not directly contribute to understanding the adult sexual body, inasmuch as the focus is on improving the socially perceived status of homosexuals. In one of the most careful studies, *Male Homosexuals* (1975), Martin S. Weinberg and Colin J. Williams conclude with a recommendation that homosexuality be conceptualized in terms of social statuses and roles rather than as a condition:

> .... In other words, the concept of "the homosexual," for some purposes, can usefully be seen as a cultural product, a status. This status is not inherent in the individuals associated with it, but it influences them by organizing other persons' reactions to them and giving those persons who occupy the status a stereotyped set of traits to orient their own behaviors and attitudes toward themselves .... It is our wish ... that societies come to conceptualize homosexuality in less negative terms, and as not being "deviant," thereby reducing the differentiation of human beings on the basis of sexual orientation. (1975, pp. 387-388)

The authors thus carry through their choice of "social reaction theory" to analyze their data. For purposes of social justice, this is a good approach. The unfortunate concomitant, however, is that nothing is said of the adult homosexual body.

To their surprise, Weinberg and Williams found that their investigation did *not* show that homosexuals living in the less homophobic cultures of Denmark or Holland had significantly fewer psychological problems than those living in the United States:

> The most unexpected result is that, contrary to the widely held belief that greater societal rejection leads to greater psychological problems, virtually no such differences appeared between American and European homosexuals. (1975, p. 180)

Possibly, this disconfirmation was due to weaknesses in their research design, as they suggest. But it is also an indication that the adult homosexual body might be better understood if the approach chosen were not disposed to focus on social role interactions and on the images held by groups of each other's sexual orientation. In the well-regarded study, *The Homosexual Matrix*, C.A. Tripp stated that there is a "fatal weakness" in the theory that homosexuality will flourish in societies where it is not penalized or restricted, namely that it is in just such societies that "the very lowest frequencies of homosexuality occur . . ." (Tripp, 1975, p. 270).

Developmental, longitudinal studies of homosexuality as orientation could be attempted. But the influential article by Simon and Gagnon (1967), "Homosexuality: The Formulation of a Sociological Perspective," urged that social scientists and psychologists move away from study of infancy and family situation, and try to understand homosexuality in terms of later events, particularly "the social structures and values that surround the homosexual after he becomes or conceives of himself as homosexual . . ." (Simon and Gagnon, 1967, p. 179). This recommended shift of emphasis has been largely accepted in the years since their article; it has tended to bifurcate research concerning the sexual body into one branch facing infancy, psychosexuality, and childhood in their family setting, and another looking toward adolescent or later years in the context of widely diffused social-sexual stereotypes and values.

In a more recent major study of sexual preference (Bell, Weinberg, and Hammersmith, 1981), the focus shifted dramatically, from the study of male and female homosexuals in their social context as adults, to the origins in earlier years of their sexual orientation. The instrument, however, was the questionnaire eliciting recall of life events, which insured that very little would emerge concerning infancy or very early childhood. The study reaches the conclusion that there is virtually nothing in the events of a homosexual life history that differs from events in a heterosexual life history. With this result in hand, the authors now suggest that homosexuality is chiefly *biological* in origin, thus reversing the earlier focus on social factors. The authors acknowledge that their approach does not attempt to get below the surface of conscious thought, but are rather proud that in this way, as in most others, their approach cannot be correlated or reconciled with psychoanalytic expectations.

It is conceivable that the AIDS emergency in the homosexual community will move researchers toward a new interest in the sexual body. It is sobering to find that a number of editors of gay newspapers and journals have concluded that the gay press has not handled the AIDS story any better than has the "straight" press (Lieberson, 1983). There has been such an extensive background of concentration on the social mission of gay journalism and scholarship that a direct threat to the sexual body of homosexual males could only be handled by defensive and evasive comment in the gay press, complemented by hysterical reactions elsewhere.

With regard to the sexual body of lesbians, recent research has something substantial to say. In a book as recent as Tripp's *The Homosexual Matrix* (1975), and one with great empirical pretensions, it was stated that lesbian couples who stay together rapidly lose sexual interest in each other (Tripp, pp. 153-154). A similar statement was made about homosexual male couples. The recent study by Blumstein and Schwartz shows that 27% of lesbian couples who have been together ten years or more have sex at least once a week, as compared to 45% of male homosexual couples who do the same (Blumstein and Schwartz, 1983, pp. 195-198). These figures do not warrant Tripp's generalizations. On the other hand, Blumstein and Schwartz do find a lower overall frequency of intercourse for lesbian couples than for any other group. Married heterosexuals with over 10 years together had sexual intercourse at least once a week in 63% of the sample, while 72% of unmarried couples who had been together that long did the same. Inasmuch as the longterm lesbian couples do not generally engage in sex outside of their relationships, these findings seem to support a hypothesis of difference in sexual body need between lesbian couples and other couples. The sources of this difference remain unknown, despite speculations (Tripp, 1975, p. 154) that women just have less libido.

One reason for the lack of reliable insight into this difference has been the "failure to explore the full meaning of eroticism in lesbian lives," as Zimmerman (1984, pp. 680-681) shows in her review-essay on lesbian personal narratives. Much current discussion in lesbian sources is hampered, Zimmerman argues, by the attempt to label sadomasochist role-play, or the "butch-femme" division, as inherently evil.

> As long as lesbian sadomasochism, or any other personal practice or identity, is considered to be evidence of virtue or vice, it is unlikely that we will be able to listen very carefully to one another. (Zimmerman, 1984, p. 681)

Zimmerman's call for change in this essay, published in *Signs*, which is probably the most central feminist scholarly journal in the United States, may signal the beginning of a new effort to understand the lesbian sexual body.

Although Tripp's generalizations on the rapid demise of intercourse among gay couples were not confirmed, the male homosexual couples in the Blumstein and Schwartz sample do confirm the belief that the frequency of sexual intercourse declines after the first few years. The finding is strengthened by that of David McWhirter and Andrew Mattison, a psychiatrist and a psychologist, respectively, and themselves a male couple. Their new study of 156 male couples shows that for most such couples, "the passion of the sexual encounter begins to dwindle rapidly within three to four years, and the couple begins to seek sex outside of the relationship" (McWhirter and Mattison, 1983).

Another and very different approach to the study of sexual orientations is through the investigation of hormonal influences on sexual gender, sexual identity, and role. Goy and MacEwen (1980)—summarizing the state of research on the question, Is there an endocrine basis for homosexuality among males? (1980, pp. 64-73)—admit that there are "major empirical obstacles to be overcome before this hypothesis . . . can gain wider acceptance" (p. 72). They insist that the evidence to date does warrant a continued interest in this hypothesis: "Let us all recognize the fact . . . that the hypothesis is here and cannot be dismissed" (p. 73). Notably, John Money and the group of researchers working with him at John Hopkins have investigated hormonal influences on gender identity and sexual orientation (Money, 1980; Money and Ehrhardt, 1974). One line of investigation sought to ascertain if gender identity and role could be determined by post-natal rearing, supplemented by surgical correction of genitalia and hormonal injections. A number of cases involve babies born with sexually ambiguous genitals but still technically males; these were raised as females and eventually had a facsimile of normal female genitalia built up by surgical intervention. Another line of investigation observed the development of androgenital syndrome in girls. These girls are hormonally "masculinized before birth" due to a chromosomal abnormality, but in the treatment by Money and colleagues, a number of these girls have been given cortisol. They now have been observed over a period ranging from birth to adulthood. A main finding is that "as they grew up, the features of behavior known as tomboyism" occurred with unusual frequency (Money, 1980, p. 27). They elected female gender identity and gender role, despite a long delay (three to nine years later than the average) in beginning to take romantic and erotic interest in males.

It is difficult to say what conclusions may be drawn from such research on the hormonal impact on sexual gender identity and role. Research descriptions and discussions by writers such as Money and Ehrhardt, Goy and MacEwen, and several others (see Parsons, 1982) show a high degree of awareness of the multiple variants involved, as well as awareness of the social issues concerning the rights of individuals with different sexual orientations and the dangers of sex-role stereotyping. This will not prevent such research, however, from indicating that sexual identity and role are in some way connected with abnormalities in the sexual body. To the extent that such a suggestion is made, it inevitably will threaten the fragile social consensus which accepts being gay as a sexual orientation. Is there a way to avoid this danger, short of banning the research or ignoring its findings? Some of the findings themselves have been subjected to a severe, even withering methodological critique by the feminist neuroanatomist Ruth Bleier (Bleier, 1984, pp.

98-103), but even assuming that Bleier's criticisms are well taken, it would appear that the door cannot be shut permanently: the hormonal line of inquiry into sexual development and gender-related behaviors is not likely to be abandoned. From the point of view of empirical theory, in which "artifacts" can easily be created by the investigator, it is good to see the conclusions of Helen Longino and Ruth Doell, a philosopher of science and a biologist, respectively. Reviewing the field of hormonal related sex research, they do criticize such work as that by Money and by Goy and MacEwen, but conclude that despite their own reservations as feminist scientists, "Sexism does not seem to be intrinsic to data as evidence for physiological causal hypotheses" (Longino and Doell, 1983, p. 225).

One can react to hormonal investigations with avoidance and anger, on the one side, or by subtly appropriating the value of the research efforts as a prop for the "straight." Either attitude would lose the complexity and challenge of the sexual body. For one thing, as Goy and MacEwen note, when we discuss "masculinization" and "feminization," we are also recognizing the possibility of "spontaneous bisexuality" which we might not be able to think about within some other theoretical vocabulary (Goy and MacEwen, 1980, pp. 5-6). Freud would have welcomed this observation; it may point to a closing of the gap between psychoanalytic theory and "sexual biology" (Freud, 1971) which distressed him and which is incompatible with the perspective of the sexual body.

Research such as Money's should be critically appraised; for anyone trying to understand the sexual body, it must be considered. The emphasis on hormonal effects, however, rather limits the possibilities of this approach to bringing about an understanding of the sexual body in all its complexity. A much broader approach to understanding the adult sexual body in its homosexual existence is being developed. The Society for the Psychological Study of Social Issues (a division of the A.P.A.), Task Force on Sexual Orientation, has now published what is designated "the *first* in-depth analysis of homosexuality and the social, biological, psychological, and public policy issues surrounding it" (Paul, Weinrich, Gonsiorek, and Hotvedt, 1982). The volume also explores lesbian relationships, the lesbian as mother, and the children of lesbian mothers. The book is strongly supportive of gay rights and is alert to all the stereotypical prejudice in its field, but it is also open and receptive to threatening findings. There is an avoidance and disavowal of the attempt to portray the homosexual as the possessor of superior mental health (Gonsiorek, 1982, pp. 76-77). The hormonal etiology of homosexual orientation is examined by Gartrell and found almost entirely wanting (Gartrell, 1982), but the one possible exception is carefully noted, both by her and by Weinrich:

> There is one suggestive finding that might connect *prenatal* hormone levels with adult sexual orientation in at least some individuals. (Weinrich, 1982a, p. 209)

Rather than idealizing the gay community, this volume contains a frank admission of one major problem within it, concerning child-rearing, namely that lesbians tend to reject rather than give support to other lesbians who are mothers (Lewin and Lyons, 1982, pp. 260-261). Far from attempting to pretend that there is no fundamental difficulty in solo parenting, Hotvedt and Mandel state that "Indeed, two parents are better than one; that is really not under debate here" (Hotvedt and Mandel, 1982, p. 284). On the other hand, Lewin and Lyons show that lesbian mothers as well as heterosexual mothers who raise children without the presence of a male in the household often make special efforts "to strengthen the children's relationships with their fathers" (Lewin and Lyons, 1982, pp. 267-269). Which is not to say that the fathers are always interested! Often they are not. The ideological concept that a network of supportive friends can take the place of the absent male parent is treated sceptically, although the role of friendship ties is recognized as important (Lewin and Lyons, 1982, p. 264).

One main emphasis of the book is on the situational similarities faced by all couples, whether gay or straight, and of all mothers, whether gay or straight (Peplau and Amaro, 1982, p. 238). Mothering is a huge part of a life, and this limits any attempt on the part of a lesbian mother to live in a manner which would ignore this fact in favor of purely lesbian relationships. Moreover, even if it is true that many homosexuals who appear in therapy have disturbed or unsatisfactory sex-lives, what can we conclude?

> This should not be surprising; heterosexuals disturbed because of their sexuality fill many therapist's case-loads. Because sexual expression is one of the most intimate, psychologically rich, and complex of all human interactions, it is not surprising that individuals who are troubled or disturbed will likely manifest problems in their sexual relationships, regardless of orientation. (Gonsiorek, 1982, pp. 79-80)

From the perspective of the sexual body, this point is very well taken; it seems to signal a turn in research interests from the political-social-stereotypical context of the homosexual body to the sexual body itself.

The volume also contains interesting theoretical work and a range of speculation that is fitting for the unknown contours of the perspective of the sexual body. For example, it might be that the genes *do* have something to do with homosexuality: something positive, that is. The evolutionary function of homosexuality might be explained partly along sociobiological lines: E.O. Wilson (1975) has argued that there is a genetic component in humans which does not directly contribute to reproduction but which does contribute to social living. To the extent that homosexuals are

> freed from the need to direct energy toward raising their own offspring, [they give] a special advantage to their kin by providing various forms of help which would not have been available to kin groups lacking homosexuals (since all members would be competing to raise their own offspring). (Kirsch and Rodman, 1982, p. 191)

This is but one of three possible genetic arguments which can be advanced on scientific lines as hypotheses which are in principle confirmable, although the hypotheses remain speculative and the empirical tests are difficult to envision. The editor of this volume ends it, however, on another theoretical note entirely. Referring to "the Popperian ideal of the falsifiable hypothesis," Weinrich maintains that

> a scientific theory is discarded not when an experiment definitively falsifies it, but when a string of false predictions of a theory's proponents becomes embarrassingly long. The existence of such a string is itself a bit of metascientific data—admittedly one difficult to apply a statistical test to, but telling nevertheless. So this book can be seen as another step in the scientific debate, embarrassing its share of those who (say) reach the same conclusions before and after their data change. (Weinrich, 1982b, p. 382)

Perhaps the most challenging article in the book is that by Joel D. Hencken, who proposes a move toward "mutual understanding" between homosexuality and psychoanalysis. Hencken argues that there are ways in which psychoanalytic theory and therapy can contribute toward a "non-illness" understanding of homosexuality. He is aware of the antihomosexual bias of many in the psychoanalytic community and duly samples statements from the psychoanalytic literature which demonstrate this bias (Hencken, 1982, pp. 108-111). But he does not allow these analysts to speak for all of psychoanalysis. Thus Hencken opens the way for constructive use of psychoanalytic theory by researchers into homosexuality, and at the same time invites psychoanalysts to join in this effort, thus allowing for a blend of developmental and social perspectives that has thus far been largely lacking.

The analysts who think that "gay is ill," however, are not giving up. Socarides, one of those cited for his bias by Hencken, has recently gone into lengthy, bitter detail about the machinations of those gay therapists and their sympathizers who deceived the American Psychiatric Association into removing homosexuality from its official diagnostic manual (Socarides, 1984). Socarides in fact raises many procedural points which show considerable skulduggery and bureaucratic manipulation leading to that decision, with which he was familiar as a dissenting insider. Of course the account given is Socarides' own. His enmity is made clear by his choice of a final quotation to end his article, from a letter sent to him by Abram Kardiner, who wrote: "Homosexuality is merely a symptom (in its epidemic form) of social disintegration..." (Kardiner, personal communication to Socarides, 1974, quoted in Socarides, 1984, p. 94). Kardiner also felt that homosexuality "destroys" the function of the family as "the last place in our society where affectivity can still be cultivated" (ibid.).

As recently as 1979, Socarides, who is himself an expert in the psychoanalytic study of sexuality (Karasu and Socarides, 1979), has classified homosexuality as one of the "sexual perversions," and under the guise of arguing for a unified theory of such perversions, maintains that the real problem for research is to learn why one "perversion is chosen over another" (Socarides, 1979, p. 188). On the contrary, I would say that a more important research task is for psychoanalytic theory itself to understand why it has consistently presumed that mature sexuality is heterosexuality. In support of Hencken's view that such analysts as Socarides do not speak for the entire psychoanalytic establishment, I would refer to Stoller's much more serious study of "perversion," a term that Stoller defends as both socially dangerous and theoretically indispensible (Stoller, 1975). Stoller is by no means willing to leave some aspects of homosexuality out of his account of perversions, but in his fine discussion of what a diagnosis is, and of the general weaknesses of the whole psychiatric diagnostic system as it exists, Stoller concludes that homosexuality is *not* a diagnosis (Stoller, 1975, p. 199). It is interesting that although Stoller cites some of the work of Socarides to warrant his conclusion that there are many sources of homosexual object-choice (p. 199), Socarides does not cite Stoller's work in his own, later "unitary theory of the perversions." Socarides is holding the line, but Stoller is correctly credited by Hencken (1982, p. 139) with beginning to implement a more promising and open psychoanalytic approach.

It has been suggested that earlier psychoanalytic research and speculation about homosexuality might have been based on a partially correct but basically misleading observation that adult male homosexuals had suffered through particularly unhappy childhoods, during which they had been dominated by overprotective mothers (Bieber et al., 1962). Recent research by Bullough, Bullough, and Smith (1983) has led to the conclusion that a group of subjects which reports having had unhappy childhoods is one which designates itself "transsexual," a category not in common use until the past quarter century. In older studies, such subjects were probably designated homosexual. Although it is not clear what bodily features would be taken as evidence that any person is a "transsexual," the most common definition in use by those who so designate themselves has this key element: "He (in the case of males) feels like a woman trapped in a man's body or vice versa" (Bullough, Bullough, and Smith, 1983, p. 240). In the Bullough et al. research sample, the 32 respondents calling themselves transsexuals reported a history of unhappy childhood much more frequently than did the 51 respondents who simply considered themselves homosexuals. The male homosexuals did not report a higher incidence of unhappiness in childhood than did the 61 respondents whose sexual orientation was unspecified (Bullough, Bullough, and Smith, 1983, p. 248). It is conceivable that a homophobic bias in psychoanalytic thinking over a period of decades had produced a confirming artifact through the selection of patients who would report early childhood unhappiness; such patients would be unrepresentative of those now considering themselves to be homosexuals, but would have been drawn in great part from the "transsexual" minority. Although this possibility is only a speculation, the research effort from which it came is a good example of the clarification which might be obtained by taking the new categorizations of sexual body gender orientations seriously. It is worth noting that Bullough et al. also studied 64 "transvestite" informants in this research project, but did not discover any outstanding variables in comparison to the transsexuals, homosexuals, and unspecified males in their study. From the perspective of the sexual body, however, it would be advisable to regard the conclusions of this study as tentative, inasmuch as the deeper psychological processes and possibly traumatic but repressed experiences would not have been reached by means of the questionnaire method.

The present discussion of the homosexual and lesbian sexual bodies in relation to current research issues may be sufficient, not for saying anything definitive, for the topic is too complicated for brief treatment, but for showing once more that the sexual body is still not understood, and that some of the issues concerning it are controversial and highly consequential. The therapist Stanley Keleman's recent book, *In Defense of Heterosexuality* (1982), for example, makes claims for the biologically central role of the nuclear family as a source of love in the world, as opposed to the concept that *any* sexual orientation is a primary source of love in society. This is not a reduplication of Kardiner's bigotry, which holds that the family is the "only" source of affectivity we have left, nor is it a call for anyone to change orientation or to classify himself or herself as diagnostically ill. But it is a question for thought, posed by a therapist who shows in his other writings that he has been able to work empathetically with homosexual patients. The case history of a patient named "Harry" (Keleman, 1975, pp. 146-165) is one example. The reader of the present study who has not read Keleman may ask himself or herself (a) what sort of evidence and argument Keleman might be offering, and (b) whether it would be possible to give his book a reasoned, critical reading, such that would satisfy one's own most cherished sense of fairness. That standard is the one suggested by the Deweyan literary critic, Louise Rosenblatt (Rosenblatt, 1978, p. 171).

The adult sexual body as actively bisexual is a further challenge to interdisciplinary study. Wilson and Fulford (1979) have concluded that bisexuals should be considered a separate category, and not regarded as some sort of mid-point between heterosexuality and homosexuality (1979, p. 292). The 45 bisexual males in their study differed in several measures from the 116 heterosexuals and 30 homosexuals; the bisexuals had had more sexual partners, had begun having intercourse at an earlier age, and showed "higher mean values for both testosterone and oestradiol" than the other two groups (1979, p. 292). The category of married homosexuals poses a special problem for non-moralistic research and personal understanding. It is interesting that research writing seems to assume, through the adoption of this category, that a married man who is bisexual must be a "married gay" (Harry, 1983) and a woman who has given birth but is now living with another woman in a sexual relation, is classed as lesbian rather than bisexual (Blumstein and Schwartz, 1983, pp. 43, 460-461, 494-497). An exceptionally lucid, fictionalized autobiographical account of the life of one married bisexual is given by Glazier (1975). It is disheartening to report that Glazier, a creative writer, now finds himself frequently rejected by "gay" publications which take a negative stance toward anyone not clearly either labelled as of one sexual orientation or the other (Glazier, personal communications, 1982-1983). Weinberg and Williams (1975, p. 341) remark, astonishingly, that *"the only psychological problem on which homosexuals living with wives stand out is guilt, shame, or anxiety regarding their homosexuality*," which might reflect the conflicting involvements and commitments peculiar to their situation" (emphasis added). If this is their "only" psychological problem, it would still appear huge.

The Sexual Body of Mentally Retarded Adults

Another large segment of the adult population which is just beginning to have a sexual revolution consists of the mentally retarded. Evans (1983) has argued that "retarded persons can engage in responsible sexual expression" (1983, p. 259). He reports that parents of retarded people in special residences frequently attempt to prevent their "kids" from having sex, even though the kids are over 21 years of age. In a society that offers a high level of visual sexual stimulation, it is especially difficult for retarded young adults to resist "coming on" to people they might meet in public. This is one reason they are put into residence homes in the first place. If the retarded adolescent is female, her sexuality will bring drastic action: "Sexual behavior of retarded women over the age of fourteen is the single greatest cause of their institutionalization" (Evans, p. 257). Of course the label "retarded" is problematical, so it is difficult to say if 3% of the population is retarded—a figure that is often accepted by specialists in the U.S. and Europe—or if a smaller percentage is involved, as Evans suggests (1983, pp. 23-25). A special problem too is that substantially more males than females are classified as mentally retarded (Evans, 1983, p. 25). The retarded population would thus have problems specific to its own conditions, even were social attitudes toward the retarded more advanced than they presently are. Evans leaves no doubt that up until recently, the retarded were considered unworthy of having sexual lives. The sex education they did get was contradicted by the expectation that they would not have sex. This left them with a sexual body but no outlets except masturbation, although some ingenious and non-exploitative sexual arrangements among the retarded within institutions are described by Evans (1983, pp. 251-259). One institution had a "privacy room" for residents, which, combined with contraceptive counseling, gave opportunity for sexual gratification—the best that these adults had ever known (Evans, p. 258).

In an earlier book, Michael and Ann Craft argued for the acceptance of the sexual body of the mentally retarded (Craft and Craft, 1978). One of the myths they dispel is that the mentally handicapped are "irresponsible," meaning that they cannot practice self-control. They cite an American research project in a 2,000 bed hospital, where the mentally retarded residents showed great capacities for sexual denial, despite the presence of abundant opportunities for having sex (Craft and Craft, p. 5). But Craft and Craft cite this not as a recommendation that sex continue to be denied but that the mentally retarded *not* be taught to have a negative attitude toward their own sexual bodies.

These comments should not be taken as disparagement of the disciplines of mental retardation. Most of the professional workers do not seem to be greatly different than the surrounding "normal" population in attitude toward sexuality for the retarded. Some, such as Evans himself, clearly are more progressive. The astounding thing about the topic of sexuality among the retarded is that it has come up at all. Evans observes that it is extremely rare for any (modern?) society not to take an unfair, negative, attitude toward its mentally retarded members (1983, pp. 298-299). Only because there has been a sexual revolution in progress for decades is the adult sexual body of the mentally retarded person now beginning to be thought human. The field of research on the adult mentally retarded, however, still seems badly in need of non-moralistic approaches which avoid the current fascination in psychology with cognitive science at the expense of all else.

The Badly Injured Sexual Body

The sexuality of heart attack victims is no longer a tabooed topic; magazine articles discuss it openly. However, the medical profession did not exactly blaze the way. As Alex Comfort has put it, medical men for the past century have an unwritten tradition of standing on the side of prohibition of pleasures, rather than helping the victims of disease or injuries to enjoy what sexual life they might be capable of (Comfort, 1967). Much of the pressure for change has come from outside the profession. For example, the need to keep soldiers in fighting trim during World War I was what gave medical science a decisive boost toward eradicating or controlling venereal disease, according to Comfort. In the case of serious injuries or diseases which threaten adult sexual life, it still seems to be true that pressure for change comes from extra-professional sources. An excellent example is the book by Ellen Becker (1978) entitled *Female Sexuality Following Spinal Cord Injury*. Becker was a victim of such an injury who became dissatisfied with what her doctors could tell her, or would tell her, about her chances to have and enjoy sex. She developed a useful pool of information on the subject by inventing a detailed questionnaire which she administered to other women who also had suffered spinal cord injuries. Sex was not nearly as absent or pleasureless for most of these women as had been supposed. The resulting book is now used in treatment of such victims. One significance of her book for a general understanding of the sexual body is that the boundary line between "popular" and "scientific" is interestingly blurred. The data assembled by Becker will not measure up to the highest standards of validation in academic psychology, but her book will serve a therapeutic, sex-affirmative function until such time as someone does her work better.

The disciplines of the badly injured sexual body are remarkable for the prominent participation of patients themselves and of professionals who have crossed conventional disciplinary lines. The volume *Sexuality and Physical Disability* (Bullard and Knight, 1981) is largely a compilation written by the disabled. Michael Barrett, author of *Sexuality and Multiple Sclerosis* (1982), is a professor of zoology at the University of Toronto. He is also highly active in CSIEC (Council of Sex Information and Education of Canada). A three-day conference on *Sexuality and the Disabled* at Royal Ottawa Hospital in Toronto was sparked by the opening address by Beverley Thomas, a quadriplegic who was also a Director of Planned Parenthood in British Columbia at the time of the conference (Finch, 1977, p. 13)

> With a mixture of gentle humor and self-disclosure, [Thomas] opened the door to the forbidden area of sexuality and made it possible for those present to begin taking a long, hard look at their own values and beliefs, as well as the taboos, myths and misconceptions surrounding sexuality in general and sexual practice in particular. (Finch, 1977, p. 13)

Finch, who attended this conference, and whose field is nursing education, concludes that it is essential for nurses dealing with the sexually disabled to accept their own sexuality (p. 14); failure to be comfortable with one's own sexuality is a virtual guarantee of being ineffective in helping others who must undergo more "embarrassment, fear, and vulnerability than most of us could ever imagine" (p. 14). It was the consensus of the professionals at the conference that privacy for disabled patients who wished to attempt to be alone with a sexual partner is a human necessity in this branch of nursing. In terms of institutional policy, this means that there must be self-regulation "by the disabled persons in all non-medical matters" (p. 14). But such provisions are not easy to come by, as Robert T. Baxter testifies (Baxter, 1978). Baxter, a quadriplegic, was also Adjunct Professor of Health and Recreation, at Kean College, New Jersey. He tells of attending a day-long seminar on sex for the spinal cord injured, in which "all of the patients felt degraded," as if they were freaks on display for the benefit of normal people in the audience (Baxter, 1978, p. 48). He stresses the importance of psychological sensitivity to the sexual problems of the disabled, rather than a purely functional physical approach, which can cause depression. Most of the effective counselling comes from nurses; "on the other hand, most doctors I've asked about sex have been speechless or turned red from embarrassment" (Baxter, 1978, p. 48).

Baxter also gives an account of how a spinal cord injured man—divorced by his wife of 25 years because his injury made him repellant to her—was able to begin a sexual relationship with a woman. This required going to a hotel which had no architectural barriers, and it took the help of an aide who "undressed him, removed his catheter, and put him in bed" (Baxter, p. 51). The aide was hired by the patient, but on the second visit to the hotel, the patient's girlfriend helped "with the preparations herself, a practice they have continued" (*ibid.*). Another quadriplegic, a 23-year-old man who broke his fifth vertebra while diving into a swimming pool, has given a comparative account of two rehabilitation centers. In the first, where he spent 13 months, sexual counselling was never mentioned, although it may have been available, but in the second, sexual counselling from a psychologist was a regular feature of the program ("Difference?," 1984).

Spinal cord injuries have very different sexual body effects on men and women. Women who have sustained such an injury may become pregnant, once menstruation is restored, which usually occurs "in almost all women within a year" (Keller and Buchanan, 1984, p. 4). In fact "most are capable of vaginal deliveries" (*ibid.*). Spinal-cord injured men have virtually normal testicular and pituitary function; their relatively normal "circulating levels of testosterone" account biologically for the "preservation of libido that is generally seen under these circumstances" (Kolodny, Masters, Johnson, and Biggs, 1979, p. 263). But there are serious impediments to sexual gratification. Some medical writings have given the impression that capacity for erection and ejaculation in the spinal-cord injured man is equivalent to sexual pleasure, but in fact those erections which are "reflexogenic"—that is, which occur without the man's realization that he is having an erection—"are often extremely brief in duration and do not usually produce pleasurable physical sensations for the man," although there may be pleasure associated with the fact of noticing an erection at all (Kolodny et al., 1979, pp. 259-260). "Psychogenic" erections, which the man is aware of, may last longer but "are usually independent of tactile temperature, or sensory awareness of the genitals" (p. 260). Kolodny et al. are led to observe that "orgasm is a total body response" (p. 260), thus marking a rare point of agreement with Reich. They express total scepticism over reports of injured people who are told that they may fantasize their way to "mental orgasm," when in fact "none of the physiologic manifestations of orgasm occur" (p. 260).

Although "the great majority of spinal-cord injured patients are male" (p. 261), and hence not as much is known about the sexuality of female patients, one of the most interesting comments made by Kolodny et al. concerns a woman patient. The patient suffered a "complete lower motor neuron lesion at T-12," and loss of all pelvic sensations (p. 262). Gradually her erotic sensations were transferred to her breasts even though she had told Masters and Johnson in an earlier study, prior to her injury, that she did not derive much erotic pleasure from breast stimulation (pp. 261-262). In the case of this woman, the authors are not at all sceptical about her attaining orgasm through breast stimulation and without pelvic vasocongestion or vaginal sensation. They are not sceptical because they observed other "physiologic manifestations" which surprised them: "the lips of this woman's mouth became engorged to twice their normal size" as orgasm approached, and when orgasm occurred,

> a pulsating wave was observed in her lips and the swelling then dissipated rapidly—in a manner almost identical to the pattern formed at the outer portion of the vagina in non-cord-injured women. (Kolodny et al., 1979, p. 262)

Perhaps what this report brings out is the depth of sexual need in an adult body; even under wretched conditions, the body is sometimes able to learn new pathways to gratification. But even more remarkable is the recovery of a rhythmic erotic capacity which may be a subsistent sexual capacity in the adult but one that also has some connection with the sexual body of the nursing infant. As with all of the material concerning the badly injured sexual body, this woman's psychophysiology testifies to the continuation of the sexual revolution: we now are past the historical era in which we might have assumed that badly injured people cannot have, or do not need to have, adult sexual gratification. It also brings to awareness how little we still understand of the sexual body.

Many aspects of the adult sexual body have now been taken up for discussion in the pages of this chapter, while others have been merely suggested. It might be fitting to end this section with a speculative question, which I owe to John Herold (Personal communication, October 1983). Is there a potential for increased intimacy and tenderness of touch in the adult sexual body, through much of the life-cycle, a potential that is only now emerging, as the sexual revolution with its emphasis on self-regulation is allowing us to discover? That emotion continues to be developed throughout adult life is a position now taken by some leaders in psychological research (Malatesta and Izard, 1984), but once again, the sexual body seems to have gone begging in this new theory. To ask Herold's question is to suggest that there is a complexity in adult sexual development that is special to humans, and which we as yet have barely named. The adult body has not just become fully grown and developed by age 18 or age 21; as a sexual body it may develop further.

CHAPTER EIGHT

THE SEXUAL BODY, PSYCHOANALYSIS AND SCIENCE: BOWLBY, PETERFREUND, AND KOHUT

The last two chapters have shown that the sexual body is a perspective demanding a complexity of critical understanding. The complications probably exceed whatever concepts of sexuality existed at the time of Freud's classical period. The perspective demands consideration of research on sexuality in a way that never loses contact with the problematical flesh and blood realities of the body, yet it does not encourage the temptation to think that we can some day uncover the preexisting "reality" or "essence" of sexuality that we have just not happened to find previously. As Dewey would have warned, there is no certainty to be sought for in the perspective of the sexual body, although there is every reason to attempt to increase human security by taking hold of the research results we do have and using them intelligently, as Dewey also held (Dewey, 1929b). Psychoanalysis as the key discipline for this perspective has not absorbed or integrated the material presented in the last two chapters, but it remains the only discipline which is ultimately committed to do so. Although the theories of Melanie Klein, D.W. Winnicott, Anna Freud, Margaret Mahler, Erik Erikson, George S. Klein, and others in the psychoanalytic tradition have been shown to be seriously deficient in their understanding of the sexual body, there is also a set of recent theorists who provide genuine revision of certain key aspects of psychoanalytic thought. In these newer theories, the sexual body is not pushed out of sight, or at least the denials are of a different and probably less severe character. In fact, well before the recent simultaneous emergence of a series of critical issues for psychoanalytic theory, that is, before the infant research explosion, before the "trouble" in the Freud archives over Freud's virtual giving up of the "seduction" theory, and before the renewed interest in Freud as a "biologist of the mind" and not a thinker who could get along without the body, there have been highly challenging reconstructive projects under way in psychoanalytic theory. What seems to be different about the work of John Bowlby, Emanuel Peterfreund, and Heinz Kohut, in contrast to many other reformist efforts such as those of Schafer (1976, 1980), is a possibility for accommodation with the sexual body rather than an effort to dispense with it. Two of these theorists, Peterfreund and Kohut, avoid basing their work on the model of the infant sexual body; they have a real sense of adult sexual life which appears frequently in their writings, even though its position within their theoretical structures is ambiguous or even dubious. Bowlby has continued to develop theory on the basis of infant and early childhood considerations, but he has moved a long way from the object-relations school of psychoanalysis, in which he originally began developing his theory (Bowlby, 1984, p. 37). Although Bowlby and Peterfreund developed their theories without knowledge of each other's activity, they have each come to recognize an affinity between their two approaches (Bowlby, 1981; Peterfreund, 1980).

All three of these theorists have been concerned with the scientific adequacy of psychoanalysis, not in the sense of its empirical confirmation reviewed by Kline (1981), but in the sense of the validity of constructs which psychoanalysis uses. Bowlby has moved away from the highly speculative object-relations constructs and developed a theory of psychological "attachment," which he reports to be "widely regarded as probably the best supported theory of socioemotional development yet available" (1984, p. 35). It is grounded in the discipline of ethology. He accepts that psychoanalysis is both an art and a science, and believes that its scientific validity should be improved to the extent that it may be possible to do so, without denying the art of the therapist (Bowlby, 1979). Peterfreund has given psychoanalysis a reformulation in information processing terms and thus has removed it, he believes, from its reliance on scientifically worthless energy concepts such as that of the psychic libido. The late Heinz Kohut took a divergent pathway toward underscoring the scientific validity of psychoanalysis: he privileged the analytic situation itself as a form of scientific knowledge, arguing that Freud is a thinker of the caliber of Hegel, Rousseau, or Marx. Freud's psychoanalytic revolution applies to the shaping of our concepts of knowledge itself and should not simply be brought into conformity with previous notions of scientific objectivity (Kohut, 1984, pp. 39-40). Kohut still believed there is a role in psychoanalytic theory for "the experimental method and proof via statistical evidence" (1984, pp. 224-225), but these considerations cannot be allowed the primacy they once were accorded in scientific theory. All three of these theorists seem to be free of that disturbing hatred of the sexual body which I have pointed out in the earlier work by Melanie Klein, Anna Freud, and D.W. Winnicott. Yet the sexual body does not receive adequate theoretical recognition in their work. What accommodation they make for the sexual body is largely at the practical, clinical level rather than in their theories as such. A problem for examination, therefore, is whether these revisionist theories could be further revised to take full account of the sexual body, or if the sexual body's exclusion is a function of the theories themselves, despite the personal sensitivities of the theorists to matters of sexuality.

Bowlby's Defense: Ethology Overcomes Sexuality

The work of John Bowlby is probably the finest and most complete endeavor ever made to extend and revise psychoanalytic object-relations theory into a scientifically respectable discipline. Bowlby's 3-volume *Attachment and Loss*, finally completed in 1980, is the creative work of a lifetime (Bowlby, 1980a, 1980b, 1980c). The problems it deals with are much influenced by Bowlby's work for the World Health Organization on the mental health of homeless children, commissioned first in 1950 (Bowlby, 1951). His work also has the feeling of a man who loves rather than hates life. Far from endorsing the Winnicottian idea that infants must be afforded an optimal and necessarily painful experience of separation from their early maternal attachment, Bowlby has found that the "anxious over-dependency" of "spoiling" is largely an artifact: ". . . all the evidence points the other way" (Bowlby, 1980b, p. 239). There is little to be feared from an alleged "excess of parental affection" (1980b, p. 244). If we are looking for reasons why so many children are disturbed, we might look, Bowlby argues, not at purely endopsychic factors, in which he places little credence, but in such actual factors as the surprisingly high percentage of parents who die of suicide; it may be that "one father in fifteen and one mother in seventeen" dies in this way, in the U.K. (1980c, p. 381). The neglect of environmental (familial) causes for children's disturbances has "left the field clear for such traditional hypotheses as phase of development or autonomous phantasy" (1980c, p. 380), but once this neglect is overcome, as Bowlby himself has overcome it, such theories can be put aside.

> With our present knowledge . . . I believe the only safe assumption for a clinician to make is that in every case, behind the smoke of a child's anxiety, self-blame or other symptom or problem, there burns a fire lit by some frightening or guilt-inducing experience of real life. (Bowlby, 1980c, p. 380)

This bold statement forms a contrast with the careful stipulations of Winnicott (1965) that the "facilitating environment" is important.

Bowlby's major innovation has been the alignment of psychoanalytic theory of the child with evolutionary theory and especially with ethology. The human species cannot be regarded as different in kind from all other species, if we are going to speak scientifically. Bowlby's realization of this principle has influenced his rejection of widely held psychoanalytic interpretations of the nature of infancy, such as those concerning fear of strangers and the relative state of development of the human brain at birth.

Psychoanalysts had made much of the oft-observed advent of a fear of strangers in infants at about the age of eight months and had eagerly built this into their theories. This fear seemed to show how an infant, just emerging from an alleged symbiotic union with its mother, and at last gaining the capacity to discriminate one person from another, is afflicted with the realization that it is not living in a world of fantasy in which it is omnipotent master, but in a world of people where threats may destroy and needs may not be met. But Bowlby has seen that this line of reasoning would make human fear a totally inexplicable event among the equipment for survival that humans, like other species, possess. Other species in fact show analogous fear of strangers at various well-marked points in their development as infants. The most sensible construction of this common occurrence is that the awareness of fear develops sometime later than birth (Bowlby, 1980b, pp. 77-86). To quote the authors of *Emotional Expression in Infancy*:

> Most animals do not show fear at birth, yet at some later point in their development they evidence avoidance or "flight" behavior in response to certain stimuli. For example: birds show a fear and flight response at approximately 24 hours . . . , cats show fear of strangers in novel situations at five weeks . . . , dogs show a fear of novel situations and human caretakers beginning around five to seven weeks . . . ; monkeys manifest fear in response to novel stimuli at two to five months. (Emde, Gaensbauer and Harmon, 1976, p. 126)

Empirical evidence is also accumulating which shows that the infant fear of strangers, although it is a common phenomenon reported at about eight months of age, is not the sudden event that psychoanalytic theorists had supposed. They had proposed a sudden realization by an infant at that age, when the child is allegedly just starting to develop an ego powerful enough to distinguish strange adults from its close caretaker, that the infant's previous delusion of being able to exert omnipotent control over its environment had been shaken, thus producing terror and hatred for self and other. It now appears that infants go through a process of careful comparison of faces: they can see faces for some months before their fear of strangers comes into play. The fear does not seem closely related to the development of "object constancy" in their perception, contrary to much of current psychoanalytic belief (Emde, Gaensbauer, and Harmon, 1976, p. 196).

Nor is it true as many have supposed that the human infant is born in a condition of drastic biological unpreparedness, a virtual fetus forced to live outside of its womb. Physiologically-based claims which estimated the abilities of the infant's brain as inherently slight because of the lack of myelination at birth are misleading. The process of myelination, "the acquisition of lipoprotein sheath by nerve fibres during development," is credited with enabling the transmission of impulses much more quickly, regularly and accurately than would be the case in non-myelinated fibres (Gibson, 1981, p. 53). As the anatomist Gibson explains,

> Myelination at birth [in humans] is less advanced than in the monkeys, but much more so than in . . . cats, dogs, or rats. (Gibson, 1981, p. 55)

Neonatal brain weight is also comparatively great; when considered in relation to other physiological maturation factors such as onset of EEG (before birth), it could only mean that "the human infant should possess behaviours of considerable complexity" (Gibson, 1981, p. 55). Moreover, many species are at least as helpless as the human infant in the days and weeks after birth. The cubs of the black bear, for example, are almost too weak to be able to move for the first three months. The cottontail rabbit is "born blind, hairless and helpless," and has a far less than even chance of making it through infancy and into maturity (Wolkomir, 1983). An ethological approach stresses a benign explanation of all such facts: "helplessness" is only relative, and the need for parental affection and for the parents to give the infant food and affection can be seen not as dire threats to the animal or to the human psyche, but as exactly the process by which the relative self-reliance of the organism comes into being. By holding to this theoretical stance, Bowlby thus reverses the implications of many of Margaret Mahler's findings while accepting them in principle (Bowlby, 1980b, pp. 322-362). "Separation anxiety," which she and others had made so much of as a specifically human experience, is common to many species (1980b, p. 74).

The changes suggested by Bowlby—although they do take into account evidence on myelination, the common helplessness among newborn of several species, and the new data on stranger fear—do not seem to enrich the perspective of the sexual body. To a great extent, the very aim of Bowlby's theory was to escape from the old Freudian concept of instincts, whether these be sexual or aggressive, and from the instinctual "drives." Instincts so conceived, Freud had acknowledged, "are our mythology. Instincts are mythical entities, magnificent in their indefiniteness" (Freud, 1933, p. 93). Ethology, in its study of survival mechanisms, offered Bowlby a surer sense of instinct.

Processes of survival, as Bowlby showed, underlie the entire development in early childhood of the relations of "attachment" and also of "loss." Survival is not simply a matter of genetic machinery, devoid of feeling; in other words, to argue from ethology is not to reduce the human mind to a biological substrate (Bowlby, 1980a, p. 377). Yet there is something missing in this new instinctual argument, however qualitative it may be, namely the sexual. One would think that inclusion of sexuality would be guaranteed within any theory of survival, but it is of little importance in Bowlby's portrait of the human condition. Perhaps by being so very clear about what he was doing, Bowlby lost some of the valuable confusion of the early psychoanalytic theory of sexuality. In his work, says Bowlby, "I give to the concept of attachment behavior" a central place, a place "distinct from feeding behavior and sexual behavior, and of at least an equal importance" (Bowlby, 1980c, p. 2). But is the sexual actually "distinct" from attachment, or for that matter from feeding behavior? The tradition of psychoanalytic thought, with its commitment to the perspective of the sexual body, would suggest that such distinctions must prove illusory.

One of Bowlby's major interests is the theory of childhood mourning: he studies the psychological behavior patterns of mourning in adult behavior and discovers striking similarities to childhood experiences of loss. The connections between child and adult mourning are buttressed with cross-cultural supporting evidence (Bowlby, 1980c, pp. 126-136). The theory of mourning, however, did not seem applicable to neonates at all; moreover, because of problems in the sheer scope of his research, Bowlby had to limit his observations of mourning so as to largely omit "children younger than about sixteen months" (1980c, p. 412). Unfortunately, this decision limits the integration of considerations on infantile sexuality into a theory of mourning, just as the decision to take up attachment as a distinct phenomenon apart from sexuality prevents its being related to sexuality at all.

Four particular results of Bowlby's theory which lose contact with sexuality are subject to serious criticism. These are its implications for adult sexuality, its attitude toward the sexual body, its defensive constriction within certain theories of Freud, and its largely dysfunctional capacity for social criticism.

Adult sexuality, not dealt with explicitly as such, tends to be overlooked in Bowlby's major formulations about the human life cycle. If we accept that "Not only during childhood but throughout the whole span of life" human beings tend "to react with fear" to the "presence of strangers" and to "darkness" (1980b, p. 86; cf. p. 166), it would seem we prevent ourselves from understanding the exogamous features of falling in love, and of the feelings of the "unknown" (as D.H. Lawrence called it), which at times draw responses other than fear (Alberoni, 1983). As for the fear of darkness, is it really so clear that "Every study" shows it to be "as common at every age as fear of animals. . ." (Bowlby, 1980b, p. 164)? The two fears in any case are of different orders, and among adults, fear of animals depends on which adult you are talking about. But can darkness, the setting for much behavior in adult sex, be associated so closely with fear? Even in the neonate, there is now some startling experimental evidence to show that there is no such fear: Indeed a great deal of very early visual development takes place in darkness and not in the light (Haith, 1980). D.H. Lawrence, who may have had eidetic recall of such darkness, intermixed the imagery of darkness with his imagery of love (Lawrence, 1981). Modern social contexts of sexual involvement do not seem in accord with Bowlby's extrapolation of the early child's experience of trust. The child who grows up "in an ordinary good home with ordinarily affectionate parents" will go through life, we are told, with a deep assurance that "there are always trustworthy figures who will come to his aid" (1980b, p. 208). A great deal of experience tells against this; notably, many sexual love situations take people beyond anything they can rely on in previous experience, and no one outside of the situation can really come to their aid, not even an internalized image of the trusting parent. Surely there are genuinely perplexing experiences of modern consciousness where such assurance is unavailable.

Bowlby does know that the body is important. He argues, in fact, that what is important in the child's learning to be separated from its mother in normal development is not so much its ability to internalize a representation of its mother which it can hold on to while the mother is gone (an idea he suggests may actually contribute to neglect of the child), but the infant's experience of adequate presence of the mother when she is there, with affectionate contact. That is what makes "letting go" possible (1980c, pp. 431-433; see also Emde, Gaensbauer, and Harmon, 1976, p. 196). In other words, bodily presence for inter-action is the infant's real need; this fits well with recent research suggesting there is no obvious connection between the ability to represent an object and the ability to undergo separation (Emde, Gaensbauer, and Harmon, 1976). Representation is less a problem than presence. But the sense of contact, the physical affection stressed by Prescott (1979), is seldom indicated in Bowlby's formulations. In another section, he reveals a surprisingly shallow interest in the body. A five-year-old girl was brought to a psychiatrist because of several related behavioral problems, one of which was "a rigidly stiff neck for which no organic cause was found" (1980c, p. 359). Bowlby's discussion omits anything about the girl's neck; he concludes with a promise to take that up in "the section dealing with somatic symptoms" (p. 361). But there is no such section; the rigid neck of this girl is only brought back for a brief, cursory paragraph in a section on "Identificatory Symptoms: Accidents" (p. 376). That section does not contain any theory of the body, much less the sexual body, nor is there anything in the indexes of this psychoanalytic study of over 1,300 pages about "body" or the somatic. Once the body is left out of a theory, the omission of the sexual body necessarily follows. Bowlby exhibits an incredible amount of disinterest in the somatic, particularly for a work that is so humane and in many ways sane. Ethological considerations, even if they are bodily in their focus, are hardly a reason for avoiding thought about the human, sexual body. On the contrary, ethology unavoidably involves the somatic interaction of live creatures.

Bowlby and the Traditions of the Body in Psychoanalytic Thought

Bowlby's psychoanalytic orientation derives from the British school of object-relations; he notes that one of his supervisors was Melanie Klein, in fact (1980a, p. xvii). He recognizes that his own views diverge from the mainstream, and somewhat defensively declares that many of his innovations are supported in Freud's text (Bowlby, 1980a, pp. xv-xvi). He faults such co-theorists as Winnicott (Bowlby, 1980a, p. 312; 1980c, pp. 321-326), showing that he has no use for the latter's theory of the transitional object. He clearly disagrees with Spitz and Mahler, who make claims that the infant learns to have "object constancy"—only long after other researchers have shown that perceptual capacity on the part of the infant has been well in place (1980c, pp. 372-375). One of Bowlby's disagreements with Spitz in fact gives evidence of Bowlby's unspoken sense of the sexual body: Spitz, despite his own findings to the contrary, emphasized the infant's psychological need for a reliable food supply rather than for warm skin contact with the caretaker (Bowlby, 1980a, p. 375).

There is some confusion in Bowlby's departure from Freud, however, and it may partially defeat his purpose. The book in which Freud most clearly set out, as theory, the view that the infant experiences anxiety through endopsychic processes is *Inhibitions, Symptoms, and Anxiety* (1926a). In that difficult and influential text, Freud is explicit that anxiety occurs irrespective of environmental conditions, and strongly implies that the psychoanalytic thinker or therapist may as well ignore the "real" source of anxiety; ultimately only the endopsychic sources are real. Bowlby reviews Freud's book at some length as part of his general review of the literature on separation anxiety, but gives almost no hint of the crucial issue, which is precisely that Freud's heavily endopsychic emphasis now leaves no room for the very kind of environmental influence which Bowlby wishes to highlight in his study of infantile life. Instead of raising this issue, Bowlby contents himself with offering one more rehash of Freud's erroneous energy concepts, which presumed that what the infant is seeking is freedom from stimulation (Bowlby, 1980b, pp. 381-382). To further the confusion, Bowlby takes it that Freud thereby meant to limit understanding of the infant's primary needs to "those of the body" (Bowlby, 1980b, p. 381), a term by which Bowlby intends to indicate a reductive sense of the body as merely requiring food. Not that Bowlby is mistaken in claiming that his own work is also a development of Freud's revisions of 1926. Freud did give separation anxiety a special place in the human psyche, in this revision of his theory; Bowlby can lay claim to having given that emphasis a scientific connection through ethology. Yet in the process of achieving this feat, Bowlby has lost touch with the reality of the sexual body. We find Bowlby writing a book in which social interactions in the experience of the child and infant are emphasized, and where the avoidable traumas of life are looked to for the origins of illness. Yet Bowlby places that book within a world hypothesis that regards the infant's psyche as a source of innate aggression and fantasies of omnipotence. Bowlby was thus able to bond his theory to the world hypothesis of psychoanalytic thought—at least as that hypothesis has developed since 1926. But in trying also to change that hypothesis, he may have obscured matters further. By having it both ways, in other words, Bowlby may have neither. He is perceived as having made a break with mainstream psychoanalysis, which in crucial respects he has in fact done; but the great work of *Attachment and Loss* nowhere clarifies that break, because it does not recognize its presence.

Social Implications of Bowlby's Revised Psychoanalytic Theory

An issue of greater importance than the correspondence between Bowlby's theory of attachment and the theories of anxiety of the later Freud, is the social implication of *Attachment and Loss*. As I have suggested at the outset of the present study, in matters of the sexual body, the works of psychologists as well as of other scientists do have social implications, whether intended or not, and they also have social consequences. Merely having impact on the direction of research in the future is one social effect. Giving support for emotionally adequate mothering through one's research, as Bowlby has done, has a potentially huge social effect. In itself, no objections to it need be made. As the Bioenergetic therapist and theorist Liss has shown, much of Bowlby's case concerning the needs of infants can be incorporated into a therapeutic project which values the human, sexual body (Liss, 1976). However, if it is true that there is a massive social disturbance in the area of childrearing, one that did not exist until "civilized" times, as I think there is good reason to suppose (Rossi, 1977), then we must recognize that the disturbance has been both cause and effect of further disturbances all through the spectrum of human relationships. From the perspective of the sexual body, such disturbances must be assumed to be sexual in a non-trivial but as yet unspecifiable way. Even without appealing to that perspective, it is evident that in the past few decades, the human race has become a species which threatens its own survival. Nuclear proliferation, toxification of the environment, and the spread of systematic "administrative torture" to some 60 countries around the globe (Chomsky and Herman, 1979) are historically new developments which tell us all too eloquently that something is radically out of control in human existence. To suggest that repairs be made at the level of the mother-infant dyad, without considering the necessary changes that would also have to be made in the self-regulation of adults, both within the family and in other social and institutional relationships, is to point psychoanalysis toward a narrowly familial, ostensibly non-political area of social change. Although Bowlby cannot have been expected to argue a more comprehensive social theory in his warranted special inquiry, his central focus on the mother-infant dyad and the processes of separation is immeasurably more narrow than the radical social changes implied by Prescott or Reich, or for that matter by Freud in his classic period.

Because Bowlby's vast study is done with thoughtful and loving attention to the subject at hand, and with plentiful concern for objections that might be offered against his theory, it must stand as one of the great works in the field of early childhood study. True, Bowlby has finally evaded the sexual body, but if his work is taken in a scientific spirit, the sexuality that is missing from *Attachment and Loss* will be reintroduced by later investigators. In principle there is no reason why an ethological approach must evade the sexual body. Bowlby himself believes that there is only scientific gain rather than loss in his adoption of "concepts such as control system (instead of psychic energy) and developmental pathway (instead of libidinal phase)"; such concepts are "now firmly established as key concepts in all the biological sciences . . ." (Bowlby, 1984, p. 34). The concept of the "developmental pathway" comes from the work of the biologist Waddington (Waddington, 1957); it postulates a strong "self-regulative" component in the biological organism (Bowlby, 1980b, pp. 366-369). In these terminological decisions, Bowlby touches upon the sexual energy issues which Peterfreund's information processing model of psychoanalysis brings up even more sharply. But it could be observed here that a "control system" may still be significantly sexual, essentially a function of the sexual body, or seriously disrupted in that very function as Reich supposed it to be in modern life. Moreover, a "developmental pathway" is not necessarily any the less libidinous for all its being a pathway. The term seems to suggest a desexualized process, but future users of Bowlby's theory need not accept that suggestion.

My strictures should not be taken to mean that it is useless, from the point of view of social criticism, to focus on the maternal-infant relation, or rather on the infant relation to the mother (or "caregiver") in its early, post-neonatal life. There are severe limitations in doing no more than that, but there is also the assumption that at least something significant can be done to change the quality of social life through the actions of individuals, providing such actions attain critical mass, sufficient to change, eventually, the most deeply held root metaphors of the society as a whole. In other words, changes that are not total changes nor recognizably political changes do count in the quality of life. To this extent, I cannot agree with the arguments of Joel Kovel, a radical psychoanalyst. Kovel effectively exposes the bourgeois, business mentality of the psychoanalytic profession, but he is not convincing in his insistence that his clients are really suffering, at base, from capitalism, rather than from illnesses that can be alleviated in psychoanalytic therapy (Kovel, 1981). What Kovel proves is that he believes capitalism is the real problem, but not that worthwhile change is impossible through therapy and the numerous other routes that bring change. Kovel has strongly defended the theory of infantile sexuality, but his Marxist commitments lead him to postpone consideration of the sexual body until such time as Marxist theory revises its own outmoded notion of the human body (Kovel, 1978). The net result of Kovel's revision is a therapeutic project practiced in bad faith: trying to help people within a system that will not allow their improvement. The Reichian priority of improvements in the social areas of childbirth, child-rearing, adult sexuality, creative work and science, with only very selective participation in formal political action of the "party" type, makes better sense as a recommendation for intelligent social participation in a world still undergoing the sexual revolution than does Kovel's revolutionary waiting. And although Bowlby's beautifully articulated contribution toward social change is not an adequate response to the challenges posed by the continuing revision of the sexual body in social life and in specialized research, it is at least a strongly compatible ally of such change.

Information Processing and the Sexual Body

Emanuel Peterfreund's recasting of psychoanalytic theory in the terms of information processing (Peterfreund, 1971) may be one of the most serious pieces of thinking ever done in the tradition of Freud. It is important in the present study because it combines the key elements of (a) a very thorough attempt to remove psychoanalytic thought from its base in sexual "drive" theory and from its dependence on a theory of sexual energy, the libido; (b) a matrix of information processing sufficiently elaborate for the necessary assumptions of psychoanalytic therapy and theory; (c) a commitment to keep within the bounds of scientific theories which are generally accepted by modern biology; (d) a commitment to theoretical inseparability of mind and body; (e) a detailed awareness of sexuality (especially in the adult lives of analysands) in all its complexity, including, (f) the recognition that sexual orgasm is an important, complicated experience. The last two items, (e) and (f) are not made into explicit topical or theoretical headings by Peterfreund, an omission which distorts the emphasis of his argument. Nonetheless, in a theory of the dimensions just outlined, we may expect that the sexual body is not a lost cause. The topic of the sexual body becomes in this theory part of a theory of a mind-body unity marked by conceptual complexity and involving unanswered questions of empirical fact. One problem, however, is the appropriateness of such a unity. Despite a great deal of philosophical effort to resolve the mind-body problem, it still can hardly be considered to be "solved," nor is it easy to dismiss as a pseudo-problem (Efron, 1980; Feigl, 1961). Peterfreund's information processing approach, however, leads to revealing difficulties in relating mind and body; these problems once more show how the challenge posed by psychoanalysis to the human awareness of sexuality is still difficult to accommodate in an overall psychological theory.

Problems arise with the first of the elements listed above—the firm denial that there is any such thing in modern biological knowledge as "sexual psychic energy" (Peterfreund, 1971, p. 55). What psychoanalytic theory had to offer on the basis of its own tradition was a kind of "hydraulic" model for drive-discharge of energy, and a speculative assumption of "fluid" energy mobility within the organism. These, Peterfreund, finds,

> are completely inadequate. The highly specific nature of drives, motility, development, and differentiation are now being dealt with in modern biology with control systems concepts, theories concerning the genetic code, information, information processing, feedback, and so on. (1971, p. 80)

Peterfreund's book demonstrates how the new concepts incorporate and make better sense of the traditional theories. A vigorous criticism is mounted against such older theorists as Phyllis Greenacre (1960), who argued within the assumptions of a generalized psychic energy which could be hypothetically coordinated with developmental processes in the infant (Peterfreund, 1971, pp. 78-81). An even sharper polemic is raised against Edith Jacobson (1964), whose concept of "psychophysiological energy" is derided as having about as much value as a "primitive" and "composite" image, such as would be normal in a dream (Peterfreund, 1971, p. 261). In each of these arguments, however, Peterfreund overlooks rather than confronts some of the real difficulties. Though it is true that "modern biology" is deeply involved with information processing theory, especially since the discovery in 1953 of the DNA processes, that is not the *only* "modern biology" available. The "bioenergetics" of Albert Szent-Györgi (1957) is not mentioned in Peterfreund's extensive bibliography, on energy theories (p. 103). Greenacre's discussion of a labile developmental energy process is part of her discussion of the key topic in psychoanalytic theory, of innate destructive aggression; Peterfreund discards her terminology but also fails to take up the theory of aggression at all, despite his commitment to restate the psychoanalytic findings in information processing terms. Modern biological theory, at least as Peterfreund expounded it in 1971, regarded energy as a value-neutral and purely *quantitative* concept, a point of view that makes most ascriptions of *quality* to energy seem grossly anthropomorhic. But later on in his book, Peterfreund himself is obliged to inject a significant qualitative dimension into his own theory, when he credits (quite properly) the core quality of "empathy" within the psychoanalytic session itself (p. 331).

His own explanations of empathy, as well as his explanation of what Jacobson must really have meant by "psychophysiological energy," are given within the framework of information theory. This kind of explanation often leads him to say that certain information "programs" are able to "activate" feelings.

Yet feelings, if genuinely active—as they must be under a theory of mind-body unity as distinct from a theory of mind control over body—are not simply turned on like so many mechanisms. That would render them one-way recipients of messages which they must obey, despite the terminology of activations and feedback loops. A feeling (as James and Dewey would have argued) not only occurs; it is in turn felt and responded to by the human organism.

We may refer briefly at this point to Sylvan Tomkins' theory of "affect as amplification." After decades of experimentation and theoretical refinement of this theory, Tomkins has now concluded that there is a "powerful connection between stimulus, affect, and response" (Tomkins, 1980, p. 153). As Tomkins goes on to say, this indicates a deep rift between the Kantian notion of the human mind, essentially cognitive, and the mind considered in relation to the "innate affects" which color every experience (pp. 153-154). Information systems language seems unable to credit such a rift; instead it attempts to translate affect into program. Peterfreund shows how well this can be done, but there remains a gap between his enlarged sense of "information" to include affect, and the root metaphor of information as a purely cognitive, affectless signal system.

Is Information Processing an Adequate Root Metaphor for Sexuality?

Beyond the terminological problems are the substantive issues that give rise to the difficulties. These issues have to do with information processing theory itself. I suggest that these issues became unmanageable once information processing theory disposed of the energy concepts such as libido that were scientifically embarrassing to psychoanalysis, according to Peterfreund and many others. But the energy concepts point to a broader problem in psychology and, inevitably, in thinking about human biology. Lewis Wolpert perhaps reveals the general problem in this statement:

> It is not easy now to realize that as late as 1947, the great geneticist Muller thought that the chemical role of DNA was to channel energy changes in the cell. Only when the genes and DNA were thought of in terms of information transfer did the revolution in molecular biology begin. (Wolpert, 1983, p. 216)

The great shift in biological paradigm, unless further elucidated, leaves out the question of *how* information is transferred. What makes it move? What energizes a "process"? Our studies of brain physiology, replete with references to "neural firing," hardly suggest that there is anything that goes on without energy. A fire may give us information, but it still has to burn.

Such terminology is admittedly metaphorical, but it is at the root metaphor level that the issues finally reveal the differences at stake between a theory informed by the perspective of the sexual body and one that attempts to stay clear of that perspective. It is interesting that Peterfreund is aware how loaded with metaphorical language information processing theory is (Peterfreund, 1971, p. 73). However, he maintains that there is no problem because these "anthropomorphizations" in theory are sufficiently redeemed by a high level of explanatory power, which the metaphors of energy lack. A fundamental feature of theory itself, however, is the manner in which explanatory power is always given in terms of one or another root metaphor, according to Pepper. As Hoffman and Nead (1983, p. 517) have shown, information processing theory is replete with *unrecognized* metaphorical terminology, grounded in an eclectic combination of Pepper's Mechanist and Formist world hypotheses. Because of the deep involvement that information processing theorists have with a root metaphor for the mind, the mere fact that Peterfreund probably was not thinking of DNA when he wrote his theory is no objection to the present discussion.

By now, the deep hold on the scientific imagination that information processing has as a root metaphor for life processes has undoubtedly been affected by the profound impact in the sciences of DNA and RNA coding discoveries. In fact the psychoanalyst Stanley Palombo, who followed in Peterfreund's footsteps, ended a book which displayed an information-processing model for the understanding of dreaming and memory, with a kind of salute to the DNA: "For everything of value in life begins with the binding of what is new to the accumulated knowledge of the past, from the DNA molecule to human love" (Palombo, 1978, p. 222). Moreover, in Peterfreund's own model, "information" is a term stretched well beyond its usual meanings, to metaphorically cover all psychological processes, including those requiring the activation of body processes. The problem of energy is still present in his use of "information processing."

There is a comparable difficulty in the earlier suggestion by Robert R. Holt, a prominent psychoanalytic theorist, that energy is not *transmitted* neurally; the nervous impulse could be compared to "the traveling flame of an ignited train of gunpowder" (Holt, 1965, p. 109). What "ignites" this "flame"? Recent exposition of how DNA is "transcribed" into RNA is also thoroughly infused with energy language, but contains no recognition of the fact. Thus Darnell (1983) writes that the "transcribed sequences *are transported* to the cytoplasm . . ." (p. 90, emphasis added). The transcription "is accomplished by" an enzyme process, which "binds" to the DNA, "selects" a location on the DNA nucleotide, and "then moves rapidly down the DNA chain" (p. 91). Darnell is thus led to use an action verb, "moves," and to give it attributions of speed and changing location. There is no reason, as far as I am aware, not to say that these RNA processes involve "motility," traditionally a function of living organisms, and one of the concepts Peterfreund rejects. Recently, at a conference on the state of knowledge concerning DNA, a further suggestion was made: Mark Ptashne of Harvard University reported on research showing that certain proteins "control" whether a gene will activate cells in its DNA pattern or not; DNA could also be turned off, as it were, if the protein contacts it at a different site. This protein process is known to occur in bacteria and is strongly suspected to occur in higher organisms as well (Ptashne, noted in Schmeck, 1983).

In 1984, a new theory of how cells transfer energy was reported by Samuel Besman of U.S.C. The old theory held that energy is carried throughout cell production by a compound called adenosine triphosphate, or A.T.P. New evidence however suggests that for brain, heart, and muscle cells, where energy requirements are comparatively high, a special substance called creatine, produced in the liver, is the effective carrier. While A.T.P. remains at the local cell site where it is produced, creatine moves in a circular pattern, from mitochondria to the wall of a muscle fiber and back again to the mitochondria where it acquires more of the energy molecule, a phosphate, from the A.T.P., and sets out again for the muscle wall fiber. This micro-pattern of energy movement is affected by macro-movement of the organism as a whole: "Exercise stimulates energy production, Dr. Besman said . . ." ("Cells Transfer," 1984). This suggests that chronic energy blockage in the organism such as Reich described under the heading of "armor," even chronic feelings of tension and slackness, are connected with decreased energy production in the body, potentially down to the level of the cell.

The brain cell, which seems to be the part of the body that information processing theorists adopt as their unacknowledged body metaphor for how processing actually occurs, has also come to be seen recently in a new way. As with the transfer of energy by the cells which I have described, the process is now viewed as a two-directional flow pattern. The old model of the neuron (as depicted in textbooks until 20 years ago or even more recently) had a "stalk-like main tube," down which a signal was transmitted, much as if it were a wire.

> But transport in the axon is no longer thought to be a one-way flow. It is now known that there is also a retrograde, or reverse flow, by which substances needed by the cell are brought back up the axon to the main cell body, sometimes even beyond the synapses. (Schmeck, 1984, p. C7)

Since 1975, "many previously unknown neurotransmitters" in brain chemistry have been discovered. In the minute bubbles called "vesicles," near the synapse, it is now believed that more than one such neurotransmitting chemical may be contained in a single site. The technical nature of these findings, their empirical adequacy, and their precise implications are beyond the scope of the present study, but the discoveries lead to one pertinent generalization: energy considerations are crucial to information processing at any level of "information," and all such levels involve the mind-body organism. Moreover, not only are these energy processes crucial, they are also complex. They can no longer be taken for granted by anyone who wishes to propose an information processing theory of psychoanalysis or for that matter a theory of cognitive science. Peterfreund's belief that the "highly specific nature of drives, motility, development and differentiation" (Peterfreund, 1971, p. 80), are given more sophisticated delineation in information processing terms, must be reconsidered in light of the new work which shows that energy processes themselves are not so "highly specific," that is, unidirectional, as was once believed.

A similar argument can be made with respect to mind-body emotional relations. Recent research on the nature of emotion has shown that the human body is more complicated than had been thought: formerly it had been assumed that the physiological basis of emotions is approximately similar for a whole range of emotions from love to fear. But as Richard J. Davidson reports, we now have discovered neural patterns which "strongly suggest that there are unique brain pathways which orchestrate each emotion" (Davidson, quoted in Goleman, 1984c; see Davidson, 1984). These unique brain pathways would not be necessarily incompatible with information processing theory, but they suggest a different and more interesting human body which underlies information as a metaphor for describing human life. The commonly used metaphor of a "feedback loop" now seems to imply an unconscionable simplification of the functional processes of the DNA/RNA, the brain cell, and the mind-body relationships in emotional experience. Information processing theory as it existed at the time Peterfreund wrote his book would now have to be modified to provide an adequate metaphor for describing the human organism, whether in psychological or physiological terms. An energy component has to be incorporated thoroughly into any such theory in order to obtain persuasive force in the context of current research in several disciplines.

In a later revision of his own theory, Peterfreund has stated that the model of the psychoanalytic process which he has constructed has a long way to go before it can make a claim to adequacy of precision: he now regards the various flow-charts of information processing and the explanations he offers as valuable for understanding the "conditions for the occurrence of experiential phenomena" (Peterfreund, 1980, p. 333), but they are not usable as yet for understanding what those phenomena are, in psychological terms. Although he has by no means reversed his opposition to the use of energy constructs, I would interpret his later clarification as at least providing an opening for their reintroduction into theory.

In addition to denying the general notion of psychic energy, Peterfreund has often argued along a complementary axis: not that there is *no* psychosexual energy involved in a psychoanalytic theory of the mind, but that there is no "special" energy. There is only (as one of his quoted sources puts it) "the energy from the metabolic mechanisms that lie behind all the cellular activity involved in behavior" (Dethier and Stellar, 1964, quoted by Peterfreund, 1971, p. 80). But Peterfreund both declines to discuss such energy, and to consider how any energy of whatever description is present at the many levels of his multilevelled information processing theory. Thus his conclusion that there is no *special* sexual psychic energy becomes assured, a function of his choice of terms. In fact, he prevents asking himself pertinent questions about energy and the mind by first constructing a dichotomy between "physical energy" which is lawful, biologically sound, confirmed, and scientifically respectable, and "psychic energy," which is arbitrary, conceptually chaotic, unobservable, and not accepted by modern biology (Peterfreund, 1971, pp. 49-59).

From the perspective of the sexual body, it would have been preferable for psychoanalytic thinking to keep the theory pathways open, provisionally, even with such concepts as "psychophysiological energy," until such time as science begins to develop usable psychic energy findings. There would then be time enough to decide whether the term "libido" should be taken literally (as Peterfreund does) to specify an energy different from all others in the human organism (pp. 54-55), or if it indicates a sexual quality of energy that is compatible with an understanding of the human organism and indeed necessary to make sense of sexuality as well as of the fundamental psychoanalytic generalizations. In this regard, it is significant that Otto Kernberg, in his own reformulation of a psychoanalytic model of the human mind, is led to introduce certain mysterious entities which he labels "affect dispositions" to account for the fact that the processes of object-relations have got to be energized by some force; else they do not function as processes (Kernberg, 1975, pp. 339-341). Energy just does not seem to be avoidable as a concept necessary for understanding the sexual body.

Peterfreund and the Sexual Body

Peterfreund is among the very few analysts to grant that empirical findings which have strongly correlated male erection with REM sleep patterns are significant for psychoanalytic theory (Fisher, 1966). But he does not follow up on his own recognition that these findings tend to confirm Freud's belief that "sexuality has a special place in dream formation" (Peterfreund, 1971, p. 250), except to say that the erections are "sexual stimuli" which may activate "new sources of information and new programming levels" during sleep (p. 285). I cannot agree that the neurophysiology which links the penile erection and the dream process (during REM sleep) is made intelligible this way. Here, just where psychoanalytic information processing theory should be sharpest, it appears helpless. Nothing is gained by calling erections "sexual stimuli."

It is Peterfreund's hope that information theory can be united with the findings of biology to produce a unified theory of mind and body, but his own distinction of physical energy from psychic energy serves to separate the two and to give his theory a mentalistic cast. "Information" thus can easily become a root metaphor that presupposes a mind to read it, rather than a body-mind organism to experience it. Another theorist who has contributed to the further development of the information processing model of psychoanalysis, Robert Rogers, has pointed to "a cognitive bias in Peterfreund's arguments" (Rogers, 1980, p. 29). Rogers argues that Peterfreund was warranted in rejecting Freud's instinctual drive concepts, but not in rejecting wholesale everything that was entailed by these concepts (Rogers, 1980, pp. 29-33).

Rogers himself has gone on to develop the connection of information processing and psychoanalysis in the area of dream interpretation. He shows how certain dreams and the analytical comments on these dreams by the dreamers themselves may be fitted into an information processing framework in such a way that their "textuality" becomes susceptible to determinate interpretations. Yet in this successful application of information processing to psychoanalytic dream interpretation, Rogers, like Peterfreund, takes little note of the specifically sexual content of the dreams. Both of the specimen dreams he analyzes in his article partake heavily of sexual detail. In one of these, a woman struggles to fend off sexual advances, and then, while no longer dreaming, acts out a fear of becoming pregnant. In an interesting feat of analysis, Rogers brings both the dream and the wakeful behavior into one unified framework of information processing (Rogers, 1981, p. 442). In the second dream, the dreamer (this time a man) describes and orders his dream in terms of "anal erotism." The dream ends with the man waking to his own hysterical laughter, which he himself interprets as a symbol of sexual gratification (Rogers, 1981, p. 443). Given the prominence of sexual body imagery in these dreams, I would expect some comment on sexuality and its importance within the information processing theory of psychoanalysis, but none is forthcoming from Rogers, who thus appears to forget his earlier insight into the excessively cognitive orientation of Peterfreund's work.

To return to the work of Peterfreund, we may ask what is the source of his (as well as Rogers') excessive weighting of the cognitive, other than a theoretically insignificant matter of personal taste? Like many information process theorists, Peterfreund's diagrams and vocabulary suggest that the brain (as Lewis Thomas put it) is some sort of "intricate but ultimately simplifiable mass of electronic circuitry governed by wiring diagrams." That might have been a reasonable assumption in the 1950's, but it now appears, Lewis Thomas writes, that the brain might be more like

> a fundamentally endocrine tissue, in which the essential reactions, the internal traffic of nerve impulses, are determined by biochemical activators and their suppressors. (Thomas, 1979, p. 167)

The combination of glandular (endocrine) tissue and biochemical processes suggested by Thomas as the nature of the brain, provides the rudiments of a terminology that is compatible with the perspective of the sexual body. The endocrine system, which Dewey long ago pointed out was involved in even the most abstract thinking (Dewey, 1934, p. 157), is one of the "ductless" glandular sources, providing input directly into the bloodstream, and connected with hormonal adjustments. Thomas' terminology suggests a model of the brain and its functioning that is more scientifically probable than that which Peterfreund had in mind in his concern to align psychoanalysis with science.

Orgasm and Information Processing

There is one especially interesting internal strain within Peterfreund's writing over the issue of the sexual body versus the information-processing brain. His several comments on the orgasm illustrate not merely the point he wishes to make—namely that traditional psychoanalytic theory hopelessly simplifies sexual description down to a matter of drive and discharge—they also reveal a centering of his attention on sexuality that is classically Freudian, but which is nowhere given theoretical recognition in his information-theory terminology. Thus, while his case histories center strongly on sexuality and its problems, there is no chapter or section on the psychoanalytic information-theory of sex.

Orgasm represents a physiological event of "extraordinarily intricate neural, hormonal, muscular and visceral attention" (Peterfreund, 1971, p. 55). To understand it, it is useless to think of the libido "because no relationship has ever been established between sexual psychic energy and the world of biology and neurophysiology" (p. 55; see also p. 154). Reich would certainly have disagreed here, but Reich is not cited. As Peterfreund attempts to make good on his claim that information theory can deal with the theory of orgasm better than classical analysis ever could, he sounds far more classical and even more Reichian than he is aware. Sexuality, Peterfreund holds, is "a highly complex, multidetermined phenomenon which ranges from mild activation to full orgastic discharge . . ." (p. 269). This is undoubtedly so, but the multilevels involve more than a quantitative difference along the progression from mild to full; the "full" orgastic discharge is by all accounts a qualitatively loaded event. In another passage, given in the context of a discussion of the theory of analytic process from the perspective of information theory, Peterfreund comments:

> . . . continued sexual excitement which cannot be consummated (fully abreacted) can be accompanied by tension and stress and a consequent longing for a full discharge. Considerable relief of tension and stress occurs when the full discharge takes place. (1971, p. 353)

Here, the concept of "longing" is a qualitative energy consideration, not well integrated into Peterfreund's theory. The notion of "full discharge" is Reichian, and the emphasis on the "relief of tension and stress" through this discharge is straight out of the classical drive theory of Freud. More important, Peterfreund is using all this sexual material to construct his root metaphor for the dynamics of the analytic process itself. But to subsume all this sexuality under the following abstract axiom merely blurs the sexual emphasis:

> The optimal analytic process makes possible the full activation of many partially activated control systems related to drives and emotions. Clinically, this results in the phenomenon of abreaction. (1971, p. 343, emphasis in original)

The full orgastic discharge and the longing for it when it is blocked suggest a much more sexual metaphor than anyone would guess from the phraseology just quoted; it is not merely one of several "control systems" which are "related to drives and emotions." As if to acknowledge that the statements on orgasm in *Information, Systems and Psychoanalysis* (1971) are not enough, Peterfreund has returned to the problem of representing orgasm and the "sexual control system" in a later publication (Peterfreund, 1980), but has now been careful to admit that the flow-chart he offers is necessarily a highly simplified and schematic one (1980, pp. 339-340). Possibly the very labelling of the orgastic process as a "control" system provides new obscurity; Peterfreund specifies that orgasm involves a loss of voluntary control and a dimming of consciousness.

The liberatory impetus of the classical Freudian assumptions about sexuality within culture is also blurred by Peterfreund, but it is not really buried. In another section of *Information, Systems, and Psychoanalysis*, Peterfreund offers a fine description of how biological activity, including subjective psychological experience, may be understood in terms of information programming at different, inter-related levels (1971, pp. 169-179). In his illustrative examples, however, he again becomes more specifically sexual than his terminology allows, and this time, he also implies a value judgment that has nothing to do with information process theory. Several of his women patients who "had highly traumatic early experience, including repeated enemas," had developed as adults a great fear of intercourse. In effect, they had become subject to an inner voice, "a monitoring conscience," which said to them, "You must not" (p. 172). I see no difficulty in accepting Peterfreund's description of this sort of conscience as a "subroutine" which interferes with "the information processing necessary for normal sexual activity," such as the "activation" of a pleasurable body-image (p. 172). The value judgment, however, should be made explicit: the analyst is in favor of the dissolution of the interfering conscience and the capacity of the woman to have fully gratifying sexual love.

This value judgment of the analyst could be called his "program," but such designation would not change the fact that a value is at stake, one that denies the right of the authoritarian family to inflict repeated enemas on the sexual body of a young girl. Similarly, it is one thing to say, as Peterfreund does, that the analytic situation calls for a "reprogramming" of sexual curiosity, and another to define that reprogramming as "freedom of expression of sexual curiosity in the analytic situation with minimal inhibition of anxiety" (pp. 263-264). The first formulation has the value-free coloration of information processing, while the second honestly makes a culturally sensitive—and complicated—value judgement about sex and the knowledge of sex.

Interestingly, Peterfreund can refer to "a feeling of joy and life," and "an inborn urge to touch," when he is talking about the mother-child relationship (1971, pp. 356-357). Here his opposition to vitalism does not seem to deter him, as it does in theorizing about adult sexuality. In a rhetorical question, Peterfreund asks his readers "what words can describe the qualities of the experiences of love, sexual passion or the sexual orgasm?" (p. 331). He does not describe these qualities, but he knows they are there, somewhere outside his theoretical discourse. Throughout his book, there is a tension between feelings for life, including Peterfreund's astonishment that life goes on at all, and his need for order (see especially p. 99). This tension, however, is a common one, and the psychoanalytic revolution has pointed to the area where that tension is most acute, namely in the dynamics of the sexual body.

If another theorist interested in the uses of information processing theory (and in other cognitive science projects such as Artificial Intelligence) were to reconsider Peterfreund's version of the psychoanalytic process, and if that theorist were not besieged by the contradictory attractions of vitalism and schematic order, than there might be some way to answer the question posed earlier, namely of whether information processing theory is capable of providing a suitable root metaphor for the sexual body. Certainly there are fundamental objections to Peterfreund's reconstruction of the mind in terms of a series of schema which exist in relations of connectivity. Such objections could be derived from Iran-Nejad and Ortony's recent biofunctional model of memory, mental content and awareness, which dispenses with the notion of relatively permanent structures of schema in the mind (Iran-Nejad and Ortony, 1984). I myself would not wish to try to resolve the issue by showing, in the manner of Iran-Nejad and Ortony, that the reality of the sexual body cannot possibly fit the dimensions of Peterfreund's theory, although many aspects do not fit the theory as it stands, as I have tried to show. Rather than a dispute resolvable through an appeal to the facts, I suspect that ultimately what is at stake in the differences of approach to psychology in the work of Peterfreund versus that of, for example, Iran-Nejad and Ortony, is their respective world hypotheses, underlying their respective root metaphors. Iran-Nejad and Ortony do not cite Pepper, but they would rightly be classified as Contextualists in Pepper's categorization of world hypotheses; Peterfreund, insofar as he allows his need for order to dominate his sense of the sexual body, would be an archetypal Formist. To point out these divergences is not to preclude an improved treatment of sexuality and of life energy within information processing theory, even on a Formistic basis. Once that is attempted there will then be opportunity for reassessment.

Kohut's Innovation: The "Self" and the Sexual Body

Given the willingness with which most psychoanalytic thinkers have accepted the notion of innate destructive aggression as a part of human nature, the rise to prominence since the late 1970's of the theories of Heinz Kohut is especially striking. For Kohut did explicitly reject the theory of innate, destructive human aggression. He did this in the course of developing his theory of the Self, and partly in response to criticisms raised regarding his neglect of the topic of aggression in the volume, *The Analysis of the Self* (Kohut, 1971; see Ornstein, 1978, pp. 103-104). The late inclusion of aggression into his theory is hardly a chronological accident; it reflects Kohut the man. Unlike the purveyors of the image of the infant as a little sadist and as asocial raw material to be made into a fit member of society, Kohut is not at all all fascinated with infantile hate and destruction. When he discusses evidence for his theories built on childhood memories, his words seem to glow with delight in describing those phases of mother-infant interaction, such as the game of "little-piggy," in which contact is close and warm. Kohut saw this favorite example as evidence of the infant's ability to experience in play its very early sense of a "cohesive body-self" within the beneficial context of the mother's embrace, "just at the right moment," when the child offers its "total self" for the enjoyment and "confirming approval" of the mother (Kohut, 1978, pp. 742-745). Kohut's sense of destructive aggressive behavior did not center on the infant at all, in fact; he did not even think that adult destructiveness was mainly a matter of people individually losing control of themselves:

> The most gruesome human destructiveness is encountered, not in the form of wild, regressive, and primitive behavior, but in the form of orderly and organized activities in which the perpetrators' destructiveness is alloyed with absolute conviction about their greatness and with their devotion to archaic omnipotent figures. (Kohut, 1978, p. 635)

The speeches of Heinrich Himmler are offered as an instance (Kohut, 1978, p. 635).

Kohut's theory of the infant includes several features that remove it from most current, prevalent psychoanalytic models. For one thing, he eventually came to assume, although in a qualified way, "that even at the very beginning of psychological life," the instinctual drives "are already integrated into larger experiential configurations" (Kohut, 1978, p. 790). Initially, Kohut had assumed that "the child's experience of himself as a body-mind unit" was slowly built up out of "the experiences of single, unconnected body parts and of isolated bodily and mental functions." He points out that this was the assumption of most of his psychoanalytic colleagues. But in his theory of the self, Kohut became "doubtful" about the wisdom of such a view (Kohut, 1978, pp. 746-747). There might even be evidence, he thought, for the existence of "a rudimentary self at the beginning of life . . ." (p. 756). In any event Kohut was not afraid of that possibility, nor did he prefer to place major theoretical weight on evidence extrapolated from the neonate; "we stand on firmer empirical ground" with evidence from early childhood (p. 756). Evidence for at least a rudimentary self in childhood occurs in abundance within the reconstructions of psychoanalytic treatment.

It is the psychoanalytic transaction of analyst/analysand which Kohut values above all else for providing the strongest evidential base for the theory: there, during the prolonged empathetic immersion of the analyst in the mind of the analysand, arises the material that is distinctively psychoanalytic and which cannot be subordinated to conventional empirical canons of evidence. Although Kohut shares little with Reich, he might have agreed with Reich's axiom that "correct clinical observation never leads one astray" (Reich, 1968, p. 34). The problem is that of determining what makes such clinical observation "correct." At least Kohut, like Reich, did not make the error of assuming that the aggression he observed clinically, in the process of conducting analyses, was direct evidence for the existence of an innate destructive instinct in human nature.

Kohut also showed a strong awareness of the differences between the child's "balance of psychic forces" and that of the adult (1978, pp. 861-862); this distinction is not an obvious one in most current psychoanalytic theory which tends to extrapolate entirely from the infant mind to that of the adult. These differences between Kohut and the predominant theories make his divergence on the issue of aggression all the more serious. His contribution may be part of a new theory that carries the original impetus of Freud's work without the moralizing retreats into analogies of sin and evil that have characterized many other adaptations, including some by Freud himself.

We are ready to ask, then, what Kohut's theory of aggression was, as he expressed it in his most advanced work. In *The Restoration of the Self* (1977), the book in which Kohut presented for the first time his actual theory of the self (1977, p. 207), the status of destructive aggression within human nature is taken up directly. "The child's rage and destructiveness," Kohut says, "should not be conceptualized as the expression of a primary instinct that strives toward its goal or searches for an outlet" (1977, p. 118). Kohut is deliberately going against or beyond *Trieb*, or drive-theory; given that, his statement may not be remarkable, although it does tell us that rage and destructiveness are not *primary* instinctual equipment of the human being. What is more, they are not primary within the self either:

> They [rage and destructiveness] should be defined as regression products, as fragments of broader psychological configurations, [they] should be conceived as fragments of the broader psychological configurations that make up the nuclear self. (Kohut, 1977, p. 118)

Nor does emotional expression in infancy prove anything to the contrary: "Although traumatic breaks of empathy (delays) are, of course, experiences to which every infant is unavoidably exposed, the rage manifested by the baby is not primary" (1977, p. 118). Destructiveness of course often occurs. Kohut has no intention of concealing the uglier facts of human nature. But he believes that these should be taken as a secondary line of development.

Kohut in fact arrives at a position much like that of Pepper, writing over 25 years ago. For Pepper, aggression is an "injective," something that is spontaneously injected into a more primary drive toward satisfaction. Once the object of the act is attained (unless it turns out to be a false object) aggression subsides into its usual subordinate position. It is not the basic thing, nor even one of the basic things, people want (Pepper, 1958, pp. 160-166). Although Kohut is arguing a theory of the self as primary rather than a theory of drives as primary, he talks much the same language as Pepper: "Normal, primary, nondestructive aggression, in its primitive as well as in its developed form, subsides as soon as the goals that had been striven for are reached . . . ." However, if there has been a history of chronic and traumatic frustration "in childhood, then chronic narcissistic rage, with all its deleterious consequences, will be established" (Kohut, 1977, p. 121). Explicitly, Kohut disagrees with the Melanie Klein school: there is no need to consider any of the infant's fantasy life nor its expressions of rage "as a primary given—an 'original sin' requiring expiation, a bestial drive that has to be 'tamed' . . ." (1977, p. 124).

Kohut was not guilty, therefore, of one thing he has been accused of by his suspicious colleagues: "elaborating on the contributions of the English object-relations school" and failing to acknowledge that fact (Gargiulo, 1978, p. 616). One effort to show that Kohut derives from the object-relations theory of Fairbairn (Robbins, 1980, pp. 484-488) fails to show how Kohut's theories of the self have any relation to Fairbairn's basic idea that the infant's first psychological internalization of an object is "a defensive measure" brought about by the "unsatisfying" nature of the so-called "original object," namely "the mother and her breast" (Fairbairn, 1965, p. 224). A recent effort to align Kohut with Mahler, on the grounds that both of them envision an early narcissistic phase in the infant (Hamilton, 1982, pp. 41-42) is also wide of the mark. Mahler found the infant at first to be subject to autism and then psychosis, and certainly did not invent or theorize a model of the infant whose "self" was of any positive value.

It is evident that Kohut situated his theory of aggression within assumptions about human nature that were very different from those of Melanie Klein, Anna Freud, or Winnicott. Where they looked at the infant's sexual body and read a message of sadistic hatred or of sexual instincts which will threaten to retard or interrupt character development (A. Freud, 1935, p. 20), Kohut looked at the young child and found a problematic of the self. Kohut also had a different aim: although, like almost all makers of psychoanalytic theory after Freud, he too wanted to get away from the emphasis on "drives" (sexual and other), he saw a clear need to extend the theory in such a way as to make it a world hypothesis in its actual as well as its intended coverage.

Let us now consider two main components of Kohut's special theory of psychoanalysis and attempt to place these with the problems of sexuality and the sexual body which I have located as the most important cultural heritage of psychoanalytic thought. The first of these components is Kohut's proposal for an extension of the psychoanalytic method into the normal practice of all the sciences, and the second is his major theory of the self.

Kohut took the nature of psychoanalytic analysis, with its prolonged, empathetic, introspective immersion by the analyst in the inner life of the analysand, as the primary source of its generalizations as well as the core of its method. Recognizing that this method is seriously different from the time-honored ideal of objective, noninvolved observation, he maintained that it was exactly in its difference that psychoanalysis could make its great contribution. In the near future, Kohut looked forward to the possibility that the analyst would

> become the pacesetter for a change in the hierarchy of values of all the branches of science concerned with man, through a shift from a truth-and-reality morality toward the idealization of empathy, from pride in the scientifically controlled expansion of the self. (Kohut, 1978, p. 676)

Such an expansion would bring human beings together in social relations by uniting science with social values. In outlining this new ideal of science, Kohut immediately recognized certain objections which were soon raised. He did not always have a firm answer to these objections. One such objection was raised by Bennis (1974), namely, that empathy in human social interaction, far from advancing social values, could be (and usually is) used for destructive and manipulative purposes (Kohut, 1978, p. 706). Kohut did not give a direct answer here, except to revert to showing the essential uses of empathy throughout the development of human psychological and social life.

A serious difficulty arises in his further discussion, however, concerning the qualities of empathy itself. In these, the problem posed by the perspective of the sexual body to theory appears just beneath the surface language. Kohut is constrained to avoid the charge that the observer using empathy scientifically would fall back on intuition alone, without the possibility of correction. The analyst resists such "empathic pseudoclosures" by patiently beginning "the greatest variety of possible configurations" and evaluating the emerging factual material in their light, in order to test "the correctness, the exactness, and the relevance of the meaning" that he, the analyst, has given to the materials (Kohut, 1978, p. 711). As a defense of objectivity, this may do, but it is difficult to reconcile this reserved kind of scientific "trial empathy," as Kohut calls it, with the greater claims he makes adjacently for the empathy as a "power that counteracts the human's tendency" in our own era "toward seeing meaninglessness and feeling despair" (p. 713). An "insufficient or faulty empathetic responsiveness" is the cause of psychological distortions of personality; such deprivations produce "intense needs" to be valued and accepted (p. 713). Empathy by its nature is a feeling process, and thus involves emotional processes that are not purely cognitive. To deal with "intense needs" empathetically will require emotional depth and intensity.

Inevitably the range of feelings in this process involves the whole human being, and unless we wish to say that the body and sexuality are disconnected from intense feelings, it involves the sexual body as well. From a Reichian perspective (which Kohut would have rejected), the answer to Bennis' objection cannot be found by reverting to the provisions for caution in the cognitive applications of empathy—these may actually destroy the empathy unless they are followed only as one phase of psychoanalytic inquiry (cf. Dewey, 1934, pp. 144-145). Nor could the intense needs be met without a consideration of the psychological health of the analyst. This would involve a value judgement about sexual health that Kohut declines to make, inasmuch as for him, psychoanalytic training in itself, when completed and followed in good faith, would take care of any problem of destructiveness in the analyst. Other sciences, outside of psychoanalysis, would benefit from an interchange with it, and an acceptance of its empathetic method would also eventually bring the socially destructive uses of their disciplines under control. But the question of the analyst's psychosexual health is inseparable from the basic question asked from the perspective of the sexual body: does psychoanalytic theory in its revised form adequately accommodate sexuality in its extended sense, as Freud proposed? Nor are Kohut's own statements on sexuality very encouraging, as I shall show in a moment. Nonetheless, it is apparent that the problems of science in society that Kohut was addressing are real.

In his psychology of the Self, Kohut extended psychoanalytic theory to reach vital questions that it had so far been unable to address. He emphasized among these the profound feeling of despair—and it is a despair without guilt—of analysands in late middle age over their failure to carry out aims set for themselves in earlier years by their own selves. The resulting "incompleteness" of the self is a major clinical datum, not to be accounted for or dealt with through traditional theoretical equipment. This despair is part of a broad historical shift in the kinds of disturbances psychoanalysts were encountering. The new patients had come from a background of coldness and impersonality, to the extent that the anonymity of the Trial in Kafka's novel has become a common experience.

> Most analysts will, I believe, agree with me that the forms of the psychic illnesses we are treating are changing, that, even though they might still be in the majority, we are seeing fewer people whose disorder is the result of unsolvable inner conflicts, and increasingly more who suffer from having been deprived of the give and take with a close and interested environment that would have enabled them to shed the asocial grandiosity of infancy and thus become self-confident and secure participants in a meaningful world of adults. (Kohut, 1978, p. 681)

Again, Kohut is addressing a most serious cultural problem. It is one that Bowlby has seemed to bypass, in his concentration on the mother-infant dyad. That Kohut could realize, after years of attempting to deal with the new problems within the framework of theory he had already learned (and which he taught to others), that new theoretical developments were needed to meet the new challenges, is entirely to Kohut's credit.

Thus he developed his psychoanalytic psychology of the self. In doing so, however, he tended to separate self and the human body, self and biology, self and sexuality. Indeed one of Kohut's most unsatisfactory innovations is his stipulation that the self arises in the psychological experience of the infant "next to and, more and more, above his experience of body parts and single functions" (1978, p. 749). There is warrant within Freud for regarding auto-erotism as a matter of gaining pleasure from a part of the body, while narcissism represents a more unified kind of self-pleasure. The problem with Kohut's extension of this line of thought is that it tends to ignore the body altogether. Like so many others, Kohut wanted to discuss "broad reconstructions of total feeling states in childhood rather than . . . narrow dynamic interpretations of drives versus defenses" (1978, p. 883). The discussion of drives, he maintained, had led to a mechanical, virtually subhuman discourse. At one point, Kohut compares drive psychology to trying to understand the living organism by means of the psychoanalytic equivalent of organic chemistry (1978, pp. 883-884). Kohut realizes that Freud had taken

> a psychobiological stance when he formulated his observations in terms of drives and psychic energy [but believes] the basic meaning of Freud's theoretical system had gradually changed, that . . . the terms Freud originally meant to fit into a biological frame of reference have now indeed become metaphors that refer to psychological data and psychological relationships. (1978, p. 904)

Even the concept of energy and its "cathexes" should be taken now as a kind of "symbolic logic" of psychology (p. 904). So far as we know about sexual "drive" in psychoanalysis, we know it only as a general quality of driveness that appears in various degrees and functions during our "introspective investigation of inner experience" (p. 227).

Not only can drive not be analyzed in the empathetic transaction except to say that it is an abstraction; if I read Kohut rightly, he is saying it need not be investigated further (1978, p. 227). What this means in effect is that biology may as well be forgotten. But such sidestepping is not convincing. After all, sexual drive sometimes occurs quite dramatically, and not as a mere abstraction that shares a quality of driveness; the belief that Freud's original psychobiology has "gradually" changed to metaphor is wishful; indeed it is virtually magical thinking on Kohut's part, with nothing less in mind than the "gradual" dispersal of sex into verbal metaphors and symbolic logic. If drive psychology eventually degenerated into some version of inorganic chemistry, perhaps that is more due to the cultural habits that tend to classify the human body as an inert corpus rather than a living organism. Besides, if we go back and read Freud's early statements on sexuality, we will find that he did not treat it as mechanical drive, later to be given its metaphorical aura; he spoke daringly of the baffling intermix of physical (sometimes gross physical) sex with sexual symbolism and with figurative language.

Without meaning to, Kohut is following the conceptual trajectory taken by George S. Klein, who also wanted to avoid mere chemistry. Klein, in a serious reconsideration of Freud's theory of sexuality, candidly began by admitting that something has been lost with the failure of the term libido. He admitted that present theories are devoid of any account of what psychic energy is. Then, after a glance in the direction of the old libido concept (Klein thought it not too bad) and perhaps also in the direction of instinctual drives, Klein went on to say that data of a chemical or glandular nature are not useful, because the theory of psychoanalysis is concerned with the "cognitive meaning" of the sexual (Klein, 1967, pp. 178-179). The remarkable thing about Kohut's similar view is that he was not one of those who placed supreme value on the cognitive. In one exchange with a critic, he even affirmed that if it were possible to produce a completely rational humankind, he would not wish to do so, because passion and the irrational are also part of life (1978, p. 915). The cultural pressures toward evading the sexual, however, are so strong, so embedded, so "overdetermined," as psychoanalysis would put it, that Kohut ends up not far from Klein on this matter of the sexual.

What should have been done? Second guessing an original theorist like Kohut is too easy. He took the risks, and his commentator can only follow his thought. But an obvious suggestion must be made. Instead of moving with most other theorists to eliminate drive theory (and with it sexuality), Kohut and others might have read their mandate as one of enlarging and reformulating the theory without losing its core. Thus while "drive" might go, sex cannot. The theoretical demands here are by no means unreasonable. A way of achieving the shift successfully from drive to a better concept of sexual need was opened by Reich in 1921, while Reich was still a young and loyal member of the Viennese psychoanalytic school. Entitling his paper, "Concerning the Energy of Drives," Reich argued that it would never be possible to clarify what the term "drive" meant, at least not in scientific terms suitable for psychology. Yet the term was central. It was therefore advisable to shift the level of inquiry "to the psychological and functional peculiarity of sexual pleasure," which entailed an understanding of the human mind's capacity to "re-experience" that pleasure through its mnemic function. In other words, sexual instinctual drive is better understood in functional terms which explain how the individual self is "assimilated" into the experience of pleasure (Reich, 1975, p. 153). Reich realized that the purely quantitative nature of Freud's notion of an instinctual drive would never permit an adequate grasp of what was at stake in this central function of the human sexual body. Reich's own later work is largely free of any reliance on the "drive" concepts, despite his deep involvement in the dynamics of orgasm. Reich's shift in the level of inquiry worked for him as a way of retaining the sexual body in theory. Kohut, in the final pages of *The Search for the Self*, similarly speaks of his aim to invent a framework which would "not disregard" the value of the old (1978, p. 937); but it appears that he was more successful in relating his theories to what he calls "the group self in the psychoanalytic community" (p. 937) than in continuing Freud's unfinished advance into sexual complexity. It will remain for future users of Kohut's theory to reinvest it with the libido—or with a more sophisticated sexual energy concept—which it needs.

Kohut and the Sexual Body in Therapy

I suggest that Kohut's very language of the self calls for the missing element of the sexual. If we can refer to a "tension arc" between two major elements of the developing self, as Ornstein does in describing Kohut's theories (Ornstein, 1978, p. 99), then we will be led eventually to ask what that "tension arc" consists of in bodily terms. How is such tension felt? What are its physiological correlates? Let us accept Kohut's conclusion that the self does not satisfy itself in the manner of drive tension and release, but instead that it has its fulfillment in "the glow of *joy*," and its blockage in "the anticipation of *despair* e.g. of shame and empty depression" (Kohut, 1978, p. 757). Then let us ask what all those feelings are like, in the body. The glow of joy is going to be connected with the capacity for joy; the glowing quality may even be a feature of what Reich called orgastic potency. The empty depression is also a bodily feeling, an *energy* blockage. Let us also recognize that the plight of the new patient, caught in a "cold" social world and starving for "give and take with a close and interested environment" (Kohut, 1978, p. 681) is experiencing a feeling of contactlessness, which is an energy disturbance. As for the self rising aside from or above the body (which is the implication of Kohut's theory), the suggestion cannot be anything but misleading. It is even possible that the self is a fundamentally *biological* feature of organic life. At least some biologists speak about the distinction between "self" and "not-self" in lower invertebrates (Theodor, 1970, cited by Thomas, 1974, p. 8). Apparently, certain sponge cells will not accept transplants from others of the same species, but will accept such transplants if the donor is taken from closely adjacent organisms of exactly the same features as those which are rejected. Biologists speculate that this cannot be explained on any grounds except that of the self, which is therefore not the highflown self of the human mind. It is very much a body self.

But Kohut eventually had little use for the body in his theory, even though he himself occasionally refers to the "body-self." His description of a patient named Mr. W. is a key instance. After much therapeutic work, Kohut found that it was "the influence of the mother's personality" that lay behind Mr. W.'s troubles. This is no news in psychoanalysis, of course, but it is intriguing that what Kohut says of this mother is that

> while her attitude had been one of dutiful caretaking, of a fulfillment of obligations, she had not been able to relate to the child with calming emotionality. She emerged as a woman . . . deeply insecure about herself—especially about her own body. (Kohut, 1977, pp. 160-161)

Here I perked up, expecting that "body" would have to be a categorical term for the self. But in fact that does not occur. The "body-self" Kohut refers to does not even merit an index entry among the approximately 100 terms glossed under the headings Self, Self-object, and Self-psychology. The Self, Kohut finally says, if taken broadly as "the center of the individual's psychological universe . . . is, like all reality . . . not knowable in its essence. . . . It cannot be defined, now or ever" (1977, pp. 310-311). All that we *can* know is the self "as a specific structure in the mental apparatus" (p. 310). On the one hand it is the very omission of the body which makes self a mystery like that of Soul; on the other, such an omission reduces self to the level of part of a mind machine. If it is true, as one report has it, that Kohut ended a major lecture on his theory before a New York psychoanalytic audience with the fervid question, "*What if man is not an animal?*" (Malcolm, 1983, p. 120), then the resistance to his theories by traditional analysts takes on a more than merely reactionary cast.

To be sure, denials must be expected here: Kohut, just because he doesn't talk body language does not for a moment wish to deny the body; there could be no self worthy of the name that was not first and foremost a body self, and so on. But these protestations cut no theoretical ice, since what they amount to is saying that if we talk a language of mental constructs and of cultural forms such as "ambitions and ideals" (Kohut, 1977, p. 234), and have good motives in doing so, the body will take care of itself. Well, it won't. A gross fact of Mr. W.'s mother being deeply disturbed about her own body gets lost: her sexual body has no theoretical resonance, let alone recognition. And were it to have that recognition, it would only raise the whole question of whether that sort of basic problem should even be thrown into the theory of the Self, or if it is best discussed in terms of natural energy, sexuality, drive, instinct, repression, or denial—indeed in all those terms which are now considered outmoded in psychoanalysis.

Kohut and the Renewal of Sexual Candor in Psychoanalytic Biography

Despite these deep antipathies to the sexual body within Kohut's theory, there is another side to it which encourages the open discussion of the adult sexual body. In his divergence from other psychoanalytic theories of development, Kohut allows for a recognition of the inconvenient or "unruly" aspects of sexuality which do not fit civilized norms, and he does not tilt the balance toward a negative evaluation of these aspects of sexuality. His concept of a "grandiose self," which he postulated as one of the necessary components of the mature self, contradicts the moralizing direction of other psychoanalytic theories: the person's self develops not by becoming progressively attuned to the real world and to the responsibilities it brings, but (in one of its major phases) by constructing a "grandiose self" and to some extent acting upon it. Kohut did not suggest that this aspect of the self was the core of the self, or the sole determinant for maturity. The concept of a grandiose self is a part of his long-term theoretical work on the theory of narcissism. But in that work, and not only in the concept of a grandiose self, Kohut created nonjudgmental theoretical concepts for those needs of the self which could not be confined within conventional notions of mature behavior. In particular, Kohut's creation of the category of the "grandiose self" (which is not to be mistaken for the whole self) serves to allow nonjudgmental thinking with regard to adult sexual contact and sexual relationships, where other theories either insist that sex be a part of the ideal of love or that it be labelled as pathological. His more traditional colleagues in psychoanalysis have taken him to task for such theorizing (see for example, Giovacchini, 1977; Tuttman, 1978). What these abstract formulations on the self might mean in a life situation is shown, I think, in the autobiography of the psychoanalyst Richard C. Robertiello, M.D., a self-acknowledged follower of Kohut (Robertiello, 1979a, p. 7; 1979b, p. 128). Robertiello discusses with candor and self-criticism, but not with self-reproach, his adult sexual life. This includes his several marriages and a number of love affairs outside marriage, including two "primary love relationships" with schizophrenics (p. 119). This is not to suggest that Robertiello's book is devoted to an account of his sexual relationships; indeed the bulk of the book is about his life as a son, a father, and as a grandson, in the light of psychoanalytic concepts he has integrated from Kohut and from other branches of psychoanalysis. It is all the more impressive that he has integrated his self-analytic account of adult sexuality with his childhood experiences. This is no small achievement, and goes a long way to make his book an important addition to the literature of Kohut's theory, as well as to the field of autobiography.

Robertiello's book could signal the beginning of a renewed personal candor in psychoanalytic writing, concerning the analyst as sexual being. Freud had revealed a great deal of himself—over 50 of his own dreams are analyzed in *The Interpretation of Dreams* (Freud, 1900)—but this beginning was not carried very much further by his followers and successors during psychoanalysis' long struggle for professional survival and acceptance. Ernest Jones' long and non-monogamous relation with Loe Kann, a patient of his whom he married (Brome, 1982), has only recently become known; it would appear in fact that Jones had a troubled, not entirely controllable sexual life which is not reflected in his carefully nourished persona as the highly stable pioneer for Freud (Brome, 1982). I suggest that Jones defended against a fear of exposure (to which Brome alludes) by casting aspersions in his biography of Freud against the stability and the character of his rivals among the psychoanalytic pioneers such as Otto Rank and Sandor Ferenzi (Brome, 1967). Robert Coles, Erik H. Erikson's admiring biographer, as well as Erikson himself in autobiographical accounts, showed a great deal of avoidance when it came to dealing with the psychodynamics of Erikson's having been abandoned by his father before birth, being adopted by his Jewish stepfather, Dr. Theodore Homberger, and later changing his name to Erikson and his religious orientation to Christianity (Coles, 1970; Roazen, 1976). Coles' biography in fact is largely silent on the sexual body. It begins with a chapter on Kierkegaard, as a way of introducing Erikson who also lived in Denmark, but well after Kierkegaard had died—an ennobling but evasive strategy. Melanie Klein did not offer a self-analysis of her highly traumatized childhood, in which siblings, with whom she was closely involved, died (Lindon, 1972). When Heinz Hartman was honored with a volume of essays by other analysts, the biographical sketch resembled hagiography, rather than biography, much less Freudian biography. Hartman had lived his adult life, apparently, in "serenity and freedom from conflict . . ." (Eissler and Eissler, 1966, p. 13). David Rapaport seems to have worked himself to death; for example, he sometimes climbed the four flights of stairs to his office at N.Y.U. if he happened to arrive before the elevators started running. At the time, Rapaport was taking a sabbatical from his position as therapist. He did the climbing even though he had a heart condition and chronic leg cramps. Rapaport died of a heart attack in that sabbatical year, 1960, at the age of 49. The account of his life by his friend, the psychoanalytic theorist Robert Holt, is devoid of psychoanalytic comment, although it provides the details I have mentioned (Holt, 1967). Robertiello's autobiography would make such a eulogistic biography uncalled for in his own case; his failings would not need to be concealed. His book is a contribution to the acknowledgement and even the celebration of the analyst as a person with a sexual body, rather than the analyst as idealized mind. Without

Kohut's theoretical advance, Robertiello might not have written what he did, or at least not for publication. In this instance, Kohut's theory helps to make the sexual body comprehensible, even though formally Kohut moves away from it.

Such hopes for a connection between Kohut's theory and the psychoanalytic theory of the adult sexual body, however, are probably futile, at least as the theory stands. With the posthumous publication of Kohut's completion of his theoretical work (Kohut, 1984) and the rise of a "school" of Kohutians, the high cultural status of the "self," conceived in asexual terms, is rapidly obliterating any trace of the sexual body. The ominously entitled volume in Kohut's honor, *The Future of Psychoanalysis*, edited by Arnold Goldberg (Goldberg, 1983) lacks discussion of sex, sexuality, the sexual body, or the body at all. A chapter called "The Phenomenology of the Self" (Meissner, 1983) contributed to this volume by Father W.W. Meissner, S.J., a prominent psychoanalytic theorist and anti-Reichian, is asexual; Meissner does not so much as mention the excellent phenomenological theory of the body by the philosopher Richard M. Zaner (Zaner, 1964, 1967, 1981). The program for the *Seventh Annual Self Psychology Conference*, held in Toronto on October 19-21, 1984, does not breathe a whisper of anything bodily or sexual in its numerous titles for paper and workshops, despite the fact that the focus of this Kohutian conference is given as "Questions and Controversies." Robertiello does not appear as a participant, nor did he contribute to Goldberg's anthology on Kohut's theory. Robertiello's book itself has attracted no attention in the psychoanalytic literature.

There is one interesting exception, however, to the general pattern of desexualization among those theorists dealing with Kohut's innovations. In the volume entitled *Kohut's Legacy* (Stepansky and Goldberg, 1984), Joan A. Lang (1984) takes up the theme of gender identity in the light of Kohut's work. Lang notices that the psychology of the self thus far lacks any specific treatment of gender identity, and locates the source of the omission in the theory's "deemphasis of drives and instincts," as well as in Kohut's unexamined assumption that "sex and gender differences" are fairly obvious biological matters (Lang, 1984, pp. 52-53). Although Lang is correct to deny that obviousness, she makes a dubious choice of empirical evidence for her own point of departure regarding the sexual body. For her, it is "clearly demonstrated" that gender identity is fixed within the child by the age of eighteen months, "in conformity with parental beliefs about their child's sex, regardless of the chromosomal reality" (Lang, 1984, p. 53). But is this actually a clearly demonstrated fact? Lang cites in support the work of Stoller (1968) and Money and Ehrhardt (1974), but as I have argued in "The Adult Sexual Body" (above), the conclusion that gender identity is fixed in accordance with parental beliefs is by no means warranted in view of more recent studies, such as that of Imperato-McGinley et al. (1979). A closer look at research on gender identity and chromosomal factors might have made Lang hesitate in reaching her conclusion that the gender of the parent who serves a "mirroring" function for the infant, usually the mother and therefore female, should not make any difference. Either parent could serve equally as "mirror" or as idealized "selfobject," Lang suggests, and she holds that Kohut supplies no impediment in theory toward this position (Lang, 1984, p. 68). Although I would not accept her reasoning, based on a different perception of the relevant research evidence, I do not wish to dismiss Lang's tentative effort to relate Kohut's theory of the self and the sexual body. Once the problem has been broached, and the theory of the self has been opened to the range of evidence available in research on sexuality, then a major step toward giving the perspective of the sexual body its due has been taken. Any errors of fact and disputes over the interpretation of fact will be resolved, given sufficient investigation and granting a recognition of the incompatibilities of differing world hypotheses.

There are also a few rumblings of discontent in another recent volume devoted to the psychoanalytic theory of empathy, with an emphasis on Kohut's pioneering work in this problem (Lichtenberg, Bornstein, and Silver, 1984). Although 13 of the 15 essays in the volume seem to be quite devoid of any interest in sexuality or the human body, the remaining two essays form an interesting contrast. In one of these, on the topic of infantile experience, Virginia Demos warns that feeling is still important; affect must be given a central role in the understanding of infancy, and we may be making a mistake in expecting that the concept of "empathy" will allow us to remain in touch with affect (Demos, 1984). The other dissenting essay is by William Condon, whose controversial work on the synchrony between infant body movement and adult speech I have discussed in Chapter Six (Condon and Sander, 1974a, 1974b). In his contribution to this volume on empathy, Condon argues eloquently for a consideration of "communication" as something more than the transmission and processing of "information bits" (Condon, 1984, p. 56). But it is plain from the tone and context of this essay that Condon is arguing as an outsider whose ideas have little connection with those of the other contributors, except for that of Demos. Nonetheless, the inclusion of these two essays may prove fruitful to the development of a sexual body perspective within Kohutian theory.

Kohut's own last essay on a recognizably sexual body topic, "A Reexamination of Castration Anxiety" (Kohut, 1984, pp. 13-33), is a disappointment, a disembodiment. No one would guess, while reading this essay, that castration anxiety contains a fearful reference at some point (unconscious or not) to the male sexual organ which is threatened with being cut off. Instead the anxiety is neatly placed within a succession of defects in internalized "selfobjects" (representatives of the person's human surroundings and "available to him as sources of idealized strength and calmness" [Kohut, 1984, pp. 51-52]). Castration anxiety is given its theoretical position in that developmental succession, as is every other sort of crisis, trauma, or neurosis. Not that this is an error. If one grants the basic theory of Kohut's "self," there is no choice but to so place castration anxiety—but the excision of the sexual body does not necessarily follow as a consequence of the theory. In practice, there could be much more attention to the sexual body than within the theory, as Kohut himself showed through most of his career as therapist; but in theory there will have to be a revision which explicitly restores the self to its sexual body connections. Otherwise Kohut's followers will find themselves outside of the psychoanalytic Freudian tradition, operating with a set of concepts that are "above it all," or with too much of a "good thing." Like all adherents to the innumerable split theories of human life referred to by Dewey, they have already come to regard "the higher and ideal things of experience" as essentially disconnected from the flesh (Dewey, 1934, p. 20). In this mind-body split they would find affinity with other psychoanalytic theorists of the present, however. It has been observed that M. Masud R. Khan, the psychoanalyst who has attempted to deny the importance of the recent challenges to current orthodoxy, "considers the self to be an almost mystical source of strength" (Gordon, 1983). And as Gordon points out, there is a fundamental difference with Freud in Khan's attitude. The current orthodoxy thus defends something that Freud would not have recognized, a self beyond the sexual body.

The Case of the Brief "Peck": Theoretical Implications

Kohut's case history material does more than counter his tendency to direct his theoretical efforts away from the problematics of the sexual body; his clinical vignettes are full of suggestions, often implicit or unstated, for further thought regarding the nature of psychosexuality. One such case, discussed in Kohut's last book (1984, pp. 156-160), provides an especially rich context for speculation about the place of the sexual body within self-psychology. This is the case of a man in his mid-forties who repeatedly brought up a certain childhood memory in his analytic sessions with Kohut. The patient had been a very lonely child; once his parents moved from a small town to Chicago, when the boy was four or five years old; here the boy no longer enjoyed "the lively company" of either adults or children. From that point on, his parents were largely absorbed in their professional careers (Kohut, 1984, pp. 156-157). The vivid memory in question is one that moved Kohut; it had "great poignancy" for him (p. 57). It made him feel "a stirring of compassion" for the patient, and this access of emotion in the therapist disrupted the therapeutic quality of empathy which Kohut believed to be essential (p. 157). The memory consisted of "a single, vivid image" of the patient's mother (p. 157), but the father who also was recalled as part of the context of this image, was very important for the meanings which emerged from it. Kohut describes the patient's key memory as follows:

> Dressed up as Madame Pompadour, she [the patient's mother] was giving him a quick goodbye kiss—a "peck," as he called it—carefully avoiding closeness so as not to disturb her elaborate makeup and wig, and then leaving him quickly for a costume ball despite the fact that he was quite sick with high fever and the measles that evening. (Kohut, 1984, p. 157)

The father, who had been waiting outside the child's room, was "dressed up as a knight" (p. 159); evidently the child did see him even though he did not join the goodnight kiss or "peck."

One of Kohut's major points regarding the interpretation of this seemingly bizarre image is that it did not fall into place in a classical Freudian schema: the patient's vivid scene in memory might have turned out to be a screen memory masking deep Oedipal conflicts (p. 158), but no such meaning emerged. On the face of it, the patient's memory might well have been a "moment that bore witness to his early emotional deprivations" (p. 159), but this commonsense idea also turned out to be quite mistaken in the network of associations and psychological needs which the patient came to explore.

The memory kept recurring, even after Kohut had attempted to get the patient past it, and into presumably more significant material, by communicating his compassionate "emotions" to the patient (p. 157). No progress was made until Kohut asked himself why he had felt such compassion in connection with the telling and re-telling of the memory of the "peck." Once Kohut did change his focus to a self-analytical one, he noticed that the memory had an affective context, one in which the body language was important:

> I began to notice . . . that the memory was very vivid, that it stood out in bright colors, so to speak, against the gray-on-gray dreariness of his accounts of lonely childhood masturbation and masturbatory eating. And I was also able to notice that the patient's mood and tone of voice were not depressed when he told of his mother's early leaving. On the contrary he described her in her exciting costume and the waiting father in his knight's outfit with a degree of vitality and pleasure that was completely absent from the accounts of this otherwise dreadful period of his life . . . . (Kohut, 1984, p. 158)

These affective clues did not prove deceptive. What was so valuable for the patient in this memory was a feeling of joyousness in the context of his parents' celebratory mood. The "peck" was an essential component of the cherished image. This memory was not exactly one of having been happy, but it was perhaps the next best thing: it was "a moment in his life from which he tried to derive strength and vitality . . ." (p. 159). Contrary to Kohut's conventional psychoanalytic expectations, the memory did not collapse into, or serve as the denial for, a meaning quite the opposite of its joyous feeling-context; it really did seem to be this patient's psychological equipment for survival and even the nucleus for the development of psychological health. The fact that his parents could be felt, in this one vivid image, as being together and vital was the important thing. The costumes they wore gave their "imagoes" a twofold aspect (p. 159) which did not connote falsity for this patient, but instead permitted the merging of their usual unaffectionate mode of relating to the boy with a greatly amplified sense of their vital union as parents. He could at least *attempt* "to derive strength and vitality from this image" (p. 159). It took many long years, however, before the potential value of this image could be brought to fruition in the context of the analytic situation. Kohut maintains that his ability to empathically understand and value the meaning of this patient's cherished image—and not the therapist's compassion—was what accounted for a decisive shift in the transference. The memory did *not* recur after this shift, and the man's analysis, Kohut reports, led "ultimately . . . to a result that I can without hesitation characterize as a cure" (p. 159).

The absence of the classical "Oedipal triangle" (p. 158) in this vignette is in one sense its theoretical point: It was not a matter of the instinctual drives of aggression and sex, but the needs of the human being struggling to develop as a self. However, the perspective of the sexual body would lead to the assumption that even without a preponderance of Oedipal dynamics, the self is significantly sexual. Here the key element may be the interpersonal constellation within the image of the boy's parents in joyous union and his own sense of himself as the child of such a union. I would suggest that Kohut is rediscovering, in the patient's progression through analysis, the importance of a particular kind of sexual fantasy, which has been described in another psychoanalytic case history dating from the year 1969.

In fact, Marion Milner's *The Hands of the Living God* (Milner, 1969) is probably the most detailed case history in the entire literature of psychoanalysis, and probably one of the longest case histories produced by any of the various psychotherapies. At the climax of the 16 years of Milner's treatment of her schizophrenic patient, Susan, was the key fantasy that the patient finally was able to create: a fantasy in which she had "loving parents in her inner world" (Milner, 1969, p. 337). Milner formulates the theory behind this creation as follows:

> Psychic health seems to be conceived of, unconsciously, as a state in which the two parents are felt to be in creative intercourse within the psyche. (Milner, 1969, p. 362)

Milner describes this fantasy as a "psychoanalytically-observed fact" (p. 362), but I do not think it has been observed at all frequently. It may have been discovered first by Milner herself insofar as it has had any recognition in the field of therapy. In any case, it is hardly a well-known theory. Kohut, in his vignette, seems to have rediscoverd the curative value of a fantasy that Milner found in her work, but one that she did not theorize as part of the dynamics of self-psychology.

Milner's reference to the "creative intercourse" of the internalized parents is phrased in language suggesting sexual union, while Kohut's description of the couple includes the highly sexual image of Madame Pompadour, who is mirthfully involved with a "knight" who is "dressed up" but hardly armored. Milner, in another passage, seems to imply that the fantasy is one of procreation, though not simply of the birth of a child but of a capacity to create basic emotional well-being:

> The task of growing to maturity requires the capacity to set up inside one the fantasy of containing parents who love each other and can be conceived of as creating, in an act of joy and mirth. (Milner, 1969, p. 399)

In terms of Milner's formulation, the mature psyche must "contain" the pair of joyous, loving parents. Her suggestion of "joy and mirth" is not unlike Kohut's patient's perception in his memorable image of his parents dressed in party costumes, but with the complementary feeling of the parents being the ones who joyously contained him in their mirth. From the perspective of the present study we may postulate that the life-sustaining fantasy of Kohut's patient as well as that of Milner's patient contains a reference to the sexual body. It is not a representation of separate parental figures in isolation but of loving parents whose relation implies positive sexual feelings for each other, in fact with each other. Although Kohut was right not to find this fantasy a screen memory for Oedipal conflicts, he is misleading in his apparent assumption that he is dealing with the dynamics of the nuclear self and its "selfobjects" without reference to sexuality.

It should be acknowledged that Milner's patient may warrant the use of Milner's descriptive phrase, "parents who love each other," insofar as her fantasy is concerned, whereas Kohut's patient may only have been able to lay claim to a fantasy of parents who enjoy each other and who include him in their joy during the intense duration of the experience recalled repeatedly in his memory. In the Milner case history, one therapeutic goal was to develop the enabling fantasy of mutually loving parents who create in joy and mirth, while in the Kohut case history, the object was not to create, but to focus empathically upon a fantasy the patient had already developed but which could not function adequately in the interests of the patient's own psychological health until that fantasy was incorporated into his analytic process. Susan, Milner's patient, assuredly did not have any better childhood experience than did Kohut's patient, even though there were many ways in which the two childhood life narratives were not comparable. Despite the considerable differences between the two cases, both histories can be interpreted as evidence that a minimum of affectionate somatosensory contact with the parents during early childhood was vital for the creating of whatever degree of joyous, self-regulated functioning these patients finally were able to attain. The Kohut case vignette is especially interesting theoretically for its suggestion of how one, seemingly very slight, episode of the "peck" could become the effective source for survival, and later in life, for the "cure" which Kohut is able to report. A process of "amplification" of affect (Tomkins, 1980) must have taken place. What these two cases suggest is that in psychoanalysis the therapeutic goal is defined by the capacity of a patient to successfully amplify certain prized or cherished emotional experiences of the sexual body after recalling them to consciousness. This statement of a goal implies that if either Kohut's or Milner's patient had had *adequate* affectionate somatosensory contact during infancy and childhood, it would not have been necessary for them to fall back upon their capacity for the amplification of affect in order to bring themselves to maturity. Amplification is in this context a kind of survival mechanism. It is in this context also a process which requires that there be some genuinely joyous affect which may be amplified; in other words, if Kohut's patient had never experienced anything like the "vital" pair of parents who came into affectionate somatosensory contact with him, even in the minimal form of the "peck," then he would not have been able to progress in his therapy nor in his maturation as an adult. The sexual body basis of health may be glimpsed in these two cases, not in the straightforward sense outlined by Prescott (1979), but in a therapeutic context. From the perspective of the sexual body, the "peck" received by the little boy was essential for his development of what Kohut calls his "nuclear self" (Kohut, 1984, p. 159).

The vignette of the little peck suggests questions for all three of the theories discussed in the present chapter. How does some semblance of "attachment" occur finally, through therapy, when in fact during most of the duration of the childhood of Kohut's patient, such bonding was not in evidence? How does the information processed through this vivid image of the body briefly kissed by his costumed mother become transformed into a life-sustaining fantasy? Perhaps there is significance in the fact that the scene occurred during a time of illness, in which the little boy was "quite sick with high fever" and with the measles (Kohut, 1984, p. 157). This situation may have been one that produced an especially receptive bodily condition, and an amplifying process might have been activated by the fever. For Kohut's self-psychology, some problems might be to understand how the nuclear self incorporates an image of the joyous parental couple, and why it is important that there be an implicit (or explicit) sexual connection between the two members of this couple.

Ethology, Information Processing Theory, and Self Psychology: Current Biases and Long-Term Prospects for the Sexual Body

There seems to be no serious reason why any of the three major revisions in psychoanalytic theory discussed in this chapter could not begin to incorporate a great deal of increased consideration regarding the sexual body. Such biases and omissions as I have brought out in each of the three point to current fissures which cause these theories to lose contact with the sexual body, but there is no reason to regard these fissures as central. Bowlby may have chosen a relatively asexual version of ethology on which to model his theory of attachment; Peterfreund may have been overconfident that he need pay no heed to energy consideration; and Kohut may have succumbed, finally, to the traditional temptations of the theory of the self, namely to erect the theory at a level where it can have no contact with the biological human organism.

These are serious faults and should be recognized as such by any who are concerned that the psychoanalytic tradition continue to speak for the complexity of the sexual body, no matter how professionally embarrassing or institutionally inconvenient it may be to carry on the tradition of Freud. But the faults may be corrected in future revisions of these three theories. The three constitute a group of extraordinary efforts to align psychoanalysis and science. Nor is it science in some futile "quest for certainty" (Dewey, 1929b) that these theorists have in mind. Kohut's interest in the problem of the analyst's active participation in the clinical evidence that his theory values so highly, places his self-psychology within the manifold of projects which recognize that theories are creative constructs. Yet Kohut's self, Peterfreund's conscious and unconscious information processing, and Bowlby's ethologically grounded theory of basic human emotional attachment all stumble continually against a number of unavoidable problems concerning the sexual body. An encouraging recent development is Peterfreund's own honest report of his patients' frequent complaint, during follow-up interviews conducted years after analysis, that far too little attention had been paid to their sexual problems (Peterfreund, 1983; see also Whitman, 1984, p. 383). Perhaps this report indicates the beginning of a change in emphasis in which the sexual body will again begin to receive attentions from some branches of psychoanalysis. While the obvious recommendation of this chapter would be to focus upon sexuality in all three of the theories, I am well aware that psychological theories are most often prized precisely because they do not get very close to the body or to sex at all.

CHAPTER NINE

LICHTENSTEIN, HOLLAND, AND LACAN: AMBIVALENCE TOWARD THE SEXUAL BODY, COOPTATION, AND DEFIANCE

In this chapter I wish to examine the recent psychoanalytic revisionist theories of two more thinkers, Heinz Lichtenstein and Jacques Lacan. Lichtenstein's theory contains provisions which appear to be most favorable to the sexual body, perhaps the most explicit which have been made in the past twenty years within a large comprehensive theory. This explicit emphasis on sexuality is probably exactly what guaranteed that Lichtenstein would be either ignored among other psychoanalytic thinkers or that he would have his theory taken over, co-opted, by others who would de-sexualize it. The desexualization in fact took place in the one field where Lichtenstein has made an impact, that is, in the literary criticism of Norman N. Holland. Lacan's theory, on the other hand, appears to be flourishing even though—unlike Lichtenstein's—it is expressed in terminology that is thoroughly innovative and in language that is extremely hard to comprehend (as almost all his readers agree). Perhaps Lacan made certain that his theory would not be taken over or co-opted by those who might wish to bowdlerize it; he seems the perfect exemplar, in fact, of C.S. Peirce's insight into the "moral aspect" of scientific terminology. Peirce maintained that if you do not want your theory taken over by "loose thinkers," then it should have a "technical vocabulary" which is "composed of words so unattractive" that only serious investigators will dare to adopt it (Peirce, quoted by Hyman, 1955, pp. 369-370). As Alderman points out, there is a strong tradition of semi-deliberate obscurity in European thought, especially in thought that aspires to impart radical insights (Alderman, 1977). Lacan is certainly part of that tradition. But the flourishing of Lacanian theory is also due, I suspect, to its definitive and sophisticated effort to separate psychoanalytic thinking from the sexual body once and for all.

Lichtenstein's Truncated Human Identity

By 1970, when the distinguished psychoanalyst Heinz Lichtenstein published a new theory of sexuality in which the orgasm had a central adult role, the mainstream of psychoanalytic thought had long been turned in an opposite direction. The article, "The Changing Concept of Psychosexual Development" (Lichtenstein, 1977, pp. 263-279), argued that the typical perceptual change during ecstatic orgasm could be regarded as a temporary loss of "object constancy" (Reich called it a "dimming of consciousness"), by means of which the adult was able to renew contact with the deepest, pre-verbal bodily sense of his or her own existence. Lichtenstein was making an attempt to give a biosexual ground to his radical perception, rare among today's psychoanalysts, that what Western civilization would now regard as "normal" social behavior could well be mass illness. The orgasm is the adult's way of getting back to a basic sense of existence, one far more authentic than anything afforded by society's roles.

Lichtenstein's departure from the prevailing asexuality in psychoanalytic thinking is matched by his sharp awareness of the irrational condition of culture in a modern world that has undergone violent disruption, both through wars and social upheavals, and in its sense of values. Taking serious issue with Heinz Hartmann's ego psychology, which holds that human development may be presumed to occur within "an average expectable environment" that is basically favorable to healthy life, Lichtenstein would see that the child's basic need for love and caring is rather more brutally disappointed in today's technological and mass society than it used to be in earlier stages of history, when relatively small communities tended to maintain a kind of parental interest for any member throughout life (1977, pp. 327-331). By the 1970's it made little sense, Lichtenstein said, to tell young people that their adaptation to society's values would help them to fulfill themselves, when in fact "the average *expectable* environment has been transformed into an average unpredictable one" (1977, p. 327).

The radical elements in Lichtenstein's thought also included his position on aggression: unlike most psychoanalysts, Lichtenstein tended to regard aggression as a drive that is less than basic. Aggression is not an "independent variable" on a par with libido, Lichtenstein concludes; it *appears* to be a basic drive only when "the affirmative function of pregenital and genital libidinal satisfaction fails . . ." (Lichtenstein, 1977, p. 275). Indeed a surprisingly Reichian element in Lichtenstein is his belief that libido, far from being a vague unobservable energy, "is relatively accessible to clinical observation . . ." (p. 271). In contrast to others who have labored to remove all trace of energy theory from psychoanalysis, he holds that problems of "energy transformation" within psychological make-up have been "indispensable" to psychoanalytic understanding "because they alone can give account of many important transformation phenomena both in mental development as well as in pathology" (1977, pp. 243-244). Lichtenstein also clearly recognizes that in Freud's "original conceptualization of psychosexual development, the independent variable in the complex processes of human individuation was unquestionably sexuality as it unfolded through the various libidinal stages" (1977, p. 268). Lichtenstein does not believe this emphasis on sexuality was decisively altered until late in the 1930's, when Hartmann proposed "several independent variables of a nonsexual nature" (Lichtenstein, 1977, p. 268). Lichtenstein's theories of sexuality, of its psychoanalytic primacy, and of the chronic disturbance of modern civilization, are enhanced by his awareness of the metaphysical underpinnings of theory, and his acknowledgment, indeed his claim, that psychoanalysis is not merely a psychology but part of a world hypothesis: psychoanalysis has moved "toward a general concern with the psychological fundamentals of the human condition" (1977, p. 365). It asks "more radical questions than any" comparable theory, and it is a tool for changing the world. "In a time of crisis, psychoanalysis should be on the firing line" (1977, p. 367).

On this note, Lichtenstein ends his book, *The Dilemma of Human Identity*. Yet none of his work along the lines just described seems to have had an impact on his own field. His more refined theory of human identity, however, which is offered in the same volume, has been a highly formative influence in a theory of literature developed by Norman N. Holland, who knew Lichtenstein during the latter's long residence in Buffalo. As Lichtenstein acknowledges (1977, p. x), a close relationship existed between Lichtenstein and the so-called "Buffalo School" of critics, and with the Center for the Psychological Study of the Arts at SUNY-Buffalo. Lichtenstein's theory of identity shows many of the problematic marks of theory I have been discussing; as such it provides a recent illustration of how in recent years, even the most radical psychoanalytic thought comes to represent its opposite. Not accidentally, the two elements of Lichtenstein's theory which give it its radical cast, his emphasis on orgasm and the importance of the sexual body in psychoanalytic thought, and his recognition that there is no "normal expectable" society any longer, are exactly what are omitted from consideration in the adaptations made from his work.

But there was also within Lichtenstein an ambivalence of his own toward his radical side, a deep doubt about the sexual body and its potential value, which helped to defuse his innovations and render them harmless. The reversal begins not surprisingly within Lichtenstein's own formulations. His key monograph, "Identity and Sexuality" (1977, pp. 49-122), was originally published separately (Lichtenstein, 1961) with the title, "Identity and Sexuality: A Study of Their Interrelationship in Man," indicating his work's broad, cross-cultural intent. The subtitle was later dropped. The first section is devoted to a consideration—prominently mentioned by Freud in his discussions of the nature of sexuality—of "nonprocreative sexuality" within the human species. In human biology, "sexuality becomes largely independent from the procreative cycles and begins to pervade all human behavior to a much more complete degree than seems to be the case in animals, particularly in the lower animals" (1977, p. 54). Such biological theorizing would seem to be an almost perfect introduction for the topic of psychoanalytic psychology, assuming that one wishes to emphasize its basis in the sexual body. However, within a few pages, Lichtenstein is busy getting sexuality out of the way: "Once sexuality has acted as a pace-setter" in early infancy, "the maintenance of human identity is accomplished by complex means, many of them of a nonsexual nature" (p. 59). It is in clinical findings on human identity that we will see this transformation. What we see in this main thrust of the monograph is, first, a review and fairly uncritical acceptance of the doctrine of infant-mother symbiosis established by Margaret Mahler (Mahler, Pine, and Bergman, 1975), and second, Lichtenstein's own theory of identity as a form of "imprinting." Each of these apparently biological approaches leads to the dubious biological postulate that the human animal alone of all creatures, is inherently imbalanced. "Man," Lichtenstein affirms at the end of "Identity and Sexuality" is "this particular living being whose fundamental biological imbalance can only be stabilized through a never ending process" of identity-making (1977, p. 120).

The assertions on symbiotic lines cannot be maintained in the face of evidence I have adduced from recent research. We can no longer assume, as Lichtenstein does,

> the fact that the relation between mother and infant does, from the infant's viewpoint . . . represent an inner state of oneness, in which there is no differentiation between the infant's I and the mother. (Lichtenstein, 1977, p. 65)

". . . I am inclined," Lichtenstein wrote in another passage, "to see in the early mother-child unit, and not in its breaking up, the primary condition for identity in man." It is "the very extremeness of the symbiotic relation of the human child to his mother" that "becomes the very source of the emergence of *human* identity" (1977, p. 72). This language, with its repetition of the intensifier, "very" and the "extremeness" that Lichtenstein assumes into the dyad, shows that Lichtenstein had not been taking into account the kinds of data I have discussed, where the process of fusion and separation is too flexible to even call for the notion of a "breaking up." In the light of more recent evidence, the idea of a symbiotic unity of infant with mother may now be taken with several grains of salt. Lichtenstein's assumption that unconscious preverbal communication between mother and infant is evidence of the singleness of their two persons was not a logical necessity even in terms of his own theory at the time he wrote his essay. Indeed there could be no communication, strictly speaking, if the two are already fused. Early undisturbed infant-mother contact could make sense as support for a theory of undistorted communication between a mother and an infant who had some sense of being separate, prior to the infant's learning of language. But that would be something quite different than a single state of consciousness in two people.

The point at which Lichtenstein diverges from Mahler is in his explanation of the creation of human identity through the process referred to in ethology as "imprinting." Lichtenstein is aware that he is employing the concept of imprinting as an analogy, but seems unaware that it is, even in the animal kingdom, an abstraction—a metaphor in fact—of how identity passes from mother to infant. As Stratton now argues, psychobiologists themselves have come to realize that when we try to explain identity by means of imprinting, "this amounts to explaining one unknown by another, possibly even more obscure, mystery." It may now even be more feasible "to explain animal imprinting in terms of what we have discovered about human bonding" (Stratton, 1982b, p. 394).

Lichtenstein's ambivalence toward the sexual body stems in part from his intellectual roots in the European Humanist tradition. He is able to say that human imprinting results in an individual identity, whereas animal imprinting leads to a species identity without significant individuation. However, the very metaphor of the imprint serves to render this distinction powerless to delineate what is preciously human. Whereas the animal at least has at its disposal the adaptational repertoire of its species, the "unique" human identity would lock the adult into the range of behavior (allowing for the play of identity "theme") that was originally imprinted by the mother. The question might be raised, what function could the mechanical concept of imprinting have for a psychoanalyst who really wishes to stress psychosexuality and the irrational social world of the late twentieth century? I suggest that his emphasis on imprinting is a function of Lichtenstein's ambivalence toward the sexual body. I say this because, in his exposition, imprinting soon takes on a thoroughly mentalized aspect. It is as if the mother transmits a code by way of brain waves to the infant and imprints it. Needless to say, this idea interferes mightily with Lichtenstein's stated goal of avoiding decisively the Cartesian ideological bias of mind over body (Lichtenstein, 1977, pp. 67-68; 267). Indeed, Lichtenstein's admirable attempt to reintroduce the adult orgasm into his psychological theory is hampered by his simultaneous insistence that adult, sexual, ecstatic states are modelled structurally after the early fusion in contact of mother and infant: "In the primitive sensory interchanges taking place between mother and infant one could see the precursor of adult sexuality" (1977, p. 77). However, if these early exchanges are pregenital, as Lichtenstein has acknowledged (1977, p. 207), then the change to genital contact in the adult is unaccounted for in this infantile precursor. Given the terms of the theory, it cannot be accounted for: within the theory of Lichtenstein, as he puts it, "man cannot ever experience his identity except . . . within the variations of a symbiotically structured *Umwelt*" (1977, p. 73). "Cannot ever" is a terribly long time, covering all of adult life as well as all human life throughout history.

These objections are not meant to deny the reality of whatever impact mothers have on the identities of their babies. Such effects surely are major. The point is that it is inept and even socially dangerous to state that the process is one of special human imprinting, and to pay no attention to the bodily, physiological qualities and conditions, nor to the qualitative differences between individual adult female bodies. Thus a mother who transmits an identity to her infant, whatever that process may really be like, but does so with her emotional capacity held back or hampered, will be doing a much different thing from a mother who enjoys a context of emotional well-being. The fact that both babies will survive except under the most extreme conditions, and that both will have "identity themes," tells us only what we can learn through the lowest common denominator, which is to say very little.

The qualitative differences might be highly affected by a process of the sexual body to which I referred briefly in an earlier context in Chapter Six: Suppose that it should turn out to be the case that the emotional bonding of mother and infant is more easily facilitated in cases where bodily contact is maintained for some hours just after birth. For this supposition we have some evidence, as Alice Rossi has argued (Rossi, 1977, p. 19), although this evidence is insufficient to warrant a claim of verification. Rossi suggested that the process of early bonding has an inherent relation to the fact that in pregnancy, estrogen levels increase by a factor of 10 while progesterone goes up to 100 times its usual level. These levels are still relatively high just after birth (Rossi, 1977, pp. 19-20). The hormonal levels then decline over a period of days or weeks, with varying rates, and with individual differences among mothers (Rossi, personal communication, August 8, 1983). It is one thing to say that the meaning of such hormonal data is as yet unknown; it is quite another to ignore the data and to speak solely about a single process of imprinting. What Lichtenstein does is create a metaphor for identity formation which seems to be that of the template. It is as though there were a preformed template within the mother's mind, through which an identity theme is transmitted to another receiving template in the infant, thus systematically bypassing any physiological variables. That the earliest mother-infant interactions are crucial to Lichtenstein's theory of imprinting could not be denied, but neither could the sexual chemistry. As Rossi points out, the process is sexual for a long time: "The infant's crying stimulates the secretion of oxytocin in the mother which triggers uterine contractions and nipple erection preparatory to nursing" (Rossi, 1977, p. 6). It is during the months of the occurrence of this process that Lichtenstein proposes a biological principle at work which is unique to humans. If we choose to redefine reality despite the original psychoanalytic terms, and find that reality, especially that part which sustains human identity, is nonsexual, then we merely add to the reinvention of the asexual infant that I have discussed in an earlier chapter.

The confusion caused by the unacknowledged template metaphor is not relieved by referring to body surfaces, that is, to the series of touch contacts that goes with the transmission of identity, since this merely makes the entire body into a template—an elaborate information processing machine with nothing to account for the fact that it runs, and that it can run in radically different ways. We still have to distinguish what it is that makes some transmissions warm and emotionally sustaining while others are emotionally crippling and produce a rigid personality incapable of change or growth.

Holland's Denial of Adult Experience

Lichtenstein's theory of human identity has found a reception in literary criticism. Norman N. Holland, who has adapted the theory of the "identity theme," is the preeminent theorist of a network of recent psychoanalytic critics of literature. Social psychologists would do well to take note of the phenomenon of the growth, within the nominally unscientific field of literary study, of a theory such as psychoanalysis which has not been able to establish strong institutional support within the domain of academic psychology. Indeed one of the strengths of the psychoanalytic criticism network is the sense of community generated within a group of individuals who have undergone (in many cases) considerable psychoanalytic therapy and self-analysis, and thus have found themselves profoundly in accord with psychoanalytic assumptions; yet they perceive themselves as under continual attack from most of their colleagues on grounds that are pre-Freudian, that is, "off the board" as far as theory is concerned. Such a group may be predicted to work cooperatively and intelligently to protect and promulgate its own view of the world.

A leader like Holland, who offers a way out of traditional literary analysis by reducing reading experience to whatever it may mean within the individual's private "identity theme," can serve not only to meet the needs of such a group, but to attract many additional professional readers of literature who might be otherwise troubled by literature's radical social illuminations (Efron, 1968). Holland's approach has the further advantage, not available to clinicians, of denying that psychoanalysis has to meet any test of effectiveness: by making "identity theory" central to psychoanalytic theory, "psychoanalysis need no longer try to present itself in a medical package of diagnosis, procedure, and prognosis." Identity theory has no connection with the classical topics, now exhausted, "of early clinical generalization—Oedipus complex, penis envy, castration anxiety, neurosis." Instead, identity theory aligns psychoanalysis "with the strong tradition of psychological experimentation on perception" (Holland, 1978, pp. 466-467). The earlier distressing topics, with all their reference to the sexual body, thus may be left behind, in favor of a new focus upon the "higher mental processes" through which humans construct their realities. This focus, however, harbors ill for any continuation of the psychoanalytic tradition, which has stressed the unconscious motivations rather than the so-called higher processes. Moreover, the phrase "higher mental processes" is taken by Holland from Neisser's *Cognitive Psychology* (Holland, 1978, p. 467, quoting Neisser, 1967, pp. 10, 305). That Holland is drawn to Neisser's branch of cognitive theory accords well with the use of Lichtenstein's identity-theme concept to deny the possibility of adult change. One of the difficulties with Neisser's theory is precisely its inability to account for the incorporation of new, dissonant, "information" into the mind. For Neisser as for Holland, "people only learn what they have schemata for and ignore everything else" (Iran-Nejad and Ortony, 1984, p. 200, referring to Neisser, 1976). The trouble is, people who are not totally defensive can be observed to take startled notice of many perceptions which do not fit their preestablished schemata and which are for that reason troubling, challenging, or delightful. Holland's move toward a cognitive emphasis in the late 1970's prefigured his recent further deemphasis of psychoanalytic theory in his book *Laughter* (Holland, 1982) and in his article with Kintgen (Kintgen and Holland, 1984); the latter is almost free of psychoanalytic thought, attitude, or terminology, even as it continues to argue for the controlling force of individual identity in the reading processes.

In this transition out of the psychoanalytic world hypothesis and into cognitive psychology, the major problem for the perspective of the sexual body occurred through Holland's mode of extensive borrowing from Lichtenstein. Although he relies almost exclusively on the monograph "Identity and Sexuality: A Study of their Relationship in Man," Holland writes as if the identity theory had no connection with sexuality. Identity becomes a largely cognitive matter, although unconscious processes remain important. This is no small job of bodily and genital excision, inasmuch as Lichtenstein's monograph centers on the case history of a woman patient who was deeply involved with alcohol, prostitution and lesbianism. These sexual body dimensions simply disappear in Holland's appropriation of Lichtenstein's theory, as does all of the sexuality. In an empirical study of how different readers respond to literary works, Holland holds that "bodily derived drives are far from fine enough" to tell us anything worth knowing about the reading process (Holland, 1975a, pp. 53-54). His statement illustrates my contention that "the drives" are convenient straw men for theorists who would prefer to dispense with the sexual body. Holland's long-term associates at Buffalo, Murray Schwartz and David Willbern, believe that psychoanalytic theory and the literary criticism deriving from it underwent "an advance" as the theory shifted its focus and its base, "from a somatic to a social world" (Schwartz and Willbern, 1982, p. 210). Schwartz and Willbern refer to "Lichtenstein's and Holland's uses of 'identity themes'" (p. 211) as if there were no distinction to be made between the two thinkers, and without mentioning that for Lichtenstein, identity was inextricably bound to sexuality.

Holland's adaptation of Lichtenstein's theory is explained in terms which are themselves highly cognitive in orientation, despite his use of an analogy from music: "We can be precise about individuality by conceiving the individual as living out variations on an identity theme much as a musician might play out an infinity of variations on a single melody." The theme, however musical, can be deduced ("we discover" it) "by abstracting it from its variations" (Holland, 1975b, p. 814). The origin of this theme is to be found in the mother-infant interactions during the first year of the infant's life. Despite attention in some of Holland's formulations to the needs of the *infant's* "style" (a theoretical decision which allows for the inconsistent notion that a precursor of identity already exists prior to the imprinting of the "primary" one), as well as to the style of the mother (Holland, 1978, p. 452), the direction of imprinting is entirely clear: from mother onto infant. "The mother . . . imprints on the infant . . . a 'primary identity'," which remains "invariant" throughout all the experiences of life, providing "an unchanging inner form or core of continuity" (Holland, 1975b, p. 814). Overlooking the implications of his own terminology here, Holland also stipulates that the *unchanging* core is capable of "infinite" variation. In the adult, Holland also assumes "such an invariant identity theme," which can again be deduced from its variations to reveal "the invariant sameness," or "an unchanging essence" of the human being (Holland, 1975b, p. 815). How an "invariant sameness" can have "infinite" variations is hardly clear, although the quest for certainty (Dewey, 1929b) in the "unchanging essence" is clear enough. It is also clear what we are to do, according to this theory: as we read a work of literature, "all of us" use the new work to reconstruct once more the old theme; we use the work, not only to symbolize ourselves, but "finally to replicate ourselves" (Holland, 1975b, p. 816).

A feature of Holland's theory especially relevant to the energy functions of the sexual body is the stipulation that the reader must also employ the "particular pattern" of defensive mechanisms and adaptational strategies, fully consistent with the identity theme, "that he keeps between himself and the world" (1975b, p. 817). In Holland's reasoning, this defensive layer is what enables the experience to take place at all. From my own Deweyan assumptions, it is that very buffering which is guaranteed to neutralize new experience—whether literary or other (Efron, 1977). To insist on keeping something between oneself and the experience is ultimately to deny its qualitative impact. In literary experience, the defensive barrier prevents any aspects of a literary work which might not fit comfortably with the established, unchangeable identity theme from reaching the reader's self. A defensive buffer maintained in human relations would make it impossible to have anything like spontaneous interaction or direct human contacts.

The facts of infantile psychology and development are again at stake here. Following Lichtenstein, Holland assumes that identity is noninstinctual: "In animals, identity is expressed in fixed instincts . . . . But we are not given an identity by instinct. Rather we are seduced into becoming ourselves by the love and nurture we receive in infancy" (Holland, 1978, p. 468). This is far too sharp a distinction, however, to accord with what is now known of animal or human identity: we could as well say the young mammal or bird has no instinctually given identity because it will not develop normally (perhaps will not even survive) unless given maternal attention (not just feeding), and that the attentions given by Harlow's mother monkeys to their young are a way of seducing and loving them into becoming themselves. It is not out of the question to suppose that monkeys too have their identity themes; a theory which holds that an infant *homo sapiens* needs love and nurturing so that it can develop identity is perhaps no more than a partial restatement of Prescott's findings of the importance for human development of affectionate somatosensory contact. Whether one wishes to refer to "instinct" or, tendentiously, to "fixed instinct," within the somatosensory contact processes is a secondary matter. The prime point is that the body is integral to identity, whether in the infant or the adult. In the tradition of Freudian psychoanalysis, the body also is sexual.

Holland often contrasts the cognitive life, the creation of meanings and the maintenance of identity, with all that is instinctual and physiological. Identity is not a matter of "physical and chemical laws" (1978, p. 468). Yet despite his denigration of such laws, Holland refers in adjacent paragraphs to the incorporation of chemical processes such as the triggering of brains cells in perception (1978, p. 468) within a "holistic" approach. This is a somewhat confusing combination, but it is an acknowledgment, however subordinated, that physical and bodily processes must be included in any psychology that hopes to be persuasive. It remains extremely doubtful whether any psychoanalytic psychology can dispense with the sexual body. In this respect, it is worth noticing that Holland retains a certain amount of reference to anality and (especially) orality, from the classical Freudian developmental stages in his work, and he also refers favorably at one point (Holland, 1975a, p. 258) to the bodily correlations of psychoanalytic concepts developed by the psychoanalyst Franz Alexander in the 1930's. But Holland's own thinking about the body is undeveloped. Despite his affirmation of the "holistic" approach, he is still confident that there are "fixed, transpersonal entities like pancreas or femur," but these contrast in their fixed nature with the processes of human identity (1978, p. 467). His own preference for such terms as "invariant" and "exactly matched" and "replicate" to describe identity deprive this contrast of its rhetorically intended effect. More important, the facts of the human body do not sustain the contrast either, even though the body is generally made to seem "dumb" by cognitively oriented theorists. Thus, to take the example of the femur: far from being a fixed entity, there is evidence that like all human bones it is part of a bioenergetic process. Emotions affect bone processes, and those processes include the formation of blood within the marrow. Ladenbauer-Bellis, a Yale biochemist working in the department of orthopedic surgery, has given a preliminary description of the relation between bone and emotion. Bone is crucial to movement and posture, and hence to any psychology that takes the body seriously. Its calcification processes are not independent, but require muscle activity. Armoring, in Reich's sense, is pertinent here (Ladenbauer-Bellis, 1980a, 1980b) since it could interfere with these processes. The bioenergetic therapist Curtis Turchin has described a method of "Working with Bone" (1979, p. 68).

Two highly effective statements of Holland's theory are given in his examination of the identity themes of George Bernard Shaw and Robert Frost (Holland, 1975b, 1978). Both studies may serve to illustrate my own argument that psychoanalytic theory now aims to deny adult sexual reality and the related radical social insights of the early psychoanalytic revolution itself.

George Bernard Shaw's Desexualization

Using psychoanalytic theories of orality, Holland gives a certain amount of attention to Shaw's bodily life in early childhood and infancy; Shaw had a lifelong interest in eating and orating. A neglected child, "his life-style might be a response to an absent mother and an empty mouth" (1978, p. 479). From such considerations, Shaw's identity theme is duly abstracted, and what it gives Holland is an astonishing sense of certainty: "an unchanging inner core with which *I can understand how Shaw shaped every phase of his life from the most public to the most personal*" (p. 457, emphasis added). The hazards of reducing Shaw's many plays to the dimension of Shaw's own motivation, his need to reassure himself that his absent mother had neither abandoned him nor mis-nurtured him, do not worry Holland: "we have got what was wanting, a way of talking *rigorously* about the individual human being" (Holland, 1978, p. 465, emphasis added).

There seems to be no reason to take seriously Holland's claim that he can understand the shaping of "every phase" of Shaw's life, since such a feat would imply an understanding of the literary creations in Shaw's plays, and of their complexity as explorations and criticisms of Western culture. But if the identity theme has the merits claimed for it, then at least we *should* have here a valuable way of talking about Shaw the man if not of Shaw the artist. In Holland's own practice, however, the infantile derivation of the theme is only imposed over Shaw's adult sexuality. The crux of the problem is Shaw's statement on sex to Frank Harris, analyzed by Holland:

> I liked sexual intercourse because of its amazing power of producing a celestial flood of emotion and exaltation of existence, which, however momentary, gave me a sample of what may one day be the normal state of being for mankind in intellectual ecstasy. I always gave the widest expression to this in a torrent of words, partly because I felt it due to the woman to know what I felt in her arms, and partly because I wanted her to share it. (Shaw, quoted by Holland, 1978, p. 457)

In Holland's analysis, Shaw is credited with virtual contempt for "physical, not mental, ejaculation . . ." (p. 457); Shaw has that "frank lack of emotion in a man who is at home only with fantasies, puppets, disguises, and applause" (1978, p. 464). To be sure, Shaw in the statement quoted above is describing his habitual manner of promptly translating sexual experience into an augury of social-utopian intellectual ecstasy, and of "sharing," that is imposing, this view on the sexual partner. From virtually any psychoanalytic perspective, including the Reichian, there is an indication in this intimate account by Shaw of sexual disturbance. However, the fact is that Shaw obviously knew that he could only get this great peak of "emotion and exaltation of existence" through physical lovemaking or "sexual intercourse." Sex therefore was not some mental puppet which could be used to perform certain identity functions, nor was it merely a fantasy without sexual body participations. On the contrary, it is a sexual body experience which makes possible an elaboration in fantasy that Shaw cherished. Holland introduces the misleading consideration that "Shaw did not prize sexuality as an end in its physical self" (p. 457). But no one who has examined the function of the orgasm would prize it for that either, if by "physical" is meant the exclusion of emotion. Thus, Holland's claims for the all-knowing power of the identity theme falls to the complexities of adult sexual experience.

Robert Frost's Clarification of the Suffering of the Body

Holland's treatment of Robert Frost brings up a problem of a different order. Frost, in a statement on poetics which Holland himself regards as highly characteristic of the man and his identity theme, said that a good poem, after beginning in delight, assuming direction, and running "a course of lucky events," then

> ends in a clarification of life—not necessarily a great clarification, such as sects and cults are founded on, but in a momentary stay against confusion. (Frost, quoted by Holland, 1975b, p. 820)

The problem here is not only whether this statement can be made to fit within Frost's identity theme, nor even if Frost's poetry entirely fits that theme, but whether, given the terms of that theory, there could be room for any "clarification of life," even one that is a purely momentary "stay against confusion." In terms of Holland's theory, these words of Frost would be part of the poet's efforts to "avoid emotional and cognitive dissonance" (Holland, 1975b, p. 818), a task for which the identity theme is, presumably, well equipped. However, if "clarification" is meant to *refer* to anything in cultural, historical, or social life, the identity theme theory has only reductive force. We can imagine through considerations of identity how Frost might have been transforming a personal infantile fantasy into a "total experience of esthetic, moral, intellectual, or social coherence and significance" (Holland, 1975b, p. 818); but Holland, as a reader immersed in his own theory of the identity theme, is obliged simply to transform that cultural significance back to its meanings within Frost's infantile needs. In this, Holland is an exemplar of the results of psychoanalytic theory's own immersion in the fantasy-besieged infantile body for more than half a century (see Chapters Three and Six, above).

To bring out the implications for the perspective of the sexual body in Holland's theory of the literary artist when it is applied not to the man but to the man's work, I would like to consider briefly Robert Frost's "A Masque of Reason," composed in 1943 (Frost, 1949, pp. 587-606). In this work, Frost attempts a "clarification of life"—*human* life and not only his own identity— through a reconsideration of the ancient Biblical drama of the trials of Job. By virtue of its scope, this work challenges the identity theme Holland ascribes to Frost, namely, to deal with "*huge unknown forces of sex and aggression by smaller symbols,*" or "*to manage great unmanageable unknowns by means of small knowns*" (Holland, 1975b, p. 818; emphasis in original). Frost's direct presentation of God, the Devil, and Job (as well as the creation of Job's wife, Thyatira) does not fit the formula of dealing with the great unknowns by means of smaller scale symbolization. "The Masque of Reason," furthermore, was regarded by Frost as a major work: Frost once confided that the "Masque of Reason" is his central work: "All my poetry is a footnote to it" (Frost, quoted in Nitchie, 1978, p. 151).

The first extended speech in the poem, as Thompson and Winnick (1976, p. 118) point out, is "God's Speech to Job." God undertakes to thank Job for his services to God. But God also explains why it has taken some one thousand years for him to say this to Job.

> I have no doubt
> You realize by now the part you played
> To stultify the Deuteronomist
> And change the tenor of religious thought.
> My thanks are to you for releasing me
> From moral bondage to the human race.
> The only free will there at first was man's

> Who could do good or evil as he chose.
> I had no choice but to follow him
> With forfeits and rewards he understood—
> Unless I liked to suffer loss of worship.
> I had to prosper good and punish evil.
> You changed all that. You set me free to reign.
> You are the Emancipator of your God,
> And as such I promote you to a saint.
> (Frost, 1949, pp. 589-590)[1]

We may fairly consider these lines as part of an attempted "clarification of life," in which the subject matter is the relation of Man and God in the Judeo-Christian tradition. The clarification attempted here consists of an exhibition of arbitrary contradictions within that arrangement. Frost conveys a certain gratification in making this exposure, and we may join with the poet in this feeling. But the *significance* is not his identity theme. Indeed, this poem challenges the validity of the theme Holland constructs: is Frost avoiding "emotional and cognitive dissonance" (Holland, 1975b, p. 818) here, or is he actually creating it? Using Holland's theory, the latter possibility cannot even be considered. For one thing, the identity theme theory requires that the literary production be a unified product of both unconscious fantasy and conscious literary effort. But the theory thus loses the possibility of unconscious meanings, unintended by the author, which sustains "emotional and cognitive confusion" as a positive aesthetic experience. In "A Masque of Reason," such unconscious intention did have a powerful effect on the play. Thompson and Winnick (1976, pp. 117-121) leave no doubt that consciously Frost did not intend the play as a criticism of God nor of any of the traditional cultural arguments which justify the suffering of human beings. He intended just the opposite. Yet God's speech to Job unavoidably suggests a satiric, highly critical attitude toward these very justifications. In fact, Lawrence Thompson, who was later to become Frost's authorized biographer, wrote a review in 1945 of "A Masque of Reason" in which he commented on the irreverence and unorthodoxy of the play. Frost was infuriated; he soon took Thompson aside and attempted to explain the basic "piety" of the play to him (Thompson and Winnick, 1976, p. 401). But the literary text refused to obey Frost's conscious specifications; indeed a few years later, an anthologist included "God's Speech to Job" (but none of the remaining passages in "A Masque of Reason") in a section on "Satire" for a book on modern poetry (Rodman, 1951, pp. 113-114). It would appear that Frost's unconscious need, the intention most relevant to psychoanalytic thinking, was not to create emotional and cognitive coherence through the play on Job's ancient sufferings, but to express dissonance for his readers and for himself.

---

[1] From *The Poetry of Robert Frost*, edited by Edward Connery Lathem. Copyright 1945 by Robert Frost. Copyright © 1973 by Leslie Frost Ballantine. Reprinted by permission of Holt, Rinehart and Winston, Publishers.

Let us return to God's speech to Job. Obviously God is saying things in this extract which offer an experience of "emotional and cognitive dissonance": God's thanks for having part of the Bible stultified, God's recollection that in the bad old days, God had no choice but to follow Man, and God's mentality of the corporation world, by which he can "promote" Job to a higher position in the organization. This is a God who enjoys ruling as a purpose in itself, without moral pretensions. The implication is that Job's bodily sufferings, both in his own body and in the cruel loss of the fruits of his generation, his children, were for the pleasure of this God. As God goes on to say:

> I'm going to tell Job why I tortured him
> And trust it won't be adding to the torture.
> I was just showing off to the Devil, Job . . . .
> (Frost, 1949, p. 600)

Although God goes on to explain further that there was a serious purpose in this "showing off," the dissonance is never overcome. Perhaps, given Frost's own life experience of bodily suffering, it could not have been: Frost had lost his first child, a son, to an infantile illness, and later on, in the years prior to writing "Masque of Reason," "a daughter, wife and son within a space of six years" (Thompson and Winnick, 1976, p. 118). Even if we grant the truisms that Frost derived personal gratification from writing God's speech to Job, and that Frost had a certain type of personality which set limits to just what sort of poetry he would find satisfying, we have done nothing to confront the satiric significance of the poem. What would be needed for such consideration would be a theory that permitted the relating of cultural historical themes and conflicts to the poet as an adult with a sexual body, rather than the reduction of the conflicts to a mere function of the infantile identity theme. In this regard, it is unfortunate that Erik Erikson's epigenetic theory (Erikson, 1982) is not a theory of the sexual body. Erikson realized that to understand *psyche* and *soma*, mind and body, it is necessary to think of their context within *ethos*, the cultural forces, some of which might be seriously rejected by the creative artist. By foreclosing the possibility of cultural criticism Holland simply avoids contact with the problem that has confronted the originators of psychoanalysis from Freud onward: how to deal with the implications of a psychological theory that fundamentally challenged civilized morality.

Meeting this challenge has proved to be extraordinarily expensive in reducing the scope of psychoanalytic interest. The criticism of cultural authority evoked by the brief passage I have quoted from Frost's "Masque of Reason" is nothing by comparison to the whole wealth of radical social thought that the psychoanalytic revolution originally implied. Holland's revision of the theory removes its troubling contents and transports it into cognitive psychology.

But once the sexual body was excised from the theory which Holland took over from Lichtenstein, it became easy for psychoanalytic thinking, in his hands, to avoid contact with the radical critical element.

Nor is Holland's project a narrowly specialist or "literary" one. Holland is well aware that his new mode of psychoanalytic theory is actually a whole way of viewing the world; he even suggests extending the theory to scientific theories in general, and calls for their incorporation within identity themes (Holland, 1978, pp. 468-469). "Psychoanalysis enables us to go *through* science, as it were, to a psychological principle that itself explains science . . ." (1975b, p. 821). As a world hypothesis, identity theory convicts itself on the grounds of inadequate scope (Pepper, 1942, pp. 74-77): implicitly it calls for the narrowing of human cognition, from that which is adequate to warrant knowledge in the face of all the evidence—which is Pepper's interest in the cognitive value of root metaphors—to the concentration on a fixed, personal constellation of responses, repeated and elaborated through one's life, designated one's "identity theme." The inadequate scope of Holland's theory is the result—though also perhaps the intended function—of its denial of the adult sexual body.

The New Psychoanalytic Mystification of the Natural Body

Holland's success in adapting and de-radicalizing psychoanalytic theory within literary criticism does not seem to have closely matching analogues in the other arts and art criticisms. A less violent adaptation is that by the distinguished British art critic, Adrian Stokes. Because the central issue of his theory might be said to be the human body, it will be worth taking up briefly here. Ostensibly, Stokes is continuing the early psychoanalytic insistence on body energies, libido, and on instinctual drives which were placed theoretically at the borderline where psyche is rooted to soma. Thus Stokes (1972) writes: "There is a sense in which all art is of the body." But what he meant by that remark is, in his own words, that the various art media "represent . . . the actualities of the hidden psychic structure made up of evaluations and fantasies with corporeal content" (1972, p. 122). The body can be permeated with mental significance, with fantasies, in other words, and then talked about with some sophistication, but this is a long way from looking at the body. Stokes, however, would have had a tough time looking at it, judging by his assertion a page or two earlier that "almost every product of the body . . . continues to revolt us" throughout our adult life (Stokes, 1972, p. 120). My point of course is not to make a personal accusation. By putting Stokes' readers into contact with the body rejection that informs his sense of the self, I hope to reinforce my argument that present-day psychoanalytic theory attracts this kind of unresolved body rejection *because* it no longer has a viable concept of the sexual body in its own assumptions. Or rather, it does have an unacknowledged concept of the body, one that regards it with pre-Freudian disgust and hatred. We can see in a new way what it means for Stokes to say that what art preserves and restores—and this is true no matter what form of art we are talking about—is "the mother's body." That, in theory, automatically should mean the human body itself, but there is a gap evident in Stokes' language (p. 120). He is referring to the symbiotic union of infant with mother in which the sexual body is enveloped, or thoroughly obscured. Nonetheless, Stokes, like all psychoanalytic theorists including Holland, is still obliged to refer to the sexual body in some way.

Lacan and the Fragmented Sexual Body

The great advantage of Jacques Lacan's theory is that alone among the psychoanalytic variants, it does not fudge the issue: Lacan in fact has a theory of the body, but not of the natural body; his theory, moreover, would have it that we constitute our selves in terms of an "Other," but this is not merely the biological mother. It is the mother, to be sure, but this "Other" is also the inscriptions of culture through the medium of language upon the early infantile psyche that form identity. Moreover, the identity so formed is no stable, invariant "identity theme," but a constantly endangered and unstable alloy of conscious and unconscious components. The result is never a unified "Self" such as virtually all other theories presuppose as the desirable and possible ideal. Self-formation in Lacanian terms can only be tenuous; human nature is a divided nature, and hence any world hypothesis that presumes to deal with the human being as a unified organism, or as a mind that makes up a "unified subject," is engaging in fabrication, and dangerous fabrication at that.

The conceptual and semantic difficulties of Lacan's theory are so formidable as to have already called for several lengthy explications. A "reader's guide" to nine essays selected by Lacan for the English edition of his *Écrits* (1977) runs to 433 pages (Muller and Richardson, 1982); the commentary and explanation are thus longer than the *Écrits* volume itself, which has 338 pages. Other books explaining Lacan include works by Lemaire (1977), Schneiderman (1980, 1983), Clement (1983), and Smith and Kerrigan (1983). Chaitin's review of the last work (Chaitin, 1984) makes it evident that with all the explication, substantial difficulties of interpretation remain. My own understanding of Lacan is heavily indebted to the writings of Ellie Ragland-Sullivan (Ragland-Sullivan, 1979, 1981, in press) to which I refer the reader.[2] It should be anticipated, however, that no interpretation of Lacan will have a consensus among Lacanians today. My reliance on Ragland-Sullivan's interpretation is

---

[2] I am most grateful to Dr. Ragland-Sullivan for allowing me to read the full manuscript of her major work on Lacan, *Jacques Lacan and the Philosophy of Psychoanalysis*, and for her replies to several inquiries concerning Lacan. The book is scheduled for publication in late 1985.

almost certain to be judged a somewhat arbitrary decision, and it may also be faulted for simplifying her argument. The purpose of the present discussion, however, is not to supply a comprehensive reading of Lacan or his commentators, but to focus on issues concerning the sexual body.

Lacan's Theories of the Neonate and Infant

In the 1930's, when Lacan began his theorizing, he had already been impressed with studies by Henri Wallon of "imprinting" in animals (cited by Ragland-Sullivan, in press), but unlike Lichtenstein, he placed the stage for human imprinting from mother to child at a point several months into life, reserving the first six months for a period of unawareness and radical cognitive insufficiency, regarding body and self. Prior to reaching the famous "mirror stage" (Lacan, 1977, pp. 1-2), where the crucial shift is begun from this early insufficiency to the delusive unified identity of civilized existence, Lacan has a definite theoretical supposition of the neonate's body upon which he relies as if on a firmly supported empirical finding: the infant can only experience its own body as a "fragmented" one (Lacan, 1977, p. 4). Within this fragmented corpus, the infant, insofar as it has any feelings of its body prior to reaching the mirror stage, has only experienced the "turbulent" movements of energy within it. The term pays homage to the influence within French child psychology of H. Wallon's book (1925), *L'Enfant turbulent*, where the supposition that the neonate could have a functioning representation of its own body was considered absurd. In Lacan, the postulated turbulence is felt by the neonate as chaotic, formless; in no way is it regarded by the very young mind as valuable.

Despite the cognitive insufficiency with regard to its own body, however, the infant can receive language at once, in the form of sounds and phonemes, in such a way that these begin to structure the psyche. What the infant does not become aware of, however, is that these traces of language, now a part of itself, are not its own, but are fused with the emotional needs (the "Desire") of the mother, who is the major (but not the sole) early representative of all that is Other; nor does the infant realize that it originally took on a firmer identity only in order to paper over, as it were, an original radical gap in itself. But this gap remains, actively operating as a dynamic force throughout life.

The seriousness of Lacanian belief in the initial confusion of the neonate is indicated by this remark by the Lacanian psychoanalyst Michèle Montrelay: for the neonate, the perceptual world is one of "confusion and coincidences: hearing is very close to the eye, which is seen [sic] by the child as an eye-ear, an open hole" (Montrelay, 1980, pp. 82-83). During this highly confused phase, mental representations or "images" do occur through the pressure of verbal-visual impact, and these Lacan has specified to be approximately the same catalog of horrors familiar to Melanie Klein: castration (for both girls and boys), mutilation, dismemberment, dislocation, evisceration, devouring, bursting open of the body, and so forth" (Ragland-Sullivan, in press, chap. 1). At another level of his theory, Lacan posits certain "objects of Desire" which the infant makes use of in an effort to fill the gap of its own insufficiency, sometimes called an "organic insufficiency" by Lacan (Lacan, 1977, p. 4); some of these objects are again familiar ones within psychoanalytic speculation, such as the breast, the phallus, excrement and urinary flow, but others are his own innovative additions, based on his highlighting of the functions of "language" considered in his special sense: "the phoneme, the gaze, the voice—the nothing" (Lacan, 1977, p. 315).

How would a Lacanian accommodate the recent explosion of findings concerning the cognitive capacities and behavioral competencies of neonates? Ragland-Sullivan actually sets out to achieve that accommodation, commenting on a number of findings that I sent her in an earlier version of the present study. Unfortunately, I was still unaware at the time of the research by Meltzoff and associates (Meltzoff, 1981), which strongly indicates just the opposite of the Lacanian expectations of infant confusion of the sensory modalities, such as hearing and sight. On the contrary, "intermodal matching" in the newborn permits it to correctly combine perceptions of visual origin and translate them back into bodily movement that has been visualized, even after some delay has occurred between the presentation of the stimulus and the onset of the imitative movement. Ragland-Sullivan's ways of incorporating the recent research findings on infant competence seem to fall into three categories, or strategies: (a) claiming that they match Lacan's theory; (b) denying that the newborn human body is ever free of "language," and hence is not susceptible to consideration as a biological fact; and (c) conceding that present-day cultural mistreatment of newborns may indeed pose a problem for the Lacanian theory of aggression (Ragland-Sullivan, in press, chap. 1). The first of these categories is the important one for the present discussion. If we consider such findings as the newborn's very early responsiveness to voice, and shortly thereafter to the sound-spectrum of its own mother's voice (Condon and Sander, 1974a, 1974b), we may take this responsiveness as evidence that indeed the neonate is being structured by language, in Lacan's sense. However, the qualitative conditions for this assertion are not only lacking, but seem to be counter-indicated by all the research. That is, the baby who responds to its mother's voice is not having fragmented bodily experience; it is undergoing early, affect-laden experience of a highly synchronized order involving the whole body. It is completely unwarranted to imagine that there is any cognitive confusion or organic insufficiency involved. As for Ragland-Sullivan's second strategy, empirical findings may indeed tell us that the neonate can experience some aspects of language even prenatally (the fetus may be able to hear some spoken speech, for example) as Lacan rather supposed, but this does not eliminate the preponderantly natural condition of a newborn person. Even though mental life begins prenatally, as much evidence now leads us to suppose (Milton Klein, 1981b, p. 79), it does not begin as some sort of bodiless mind. Outside of the most rigid Marxist theory, a baby is not a "product" of culture in the same sense that anything else is a product. As Ragland-Sullivan recognizes, the biological facts of infancy do have to fit, empirically, with an adequate psychological theory. These facts constitute a huge area of interdisciplinary inquiry, much of it of immediate importance for the perspective of the sexual body. This field is not subsumable within a theory which would hold that all the bodily aspects of infancy are either evidences of psychological fragmentation or products of cultural formation.

Despite allowing some positive connotations for "jouisance," or sexual pleasure, Lacan is forced by the overall dimensions of his theory to thoroughly foreshorten the potentials of adult sexual union. An experience of real orgasmic gratification would have to be devalued as one more illusion of the unified subject, because in Lacanian theory "Desire" is *in principle* ungratifiable. That is, I may think that "I" am satisfied, but what I am really after is filling the original gap of insufficiency, and the only way I actually could do that would be to have the Other as my Self in bodily fact, not as delusion or fantasy. Desire is "of the Other" (Lacan, 1977, pp. 281-291), which is to say that it cannot be brought to consummation within myself, nor for that matter, with actual other people. Nor does Lacan's formulation refer to the orgasmic energy "superimposition" of male and female, as Reich would have thought; it refers to "the Other" in its fully cultural meanings.

Eternal division is implied for the adult sexual life in Lacan's reading of Freud's sexual theories as well. Lacan interprets Freud's momentous essay, "On the Universal Tendency to Debasement in the Sphere of Love" (Freud, 1912), in such a way as to make it a matter of the human archetype, rather than a description of a common pathological deformation in civilized adulthood. The adult male described by Freud could have sexual contact with a woman he loves, but could not be fully engaged with that woman emotionally, because he is disturbed by fantasies of another woman, a purely sexual object who is not loved and who cannot be loved. Lacan's contribution is to imply that basically nothing can be done about this situation (Lacan, 1977, p. 290); it is the haunting of sex by the Other. It is important to see, however, that these built-in disparagements of adult sexual gratification (which Lacan carries to the logical end of declaring that the adult *never* really "perceives" his or her body as a complete entity) (Lacan, 1975, p. 200), are required by the theory itself. They are unfalsifiable, not because they are ambiguously stated, but because any subjective experience of the subject, no matter how it feels to the subject, is less important than what the theory demands.

Probably haunting the Lacanian structure is an "Other" of its own: a deeply introjected hunger for the absolute. In French intellectual history, a sense of certainty has taken root through the prominence of the concept of the Cartesian ego. Lacan will have none of that concept. But his theory is infused with deep disappointment that the human subject is never an entity absolutely unto itself. Early infantile dependency must always offer the suggestion that our selves have been formed on the basis of weakness, or rather, on *what will always be interpreted to be weakness by those who find such dependency a threat in principle to the human self.* The biological predispositions of the infant are as nothing, when weighted in Lacanian terms against this inherent position of weakness. Reich's theory of human biological self-regulation is thus ruled out, implicitly, by not allowing that the self may be significantly biological. To say, as the Reichians do, it is "essential that the child's own organic rhythms of functioning were respected and allowed to develop naturally" (Boadella, 1973, p. 220) becomes nonsense in the language of Lacan. It becomes nonsense however, not because of a lack of evidential support, but because the language of Lacan has no other way of conceiving a theory that aligns self-regulation with the biology of the sexual body.

The Fragmented Self

Lacan's firm resolve, here and throughout his theory, is worth taking seriously precisely because it is a consistent working out of the psychoanalytic axiom that the human being is a creature of conflict. *In some sense*, intrapsychic conflict is basic to the theory. The problem is to determine whether this model of a mind in conflict with itself requires a radical, completely uncompromising interpretation, or if some ways of living can lead to a level of psychological health in which such conflict is controlled to the point where it is no longer causing a split in human consciousness between instinct and control, gratification and desire, body and mind, self and other-as-self. Reich thought such a level could be attained, though he did not propose it could be maintained at all times. The "genital character," as Baker points out, is not someone who has "ideal health"—a concept that has no correlate in the world of nature—but someone who "is well enough integrated and free enough emotionally so that he can sufficiently express and satisfy himself in life" (Baker, 1967, p. 101). The genital character "is able to solve his conflicts in an unneurotic way" (Boadella, 1973, p. 92) but does not represent a Rousseauistic ideal of "natural man" who never has to "defend himself against a hostile environment" (Boadella, 1973, p. 46). Anna Freud, on the other hand, concluded that "even the most revolutionary changes in infant care" cannot do away with "the division of the human personality into an *id* and an *ego* with conflicting aims" (A. Freud, 1968, p. 326). To suppose otherwise would be to deny human nature, or at least the theory of human nature which she had derived from the psychoanalytic world hypothesis. Thus she continued:

> According to the views presented here, the emergence of neurotic conflicts has to be regarded as the price paid for being human. (A. Freud, 1968, p. 326)

Yet the issue has not been settled, and can hardly be settled as long as there are basic questions of human nature not yet securely and empirically formed into "objects of knowledge" (Dewey, 1929b). Anna Freud herself continued to emphasize throughout her career the developmental needs of children; were she entirely convinced of the centrality of conflict, or were she fully centered on the sex-hating qualities I have located in her work above (Chapter Three), then she could never have been such a strong supporter of those needs. The unsettled debate over the issue of whether the split in human consciousness which psychoanalysis supposes must be taken radically or benignly is brought out by the work of Anna Freud's associate, Erik Erikson. Erikson, in accordance with his own idea of psychoanalysis, delineates a series of *oppositions* (such as basic trust versus mistrust) which every human being must live through, but never with the presupposition that these represent conflicts which are unresolvable in principle (Erikson, 1982). Lacan fastens upon a potential for unbridgeable intrapsychic conflict in Freud's work and makes the very most of it. He does this not through Freud's theory of sexuality or of the sexual body, but through Freud's insights into the hazards of consciously intended meanings in language. The unconscious, as Freud knows it, cannot but contradict and undercut conscious meanings and intentions throughout some great cross-section of mental functioning. Unintended associations of even a phoneme will undermine the meaning of the word of which it is a part. The resultant world is a surreal one, but Lacan, who had some connection with the Surrealist movement, is delineating such a world intentionally.

The Futures of Lacanian and Lichtensteinian Theory

The problem of the body, however, is the great obstacle in Lacan's path. The human body does not seem to provide a convincing metaphor for the permanently conflicted, divided subject. As more is known of the infant body, it will be less and less possible to pretend that the obstacle of the body has been removed from the theory.

Some of Lacan's followers, such as Schneiderman, celebrate the master's refusal to agree that "states of feeling and emotion" have a central place in "psychic reality" (Schneiderman, 1982). Once the body is regarded as a set of incoherent fragments, the devaluation of feeling and emotion follows apace. The Lacanian movement within psychoanalysis promises to fully carry out this logic, and therefore to provide a kind of limiting case of the animus toward physical sexual existence in psychoanalytic thinking.

Within its own terms, Lacan's theory is probably irrefutable. However, there may be a kind of linguistic time-bomb within those terms which will cause trouble. It is plain that Lacan does not mean to focus on the body itself; for him, the phallus, for example, is an imagined object of unconscious desire, not to be confused with the penis or with any sexual body organs. Yet, in the logic of his own theory, the deeply embedded bodily associations of such a term as "phallus" (a central term in his theory of cultural authority) cannot be extirpated by stipulation, even with the most strenuous insistence. In the logic of the unconscious, such denial of the body in thinking about psychology stimulates its opposite. Lacan's concept of the "Law of the Name-of-the-Father"—his term for the cultural heritage of authority which he believes each infant must accept and incorporate into the mind in order to avoid psychological stunting within early, bodily-fragmented infancy—will similarly come under critical examination; the old questions of "Why Repression," "Repression for what purpose?", and "Repression at what cost?" will re-emerge precisely because they have been systematically denied in Lacan's theory. Abel, in fact, has pointed out that Lacan's generalized cultural concept of paternal authority obscures the difference between the socio-political sources of male authority and the internalized psychology of the Name-of-the-Father (Abel, 1984, p. 155). By merging these concepts, Lacan has obstructed the work of Feminism, Abel suggests (*ibid.*). For a Lacanian able to confront the evidence of Prescott's far ranging hypothesis of the critical difference made in psychological and social life through the presence of affectionate somatosensory contact, the doctrine of the Law of the Name-of-the-Father will come to be highly problematical. It will no longer warrant the term "Law."

Certain unspecified presuppositions of the "mirror-stage" would also suffer exposure from any Lacanian who refuses Schneiderman's interpretation of Lacan as one who held that emotions and feelings are not central to "psychic reality"; for the basic metaphor of a mirror entails the distancing of feelings. I can feel contact with another body, but Lacan will forever tell me that if only I understood the mirror stage I would see these feelings are of my "je" or my "moi" or of an illusory combination of the two. In other words, I may feel direct contact but that is an illusion. But the visual metaphor of a mirror *guarantees* his advice on this score, because what mirrors present is an image which cannot be a source of somatosensory, body-to-body feelings, such as those Prescott (1979) describes. A mirror also *automatically* provides a reversed image which is optically persuasive and yet systematically distorted. Although mirroring processes may have an essential role in even the deepest sexual contact (which Reich specifies must entail the "considerable ability to identify oneself with one's partner" [Reich, 1945, p. 122]), mirroring can hardly be equated convincingly with sexual gratification.

An even more troublesome Lacanian term and concept is that of "castration," which Lacan applies in a special and extremely broad sense to the psychology of Desire in both sexes. He does not mean what psychoanalysts usually refer to as castration anxiety, although his complicated theory incorporates and repositions that theory. A coherent Lacanian sense of "castration" can again be stipulated so as not to commit an absurdity, but the long-term connotations of having women think of themselves (or about other women) as castratable in the same sense as men are castratable will contribute so much bodily confusion to the Lacanian theory that those who explore it fully, with a felt connection to their own bodies, will arrive at a point of beginning serious, potentially uprooting revisions aimed at giving the sexual body a positive role within it. Because of the massive series of categories, insights, metaphors, and levels of Lacan's theory, there is probably enough flexibility to allow for revision of the Lacanian theory of the body. However, if the basic issue ever becomes sharply focused, if the probability ever seems to be that the sexual body is not necessarily a set of perceptual fragments before the mirror stage, but a potentially unified psychosexual organism, then the life work of Lacan may have to be rejected, except for its value as great opposition to the sexual body.

It is more difficult to say what future there might be for Lichtenstein's theory of human identity, insofar as it is related to the perspective of the sexual body. Lichtenstein's own attraction toward the traditional "higher things," which Dewey saw in needless opposition to the flesh, has facilitated the bowdlerization of his work. But surely his linking of identity and sexuality deserves another look. In fact, it deserves a first serious look in the field of psychoanalysis, a consideration it has never been given.

CHAPTER TEN

WORLD HYPOTHESES AND INTERDISCIPLINARY SCIENCES IN INTIMATE RELATION

The perspective of the sexual body seems to have been turning up in each of the disciplines I have discussed. Such ubiquity, however, may be a mixed blessing insofar as the perspective is intended to clearly exhibit interdisciplinary relationships and at the same time make for a more valuable, coherent study of sexuality in all its dimensions. To what extent is the perspective a potentially scientific point of view? As Pepper understood the problem of scientific hypotheses, none of the hypotheses of science can be considered to have unrestricted scope (Pepper, 1982). Yet the perspective of the sexual body threatens to balloon interminably. I have attempted to show that psychoanalysis is the key discipline for such a perspective, but the key may not act as a useful control precisely because it is grounded in an incompletely specified theory of sexuality. Indeed, Freud's grasp of the necessarily open definition of sexuality, given his new insights into its psychosocial pervasiveness, was probably a saving element in his own integrity as a scientific thinker, for as Willbern has argued, Freud tended in his most intimate fantasy life (as shown in his dreams) to move toward a sense of closure and certainty (Willbern, 1979). The fact that in his theory of sexuality Freud resisted this tendency, this deep need of his own personality, gave psychoanalysis its resilience as a potentially scientific discipline; within the psychoanalytic tradition, sexuality became an unending series of "objects of knowledge" (Dewey, 1929a), rather than a hopelessly dogmatic claim to have "discovered" what sexuality "is." Sexuality might also be illuminated by disciplines outside of psychoanalysis. Freud's hope that biology would eventually contribute an understanding of the psychology of bisexuality is one instance (see Chapter Seven). It is one instance out of many in which the results of research in one discipline regarding sexuality will affect not merely one or more theories in other specializations, but will cause larger ripples in the shared social and scientific assumptions about the general nature of sexuality. What seems to occur in such cross-fertilization of the disciplines, wherever sexuality is the focus, is the development of a large, unlimited hypothesis which Pepper would not call a scientific hypothesis at all (even though it must have empirical foundations in order to be cognitively valuable). Instead, the scientific understanding of sexuality, when it includes the psychological dimensions of sex, tends to move toward becoming a world hypothesis (Pepper, 1942). The perspective of the sexual body, in other words, may turn out to be a way of focusing upon the sexual elements in any hypothesis of what the world is probably like, but it may also prove to be a generating force in theory for the construction of a relatively new and relatively adequate world hypothesis.

Rossi (1977, pp. 11-17), for example, has pointed out that developments in neuroendocrinology—a field hardly expected to have immediate impact on the overall perspective of the sexual body—alter the traditional biological metaphor of sexuality in which males are the "active" and females the "passive" elements. The notion that androgen is a male, and estrogen a female hormone, must be qualified in light of findings which show that at least some androgen is also produced by the female body. There is no neat division of hormones along a male-female divide. "Both hormones," in fact, "are present in both sexes, although in different balances" (Rossi, 1977, p. 11). Although women's bodies contain lower levels of androgen then do men's, there is some evidence to suggest that it also "takes less androgen to produce an effect in the female than in the male" (p. 11). Rossi also shows how developments in the field of reproductive physiology have a potential impact on thinking about male and female biological roles. The motility of spermatazoa, which has attracted attention and admiration from biologists since the time of Leeuwenhoek (Rossi, 1977, p. 16), is now understood in a new light. The sperm's motility now appears to depend not solely on its own forward impulsion, as it makes its legendary way up the uterus toward the ovum, but on cooperative forward-carrying motion provided by the glandular activity of the human female. Rossi realized that this information changes not just the restricted scientific theory of procreation, but the way in which we think of sexuality itself. Rossi's observations have been paralleled by those of Myron Hofer, whose discipline is called "developmental psychobiology" (Hofer, 1981). The selection of a given sperm for fertilization by the female will be effected, Hofer argues, by the woman's hormonal dynamics and potentially by her emotional state (Hofer, 1981, p. 83). Procreation thus appears as an interactional biological process, rather than an active-passive interchange between male and female.

The interdisciplinary perspective of the sexual body would provide a continuous scanning process for scientific research inquiries toward the discovery of changes of this kind. It is difficult to think of any other perspective that would do the same, although there will continue to be pertinent observations such as Rossi's from different fields. Rossi's own field of sociology, and her specialty of demographics, would not readily recognize her observations regarding sexual thought as their products, while the special discipline of sexology might acknowledge the biological findings without attempting to think of their implications for the ways in which members of society regard the nature of procreation. Hofer's study of developmental psychobiology would bring his argument under a general developmental framework without emphasizing the sexual aspects. But the perspective of the sexual body might be considered an instrument for intelligent thinking about sex in the social context of continuous new empirical evidence and the human response to that evidence.

Is a New World Hypothesis Needed?

If we are to attempt a preliminary elaboration of such thinking toward an organized theory, rather than stay witin the less formal dimensions of a perspective, we would soon encounter the question of whether a theory of sexuality could be fitted into some one (or more) of the relatively adequate world hypotheses (Pepper, 1942). The position I have taken in this study is that the perspective of the sexual body developed since the early work of Freud will not fit the traditional hypotheses, except with great strain. A new world hypothesis would have to be developed to accommodate this perspective. Possibly the final hypothesis tentatively developed by Pepper (Pepper, 1967), which he called Selectivism, could accommodate and make intelligible the various findings I have grouped under the perspective of the sexual body.

In attempting to come to terms with the problem of the sexual body as a new perspective which challenges existing concepts, I suggest a consideration of the term "the sexual self." Actually this is the title of a work by the sex therapist Avodah K. Offit (Offit, 1977), to whom I have referred favorably above (Chapter Two). If only Offit meant something serious by the term! But she reverts as early as her introductory chapter to a conventional perspective: sex must be understood "as a part of the total personality," and only when that is done, can "we move toward harmonious sexual relationship." The sexual revolution Offit reduces to its simplicities which amount to a claim for easy and instant liberation. With such a view of the problem, she easily dismisses the value of the revolution (Offit, 1977, p. 20). In her last chapter she expresses contempt to the point of hatred for the very idea that "the new sexuality" could seriously lead to a better world, and she reduces the problem to a false opposition between "only the simple hedonism of biological pairing," versus the full tragic potential of the human species that is above all that; "we are . . . a higher order of animals forever on the verge of immortality" (p. 292). A few years later, Offit went on to add a harsher comment in a revised edition of her book (Offit, 1983). Making a dubious historical generalization, she approves of the sexual revolution, but claims that the sexuality of the 1960's was not a part of that broader movement (Offit, 1983, pp. 294-295). Throughout her summarizing comments, Offit is most hostile to any suggestion that the sexual body can be important in widespread improvement in the quality of life. Such a hope would be *utopian*, as Offit sees it, and that would conflict with her major commitment to the *tragic* quality of human life.

This ideological stance aligns Offit with such psychoanalytic messengers of the tragic as the later Freud (1930), Kohut (1977) and Schafer (1976). It also connects her to a long tradition of tragic humanism which denies that any social change toward significantly unrepressed sexual and social life is possible. But in this denial, she as well as the psychoanalysts outrun their base in evidence. Were "advanced" technological society to adopt on a very wide scale the practice of affectionate, somatosensory contact shown by Prescott (1979) to be valuable for the control of sadistic impulses in numerous preliterate cultures, there is reason to expect that the "tragic" cultural prescript of the civilized world would be largely evaded. I maintain it is more mature and sensible to *reject* tragedy as the fixed, necessary fate of the human, as indeed D.H. Lawrence rejected it (Gordon, 1966, p. 87; Michel, 1970, pp. 47-48). There is an implication in the psychoanalytic fascination with the tragic, in fact, that it is advisable to put the child's sexual body through some tragedy, in the best authoritarian traditions of child-rearing. As Philip Lichtenberg put it, after Freud turned in his later years to endorsing the value of frustration, there arose the notion that "sometimes psychoanalytic theory urges us to provide tragedy for our children" (Lichtenberg, 1969, pp. 89-90). The cycle of generations would thus guarantee the definition of the human being as a tragic creature, ostensibly confirming that definition while actively producing the conditions for its repetition.

Far from meriting Offit's scorn, the claims and hopes for the social changes to be expected from the sexual revolution as a great cultural movement are no different than those of any other world view that accepts the human ability to make and re-make social reality. As the Marxist sociologist and theorist, the late Alvin Gouldner pointed out, to believe that the human condition can in fact be radically improved is to make a break with the entire tragic paradigm (Gouldner, 1976, chap. 3; 1980, p. 71). Had Offit risen to the challenge of the new sense of the sexual body since Freud, she would not have written of the conventional integration of sex within the total personality nor of the conventional subordination of personality within predefined "human" and "tragic" constraints. Instead, the basic meaning of her term, "the sexual life," would be that *the self is basically sexual*, in ways that we are still discovering, ways that are far from trivial or simplistic, and which eventually will make us revise our ideas of what it is to be human. Most of the contents of her two books (Offit, 1977, 1982) provide evidence for precisely such a conclusion. Moreover, the great bulk of the details she provides refer to the body, thus warranting from another source my own title, "the sexual body," rather than "the sexual self." The temptation to idealize human thought to the point of supposing that we belong to some "higher order of animals, forever on the verge of immortality" seems a perpetual one for the humanist psychoanalyst, as I have shown in discussing Kohut and his concept of the self. Such claims of higher-ness always avoid a serious confrontation with the sexual body.

Obstructive Synthesis Versus the Emergence of Usable Theory

To make such confrontation unnecessary, certain shortcuts in theory have been proposed from time to time. These are well-meaning, but I question whether they are wise. Winnicott, for example went so far as to say "There is no such thing as an infant," by which he meant that infants are always found within a context of maternal care, and hence we must always speak of infant and mother (Winnicott, 1960, quoted by Chodorow, 1978, p. 57). This is a neat way of distracting attention from the possibility that the infant is not always behaving in the maternal context, unless one insists that the infant's behavior is always in such a context by virtue of the fact that the infant (usually) is being nurtured by a mother. But such an insistence has long obscured the possibility of a neonate having "peer relations" with other infants during the first year of life (see for evidence of such relations among neonates, Atkins, 1983). Winnicott might not have objected to such findings, but he did not want to confront the sexual body of the infant or child. He seriously believed that in child play, "Bodily excitement in erotogenic zones . . . threatens the child's existence as a person" (Winnicott, 1971, p. 52). It was Winnicott who was threatened; how else explain this astounding claim?

Winnicott's foreshortening of theory through his declaration that there is no such thing as a baby has parallels in other formulations from non-psychoanalytic disciplines. The philosopher Merleau-Ponty presented a series of formulations which tell us that existence is sexual and the sexual is existence, one of the terms always supposing the other. D.O. Hebb, a psychologist, proposed an analogous formulation: human life is 100% biological and it is also 100% cultural (Hebb, 1959). An advantage intended by formulae of this type is to put an end, once and for all, to wrangling over whether something is sexual ("natural," "instinctual") or culturally learned: it has to be both. But the advantage thus gained is dubious. As long as we still are at the threshold of discovering what the dimensions of sexuality are, any call to fundamentally ignore the distinction between sexual as natural and sexual as cultural only contributes to the further obscuring of the sexual body.

Such moves as Winnicott's, Merleau-Ponty's, or Hebb's toward a premature synthesis of culture and nature also make it impossible to pursue the investigation of human nature, and cut off the search for universal cross-cultural emotional patterns and symbolic meanings that may underlie the vast array of cultures. The old question, for example, of why humans perceive color differentiations such as between green and blue at a certain range of the spectrum, when objectively there seems to be no division there, is hardly approachable by assuming that cultural namings such as those for colors just happen to perch at certain light spectra. It is approachable, however, by studying infant responses. In an experiment designed to test whether infant visual attention follows the "arbitrary" division of blue and green or not, Bornstein, Kessen, and Weisskopf (1975) found that it did. There is a discontinuous structure in color perception, in other words, that is characteristically human, not linguistic, and not approachable through assumptions which automatically classify all perception as both natural and cultural. But is the sexual body involved in this perception? I would say yes: the long traditions in many cultures which link perception of color with emotional perception (Birren, 1978; Itten, 1973; see also Cutler and Pepper, 1923, p. 149) are good indications that connections will be found with the sexual body. Restak points out that "neurons found in the areas of the brain specialized for the more 'elementary' perceptions such as vision are now known to be affected by sound and touch stimuli as well" (Restak, 1983, p. 23). If touch is involved, then affectionate somatosensory contact (Prescott, 1979) will be connected in some way or ways with the qualitative aspects of visual functioning, especially in the perception of emotionally significant color. Moreover, emotions are closely linked with body chemistry (as I noted earlier in Chapter Six; see Izard, 1977, pp. 9-10; McGeer and McGeer, 1980); the body is sexual. The evidence I have reviewed above, in "Reinventing the Asexual Infant," of the sexual differences in neonatal mental processes (little as these are understood as yet) is sufficient warrant for expecting further information to emerge concerning color perception and the sexual body. A considerable psychological literature, in fact, suggests universal humanly-shared patterns of emotional response, not primarily dependent on cultural conditioning, but closely connected with body language such as facial expression (Clynes, 1977; Izard, 1977; Tomkins, 1962, 1963, 1981a, 1981b). Pepper (1969c) was aware of this approach, and argued that there are certain natural symbols, such as fire, which are not entirely determined by culture.

The advanced (so-called) civilized psyche is not necessarily too refined or individualized for the sharing of referents with emotional value to occur. Recently Dahl completed a careful experiment on the referents of emotionally-loaded words (Dahl, 1983). Dahl is a psychoanalytic investigator who has falsified in this experiment certain predictions offered in current, mainstream psychoanalytic theory (Brenner, 1974). Brenner holds that the individual psyche is so removed from common, shared emotional meanings as to make any hope for a shared language regarding emotions unrealistic. On the contrary, Dahl concludes,

> the intrinsic ability of people to communicate their emotions to others successfully must surely rest on this area of shared referents for the labels they attach to their emotional states. (Dahl, 1983, p. 60)

Dahl's subjects were English-speaking Americans with college educations. Their ages ranged from 18 to 75, and Dahl used a total of 58 such subjects as judges of what some 370 different "emotion words" (p. 59) meant to them.

There is a parallel development in another branch of psychoanalytic investigation. In an empirical study of psychoanalytic aesthetic theory, the analyst Legault (1981) similarly concluded that the hypothesis of individual idiosyncratic perception of aesthetic objects proposed by Holland (1978) is quite the opposite of what actually happens when a number of observers, including some with a great deal of psychoanalytic training and some with none, look at Picasso's statue, "Man With a Sheep." From the perspective of the present study, I would expect that the sexual body provides the cognitive ground for such findings of shared referents within emotional and aesthetic experience.

We would have to look to human biology for verification of such a claim. The nature *versus* nurture conundrum is not in itself unapproachable. Recently, Jacquelynne Parsons, a developmental psychologist, has maintained that under certain conditions it is reasonable to hold that some human behaviors "are shaped at least to some degree by biological processes" (Parsons, 1982, p. 137). If there are congruent findings from two or more of the following four sources, then a biological involvement should be regarded as warranted:

> (a) demonstrations of an association between hormonal and behavioral variations, (b) behavioral patterns among infants or very young children, (c) cross-cultural universal, and (d) cross-species consistency, especially among higher primates. (Parsons, 1982, p. 137)

These guidelines have been adopted and made somewhat more inclusive by Rossi in her presidential address to the American Sociological Association (Rossi, 1984). From the perspective of the sexual body, they would seem most valuable, with the exception of (d) primate and other animal studies. Human sexuality is just too different, as I have explained in the introduction to the present study, to be compared directly with animal sexuality.

With this warning in mind, however, it should be permissible and valuable to consider evidence from a very broad range of mammals (sometimes known to include humans) which shows that sexual dimorphism of specific body organs other than the genitals is very likely a fact. Bardin and Catterall (1981) have reviewed the effects of testosterone in this light. Biological understanding is in the process of change in this area, showing that testosterone has more effects and functions than had previously been thought. Although not strictly a male hormone, the authors state that the amount of it secreted by female ovaries "in most species is too low to have biologic effect" (Bardin and Catterall, p. 1285). This statement appears to oversimplify the matter, but there is good evidence for regarding the human kidney and liver as significantly sexually dimorphic (pp. 1288-1292), and not only in the factor of size. In muscle development, the effects of "estrogenic metabolites of testosterone" are especially notable on one set of muscles in the pelvic area, "the levator ani but not on other muscles" (p. 1292). What these dimorphic differentiations mean for understanding the sexual body is a problem for interdisciplinary research, but the problem cannot be dismissed out of hand if we grant the perspective of the sexual body.

Parsons, whose four criteria for proposing that some human behavior is shaped by biological processes, "at least to some degree," goes beyond these gross dimorphic considerations to draw some psychological conclusions. Using her own set of standards, she finds that there is good evidence for concluding that biological processes are involved in several "sex-dimorphic behavior clusters," namely

> aggression and/or activity level; a set of limited cognitive skills associated with spatial visualizations and perhaps mathematical reasoning and verbal skills as well; and parenting. (Parsons, 1982, pp. 137-138)

This statement is significant not only in itself but as an indication of a new attitude among women scientists. Parsons is one of a new generation of biosocial inquirers among women in the disciplines. They are quite careful in their choice of terms not to imply support for sexism; they in fact oppose such sexism firmly and often bring a feminist sensibility to bear on the problems of sexual dimorphism—but they also insist that there is something very important to the biological dimension. (See also Kaplan, 1980; Ledwitz-Rigby, 1980; Peterson, 1980; Waldron, 1982, and the pioneering work of Rossi, 1977, 1981, 1984.) These women scientists seem to be attaining prominence in their fields at the same time that a new movement in feminist theory has revived a positive interest in female sexual pleasure (Patton, 1984, p. 4; Vance, 1984; Vance and Snitow, 1984).

In the newer biosocial research writing, whether it is by the women researchers just mentioned or by men in the same field, a high standard of complexity is maintained. The biological factors are not exaggerated, and they are never discussed without consideration of a cultural context. The biases and conceptual traps of E.O. Wilson's sociobiology are noted and avoided (Gove and Carpenter, 1982). An indication of the change afoot can be seen in the statement by Money (1980, p. 31) that certain of his research findings with regard to adrenogenital syndrome "serve to remind us all that we dare not attribute all shades of difference in gender-related behavior to postnatal social and cultural determinants." A few years earlier, Money did not include such a statement; instead he then emphasized the ways in which certain newborn infants could be "reassigned" successfully to live as the opposite sex and be raised accordingly, aided by hormone injection and surgical correction (Money, 1977). Although he has not changed his mind about that, he seems to have come to a realization that there are limits to the environmental reshaping of gender.

At least one study has offered sharply contradictory evidence concerning the theory that gender is shaped primarily by social determinants. This is a study of genetic males who had been born with deficient masculine organs, due to a prenatal (testosterone) hormonal deficiency. In two inbred villages where this syndrome occurred with some frequency, 18 genetically classified males were raised unambiguously as girls. But once adolescence set in, with its new supplies of testosterone, all of these males changed to male gender identity, and all but one to male gender role as well, either during puberty or after (Imperato-McGinley, Peterson, Goutier, and Sturla, 1979). It is interesting in the light of the perspective of the sexual body, that the "object of knowledge" this study brought into being soon led to a change in the sexual gender identity practices of the inhabitants of the two villages. The researchers shared their findings with the villagers, and now the villagers do *not* raise babies who are born with this particular genetic defect as females; they raise them as males and allow adolescence to do its work (Imperato-McGinley et al., 1979).

The whole ideological drive toward androgyny (Heilbrun, 1973) in fact has suffered setbacks in the practical sense. Bem, who had been one of the theorists and advocates of androgynous child-rearing, that is, the raising of children so that traditional gender roles were redistributed equally irrespective of sex, found that more serious difficulties than she had expected were encountered. It was as if each child was being instructed not merely to follow the gender behavior of one sex, but that each child was now being required to learn how to fulfill the gender behavior of two sexes. This proved to be too much (Bem, 1983).

Bem's revaluation of androgyny at the practical level of its operation in children's lives was preceded by an unusually perceptive critique from yet another discipline. The failure of the androgynous child-rearing program was predicted by the political scientist, Elshtain, in 1981. She maintained that when we ask children to not understand reality sexually, we ask them to ignore their own bodies: each child knows that its genitals are part of its identity, and no matter how suppressed the topic may be socially, the child also realizes there are two sexes. Elshtain argued that to carry out the androgynous child-rearing program the parent would have to vigorously distract the mind of the child from these basic matters of the sexual body, and that this would be psychologically disastrous: it would in fact make the old masturbation taboo look benign (Elshtain, 1981). Fortunately, there seems to be a growing consensus among feminist theorists and others now that the sexual body is essential to the child's view of the world. The concept of androgyny may continue to afford an ideological base from which to criticize sexism in the family, but perhaps it will not be taken as a warrant for denying the sexual body.

At other levels of theory, Bem's proposal for androgynous child-rearing also came under severe criticism by other feminists. Her hypothesis that children raised without an awareness of sexual role differention would score on personality tests to indicate a "balanced" male-female ratio, was upset by findings which showed that the term "balanced" could be applied to children with very low self-esteem as well as to those with high self-esteem (A. Kaplan, 1979). Beyond the empirical complexities, however, were more basic issues. Berzins (1979) showed in a brief survey that androgyny meant different things to holders of the four world hypotheses originally deployed by Pepper (Pepper, 1942).

Although Berzins' plea for grounding the problem of androgyny in the theory of Pepper seems to have had no direct results, there are more signs of a willingness to revise rather than avoid the basic categories of "culture" and "nature." For example, Money has offered a comprehensive and coherent schema for reformulating the "nature" versus "nurture" problem so that it no longer indicates a dichotomy (Money, 1980, pp. 9-11). There now seem to be good theoretical tools developing in the medical and psychological fields for the study of nature and culture which do not fall into the old traps of severing the two, nor into the newer traps of conceptually molding them into one "whole" that is so tightly forged it cannot permit an investigation at all. Within the world hyppothesis of Contextualism, there has always been a tendency to examine the potential conflicts between "instinctive impulse and social interest," even while realizing that these always occur in a context or situation or event in which neither instinct nor culture stand in isolation (Pepper, 1945, p. 67). The only problem is whether Contextualism—which is Pepper's name for the Pragmatist tradition—can adequately encounter the sexual body.

Formism and Survival

Pepper might not have regarded all the new evidence for, and interest in, the biological basis of sex and gender role differences as equally supportive of all four of his set of world hypotheses. During much of his career Pepper appeared to regard such evidence as Dahl's on the relative uniformity of response to emotion words by various subjects, or such evidence as Legault's on the relative similarity among different viewers' responses to a Picasso statue, as new evidence primarily for only one of the four relatively adequate world hypotheses, namely Formism. That worldview is one of the oldest of the set, and takes for its root metaphor the notion of "similarity," the matching of particular occurrences with a "normal" model. Idiosyncratic instances of feeling or perception tend to get labelled in this view as abnormal, and would be suspected of having a deficiency in human survival capacities. In Formism, the ethical and the normal are close categorical companions. People's emotions correspond to certain basic forms, cross-culturally, and their cultures are either grounded in those same forms or they lose their capacity for survival as cultures: all else is distortion.

> Distortions occur . . . in the norms of animals, men, and of human societies. These last [the norms], of course, are the basis for formistic ethics. Human and social norms are ethical standards of value. In concrete existence, especially among the more complex forms of existence, these norms seem to exhibit states of human and social equilibrium, and serious distortions are accompanied with discomfort and pain. Hence Plato's search for the perfect State, Aristotle's for the several types of social structure, exhibiting a golden mean, and the search of many modern men for the life cycle of a normal culture, or for the life cycles of the several normal types of culture, or for the normal surges of transition of culture, toward the perfect social structure. All such social studies presuppose formistic catagories. (Pepper, 1942, pp. 179-180)

It would be possible to take evidence of the human eye's propensity to divide the color spectrum in a certain way, for the human emotional range to form itself along a certain limited set of basic emotions in any culture, or for different human beings to respond in a shared way to emotionally-toned words, or to a statue by Picasso, as new evidence that somewhere the forms of the normal do exist and that these forms are also the ones that lie behind the cohesion of societies.

What has been suggested since the early Freud, however, is that sexuality has norms that are unknown, or not well-known, within culture, but which also are strongly suspected *not* to fit the other social, political or ethical norms of most of civilized society. This would suggest not a reinforcement of Formism through psychoanalysis, as Pepper sometimes argued (1949, p. 144), but a gaping disparity. What is "normal" to culture is not the human sexual body. But can culture any longer be regarded as itself "normal"? Cultures world-wide now seem to be caught in a position of increasingly probable non-survivability due to both nuclear proliferation and the hastening massive destruction of the environment. The biologists Paul and Anne Ehrlich, in their book *Extinction*, make a considerable case for the possibility of destruction (Ehrlich and Ehrlich, 1981). Cultural norms simply cannot be considered to be automatically linked to biological survival, given the present world situation. The perspective of the sexual body tends to highlight the gap between the two, and contributes to an understanding of changes that must be made for survival to be possible. For example, the cultural norms in typically impoverished societies, such as in Bangladesh or in Northeastern Brazil, call for maximum procreation leading to an extremely high birthrate, which places great strain on the ability of the societies to remain viable. Some of the changes contemplated in this study, such as the encouragement of infant-maternal bonding and of affectionate somatosensory contact, are also important for species survival, even if they have no crucial role in individual survival (see Pepper, 1969a). It may be feasible to raise a generation of humans who lack an ability to empathically relate to the possibility of bodily destruction in nuclear war, and whose imaginations are controlled by the game-playing ideology of "we" versus "they." Such people have developed to maturity. But is it really a survival strategy to do so? The affectional somatosensory variable pointed to by Prescott, which is an inherently sexual body interaction, may not be necessary for growing up and having a career or for filling any number of social role models, but it may be necessary to insure the survival of *a species which is moving toward a violent demise and which cannot feel what it is doing to itself.*

Pepper's Selectivism and Alternate Philosophical Proposals on the Human Body

Pepper continued to maintain that Formism was one of the few relatively adequate hypotheses, whatever weaknesses it might have. He did not attempt to remedy its defects in theory, partly for lack of interest in Formism, and partly because his own philosophical attitude drew him toward the development of an entirely new world hypothesis which would do justice to both the physiological data concerning the body and to the typical contexts in which the body must be understood. In "Selectivism," Pepper proposed the category of the "natural norm" for human purposive acts. He thus gave philosophical order to the psychological theory of E.C. Tolman, a friend and intellectual companion who had great influence upon Pepper in the 1920's, and probably until Tolman's death in 1959. Tolman's *Purposive Behavior in Animals and Men* (1932) is a classic in its field. Tolman showed that the human species and other animal species carry out acts in an intelligent purposive manner; for example, the cognitive mapping which animals perform without benefit of written communication is not different in principle from the mapping performed at a vastly increased level of sophistication by humans, and all animal species have developed their mapping abilities in order to protect and enhance survival. Pepper's *Concept and Quality* in fact contains a detailed exposition of the purposive behavior of a deer in the act of searching out, among a variety of edible available plants, some especially delectable lily pads (Pepper, 1967, pp. 424-438).

With the concept of the "natural norm," and a project for outlining a limited number of "selective systems" in which purposive behavior occurs, the Purposive Act became a new root metaphor for a world hypothesis (Pepper, 1967). The human body was notably included both in the subcategories of this hypothesis, and in some of Pepper's exposition. Purpose would require a body to carry it out, a truism which meant for Pepper a commitment to delve into not just the ideas or motives but also the behavioral actions and conditions in any purposive act. He regarded much of European philosophy as obviously weak in this respect, although he suggested that the omission of the behavioral "ties" including the body could be remedied in some instances, as perhaps in the work of Sartre (Pepper, 1970). Pepper also continued to think about sexuality: a few years after publishing *Concept and Quality*, in which Selectivism was described at length, he gave as an example of a minimal social situation the act of sexual intercourse, with orgasms—and as a matching example of a private situation, the act of taking a shower (Pepper, 1969a). I point this out because in considering the merits and failings of Pepper's gigantic new project in relation to alternative proposals in philosophy, it is important to keep the body in view. Pepper, for example, was somewhat anticipated in his proposed world hypothesis by the process philosophy of Alfred North Whitehead (see Reck, 1968, pp. 77-78), but he does not have Whitehead's bias against the body, a feature of Whitehead I have discussed elsewhere (Efron, 1980, pp. 249-250). Similarly, the body seems to be more integral in Pepper's "selective systems" than it is in the Systems Phiosophy of Laszlo (Laszlo, 1969), although Pepper generously credited Laszlo's book with carrying out an argument very close to his own (Pepper, 1972).

There has been a slow growth in the Western world of philosophical interest in the body, as Thomas Hanna (1970) has argued. The rise of the discipline of aesthetics in the 18th century, with its emphasis on the sensuous element in perception, contributed to this development, as David Richardson has pointed out (Richardson, in press). Nor is it feasible to maintain a clear distinction between the sensuous and the sensual in aesthetics, as Berleant (1964) has shown. In the twentieth century, Merleau-Ponty has given a profound sense of the sexual body in *The Phenomenology of Perception* (1962). It has been argued that in fact Merleau-Ponty's intentions were more directed toward the development of a specifically sexual philosophy than his commentators have realized; his central term "chair," or flesh, has an erotic connotation in French which Weiss has designated as essential to Merleau-Ponty's new theory of the libido (Weiss, 1981). Gabriel Marcel also developed a philosophical theory of the body (see Siewert, 1971; and Zaner, 1984). Julián Marías, who has reinterpreted the philosophy of Ortega in terms compatible with Catholicism, has also proposed that the body is inherently sexual, or rather, "sexuate," a distinction by which he means to refer to the inherent sexual dimorphism of human existence without emphasizing genital sexuality (Marías, 1971; see Donoso, 1982, pp. 64-68). Marías instead attaches great importance to the self-defining function of the sexuate division of humankind: I know I am a man only because I know that there are women, and for the woman, self-definition is equally "sexuate."

Without attempting to evaluate all of this work, I will merely state why I think Pepper has begun a more valuable project from the perspective of the sexual body. For one thing, Marcel's philosophy of the body was not concerned with sexuality. In fact, in reply to the comment by Marías that he had ignored the importance of sexuality (Marías, 1984, p. 567), Marcel could only concur, although he suggested that in his non-philosophical works, his dramas, this defect had been avoided. Rather startling is Marcel's declaration that "sexuality strictly speaking has not played a decisive role in my life" (Marcel, 1984a, p. 572). Marías' own insistence on the "sexuate" as an inherent category of human existence, an "installation" of life, as he calls it, is more problematical. To be frank, I suspect that the committed Catholicism of Marías (as well as that of Marcel) would not permit the full consideration of a new world hypothesis, open to possibilities which might not accord with the faith. As I have urged, the perspective of the sexual body introduced by Freud implies a break with traditional values. I doubt that either of these philosophers could make that break, which is not to deny that many of their observations and arguments on the body are valuable. Marías also often verged on what would now be called sexism in his exposition of the "sexuate condition." That is, he felt it was the inherent role of the male to exercize *senorio*, or "overlordship," while the correlative role of the woman was her "surrender" to the protection of the male, and to support his *gravedad*, a word connoting the endurance of the "burden of life" (quoted in Donoso, 1982, pp. 66-67). Although Marías did not intend these terms to have a sociopolitical meaning, it is not surprising that a woman philosopher has taken exception to them (MacGuigan, 1973), nor is it entirely clear to me how Donoso means to defend Marías against her accusations (Donoso, 1982, pp. 128-131). Probably the main issue here for the perspective of the sexual body is the question of whether Marías' type of philosophical anthropology could accommodate the historical changes in sexuality of the past century. There is some indication in fact that Marías has wished to make such an accommodation, in his recent untranslated work, *La mujer en el siglo xx* (1980). Unfortunately, Marías rejects the work of Freud in that book, not on empirical grounds, but because he believes the emphasis on sex and on a material, measurable libido in psychoanalysis can only devalue sexuality itself (Marías, 1980, pp. 126-141).

Pepper's main advantages as a philosopher in the context of the sexual body were probably first in his scope: he is offering a world hypothesis, which includes a theory of perception (see also Pepper, 1971), but is not limited to such a theory as is Merleau-Ponty's. Secondly, his empirical commitment is a great deal more serious than that of either Marcel or Marías. Pepper's lifetime of working closely in touch with empirical evidence regarding physiology and the motivation of purposes led him to a much finer descrimination of body qualities within his conceptual plan. The categories of Selectivism do not merely refer vaguely to the body as a ground for perception and experience; they incorporate such dynamic considerations as *"bodily action* and *tension pattern* arising from internal bodily changes, or environmental stimulation (the drive impulse)" (Pepper, 1967, pp. 28-30). All the categories are regarded as qualititatively felt. This amounts to saying that the world itself, on this hypothesis, is a world of qualitative feeling. Pepper's ability to relate biological, environmental and cultural categories and bring them to bear on a concept of individual purposive activity gives his original world hypothesis a potential for further development which would continue to incorporate the sexual body and all the feelings of sexuality.

Pepper shows in *Concept and Quality* how it is conceivable that the manifold of philosophical and psychological problems (indeed how all of the disciplines) may be organized under the rubric of the purposive act metaphor within an arrangement of selective systems. It would be interesting to determine if the perspective of *the sexual body could not only be incorporated* into his effort, *but* if it could have sufficient empirical warrant to be *considered as approximately coextensive with* Pepper's qualitatively grounded hypothesis. If the perspective of the sexual body is actually a version of a world hypothesis, then it would have relevance throughout the natural world, not only within human life. In this respect, the discovery by the biologist Joshua Lederberg in the 1950's that bacteria reproduce sexually is an interesting increment to the evidence warranting Pepper's hypothesis (Lederberg, Cavalli, and Lederberg, 1952). For his work, Lederberg shared a Nobel Prize in genetics in 1959. The "genetic recombination" of bacteria, by which they reproduce, is a kind of mating. As Lederberg phrased the matter, the genetic recombination of certain strains of the bacteria *Escherichia coli*, upon which he conducted his investigations, "corresponds exactly to the normal sexual fertilization in the higher organism" (quoted in *Current Biography*, 1959).

Another corroboration of a qualitative sexual world hypothesis comes from work in the study of "protolife" forms. Sidney W. Fox, of the Institute for Molecular and Cellular Evolution, has presented evidence of "protosexual" behavior in certain macromolecules (specifically thermal polyamino acids, usually referred to as protenoids) (Fox, 1978, 1980). In Dr. Fox's account of the behavior of these macromolecules,

> endoparticles combine with each other, exhibiting a primitive kind of recombinant behavior. The phenomena . . . when watched through a microscope, suggest a primitive kind of dating dance. Couples join and stay joined. Others join, break apart and rejoin. Others that break apart join with new partners. Moreover, during a typical three-day lifetime of a population, those less than half-a-day old are too young to conjugate, whereas those more than two-and-a-half days old are typically too old to conjugate. (Fox, 1980)

It might be objected that Fox is reading sexuality into these observations, a possibility he seems aware of in his own language: the phenomena "suggest" a dating dance, and they seem to "conjugate," in the reproductive process; but these terms are not the only ones he might have chosen. On the other hand, there are "couples" here, and the analogies with sexual behavior that his description reveals may be adequate to warrant his hypothesis that in fact we do find protosexual behavior at the molecular level. In working in the area of "protolife" forms, Fox is engaged in the study of the origins of life. Findings in this area concerning sexuality are frought with implications for any hypotheses of what the world is like; at a personal level, they also condition what we assume about life.

In human beings, the perspective of the sexual body implies that whatever is sexual is basic to the whole human organism, not something confined to certain parts. Recent research has highlighted the sexual dimorphism of the human brain, which takes place in the fetus (Goy and MacEwen, 1980; Hoyenga and Hoyenga, 1979). From a feminist ideological perspective, Bleier has denied that there is any evidence to warrant a claim of gender "organization" of the fetal brain; there are too many "confounding variables" (Bleier, 1984, pp. 86-93). Hoffer, however, deals with several of these variables and still concludes that "probably in humans," there is a good reason to attribute gender organization to fetal hormonal exposure in brain development (Hoffer, 1981, p. 168). Evidence for difference in degree of hemispheric lateralization between adult males and females is strong (Hoyenga and Hoyenga, 1979), and it also appears to be true that females have a more fully developed corpus callosum joining the two hemispheres of the brain (DeLacoste-Utamsing and Holloway, 1982). These findings are corroborations for a hypothesis of a sexual body root metaphor. A student who asked me why D.H. Lawrence (Lawrence, 1915/1981) referred to the "female brain" of one of his characters might have been advised to take this field of research into account.

A long tradition of mis-reasoning has labelled women as mentally "inferior" to man, on the basis of brain differences, as Sayers shows (1982, pp. 84-104). It is all the more to the credit and credibility of the neurobiologist, M. Christine DeLacoste, that she refused to jump to the conclusion that a 40% larger corpus callosum in women makes women "superior." She was urged to do so by radical women scientists at a meeting entitled *Critical Issues in Sexual Dimorphism Research*, but DeLacoste argued that we do not yet know how this larger corpus callosum area functions: it could enhance communication between the two brain hemispheres, as some feminists have said, or it could inhibit it. We do not know. But the finding opens a new avenue of thought: the difference in the corpus callosum is the first major male-female brain difference to be discovered that is not directly connected with sexual functioning

(Del Guercio, 1983). This is a good example, in fact, of a discovery where the term "sexual body" seems directly needed as a perspective which permits a comprehension of findings.

There is also the possibility of male-female functional differentiation in brain chemistry involving hormonal production and its effects. Although the meanings of such research into this problem are not clear to me, and are undoubtedly quite complex, the minimal claim by Broverman, Klaiber and Vogel (1980)—two clinical psychologists and an endocrinologist who have pursued this line of research against strong initial opposition from other professionals—is worth quoting. It is, simply: "The gonadal hormones are psychoactive" (1980, p. 74).

The bits of evidence I have been assembling in these comments upon bacterial reproduction, macromolecules, sexual dimorphic organization of the brain, and hormonal effects in the brain are intended to show that Pepper's root metaphor of the purposive act, grounded as it is in its categorial structure on the facts of a human body which has feeling, must have an essential stipulation that this body is sexual. Despite his considerable sexual body thinking, Pepper did not make this point explicit. Further, this kind of root metaphor may be extended to cover phenomena in the world, in addition to the human. Pepper's root metaphor of the purposive act thus gains credence, as he would have expected, from evidence not available when he formulated the world hypothesis of Selectivism.

As a world hypothesis, Selectivism would have to have smaller, more restricted theories within it, eventually covering all fields for which there is any evidence, such as a theory of ethics. A basically ethical consideration, for example, would be the whole area of cultural mandates concerning purposive activity. The inculcation of learned helplessness (Seligman, 1975), for example, is tantamount to destructive cultural interference with the human capacity to carry out purposive acts. But given the sexual nature of the body, interference with sexual functioning would be a way of crippling that capacity at its base. In this light, the advice of Odent, an obstetrician who follows and develops the theories of Leboyer, that the newborn infant's rooting instinct (in which the baby turns to the nipple) should be not merely an idle fact, but a kind of "infant right" that society should protect, acquires additional theoretical warrant (Odent, 1984a). Similarly, Wolff's evidence that jarring the cradle of a 4-day old infant boy can interfere with the pattern of erections (Wolff, 1966, p. 22) might cause us to ask seriously if such interference is harmful. To be sure, these erections, and the analogous bodily functions in the human female, are not purposive acts. Nonetheless, we are learning enough about the neonate to suspect strongly that any function is more than mere reflex. The "purposiveness" of the neonate erection is problematical but, I maintain, not nonsensical. The point of both these examples (rooting reflex and male neonate erection) is that Pepper's world hypothesis of Selectivism would give special sanction to a policy of noninterference with the neonate, based on the expectation that the cumulative weight of interferences will damage the ability to function in the most basic human way, the carrying out of purposes.

Formism as a Shelter for Fears of the Sexual Body

My reasons for making such suggestions are two: first, their very strangeness serves to highlight the radical possibilities of the perspective of the sexual body; and second, they are an indication of how a world hypothesis can be related to body events. I would invite comparison here with the applications of Pepper's world-hypotheses theories being made at this time by the distinguished psychologist and psychoanalytic theorist, Robert R. Holt. In two articles, Holt argues that Freudian psychology can best be classified as Contextualist, in Pepper's scheme, a conclusion with which I sympathize. However, Holt's exposition becomes vague and excessively abstract, especially as he places Pepper (and ultimately Freud as well) within a version of "Systems Philosophy" in which all levels of reality fit into one another without a single hitch (Holt, 1984; in press). I will not attempt to summarize Holt's elegant argument here; all I want to note, in fact, is that he has little to say about sexuality or the body and that he combines this reticence with some ill-considered insults (Holt, 1984, p. 153) aimed at Reich and Herbert Marcuse (1955). These are the two psychoanalytic theorists who took the greatest interest in the radical possibilities of sexuality, Reich through his theory of the sexual revolution and Marcuse in his critique of the cultural value of the myth of Eros. There is something more than Holt's personal taste involved in his disparagement: my suggestion is that the vagueness and the self-confirming levels of abstraction in Holt's exposition are a result of his loss of contact with the perspective of the sexual body. That perspective, in other words, has something to imply concerning theory formation itself. Most of the psychoanalytic formulations which I have found to be defective, as well as most of the research "explosion" in the field of the study of the infant, have avoided any extended consideration of the sexual body. It is as if researchers and theorists have run away from it. The result has been a series of reinventions of Formism within psychoanalytic theory and within research on the infant. The focus on the cognitive capacities of the infant accords with traditional interest in the human mind as a "higher" organism, well above the sexual body and its suspiciously animal correlates. The psychoanalytic world hypothesis that has emerged after the break from the early Freudian emphasis on sexual repression and human need has also been shaped through its unnoticed connection with Formism.

What I refer to here is Formism in the sense of assuming the need to match human behavior to patterns or forms that have long been known within culture. Long before the sex-hating theories of certain psychoanalysts had been developed, the baby had come to be tacitly regarded as basically suspect within the psychology of the Formistic world hypothesis, because the baby is *unformed* as yet in the patterns of culture that the adults have accepted. This helps to explain the extraordinary psychoanalytical attachment to the image of the infant as incapable of self-regulation and self-perception and at the same time full of hatred or other allegedly natural, destructive wishes. From within the world hypothesis of Formism, this notion of the infant had already been implicit. The infant's unreliable perceptual apparatus (so it was assumed to be) could only make it part of the valueless category of the "unstable." As Dewey argued, in Formism true "Being" or "Reality" was conceived to be perfect and immutable. For purposes of adequate scope, Formistic philosophy has got to acknowledge the fact of change and movement, and thus come in contact with that in existence which is unstable, but it cannot concede that this instability has its own existence: it is always teleological change *toward* the Real that is valued. The rest is considered to be chaos (Dewey, 1929b, p. 20).

> The traditional concept in natural ends . . . was that every change is for the sake of something which does not change, occurring in its behalf. (Dewey, 1929a, pp. 98-99; cf. Halper, 1984)

Such a view forces the mind into regarding infancy and childhood as existing "for the sake of maturity" (Dewey, 1929a, p. 99).

A recent philosophical consideration of the prevalent cultural meanings attributed to childhood in contemporary civilized culture, argues that there has been little change from this traditional view (Matthews, 1982). Our unacknowledged philosophical assumptions lead us to only three models: a Preformation model in which children are nothing but miniature men and women; a Specification-and-Generalization model which encourages the notion that a child is a schematic human being; and a Recapitulation model which suggests that children are primitives who must outgrow themselves. The last of these models is the great fear of Formism, while the first two are its pre-Freudian assumptions which are no longer very credible. The second model, that of Specification and Generalization, loses sight of the possibility that the neonate body could have neural pathways which are not present in later development, as some research in the newborn rat has suggested (Wiener, 1980, p. 235), or that the child of six years old has far *more* sensory receptors in a fingertip than he or she will have later on, as an adult—which is a fact, according to Schachtel (1959, p. 138). The human neonate has been found to sustain steady rhythmical sucking with its mouth, but some young adults who tried to imitate this sucking pattern could not do so: "The most stable adult performance was five times as variable as any of the newborns and the adults became tired within 2 min." (Stratton, 1982a, p. 129; Wolff, 1968). The newborn bodies do not simply "develop" into more mature ones.

Once the psychoanalytic revolution in thought had begun to occur, traditional expectations regarding the child could no longer be maintained, unless the notion of maturity itself were to be redefined so that it came to mean living in full acceptance of the sexual body. Accordingly, as the threat grew, Formist thinking began to infiltrate into the discipline of psychoanalytic thought. *Babies must be regarded as basically unfit* in order to warrant the imposition of cultural norms. The worst possible motives—innate unlimited sadism—are imputed to the infantile mind. Even when the analyst ascribes a sense of self to the infant at birth (an ascription basically at odds with current theory), he or she must do so with the proviso that this would be a self that violently rejects its situation as a dependent being. (See Hamilton, 1982, pp. 33-77 for a review of the several psychoanalytic theories regarding the neonate's ability to function as a self.)

In contrast, there was the original Freudian perspective of the sexual body. The early Freud, whose arguments presented in the U.S. in 1909 for a lessening of repression, a letting up on the civilized demands for sexual stifling of the human, threatened to break with Formism (Freud, 1910a; see also Freud, 1908). Far from envisioning a theory that would fasten upon deepseated endopsychic qualities which could not be changed, Freud wrote in 1914, in the preface to the third edition of his *Three Essays on the Theory of Sexuality*, that psychoanalysis attaches more weight to how a person develops, a course of life full of "accidental" factors, than it does to any inherent "disposition."

> For it is the accidental factors that play the principal part in analysis: they are almost entirely subject to its influence. (Freud, 1905b, p. xvi)

Five years later, Melanie Klein was one of the therapists who showed that she understood part of Freud's radical social implications. Speaking before the Hungarian Psycho-Analytical Society in 1919, and giving her first professional paper, she said:

> We can spare the child unnecessary repression by freeing—and first and foremost in ourselves—the whole wide sphere of sexuality from the dense veils of secrecy, falsehood and danger spun by a hypocritical civilization upon an affective and uninformed foundation. (Klein, 1975, p. 1)

Although Klein seems to have expected a great deal from sexual candor and sex education, her emphasis on how the therapist must be "first and foremost" among those who free the "whole wide sphere of sexuality" from civilized lies, is clearly in accord with Freud's original impetus toward social change. But Klein was soon to quit speaking in these terms; she was soon to help turn psychoanalysis around (see Chapter Three above). The later generations reversed Freud's emphasis, as the later Freud himself very nearly did.

Creation of the artifact of the self-less, helpless, destructive infant whose body exists in a state of confusion has in large part been both the method for this reversal, and its continuing justification.

The function of psychoanalytic concentration on the infant has also been that of distracting attention from the adult sexual body. The missing adult body in psychoanalytic theory cannot be explained as an omission that just happened to occur. The absence is too blatant, too much at odds with the original emphasis on sexuality in Freud to be explained away. The great threats to Formism in culture that are implied by what Reich called "The Sexual Revolution" need never be faced if only we can continue to cling to a theory of human nature that defines us as basically irresponsible due to the unavoidable facts of infancy. In such a definition, those who feared the great change could stave it off indefinitely.

Theoretical Intimacy

The sexual body posed a new problem within the life cycles of scientific hypotheses. There is something emotionally immediate, and personally intimate, in theories of what we are, sexually. This fact produces an intensification in the processes of theory that is not necessarily an advantage. By contrast, the best examples in Kuhn's *Structure of Scientific Revolutions* (Kuhn, 1970) are from the seemingly impersonal sciences of astronomy and chemistry. As Kuhn has shown, these sciences regularly have been loaded with emotional and symbolic meanings, so much so that the old notion of the purely objective institution of science has to be set aside. With the psychoanalytic theory of sexuality, however, the question was not so much whether the investigation *could* be loaded with meanings for the investigator; on the contrary, here was a topic so intrinsically intimate that it would produce instantaneous projections of a personal nature for the investigator. This condition of investigation is highly unusual, perhaps unique, in the sciences. The feeling must be something like this: "My evidence (clinical, self-analytical, empirical) is showing me what I am really like, and what others very probably are like, sexually and emotionally, and what it is showing is completely foreign to the expectations of the normal civilized person that I thought I was! Help!"

Kuhn's theory has nothing to say about such a crisis. In fact, it may have nothing to say about the cultural crises that underlie paradigmatic changes in general, as a recent criticism of Kuhn points out (Postiglione and Scimecca, 1983, p. 186). Kohut too, in his last work, expressed sharp disagreement with the use of Kuhn's theory to explain the nonreceptiveness many psychoanalysts display toward data and concepts which go against the grain of the paradigm they learned during their training analysis (Kohut, 1984, p. 163). Something more personal is at stake, a greater threat which prompts a search for help.

The "help" to which the investigator or theorist is likely to turn is the integration and normalization of psychoanalytic findings, within the manifold of other sciences on the one side, and within the traditions of humanism on the other. But would such moves toward the normal have the desired effect? At some level, perhaps an unconscious one, the investigator would be aware of a gaping discrepancy between his or her newly normalized theory of the infant and what is really felt about adult sexuality, based on what has been learned from the early Freud and from all the later supporting evidence that shows the reality of the sexual body. As a result, the theorist may go into another stage of refining and normalizing the theory, only to again be confronted with a feeling of dissatisfaction over the ever widening gap between the initial intimate perplexity and later theoretical security.

Is there anything in psychoanalytic therapy which would encourage such a process? Recently the psychoanalyst John Klauber has indicated that indeed there is. The analyst may be tempted to concentrate his or her attention on the process of interpretation as a defense against sexual impulses which could get out of control (Klauber, 1981). Not only is there the ever-present problem of the analysand's sexual body under the influence of transference; there is the analyst's own anxiety over the ability to control sexual impulses of his or her own. But while interpretations may be therapeutically correct, they may fail to defuse the intimate sexual level of the discourse, because therapeutic success itself carries an implication that the patient will become capable of acting in the manner of a sexually mature adult. Moreover, as the patient hears or mis-hears the analyst's interpretations, the message may become, unconsciously, one of sexual liberation. This complicates the transference, of course, which is Klauber's point; but it also complicates the position of the analyst. Several generations of analysts who have lived within this kind of intimate professional pressure might well evolve toward the avoidance of the sexual body delineated in the present study.

Sources of Change in the Disciplines

Because psychoanalysis is unable to abandon its roots in sexuality, it is safe to predict that there will continue to be creative dissatisfaction with its excessively desexualized theoretical revisions. The challenge of the sexual body will be revived periodically within it, even though the bulk of psychoanalytic theorists may avoid this challenge. Jacoby has argued, in fact, that the social processes of professionalization and, in the case of American psychoanalysis, the triumph of "medicalization," that is, the restriction of licenses for practicing psychoanalysis to holders of an M.D. degree, have produced a highly conservative social institution. Any hope that once might have been entertained for psychoanalysis as a source of radical change must be given up, according to Jacoby's theory of "the repression of psychoanalysis" (Jacoby,

1983). Drawing upon the Weberian theories of Burton J. Bledstein (Bledstein, 1976), Jacoby argues that psychoanalysis is not merely a special field of knowledge for which special training is necessary, but a method for the monopolization of certain skills and controlling their social applications (Jacoby, 1983, p. 144). Although there is much merit to Jacoby's argument, it seems to miss two possibilities for change which have not been closed off. One of these cannot be closed even under the conventions of professionalism: the need to change in order to conform to market pressures, such as the increased refusal of women to pay for therapy which tells them that they are suffering from penis envy. Second, there are also appropriations of the heritage of psychoanalysis outside of its own official circles, or its professional societies. In this respect, psychoanalysis resembles all of the disciplines of the sexual body: pressures for change frequently come from researchers who are acting somewhat outside of the accepted rituals of their field of specializations. (For example, it will be recalled that Kinsey was a zoologist.) With these two additional sources of change available to psychoanalytic thinking, and with the presence of courageous innovators within the field itself, the crisis of Formism is likely to recur periodically, or even continually. It will recur until such time as it is actually faced, along with the threat that this crisis poses to the entire manifold of Formistic assumptions.

It might also be noted that the triumph of medicalization—which Freud opposed (Freud, 1926b)—has not been complete. For example, Milton Klein, whose criticisms of the psychoanalytic model of infancy and whose critique (with David Tribich) of Freud's "blindness" toward the harm done by parents to children (Klein, 1981a; Klein and Tribich, 1979) I have cited, is not an M.D. As a Ph.D. he not only is a therapist but has worked as a training analyst within an institute for the training of psychoanalytic therapists. The *Review of Psychoanalytic Books*, founded in 1982, quickly established a reputation in the field, and became indispensable reading for anyone seriously interested in the range of psychoanalytic topics; yet it is edited by another analyst who has a Ph.D., and not an M.D., Joseph Reppen. Reppen's comprehensive review journal by no means selects its authors from the ranks of orthodox practitioners, although some conservative analysts, such as W.W. Meissner, M.D., S.J., who serves on its editorial advisory board and writes some of its reviews, presumably would not welcome the perspective of the sexual body. The review nonetheless succeeded in sounding a new note of theoretical work by M.D. analysts which are sympathetic to the perspective of the sexual body; one such is *Pleasure and Frustration: A Resynthesis of Clinical and Theoretical Psychoanalysis* by Leon Wallace, M.D., published by International Universities Press, the major publishing house for psychoanalytic writings in the U.S. (Wallace, 1984). Wallace argues for the primary role of pleasure in emotional development, and maintains that Freud was mistaken to give a large positive role to frustration as a developmental motivator. Wallace redefines and endorses the pleasure principle. Such an argument goes against the grain of recent psychoanalytic thinking; it is too close to the perspective of the sexual body. But it will be heard by at least a minority of analysts. It is also important that the Reichian tradition of psychoanalysis has survived, even though it is often ignored; it continues to provide challenges to psychoanalytic thinking, from within the perspective of the sexual body. There are at least some practitioners of such disciplines as psychology, neurophysiology, sociology, aesthetics, etc., who will take heed. Some of the impetus toward understanding the sexual body in other disciplines, in fact, may by now be based on a sense of sexuality within these disciplines which owes a great deal to the classical psychoanalytic period.

It would be an error, however, to credit psychoanalytic journals, books, ideas, therapists, or associations, with the power to have kept the sexual revolution in process and spreading, since the latter part of the 19th century. A deeper convergence of human needs has energized the peculiar interdisciplinary relations described in the present study. In matters of the sexual body, we are confronted not only with specific research possibilities and results, but with an area of cultural choice. The choices frequently are made before there can be any firm evidential base. For example, Wilhelm Reich in his later years regarded the hospital personnel and even the parents in the hospital birth scenes of their own children, as functionally blind and deaf: they simply did not hear or see the agonized screaming and obvious bodily discomfort of the newborn (Reich, 1983, pp. 3-4). For Reich, as for Leboyer and many others, the choice was clear: birthing must be made a situation of love, not violence. However, as far as there was any question of hard scientific evidence that distress at time of birth, or that separation from the mother in the first few hours or days of neonatal existence, actually does any baby any long term harm—Reich was lacking. Such evidence is largely still unavailable, one way or the other, and for experts such as Jerome Kagan, there is nothing to be said until and if the evidence confirms what Reich and Leboyer and some parents have felt. In fact, some of Kagan's major research on change and constancy in infancy came out just prior to the Leboyer wave, and it did deal with the relationship between "excessive crying and irritability" in infancy and later personality development. When the babies who had cried a great deal became children of 10 years, no significant behavioral differences were found between them and other, control-group children (Kagan, 1971). Kagan thus was not in a position to contribute to the change which soon began to take place in obstetric practices. As Lamb and Hwang acknowledge (1982, p. 2), the inhumanity of the obstetrics wards was obvious and inexcusable, and they are glad to see it begin to change, but they do not think science has anything to do with the change—nor should it have. This problem presents a choice: the reader may ask if he or she *wants* to encourage and support a birth process that is gentle, non-violent, and as self-regulatory on the part of infant and mother as possible, with ample body contact soon to follow, a process also involving affectional bodily presence of the father. I suspect that if the question is put this way, many could open themselves to feelings of empathy with the newborn as well as with the parents, and make an intuitive option for less pain and more love. This could be done on the grounds that it feels basically sane, basically human, to make that choice, rather than tolerate or even encourage the painful screaming of the infant that seems in most cases to be *caused* by unnecessary birth practices. We would not have to wait for evidence that better birth is beneficial in later life; being born is a part of life in itself.

The move toward gentle, loving birth, which is now a fairly strong social movement, did *not* gain its momentum from those in the fields of child development who took a neutral, purely scientific stand. Were the voices of scientists who require empirical evidence of damage in later development to have prevailed, the choice would have been made to keep having violent birth (cf. Arney, 1980, pp. 560-562). As I have noted, Leboyer did not go the route of trying to influence the obstetrics profession through publications in medical journals; instead he gave workshops and lectures and delivered thousands of babies before publishing his text—which reads like poetry—*Birth Without Violence*. Similarly, the decline within psychoanalytic therapy of the "penis envy" explanation of women's neuroses did not come about through scientific revision of the theory (penis envy would seem to be still part of the theory at this point); it came because women, living through their own growth in an age of sexual revolution, more and more refused to accept such explanations. Sexual research outside of psychoanalysis helped to change the attitudes of clinical psychology, but so did the vast psychosocial changes which have led millions of women into the work force even when they might have the opportunity of staying at home as housewives (Heckerman, 1980). The absurdity of attributing this entire social change in work to penis envy must have become evident by 1970, just as that absurdity was not obvious in the society of 1900.

The influence of a popular demand on scientific disciplines is part and parcel of the topic of the sexual body. The pop-poet Rod McKuen has had some impact, I suspect, upon reducing child-abuse or at least in calling attention to its existence, through the National Committee for Preventional Child Abuse, an organization which he has helped to organize. It has been argued seriously regarding the problem of the sexual molestation of children, that the higher the level of professional training by the social worker or family counselor who sees the child, the less willingness will there be to recognize what is going on sexually (Sgroi, 1975). If more attention has been directed toward the problem in recent years, after long delay, it may be the result of a reform within the "Helping" professions by a minority of workers who had an awareness of larger nonprofessional support. Simplified presentations such as Masson's recent *The Assault on Truth: Freud's Suppression of the*

Seduction Theory (Masson, 1984a), serve at least to sound an alarm outside of the professional journals. It would also be a mistake to dismiss as "sensationalism" certain recent articles in newspapers which describe not the theory of child abuse, but its graphic practice; a news story telling of an 18-month old boy whose rectum was found to be bleeding because his father had forcibly penetrated him, is likely to get more than a routine reading. The cumulative effects of such work will include a prurient appeal to puritan values—but also will lead to popular demand for changes in therapeutic assumptions and in the mores of the family.

Research Formulations in the Light of Popular Pressures

Unfortunately, the tremendous wave of popular interest in sexual abuse of children will also encourage the adult denial of sexuality in children altogether. The PBS program "Crime of Silence" (1984) contains the briefest acknowledgment that children are naturally sexual (but no acknowledgment that children masturbate) in a half hour of condemnations of the "Crime" along with ways to prevent it. Probably if anything is clear in the present study of the sexual body, it is that human sexuality is too complex for simple nostrums to work. Thus the idea that adult-child sexual contact must always be bad, or that incest must always be harmful, which was the implied position of the program, can only confuse matters. None of the experts continually referred to in this broadcast represented the viewpoint of the group of researchers in *Children and Sex: New Findings, New Perspectives*, edited by Larry L. Constantine and Floyd M. Martinson (1981). For the contributors to this book, it is still necessary to ask such questions as what quality of sexual contact occurred between adult and child, and it is still possible to say that not all such contact is bad. In fact one contributor, Joan Nelson, offers a brief statement of self-evaluation which will no doubt anger any moralistic guardians of sexual innocence who happen to read her article:

> This study was motivated in part by a strong personal need to know the "truth" about incest. When I was a child I experienced an ongoing incestuous relationship that seemed to me to be caring and beneficial in nature. There were love and self-actualization in what I perceived to be a safe environment. I remember it as perhaps the happiest period in my life. (Nelson, 1981, p. 163)

For Nelson, who is identified as a doctoral candidate at the Institute for the Advanced Study of Sexuality, tremendous harm came about not through the incestuous relationship but from her mother's horrified reaction upon learning of its existence. Other contributors to this volume (several of whom are women) are sensible to the damages and traumata of incest and adult-child sexual contact, but never allow themselves to be stampeded into simple

HYPOTHESES AND SCIENCES

condemnation. In their study of "forbidden sexual behavior among kin," Symonds, Mendoza, and Harrell (1981) conclude with the necessary discriminations:

> We would not condone incest if it is coercive or used by one member of the family in a power struggle, just as we would not condone other behavior used in that way. It appears, however, that where incestuous relations do not harm and have some positive aspects for those involved, the taboo should be played down rather than built up. (p. 162)

Another chapter in this volume studies childhood molestation in terms of its "differential impacts on psychosexual functioning" (Tsai, Feldman-Summers, and Edgar, 1981). The very concept that impacts could be differentiated is hardly suggested in the popular presentations, which tend to repeat unexplained shock statistics such as "one out of every three children up to 16 years of age report that they have been sexually abused." Yet from this time on, research on the sexual body of the infant, child, and adolescent will take place in a new context of an enlarged public awareness grounded in part upon a number of misconceptions. Without the misconceived aspects, however, there probably would not have been such awareness at all. Psychoanalysis, as the key discipline in the study of the sexual body, can only benefit in the long run from being obliged to give up its entrenched assumption that reports of childhood sexual abuse by clients in therapy are largely fantastic, or that even if such reports are true, they should be dealt with in the theoretical dynamics of sexual fantasy, just as if they had not occurred between human sexual bodies.

Any sharp dichotomy between professional and popular pressures toward change in the disciplines is thus misleading from the perspective of the sexual body. Those of us who work within specialized disciplines also make up some of the "popular" demands upon these disciplines; no one is specialized in all areas of life. As we absorb the perplexing evidence and controversies regarding the sexual body, we are also constantly re-forming our world view. We may revise it only to keep it the same, or we may make slow changes in how we view the world, other people, relationships, and our own bodies, as we think about the sexual body. I propose that having the nourishing flow of new problems which may be thought about and whose impact may be felt is as much a purpose for engaging in a professional discipline as is the specialized practice of the discipline itself. The new problems provide the opportunity for growth, intellectual and emotional. This perhaps is a truism, but in the disciplines of the sexual body it appears to be especially important.

To return to prospects for change within professional contexts, I would like to note two developments reported by the pioneers of "maternal-infant bonding," Marshall H. Klaus and John H. Kennell (see Chapter Six above). In their 1982 revised edition of *Parental-Infant Bonding*, they tell of their attempt to tone down their statements on the importance of bonding in order to allay the possible fears they had been creating among parents who had not had the opportunity for an early bonding experience with their newborn infant. They had also been severely criticised by professionals for this same fault. However, there was an unfortunate result in their effort

> to speak more moderately about our convictions concerning the long-term significance of this early bonding experience. Unfortunately, we find that this had led some skeptics to discontinue the practice of early contact or to make a slapdash, rushed charade of the parent-infant contact, often without attention to details necessary to the experiences provided for mothers in the studies. (Klaus and Kennell, 1982, p. 56)

Klaus and Kennell thus see themselves as caught in a "dilemma" of either having to make overstatements and popularize their approach, or allowing their work to fail to have an impact on bonding practices. From the perspective of the sexual body, it might appear that their dilemma was due to pressures brought to bear upon them—such as causing them guilt for allegedly making some parents feel guilty—by professional critics who would have preferred not to have to deal with the idea of bonding at all.

Klaus and Kennell evolved another method for meeting the related implied criticism which held that their advocacy of bonding could only cause guilt for mothers who delivered by Ceasarian section. Instead of evading this problem, Klaus and Kennell have devised a postnatal procedure for these deliveries which achieves some of the specifications of their model of early contact between mother and infant. A local anesthetic is used, and fathers are permitted in the delivery room.

> The father sits behind the mother with the anesthesiologist, receives the infant, holds the infant, and shows the infant to the mother.
> Twenty minutes following the birth, the mother, infant, and father go to the small labor room where they have privacy and the infant can be placed next to the mother with a heat panel. Here the mother can have the normal 45 to 60 minutes together with her husband and the newborn infant. (Klaus and Kennell, 1982, p. 92)

An ingenious feature of this procedure is that it takes advantage of the period when the local anesthesia is still effective, thus allowing for contact to take place before post-surgical distress and depression can set in (*ibid.*). Kliot, an obstetrician who follows Leboyer's teachings, also reports that he has developed a modified Leboyer procedure for Caesarian births. "No detrimental effects to the neonates have been observed" (Kliot and Silverstein, 1984, p. 173, endnote added by authors to offprint). Such innovations by Klaus and Kennell, and by Kliot and Silverstein, demonstrate a creative response to the social movement of nonviolent birth. Brazelton, who has taken a more cautious approach to the bonding controversy, might now wish to reconsider his view that a Caesarean section delivery automatically implies a "forced separation" of mother and infant (1981, pp. 80-104).

In a related practical application of a kind which might have been presumed to be unfeasible, Prescott, whose work on the value of affectionate somatosensory contact I have discussed, is reported to have developed a special rocker for premature infants in incubators. The device provides a facsimile of the movement the fetus would have experienced had it not been born prematurely (Utts, 1984).

The Challenge of the Sexual Body in Current Social Theory

In most theories, the very talk of making "choices" in life would be a signal that the discussion was no longer a scientific one. Dewey, however, long ago recognized that we are living in a time of history that will require choice in the realm of values, and that such choices should be intelligent ones—which means that scientific evidence will be important in making them. In *The Quest for Certainty* (1929b), Dewey's chapter on "The Construction of Good" stands as an opening statement on what must be done. For those who believe they already know what "good" is, the chapter is laughable. There is no need to "construct" what we already have. For those who would agree with me that the ongoing discovery of the sexual body is one of the developments in modern life that brings us into an unprecedented social situation, where we must both choose and make our choices in the midst of unsolved questions, Dewey's topic is crucial. To the chagrin of his critics, Dewey maintains that we will have to experiment empirically in the "field of ideas of good and bad" (1929b, p. 258). The phrase may arouse suspicions of "human research," but what Dewey had in mind was not the laboratory but the social context of modern life. The alternative to intelligent experimentation is not reliance on a set of conservative social values which have broken down; it is the indefinite extension of social chaos into the future, unless intelligent use is made of the changes already under way in science, psychology, and in society at large.

Evolutionary Theory and the Sexual Body

Although the perspective of the sexual body is inherently interdisciplinary, it may be the case that certain disciplines are so constituted as to be unable to make a positive contribution toward understanding the huge social experiment of the sexual revolution. An open question at this point is whether any of the disciplines are inherently based on assumptions that would cause them to give support to traditional values, irrespective of the modern situation. If there were such a discipline, it might be the study of evolution. Here we may consider the views of Donald Symons, in his highly praised work *The Evolution of Human Sexuality* (Symons, 1979). Symons is aware of the changing and unusual context of modern sexual life in the sexual revolution, and rightly regards it as part of a vast social experiment:

> To some extent the artificiality of modern Western environments can be considered to constitute an unplanned experiment .... By the standards of preliterate peoples, modern human communities provide an enormous pool of potential sexual and marital partners, relatively few taboos, unprecedented freedom from parental influences, and thus great scope for personal attraction based upon physical appearance. (Symons, 1979, pp. 204-205)

In Symons' reading of human sexual evolution, physical appearance is very likely tied to reproductive fitness. Symons expects that the lifting of taboos will slowly bring about a return to the "adaptive human dispositions" which have functioned throughout human existence. The problem with his formulation is that it really amounts to no "experiment" at all: we remove the taboos only in order to return to the evolutionary roots of sexual relationships in connection with reproductive success. These roots are authoritarian in their social embodiment, rather than self-regulative. Symons maintains that biological study of human and other mammalian species shows that male and female sexuality, considered separately, differ very greatly, to such a degree that the two sexes should be regarded as two different species. Symons (1979) explains his intention of showing this in his Preface:

> A central theme of this book is that, with respect to sexuality, there is a female human nature and a male human nature, and these natures are extraordinarily different, though the differences are to some extent masked by the compromises heterosexual relations entail and by moral injunctions. (p. v)

What sort of compromises and injunctions Symons has in mind are explained more fully in his chapter, "Copulation as Female Service" (pp. 252-285). In this model, heterosexual life is presented as a trade-off of male support and protection for female sexual "service"; such abstractions as "love" merely disguise that arrangement. This service "can be given freely, traded, or taken by force" (p. 284). Symons does not recommend the latter alternative, by any means. However, in order to prevent the use of force (which in the prehistoric past has shown its adaptive value), there must be both *structural barriers* which forcibly prevent a person from carrying out some sexual impulses, and *socialized inhibitions*, which are products of the socialization process (pp. 284-285). It is not my aim at this point to debate the merits of Symons' conclusions. I merely point out that they are a prescription for considerable social suppression and internalized inhibition of sexual expression. Symons argues for this prescription through a discussion of the problem of rape, where it seems to make common sense. (I say *seems* to make sense, because Reich has argued that adequate male sexual gratification will prevent the occurrence of rape impulses—which are quite another matter than rape fantasies—and that this method of dealing with rape will prove far superior to the attempt to control it through prohibitions. See Reich, 1968, p. 155.) But Symons explicitly generalizes this argument from rape to all of human sexuality. Given Symons' approach to the evolution of human sexuality, he would have to reach such a conclusion. What he argues in effect is that the only result other than self-annihilation that can emerge from the sexual revolution is a re-creation in suitable modern terms of the same repressive controls over the sexual body which have been brought into question in the first place. Nor does Symons make any concessions to the notion of alternative world hypotheses or to interdisciplinary contributions which might clarify the sexual revolution in quite different ways than his own. On the contrary, he regards his evolutionary knowledge as impeccably scientific, and presents it as if it were value free. He even denies that his book has anything to do with social policy recommendations (Symons, 1979, p. vi). Yet it obviously entails very serious recommendations, by virtue of his endorsement of the barriers of inhibition.

Symons presents important evidence that any overall interdisciplinary account of the sexual body must consider. It would seem however, that unless his own Formistic assumptions are made clear, there is nothing at issue. Once the Formism is acknowledged, it might be possible to go on to other models of the "selective systems" for survival that have been evolved thus far. In this light, Pepper's discussion (Pepper, 1967) would come into play. From the perspective of the sexual body, a critique of Symons would emphasize three points. First, if we grant that adult sexual intercourse (if heterosexual) involves the energy interactions of man and woman, then the artificial problem of trying to have two virtually distinct species, male and female, get along with each other, is greatly alleviated. Men and women can and do feel the merging of their two organisms in sex. The significance of this merging is an empathic recognition of their profound compatibility. It is not a way to feel that each sex has built-in biological interests of its own, which would ignore the needs of the other if it could only get away with it. Despite Symons' boast that the study of evolution provides the most important evidence we have for understanding the human species, it cannot operate as a solo discipline: disciplines that tell us about the relational qualities of the interactions of the sexes are vital to understanding the species.

One such research effort is the study of human love based on an oral autobiographical account by a teenage girl of her dating and courtship relations. In it, we can follow her development from dating to sexual love and commitment (Schwartz and Merten, 1980). This account by "Cheryl" might fit into Symons' capacious evolutionary categories, but it would also have the contemporary relevance of a life within a society where the pressure to reproduce has undergone a shift toward intelligent self-regulation. During most of Symons' account of the evolution of sexuality, the potentials for relationships within such a shift were not available to the human race.

Another research inquiry which focusses upon a problem which sexual evolution has not previously been called on to face is the recent book by

Frank F. Furstenberg and Graham H. Spanier, *Recycling the Family: Remarriage After Divorce* (1984). The point of their eight-year study is that marriage is not exactly duplicated in remarriage; marriage becomes a very different process for the large numbers of people who go through the transition from marriage to divorce to remarriage. Not only are there special problems such as keeping some combination of distance and maintaining communication with a former spouse; there are also new expectations which are not usually present in a first marriage. There is a greater awareness that marriage may be an unstable, impermanent arrangement. This awareness would become generalized to the experience of marriage per se, eventually. A related problem is that of the adolescent who grows up under the supervision of a divorced parent. Teenagers in that circumstance are reported to have difficulty in accepting the behavior of the parent who dates, not because of Oedipal jealousies (although these cannot be ruled out), but because the behavior of the adult seems to interfere with the adolescent's own need to think of sexuality as a matter of love. In other words, adolescent fantasy is threatened by the idea that not all sexuality on the part of a parent is necessarily connected with love, or with falling in love (Francke, 1983, pp. 171-173). But adolescent fantasy has been conditioned by a cultural prescription which equates sexuality and love. Inasmuch as divorce is not likely to become greatly less frequent than it is now, a question for research would be, how can adolescents overcome this difficulty? How, in fact, have some of them perhaps already overcome it? Why are some unable to do so? Now Symons does discuss divorce, and he does not dismiss marriage as a purely social institution about which the science of evolution can tell us nothing. But the focus of his book is simply too broad to include an examination of the pattern of remarriage. The real issue here, however, is whether the questions investigated by Furstenberg and Spanier could ever have been *asked*, from the theoretical perspective Symons offers.

Second, there would have to be a recognition within Symons' theory, as there presently is not, of the human possibilities for self-regulation in sexuality. This would not settle the question of whether other controls are needed, but it would at least allow the question to be asked intelligently.

Third, it is revealing that Symons has only very bad things to say about ethnographic description; he faults all cross-cultural evidence on sexuality as hopelessly inept and biased (Symons, 1979, pp. 66-71). Thus Prescott's theory of the value of affectionate touching cannot gain entry into Symons' discussion. Were it permitted entry, that discussion might be improved. It would definitely have to be changed. The net result of Symons' book is an excellent example of an approach grounded in an established discipline which avoids most of the problems we are faced with, even as it recognizes that we are engaged in a great social experiment during the continuation of the sexual revolution.

Experiment and Risk: Psychoanalytic Pedagogy and Self-Regulation

Of the many studies I have commented upon, only one seems to have been a deliberate attempt at an experiment in the lives of those engaged in the study, namely the autobiographical account of the free family by Jean and Paul Ritter (1959, 1976). The Ritters could hardly have carried out this experiment in the context of a professional institution; at least they could not have justified the project with all its possible risks for the children involved. Inasmuch as certain risks were taken, both for their children and for the Ritters themselves, it is important that the results of their project become known so that later "free families" will have the benefit of this experiment. Yet their experiment is not generally known. Leboyer's delivery of thousands of infants according to his method required that he take chances, not only with his career, which might have been a real risk for him, but for the infants so delivered. Would they turn out happier and healthier, in some of the meanings of those unavoidable value-terms, than would have been the case under ordinary hospital practice? By going ahead with his project, Leboyer has managed to launch it into the world. Recent research on the Leboyer birth procedure is now able to focus upon a different question than the primary one, would it work? Kliot and Silverstein (1984) are content to show that there is excellent empirical justification for saying that at least the Leboyer procedure does not hurt the health or well-being of the baby or of the mother. In other words, they have now put the issue at the level of a choice: those who find value in the Leboyer procedure are able to make that choice, without having to wait for longitudinal studies which *might* answer some of the many questions about the long term effects. Kliot reports that since writing his article (with Silverstein), he has "delivered more than 1,500 infants, incorporating the Leboyer bath into the birth management technique" (Kliot and Silverstein, 1984, p. 173; endnote added by authors in offprint).

Psychoanalytic theory at one time was complemented by a series of social experiments which were inspired by its early commitment to the sexual body. Sol Cohen has recounted that there were several experimental schools with the definite aim of freeing the child of inhibitions, even of dissolving the superego, an aim which the staid Franz Alexander could designate as "the task of all future psychoanalytic therapy" (Alexander, quoted in Cohen, 1979, p. 194). These schools of the 1920' and 1930's, in Berlin and Vienna, were an experiment in sexual enlightenment. Yet by the end of the 1930's, the experiment had been found a failure by the notable analysts who had worked in the schools as teacher-therapists, such as Siegfried Bernfeld, Willi Hoffer, and Erik Erikson. Anna Freud, whose seminar on child analysis was closely attended by several of the teachers, was to concur. By 1935, Anna Freud was able to conclude that the sexual drives of the child cannot be allowed to go uncontrolled by a superior force:

> for if they [the sexual drives] are constantly breaking through, there is a danger that his [the child's] development will be retarded or interrupted, that he will rest content with gratification instead of sublimating, with masturbation instead of learning; that he will confine his desire for knowledge to sexual matters instead of extending it to the whole wide world. This we want to prevent. (Anna Freud, 1935, p. 20, quoted by Cohen, 1979, p. 207)

How Anna Freud reached these dreary conclusions is not made clear in Cohen's article; what the article does show is a pervasive sense of "struggle" with, or rather against, the instinctual gratifications of the children. On the basis of Hoffer's description of the experimental school with which he was involved, some further clues may be gathered. The school was operating on a theoretical expectation that if the children were not subjected to sexual repression, they would develop in accordance with the phases of Freud's model, but that proved to be a problem. Latency especially "did not occur: only a limited reduction of instinctual expression could be observed" (Cohen, 1979, p. 205). The children not only remained highly "instinctual" in their behavior, but their emotional life seemed to be very disturbed, full of irritability, obsessions, depression and anxiety (*ibid.*). No doubt the analysts had indeed discovered that the pathway toward self-regulation was a troubled one, but it remains unclear how much of the "deterioration of character" (Hoffer, 1945, pp. 302-303, quoted by Cohen, 1979, p. 205) was due to their own unpreparedness for the vital life of the child, which offered little resemblance to civilized models of deportment, and how much to the analyst's expectations (cf. Hoffer, 1981). Another of these experimental schools, which lasted for nine months in the year 1920, not only expected the children to develop into free spirits who did not undergo sexual repression; the children were also being prepared for later Zionist emigration to Palestine and for Socialism (Cohen, pp. 196-197). Even with all that burden, the school appears to have given tentatively encouraging results.

The school in which Hoffer and Erikson were teachers operated for several years. Hoffer himself carried certain psychoanalytic beliefs with him which helped to guarantee that the experiment would fail. He concluded in fact that experiments in children's freedom were useless no matter how well they might be run. Arguing that it would be wrong to leave the child "alone with his various drives," Hoffer maintained that the Oedipal wishes

> are prone to frustration even without any external influence. To excite castration fear in the boy and penis envy in the girl no other stimulation from the outside is necessary than the unavoidable sight of the other's genitals. (Hoffer, 1945, p. 303)

Clearly, the "various drives" must be subjected to control. Erik Erikson, after three years of teaching in a school founded by Anna Freud and Dorothy Burlingame, declared that sexual enlightenment alone did not make for healthy children (Homberger, 1935). Erikson (at that time still writing under the name of Erik Homberger) concluded, much as Anna Freud was to do, that the child will continue to form "anxieties, fantasies, and unconscious and conscious [sexual] theories, regardless of sexual enlightenment" (Homberger, 1935, pp. 58-59). One problem here is that Erikson appears to have thought it desirable for the child not to fantasize about sex, and not to make up "theories" about it. But why that would be good for the child is not explained. If we take seriously the psychological needs of a child with a sexual body which the child remains interested in, and the child's observations of other people's bodies, then much repression would have been necessary for the disappearance of sexual fantasies. Erikson does show that some of the children did not thrive in the atmosphere of sexual enlightenment; some in fact showed signs of becoming *more* repressed to the extent of becoming unable to ask Erikson the questions about sex that were (as he persuasively infers) troubling them. But Erikson says almost nothing about the context in which these children were living.

That context could easily have been a factor in the "failure" of the experiment to produce healthy, unrepressed children. One student in the school at which Erikson taught was Peter Heller, who is now a professor of Modern Languages at SUNY-Buffalo. Heller's invaluable account of his psychoanalytic therapy as a child (age 9 to 12), when he was a patient of Anna Freud (Heller and Bittner, 1983) is especially revealing since it draws upon both his own memories and upon the notes Anna Freud kept of his case, which she generously gave to Heller for his use in writing his book. Heller has little doubt about Anna Freud's conservative attitude regarding sexual matters (Heller, 1984, p. 8), but this did not hinder her from explaining the "basics of sex" to young Peter. According to her notes, this explanation was gratifying to him, although he now does not recall the feeling (1984, p. 6). It can be seen that Anna Freud was still following the advocacy of her father's essay (Freud, 1907) on the sexual enlightenment of children. The pertinence of Heller's case history to the experiment in psychoanalytic pedagogy—for at the time that he was in therapy with Anna Freud he was also in the school where Hoffer and Erikson were his teachers—lies in its information concerning family context. Heller's parents were going through a complicated separation and divorce, involving a lengthy separation of the young boy from his mother. He developed a partial awareness of non-monogamous behavior by his parents, which was carried out *without* the condition of their enlightening him. As his case history makes clear, his disturbing symptoms, such as his night terrors which woke him up screaming, were connected with the family dynamics. But the accounts by Erikson, Hoffer, and by Anna Freud herself of the psychoanalytic pedagogical experiments make no mention of the pressures and strains which the children were undergoing in their family lives. The omission of such essential matters unfortunately serves to reinforce the impression that the experiment with sexual enlightenment, and with the sexual self-regulation of children, "failed."

Even within the context of the school, it hardly will do to enlighten children about sexuality while implying in all sorts of ways that they had best not engage in sex play, should curtail masturbation, and not drift off into daydreaming. Erikson, a few years later, began to be interested in implementing the social "organization" of the infant's "early bodily experiences and through them," of the early ego (Erikson, 1982, p. 23). His heart certainly was not drawn to the concept of self-regulation for children. In 1936, he visited a tribe of Sioux Indians and was deeply and favorably impressed with their infant rearing practices, particularly, the Sioux mother, who

> while still nursing during the teething stage . . . would playfully aggravate the infant boy's ready rage in such a way that the greatest possible degree of latent ferocity was provoked. (1982, p. 35)

The energies thus "provoked and deflected" would be later "channelized" into culturally normal activities. Erikson considered this sort of behavior by the mother as part of her "almost unrestricted attentiveness and generosity" (*ibid.*). He also felt a powerful convergence between these Indian ways of childrearing and psychoanalytic theory (p. 23). Given his assumptions, it is not surprising that his work as teacher in the progressive school founded by Anna Freud led him to unenthusiastic conclusions.

All in all, these experiments "proved" something to the founders and teachers which they were too eager to accept: namely that without sexual repression and control over children's lives, there can be no expectation of producing anxiety-free "normal" children whose sexuality would never pose a threat to their progress in schools nor threaten their teachers' most cherished values. Half a century after the demise of the psychoanalytic experiments in self-regulation for elementary pupils, Erik Erikson was still referring to the unexpected "defensive behavior of an intimidated and inhibited sort" which some of the children had developed (Erikson, 1982, p. 84). Plainly, the experience impressed him deeply; it discouraged any further experimentation on his part or on the part of Anna Freud.

Heller (1984) has remarked that there has been some effort on the part of his former teachers and his older acquaintances from the Viennese psychoanalytic circle of the period 1929-1932 to persuade him that no experiment had ever taken place—there was nothing more than a school which happened to be closely associated with Anna Freud. This advice has conflicted with his earlier impression that there had indeed been an experiment (Heller, 1984). As we have seen, the experiment was centered not on a generalized conception of childhood freedom, but on a hypothesis concerning the sexual body, namely that sexual enlightenment would lead to healthier development. Anna Freud's therapeutic practice with her young patient was also grounded in the sexual body. Not only did she enlighten the boy at a factual level, but as his account makes clear, she stressed sexuality as the key psychological factor throughout the course of treatment, often at the cost of other factors which Heller now feels might have been given more attention (Heller, 1984, pp. 5-6). She emphasized sexuality notwithstanding her own rather ascetic personal preferences. The sexual body was still central to psychoanalysis, but its relation to health was not adequately formulated.

The narrow hypothesis that sexual enlightenment in itself would prevent intrapsychic conflicts over sex may have been disconfirmed in these experiments in psychoanalytic pedagogy. A broader hypothesis, however, that sexual enlightenment combined with a consistent child rearing practice of self-regulation would lead to self-regulated children who would be capable of dealing in a relatively unarmored manner with the inevitable traumas of growing up, was not implicated. As Reich put it,

> We must abandon the mystical expectation that we are going to bring up perfectly healthy human beings. It is totally unrealistic to believe that children will grow up without traumas. . . . We are not aiming for perfectly healthy children. We are fighting against the impact of events that cause armoring. (quoted in Sharaf, 1973, p. 256)

The psychoanalytic pioneers who experimented in pedagogy thus misunderstood their project. They expected perfection through knowledge, and did not understand that knowledge is much more than honest enlightenment on matters of sexuality. Knowledge to be meaningful from the perspective of the sexual body would have to have been created in the context of the many obstacles against self-regulation which culture has erected through its "contempt for the body, fear of the senses, and the opposition of flesh and spirit" (Dewey, 1934, p. 20, once more).

In the historical context of European childrearing, it would have taken, and it still would take, a much greater effort to overcome a heritage in which children often were considered a hindrance to be disposed of as simply as possible. Elisabeth Badinter, in *Mother Love: Myth and Reality* (1981), has brought to light widespread evidence that from 1760 onward, French children of all classes were abandoned, or given to wetnurses who would be expected to insure their nonsurvival. In 1850, for example, some 80% of infants born in Paris and sent to the country for care by wetnurses died before the age of two (Badinter, 1981, p. 193). As late as 1907, 30% to 40% of all newborns in the large French cities were sent to the countryside for nursing (p. 192). The mortality rate was considerably higher for these children as compared with those nursed by their own mothers (p. 193, footnote). Badinter produces evidence to support her hypothesis that maternal indifference has been an especially strong cultural phenomenon in France; it is being slowly countered by social conditioning—of which Badinter quite disapproves—which teaches women that they "should" feel virtually unlimited quantities of "mother love." Badinter's research reinforces the work of DeMause (1974), who has maintained that parental indifference and hostility toward infants and children has been the widespread and indeed the dominant pattern in the Western world until recently. Smith (1984) concisely summarizes the research by Badinter, DeMause, and others during the past two decades, as showing "a particularly disturbing pattern in the treatment of children over the centuries" (Smith, 1984, p. A). He then draws a connection between that pattern and the "great national experiment in childcare" now taking place in the U.S. This experiment, Smith argues, is being vitiated by the neglect of children's needs, especially in the commercially operated franchise-chains of day-care centers. The day-care situation has been brought to public attention by Valerie Suransky in *The Erosion of Childhood* (1982). In contrast to the U.S., Sweden provides day-care centers in which the ratio of child to adult is no higher than 5:1, and it gives salary payment to parents (including fathers) who wish to take days off from their employment in order to take part in the child care center in which their children are enrolled (Thomas, 1984). Britain has a licensing system for childcare workers; it offers a two year study program followed by an examination which qualifies these workers, providing their health is good, their police records are not suspicious, and their references are favorable. According to Thomas, there have been no sex-abuse scandals in day-care centers in those countries (Thomas, 1984).

The broad historical context in which childcare and education outside of the family take place should be considered when evaluating the several short-lived psychoanalytic pedagogical experiments of the period 1905-1938 (Cohen, 1979). The ironic fact is that these schools were inaugurated by adherents of a theory which gave a central position to the sexual body, which focused attention on the sexuality of children, and which emerged in a culture where disregard or outright violence toward the child's sexual body had been the major historical heritage. Yet within a few years the experiment was given up. One result may have been to further delay a shared social awareness among specialists in education as well as among parents and the populace at large that self-regulation, far from having been discredited, has never been tried on a large enough scale over a long enough time span to have yet had its experimental test.

Child and Infant Research as Social Experiment

The early psychoanalytic schools were experiments such as Dewey envisioned; they dealt with the creation of values, although they were also attempting to recreate some traditional values through a new method. Their "failure" had a fateful effect on the social bearing of psychoanalytic theory, giving it further justification for its attempt to turn away from the sexual body. In a sense, it can be said that the "army of infant observers and researchers" to which Galenson and Roiphe have referred (1981, p. x) are also engaged in an experiment with the values of good and bad even though any given experiment considered individually may not seem to be part of any larger pattern of social change. Much of the literature gives an impression, in fact, of a "fallacy" pointed to by Dewey long ago. The fallacy is to assume that because a given experimental procedure is free of any application in life, therefore the entire empirical endeavor of the sciences is ultimately just as free. Science thus becomes an exercise in pure abstraction. The fallacy is a kind of occupational hazard, "easy to fall into on the part of intellectual specialists" (Dewey, 1929b, p. 154). Dewey maintained that science and its researchers ultimately exist for the purpose that all inquiry exists: to permit "added depth, range and fullness of meaning [to be] conferred upon objects of ordinary experience" (1929b, pp. 190-191). The sexual body in infant, adolescent, and adult is such an object of ordinary experience. The special problem for inter-disciplinary study is considered by Dewey, in this statement:

> The sheer increase of specialized knowledge will never work the miracle of producing an intellectual whole. Nevertheless, the need for integration of specialized results of science remains, and philosophy should contribute to the satisfaction of this need. (Dewey, 1929b, p. 312)

As Dewey goes on to say, however, this task calls for something extra, something that scientific research and theory alone cannot give:

> The need, however, is practical and human rather than intrinsic to science itself; the latter is content so long as it can move to new problems and discoveries. The need for direction of action in large social fields is the source of a genuine demand for unification of scientific conclusions. They are organized when their bearing on the conduct of life is disclosed. (1929b, p. 312)[1]

In this light, we may say that the cumulative effects of knowing a great deal more than we did about the infant will undoubtedly bring changes in child-rearing and parental marital status. For example, the single-parent family is now part of the "mainstream of American society," but there is still little research comparing the effects on children of this living arrangement with children in two-parent families (Thompson and Gongla, 1983, p. 110). Unfortunately, some distinguished behavioral scientists such as the medical sex researcher Money (1980, p. xiv) and the cultural anthropologist Naroll (1983) have condemned the single parent family out of hand, as something inherently bad for children. They have not waited to find out what the new

---

[1] As these statements by Dewey show, he did not abandon the philosopher's role of attempting to show how empirical inquiry has bearing on life, and particularly on the social practices and policies of societies. It is somewhat misleading to reduce Dewey's later position to one of advocating a culture of "aesthetic enhancement" as opposed to one in which "objective cognition" is the dominant motif (Rorty, 1979, p. 5). Although the term "objective cognition" obviously conflicts with Dewey's whole method, he continued to hold that the "objects of knowledge" which science creates are crucial for human wellbeing, even when defined aesthetically.

"object of knowledge" will turn out to be. When such research is carried out, it will be affected by recent discoveries of infant competence and the redefinition of dependency that is implied by it. But a crippling interdisciplinary defect must be faced: most of the research implies a metaphor of the infant as a de-sexualized creature. Hence it may be research that is in the long run harmful to the enrichment of ordinary human experience. There is a practical "need for direction" in the large social field of child-rearing in relation to sexuality, in which the new knowledge created by the explosion of research is brought to bear. This research itself will not merely have to be handled with caution and subjected to doubts (such is common sense); it will need to be sorted through and organized so that it becomes applicable to human sexual beings.

Research Conventions, Research Purposes

Rather than continually having to catch up, and make research applicable to the sexual body, it would be preferable to begin designing research which has an awareness of the sexual body incorporated into its program. I envision, for example, a deliberate change in much of empirical reporting, in which the "conclusion" section of an article specifies the possible bearing of the research on issues concerning the sexual body. Were this change in convention to begin to occur, it eventually would lead to a shift in the objects of inquiry among the disciplines, toward an inclusion of the sexual body. A larger recommendation is for the deliberate undertaking of research in various disciplines with the aim of learning whether and in what ways the "proposition" regarding the perspective of the sexual body applies. The proposition, which I introduced in the opening chapter, is: *any finding in science concerning human beings will turn out, upon investigation, to have meaningful connections with human sexuality.* Research into vision, for example, might explore the question of how brain dimorphism is related to visual functioning. Another approach to visual experience might attempt an understanding of the connections widely reported in therapy between variations in gaze and memory. In a recent clinical symposium, Byron Braid remarks:

> There is a body of research having to do with neurolinguistic programming that has apparently documented that memories and experiences are revived by altering the direction of gaze [in therapy], and that by looking in another direction, aural memories are stimulated, and by looking in another direction, visual memories are stimulated. (quoted in Clinical Symposia: The Ocular Segment, 1984, p. 47)

Inasmuch as these remarks were delivered in a symposium of Orgonomic therapists, my point is almost made for me: any substantiation of the connections between direction of gaze and type of memory revived will prove, according to the proposition offered by the perspective of the sexual body, to have meaningful connections with human sexuality. Reichian therapists could not assume otherwise. In this case, the psychoanalytic theory of repression and the cultural conditioning of visual perception for use in "distance" rather than emotional perception (Schachtel, 1959, pp. 279-322) might be involved.

The larger problem is not so much how to devise experiments which would permit a greater range of investigations into the sexual body in all its connections with human psychological functioning, but the fostering of an orientation toward research which could answer to the old question, Knowledge for What? In complicated civilizations, with our complicated bodies and minds, it is both "more difficult and more imperative," as Dewey put it, to find out what we are doing: will a given policy—whether it is promulgation of a cognitive emphasis in psychological research, the social protection of adolescent sexuality, or noninterference with the sexuality of the newborn—work toward creating conditions "favorable to subsequent acts that sustain the continuity of the life process"? (Dewey, 1929b, p. 224).

Freud's original "classical" theory strongly suggested that this continuity of life process had been badly disturbed, not in the sense of stopping human survival—not as yet anyway—but in blocking, upsetting, and over-riding the sexual body. The theoretical perspective of the sexual body is a way of reformulating Freud's insight. As the reader will note, the present study does not move toward the safe but perhaps sterile assumption that life is equally of the mind and of the body, or that the two are so intermixed as to make any discussion in terms of the sexual body meaningless. Instead, I have throughout suggested an "asymmetrical" balance (Efron, 1980), in which the sexual body is assumed to be indispensable for a reconnection with "the continuity of the life process," as Freud had thought. (There was one point, however, at which I speculated that in very early infancy, the mind-body relation is not only in balance, but that it may be virtually free of intrapsychic conflicts.)

As far as civilized mental functioning is concerned, I suspect that the mind is far from at ease with the sexual body. I offer as speculation the idea that the cerebellum, which Eccles has found to be the chief organ of the body with the function of *inhibiting* impulses (Eccles, 1977; Eccles, Ito, and Szentágothai, 1967), has been "selected" by modern industrial civilization as an organ to be maximally developed, and metaphorically celebrated. It is significant that Masao Ito, Eccles' associate, does not even deal with the functioning of the cerebellum during normal sleep, in his book (Ito, 1984), *The Cerebellum and Neural Control*. There is little discussion in this 580 page work of the problem of what happens during those hours of REM dreaming, when "neural control" is of quite a different order than during wakeful states, when in fact the degree of "control" is greatly decreased from the level of ordinary rationality. Eccles has described REM dream activity as another mode in which the "self-conscious mind" is constantly at work: "It is always there scanning the brain, but the brain is not always in a communicative state for it!" (Eccles, in Popper and Eccles, 1977, pp. 371-372). The cerebellum obviously is not the whole brain, but if it comes to serve as the metaphor for mind, it then will insinuate an equation, "mind *equals* control over body," and particularly over the sexual body. This equation also serves to fuel the hatred of the sexual body as precisely that which cannot be fully controlled by the artifact of a "self" metaphorically situated in the mind. As Zaner (1984) has long argued, the "body as mine" is not really mine in the sense that other property I own is mine. The sexual body rather than the body in a general, non-sexual sense, poses a special problem. As Freud stated in 1905, "I am inclined to believe that the impulses of sexual life are among those which, even normally, are the least controlled by the higher activities of mind" (Freud, 1905b, p. 149). Eighty years after Freud's statement, it is still far from evident that the various disciplines in psychology have come to terms with it. Few theorists seem concerned to understand human intelligence and mental development, for example, in close connection with emotional development, let alone sexuality. Yet intelligence in Dewey's sense, the capacity to convert "desires into plans" (Dewey, 1930, p. 255), cannot function unless desires are understood and clarified (cf. Dewey, 1935, p. 51). Plans drawn up without benefit of such clarification are bound to lead to destructive consequences, precisely because such plans are carried out without regard to what Dewey referred to as the "continuity of the life process" (Dewey, 1929b, p. 224).

At the present time in human history, unintelligent choice can prove unthinkably disastrous. Pepper's very late attention to the problem of "Survival Value" (Pepper, 1969a), and his position taken in *Concept and Quality* that the "selective system" for survival may be judged under certain conditions to take precedence over all the other value systems (Pepper, 1967, pp. 544-551), are pertinent today. The perspective of the sexual body may have more bearing upon research concerning survival and decisions taken about survival of the species than it has for any of the topics discussed in the previous chapters. It is not too much to say that "the continuity of the life process" is being risked, over this globe, in current history. Science will soon increase that risk further, in the rapid development of biotechnology (see, for example, Chargaff, 1976). The entire discussion on the sexual body given in this study will have to be reconsidered once sexual bodies come to be produced on a large scale outside of procreation and the birth process. A distinction is already being drawn in recent discussion of "noncoital collaborative reproduction" between the "gestational mother" and the "genetic mother" (Goodman, 1984; see also Keane and Breo, 1981). Human genes are entering a time of greatly enhanced mechanical manipulation at the same time that the decision has been made (with virtually no public awareness of the fact) that gene transplantation from one mammalian species to another may be carried out for medical and other scientific purposes (Schmeck, 1984). The sexual body, as well as all other objects of knowledge which we now regard as mammalian bodies, are likely to undergo changes of an unpredictable nature now that these processes are underway. Yet there are still many decisions to be made concerning these processes in their details; members of the appropriate specialized disciplines may have influence in making such decisions. My point is not to call a halt to biotechnics, but to insist that without coming to terms with our knowledge of the sexual body, intelligent decisions cannot be made in this area (nor for that matter in the many other problem areas I have discussed in this study), and survival will be risked. Moreover, even those decisions which do take into account the perspective of the sexual body will be unable to do so intelligently unless the decisions are made with an awareness of affectionate somatosensory contact such as Prescott describes in his cross-cultural study. The sexual body-haters could hardly be expected to make a fair or wise decision for the survival of humankind, nor could the practitioners of virtually affectless theoretical systems (e.g., Schafer, 1976) be expected to feel the depth of the problems.

Research and Knowledge

It remains to emphasize that research helps to create objects of knowledge, but at least in Dewey's contextualist theory, no "antecedent existence" is discovered. We never "discover" what the sexual body "is." Yet there is a point in Pepper's excellent chapter on Contextualism where he suggests a doubt about this position. Is it not a strange paradox that all our inquiry fails to give us "insight into the qualities of nature"? To maintain that any research, or any hypothesis even if confirmed, is "no more than a tool for the control of nature . . ." strikes Pepper as a harsh doctrine. He argues that this position is actually an "unnecessarily stern if not perverse interpretation" of the Contextualist notion of truth (Pepper, 1942, pp. 274-275). It would be difficult to refute Pepper, and the attempt would be little more than making an arbitrary choice to mediate between his Contextualism and that of Dewey. Perhaps the perspective of the sexual body would require that both Pepper's and Dewey's views on knowledge within Contextualism be kept active. Despite Dewey's advice, we would not want to discourage the researcher who hopes to find out what some aspect of sexual body life "is," underneath all the shifting demands of culture.

If anyone has a research inquiry which promises to tell us something about sexual body functioning that is true for the human race and that would appear to be true for as long as there have been human bodies, then why should the Contextualist or the advocate of any other world hypothesis rule that researcher out of order? I.D. Rotkin, for example, has presented results of his research on cancer of the prostate which strongly suggests a link between sexual abstinence in the adult human male and the incidence of that cancer, by way of a slow-working virus which develops in the testes of the inactive adult male (Rotkin, 1980). If there is such a link (and Rotkin's empirical evidence for it is at least indicative), then we would want to know about it, and we would take this knowledge into account in leading our lives as well as in making judgments about other lives. There would have been little point in discouraging Rotkin, before he began this research, with warnings that he should not assume there "is" a link of abstinence and disease in the sexual life of the human male which he might uncover. Rotkin, if he is right, has given us some insight into the qualities of nature, as Pepper had expected a good confirmed hypothesis to do.

Yet ultimately, Dewey may have had the greater social wisdom. He realized that you cannot suggest to the modern mind (and especially not to the mass mind) that science gives "knowledge" of that which is, and still have an inquiring society. It is exactly where research promises to give results which are threatening—which is surely the case with inquiry into the sexual body—that the need for keeping inquiry open is felt most strongly. This is all the more so when the new objects of knowledge clash with old forms of social organization, fail to comply with established mores, and upset the prevalent world hypotheses. In such unresolved cultural conflict lies the continuing challenge of the sexual body, both to the specialist in the disciplines and to the same specialist engaged in living a life.

References

Abel, E. (1984). [Review of J. Gallop, *The daughter's seduction: Psychoanalysis and feminism.*] *Signs: Journal of Women in Culture and Society,* 9, 152-156.
Adorno, T., Frenkel-Brunswik, E., Levinson, D., and Sanford, R. (1950). *The authoritarian personality.* New York: Harper and Brothers.
Alberoni, F. (1983). *Falling in love* (L. Venuti, Trans.). New York: Random House.
Alderman, H. (1977). *Nietzsche's gift.* Athens: Ohio University Press.
Altman, L. (1981). [Review of N. Smelser and E. Erikson (Eds.), *Themes of Work and Love in Adulthood.*] *Psychoanalytic Quarterly,* 50, 288-289.
Ammon, G. (1979). *Psychoanalysis and psychosomatics* (S. Ray, Trans.). New York: Springer Publishing Co.
Analyst [M. Mahler] focuses on life's early years. (1984, March 13). *New York Times,* p. C2.
Anderson, P. (1983). The reproductive role of the human breast. *Current Anthropology,* 24, 25-45.
Andors, P. (1983). *The unfinished liberation of Chinese women, 1949-1980.* Bloomington: Indiana University Press.
Appleton, T., Clifton, R., and Goldberg, S. (1975). The development of behavioral competence in infancy. In F.D. Horowitz (Ed.), *Review of child development research* (Vol. 14, pp. 101-186). Chicago: University of Chicago Press.
Arkin, A., Antrobus, J., and Eldman, S. (Eds.). (1978). *The mind in sleep: Psychology and physiology.* Hillsdale, New Jersey: Erlbaum.
Arney, W. (1980). Maternal-infant bonding: The politics of falling in love with your child. *Feminist Studies,* 6, 547-570.
Asso, D. (1983). *The real menstrual cycle.* Chichester-New York-Brisbane-Toronto-Singapore: Wiley.
Atkins, R.N. (1983). Peer relationships in the first year of life. *The Annual of Psychoanalysis,* 11, 227-244.
Ayala, D., and Weinstock, T. (1979). *Breasts: Women speak of their breasts and their lives.* New York: Summit Books.
Badinter, E. (1981). *Mother love, myth and reality: Motherhood in modern history.* New York: Macmillan.
Baker, E. (1952). Genital anxiety in nursing mothers. *Orgone Energy Bulletin,* 4, 19-31.
Baker, E. (1967). *Man in the trap.* New York: Macmillan.
Barclay, D. (1983, May 17). Study of wives finds 43% admit extramarital affairs. *Buffalo News,* AP Dispatch, p. A8.
Bardin, C., and Catterall, J. (1981). Testosterone: A major determinant of extragenital sexual dimorphism. *Science,* 211, 1285-1294.
Barrett, J. (1982). Prenatal influences on adaptation in the newborn. In P. Stratton (Ed.), *Psychobiology of the newborn* (pp. 267-295). New York: Wiley.
Barrett, M. (1982). *Sexuality and multiple sclerosis.* Toronto: Multiple Sclerosis Society of Canada.
Barthelow-Koch, P. (1980). A comparison of the sex education of prmary-aged children in the United States and Sweden as expressed through their art. In J.M. Samson (Ed.), *Childhood and sexuality: Proceedings of the International Symposium* (pp. 345-366). Montreal: Éditions Études Vivantes.
Baxter, R., with Linn, A. (1978). Sex counseling and the SCI patient. *Nursing,* 8 (Sept.), 46-52.
Becker, E. (1978). *Female sexuality following spinal cord injury.* Bloomington, Indiana: Cheever Publishing Co.
Bell, A. (1961). Some observations on the role of the scrotal sac and testicles. *Journal of American Psychoanalytic Society,* 9, 261-286.
Bell, A. (1965). The significance of scrotal sac and testicles for the prepuberty male. *Psychoanalytic Quarterly,* 34, 182-206.
Bell, A., Weinberg, M., and Hammersmith, S. (1981). *Sexual preference: Its development in men and women.* Bloomington: Indiana University Press.
Bem, S.L. (1983). Gender schema theory and its implications for child development: Raising gender-aschematic children in a gender-schematic society. *Signs: Journal of Women in Culture and Society,* 8, 598-616.

Bennis, W. (1974). Discussion remarks at round-table-conference: Empathy and the scientific method. University of Cincinnati, April 20, 1974.

Berleant, A. (1964). The sensuous and the sensual in aesthetics. *Journal of Aesthetics and Art Criticism, 23,* 185-192.

Berzins, J. (1979). Discussion: Androgyny, personality theory, and psychotherapy. In A. Kaplan (Ed.), *Psychological androgyny: Further considerations* (pp. 248-254). New York: Human Sciences Press.

Bieber, I., Dain, H.J., Dince, P.R., Drellich, M.G., Grand, H.G., Gundlach, R.H., Kremer, M.W., Rifkin, A.H., Wilbur, C.B., and Bieber, T.B. (1962). *Homosexuality: A psychoanalytic study.* New York: International Universities Press.

Birren, F. (1978). *Color and human response.* New York: Van Nostrand Reinhold Co.

Biven, B. (1982). The role of skin in normal and abnormal development with a note on the poet Sylvia Plath. *International Review of Psycho-analysis, 9,* 205-229.

Blackman, N. (1980). Pleasure and touching: Their significance in the development of the preschool child—an exploratory study. In J.M. Samson (Ed.), *Childhood and sexuality: Proceedings of the International Symposium* (pp. 175-198). Montreal: Éditions Études Vivantes.

Blasband, D. (1984). Effects of the Orac on cancer in mice: Three experiments. *Journal of Orgonomy, 18,* 202-211.

Bledstein, B. (1976). *The culture of professionalism.* New York: W.W. Norton.

Bleier, R. (1984). *Science and gender: A critique of biology and its theories on women.* New York-Oxford-Toronto-Sydney-Paris-Frankfurt: Pergamon Press.

Blight, J. (1982). [Review of R. Fine, *The psychoanalytic vision.*] *Review of Psychoanalytic Books, 1,* 15-28.

Blos, P. (1970). *The young adolescent: Clinical Studies.* New York: Free Press.

Blos, P. (1979). *The adolescent passage: Developmental issues.* New York: International Universities Press.

Blumenthal, R. (1981a, August 18). Scholars seek the hidden Freud in newly emerging letters. *New York Times,* p. C1.

Blumenthal, R. (1981b, August 25). Did Freud's isolation, peer rejection, prompt key theory reversal? *New York Times,* p. C1.

Blumenthal, R. (1984, January 24). Evidence points to anguish over seduction theory. *New York Times,* p. C1.

Blumstein, P., and Schwartz, P. (1983). *American couples: Money, work, sex.* New York: Morrow.

Boadella, D. (1973). *Wilhelm Reich: The evolution of his work.* London: Vision Press.

Boadella, D. (Ed.). (1976). *In the wake of Reich.* London: Coventure.

Boffey, P. (1983, May 31). Sexology struggling to establish itself amid wide hostility. *New York Times,* pp. C1, C3.

Bornstein, M.H., Kessen, W., and Weisskopf, S. (1975). Color vision and hue categorization in young human infants. *Science, 191,* 201-202.

Boskind-White, M., and White, W. (1983). *Bulimarexia: The binge/purge cycle.* New York: W.W. Norton.

Bowlby, J. (1951). *Maternal care and maternal health.* New York: Columbia University Press.

Bowlby, J. (1979). Psychoanalysis as art and science. *International Review of Psychoanalysis, 6,* 3-14.

Bowlby, J. (1980a). *Attachment and loss: Attachment.* London: Hogarth Press.

Bowlby, J. (1980b). *Attachment and loss: Separation anxiety and anger.* London: Hogarth Press.

Bowlby, J. (1980c). *Attachment and loss: Sadness and depression.* London: Hogarth Press.

Bowlby, J. (1981). Psychoanalysis as a natural science. *International Review of Psychoanalysis, 8,* 243-256.

Bowlby, J. (1984). Attachment and loss: Retrospect and prospect. In S. Chess and A. Thomas (Eds.), *Annual progress in child psychiatry and child development 1983* (pp. 29-47). New York: Brunner/Mazel.

Brackbill, Y. (1975). Continuous stimulation and arousal level in infancy: Effects of stimulus intensity and stress. *Child Development, 46,* 364-369.

Brady, M. (1947). The strange case of Wilhelm Reich. *New Republic, 116* (May 26), 20-22.

Brady, M. (1948). The strange case of Wilhelm Reich. *Bulletin of the Menninger Clinic, 12*(2), 61-67.

REFERENCES

Brake, M. (Ed.). (1982). *Human sexual relations: Toward a redefinition of sexual politics.* New York: Pantheon Books.
Brazelton, T.B. (1981). *On becoming a family: The growth of attachment.* New York: Dell/Delta.
Brecher, E., and The Editors of Consumer Report Book News. (1984). *Love, sex and aging: A consumer's union report.*
Bregman, S. (1975). *Sexuality and the spinal cord injured woman.* Minneapolis: Sister Kenney Institute.
Breines, W., and Gordon, L. (1983). The new scholarship on family violence. *Signs: Journal of Women in Culture and Society,* 8, 490-531.
Brenner, C. (1971). The psychoanalytic concept of aggression. *International Journal of Psycho-Analysis,* 52, 137-144.
Brenner, C. (1974). *An elementary textbook of psychoanalysis* (2nd ed.). New York: International Universities Press.
Breuer, J., and Freud, S. (1957). *Studies in hysteria* (J. Strachey, Trans.). New York: Basic Books. (Original work published 1895)
Bridges, K.M. (1930). A genetic theory of the emotions. *Journal of Genetic Psychology,* 37, 514-527.
Bridges, K.M. (1932). Emotional development in early infancy. *Child Development,* 3, 324-341.
Brody, J. (1983a, March 30). Bulimia is an out-of-control cycle of binge-eating followed by purges and, usually, guilt. *New York Times,* p. C8.
Brody, J. (1983b, October 4). Major study on couples looks at jobs and money as well as sex. *New York Times,* pp. C1, C5.
Brody, J. (1983c, December 13). Divorce's stress exacts long-term health toll. *New York Times,* pp. C1, C5.
Brody, J. (1983d, December 20). Emotional deprivation seen as devastating form of child abuse. *New York Times,* p. C1.
Brody, J. (1984, March 27). "Autoerotic death" of youths causes widening concern. *New York Times,* p. C1.
Brome, V. (1967). *Freud and his early circle.* New York: William Morrow and Co.
Brome, V. (1982). *Ernest Jones: Freud's alter ego.* London: Caliban Books.
Bronte, C. (1960). *Jane Eyre.* New York: New American Library. (Original work published 1847)
Broverman, D., Klaiber, E., and Vogel, W. (1980). Gonadal hormones and cognitive functioning. In J. Parsons (Ed.), *The psychobiology of sex differences and sex roles* (pp. 57-80). Washington-New York: Hemisphere Books/McGraw-Hill.
Brown, L. (Ed.). (1980). *Sex education in the eighties: The challenge of healthy sexual revolution.* New York-London: Plenum Press.
Brown, N.O. (1959). *Life against death: The pscyhoanalytic meaning of history.* Middleton, Connecticut: Wesleyan University Press.
Bruner, J. (1983a, October 27). State of the child. *New York Review of Books,* pp. 84-89.
Bruner, J. (1983b). *In search of mind: Essays in autobiography.* New York: Harper and Row.
Bühler, C. (1930). *The first year of life.* New York: Day.
Bullard, D., and Knight, S. (Eds.). (1981). *Sexuality and physical disability.* St. Louis, Missouri: C.V. Mosby Co.
Bollough, V., Bullough, D., and Smith, R. (1983). A comparative study of male transvestites, male to female transsexuals, and male homosexuals. *The Journal of Sex Research,* 19, 238-257.
Burgess, A., Groth, L., and Sgroi, S. (Eds.). (1978). *Sexual assault of children and adolescents.* Lexington, Massachusetts: Lexington Books.
Burgess, A., and Holmstrom, L. (1979). Rape: Sexual disruption and recovery. *American Journal of Orthopsychiatry,* 49, 648-657.
Butterworth, G. (Ed.). (1981). *Infancy and epistemology: An evaluation of Piaget's theory.* Brighton, Sussex: Harvester Press.
Buunk, B. (1983). Alternative lifestyles from an international perspective: A trans-Atlantic comparison. In E.D. Macklin and R.H. Rubin (Eds.), *Contemporary families and alternative lifestyles: Handbook on research and theory* (pp. 308-330). Beverly Hills-London-New Delhi: Sage Publications.
Buxbaum, E. (1951). *Your child makes sense.* London: Allen and Unwin.

Cacioppo, J., and Petty, R. (Eds.). (1983). *Social psychophysiology: A sourcebook*. New York-London: The Guilford Press.
Calderone, M., and Johnson, E. (1981). *The family book about sexuality*. New York: Harper and Row.
Calderone, M., and Ramey, J. (1983). *Talking with your child about sex*. New York: Random House.
Campbell, P. (1979). *Sex education books for young adults, 1892-1979*. New York: R.R. Bowker.
Campos, J., and Stenberg, C. (1981). Perception, appraisal and emotion: The onset of social referencing. In M.E. Lamb and L.R. Sherwood (Eds.), *Infant social cognition: Empirical and theoretical considerations* (pp. 273-314). Hillsdale, New Jersey: Erlbaum.
Cargan, L., and Melko, M. (1982). *Singles: Myths and realities*. Beverly Hills-London-New Delhi: Sage Publications.
Carrera, M.A. (1983). Some reflections on adolescent sexuality. *Siecus Report*, 11(4), 1-2.
Cauwels, J. (1983). *Bulimia: The binge-purge compulsion*. New York: Doubleday.
How cells transfer energy. (1984, February 21). *New York Times* (Science watch section).
Center for Constitutional Rights. (1983). Marital rape. *Docket Report*, 1983-1984, p. 13.
Chaitin, G. (1984). [Review article of J. Smith and W. Kerrigan (Eds.), *Interpreting Lacan*.] *Review of Psychoanalytic Books*, 3, 361-368.
Chargaff, E. (1976). On the dangers of genetic meddling. *Science*, 192, 938-940.
Chess, S. (1978). The plasticity of human development. *Journal of American Academy of Child Psychiatry*, 17, 80-91.
Chess, S., and Thomas, A. (Eds.). (1981). *Annual progress in child psychiatry and child development 1980*. New York: Brunner/Mazel.
Chess, S., and Thomas, A. (Eds.). (1983). *Annual progress in child psychiatry and child development 1982*. New York: Brunner/Mazel.
Chess, S., and Thomas, A. (Eds.). (1984a). *Annual progress in child psychiatry and child development 1983*. New York: Brunner/Mazel.
Chess, S., and Thomas, A. (1984b). Infant bonding: Mystique and reality. In S. Chess and A. Thomas (Eds.), *Annual progress in child psychiatry and child development 1983* (pp. 48-62). New York: Brunner/Mazel.
Chess, S., Thomas, A., and Birch, H. (1965). *Your child is a person: A psychological approach to parenthood without guilt*. New York: Viking Press.
Chodorow, N. (1978). *The reproduction of mothering: Psychoanalysis and the sociology of gender*. Berkeley-Los Angeles: University of California Press.
Chodorow, N. (1981). [Reply to A. Rossi.] *Signs: Journal of Women in Culture and Society*, 6, 504-508.
Choisnel, E. (1981). Vision and irrigation of the brain. *Energy & Character: The Journal of Bioenergetic Research*, 12(3), 55-59.
Chomsky, N., and Herman, E. (1979). *The Washington connection and third world fascism*. Boston: South End Press.
Cicchetti, D., and Pogge-Hesse, P. (1981). The relation between emotion and cognition in infant development. In M.E. Lamb and L.R. Sherrod (Eds.), *Infant social cognition: Empirical and theoretical considerations* (pp. 205-272). Hillsdale, New Jersey: Lawrence Erlbaum.
Clark, R.W. (1980). *Freud: The man and the cause*. New York: Random House.
Clarke, A., and Clarke, D. (Eds.). (1976). *Early experience: Myth and evidence*. New York: Free Press.
Clement, C. (1983). *The lives and legends of Jacques Lacan* (A. Goldhammer, Trans.). New York: Columbia University Press. (Original work published 1981)
Clinical symposia: The ocular segment. (1984). *Annals of the Institute for Orgone Science*, 1, 43-49.
Clynes, M. (1977). *Sentics: The touch of emotions*. New York: Anchor/Doubleday.
Cohen, S. (1979). In the name of the prevention of neuroses: The search for a psychoanalytic pedagogy in Europe 1905-1938. In B. Finkelstein (Ed.), *Regulated children, liberated children: Education in psychohistorical perspective* (pp. 184-219). New York: Psychohistory Press.
Cohler, B., and Boxer, A. (1984). Personal adjustment, wellbeing, and life events. In C.Z. Malatesta and C.E. Izard (Eds.), *Emotion in adult development* (pp. 85-100). Beverly-Hills-London-New Delhi: Sage Publications.

REFERENCES

Cohn, A. (1982). Violence against children. In *Britannica Book of the Year: 1982* (pp. 621-622). Chicago: Encyc. Britannica Inc.
Cohn, A.H. (1984, May). Flyer from president of National Committee for the Prevention of Child Abuse. Chicago: NCPCA.
Coles, R. (1970). *Erik H. Erikson: The growth of his work.* Boston: Little, Brown.
Collins, G. (1984, May 28). A dean of pediatricians looks at today's family. *New York Times*, p. 40.
Comfort, A. (1967). *The anxiety makers.* London: Thomas Nelson and Sons.
Comfort, A. (1972). *The joy of sex: A cordon bleu guide to lovemaking.* New York: Simon and Schuster.
Comfort, A. (1974). *More joy: A lovemaking companion to the joy of sex.* New York: Simon and Schuster.
Comfort, A. (1978). On writing books about sex. *Paunch*, #51, 88-95.
Condon, W. (1977). A primary phase in the organization of infant responding. In H.R. Schaffer (Ed.), *Studies in mother-infant interaction* (pp. 153-176). London: Academic Press.
Condon, W. (1979). An analysis of behavioral organization. In S. Weitz (Ed.), *Nonverbal communication: Readings with commentary* (2nd ed., pp. 149-167). New York: Oxford University Press.
Condon, W. (1984). Communication and empathy. In J. Lichtenberg, M. Bornstein, and D. Silver (Eds.), *Empathy II* (pp. 350-358). Hillsdale, New Jersey: Analytic Press.
Condon, W., and Sander, L. (1974a). Neonate movement is synchronized with adult speech: Interactional participation and language acquisition. *Science, 183*, 99-101.
Condon, W. and Sander, L. (1974b). Synchrony demonstrated between movements of the neonate and adult speech. *Child Development, 45*, 456-462.
Constantine, L. (1980). The impact of early sexual experiences: A review and synthesis of outcome research. In J.M. Samson (Ed.), *Childhood and sexuality: International proceedings of the symposium* (pp. 160-167). Montreal: Éditions Études Vivantes.
Constantine, L., and Martinson, F. (Eds.). (1981). *Children and sex: New findings, new perspectives.* Boston: Little, Brown.
Cornell, G. (1984, November 4). Celibacy cited in poll on drop in new priests. *Buffalo News* (AP dispatch), p. A-12.
Craft, M., and Craft, A. (1978). *Sex and the mentally handicapped.* London-Boston: Routledge and Kegan Paul.
Cranefield, P.F. (1966a). The philosophical and cultural interests of the biophysics movement of 1847. *Journal of the History of Medicine and Allied Sciences, 21*, 1-7.
Cranefield, P.F. (1966b). Freud and the "School of Helmholtz." *Gesnerus, 23*, 35-39.
Cranefield, P.F. (1970). Breuer, Josef. In C.C. Gillispie (Ed.), *Dictionary of scientific biography* (Vol. 2, pp. 445-450). New York: Charles Scribners' Sons.
Crews, F. (Ed.). (1970). *Psychoanalysis and literary process.* Cambridge, Massachusetts: Harvard University Press.
Crews, F. (1975). *Out of my system: Psychoanalysis, ideology and critical method.* New York: Oxford University Press.
Crist, P. (1984). [Review of Reich, *Children of the future.*] *Journal of Orgonomy, 18*, 99-105.
Croll, E. (1981). *The politics of marriage in contemporary China.* Cambridge-London-New York: Cambridge University Press.
Crooks, R., and Baur, K. (1983). *Our sexuality* (2nd ed.). Menlo Park, California: Benjamin-Cumming Publishing Co.
Cuniberti, B. (1983, July 28). Suicide rate increasing steadily in US. *Latin America Daily Post* (repr. from LA Times), p. 5.
Current Biography. (1959). Joshua Lederberg (pp. 251-252). Bronx, New York: H.W. Wilson.
Cutler, C., and Pepper, S. (1923). *Modern color.* Cambridge: Harvard University Press.
Dadoun, R. (Ed.). (1983). Wilhelm Reich [Special Issue]. *L'Arc*, #83.
Dahl, H. (1983). On the definition and measurement of wishes. In J. Masling (Ed.), *Empirical studies of psychoanalytical theories*, (Vol. 1, pp. 39-67). Hillsdale, New Jersey: Analytic Press.
Darnell, J. (1983). The processing of RNA. *Scientific American, 249*, 90-100.
Darnton, J. (1983, November 7). Spain grows less prudish, but not yet libertine. *New York Times*, p. A2.

Darwin, C. (1877). A biographical sketch of an infant. *Mind: A Quarterly Review of Psychology and Philosophy,* 2, 285-294.

Datan, N., and Ginsburg, L. (Eds.). (1975). *Life-span developmental psychology: Normative life crises.* New York-London: Academic Press.

Datan, N., and Reese, H. (Eds.). (1977). *Life-span developmental psychology: Dialectical perspective on experimental research.* New York-London: Academic Press.

Datan, N., and Rodeheaver, D. (1983). Beyond generativity: Toward a sensuality of later life. In R. Weg (Ed.), *Sexuality in the later years: Roles and behavior* (pp. 279-288). New York-London: Academic press.

Davidson, J. (1980). The psychobiology of sexual experience. In J. Davidson and R. Davidson (Eds.), *The psychobiology of consciousness* (pp. 271-332). New York: Plenum Press.

Davidson, R. (1984). *Emotion, cognition, and behavior.* New York: Cambridge University Press.

Darnell, J. (1983). The processing of RNA. *Scientific American,* 249, 90-100.

Davis, R. (1978, October). Literature and woman's body. *Paunch,* #52, pp. 55-66.

DeCasper, A., and Fifer, W. (1980). Of human bonding: Newborns prefer their mothers' voices. *Science,* 208, 1174-1176.

DeLaCoste-Utamsing, C., and Holloway, R. (1982). Sexual dimorphism in the human corpus callosum. *Science,* 216, 431-432.

Delaney, J., Lupton, M., and Toth, E. (1976). *The curse: A cultural history of menstruation.* New York: Dutton.

Del Guercio, G. (1983, November 12). No meeting of minds on brain differences. *Buffalo News* (UPI dispatch).

DeMause, L. (Ed.). (1974). The evolution of childhood. *History of Childhood Quarterly,* 1, 503-606.

Demos, V. (1984). Empathy and affect: Reflections on infant experience. In J. Lichtenberg, M. Bornstein, and D. Silver (Eds.), *Empathy III* (pp. 9-34). Hillsdale, New Jersey: Analytic Press.

De Rougement, D. (1956). *Love in the western world* (M. Belgion, Trans.). New York: Pantheon. (Original work published 1939)

Desmond, M., Rudolph, A., and Phitaksphraiwan, P. (1966). The transitional care nursery: A mechanism of a preventive medicine. *Pediatric Clinics of North America,* 13, 651-668.

Dethier, V.G., and Stellar, G. (1964). *Animal behavior* (2nd ed.). Englewood Cliffs, New Jersey: Prentice-Hall.

Deutsch, H. (1944). *The psychology of women.* New York: Grune and Stratton.

Dew, R. (1978). The biopathic diathesis (X): Obesity. *Journal of Orgonomy,* 12, 216-231.

Dewey, J. (1929a). *Experience and nature.* New York: W.W. Norton.

Dewey, J. (1929b). *The quest for certainty.* New York: Minton, Balch.

Dewey, J. (1930). *Human nature and conduct: An introduction to social psychology.* New York: Modern Library.

Dewey, J. (1934). *Art as experience.* New York: Minton, Balch.

Dewey, J. (1935). *Liberalism and social action.* New York: G.P. Putnam's Sons.

Dewey, J., and Bentley, A. (1949). *Knowing and the known.* Boston: Beacon Press.

Diamond, S. (1974). *In search of the primitive: A critique of civilization.* New Brunswick, New Jersey-London: Transaction Books.

Dick-Read, G. (1942). *Revelation of childbirth.* London: Heinemann.

Dick-Read, G. (1947). *Birth of a child.* London: Churchill.

Dick-Read, G. (1955). *Ante-natal illustrated.* London: Heinemann.

Diesing, P. (1971). *Patterns of discovery in the social sciences.* Chicago: Aldine-Atherton.

Is there a difference? (1984, Spring). *Rehabilitation Digest,* 15(1), pp. 8-9.

Dinnerstein, D. (1976). *The mermaid and the minotaur: Sexual arguments and human malaise.* New York: Harper and Row.

Donoso, A. (1982). *Julian Marías.* Boston: Twayne/G.K. Hall.

Dowling, S. (1982). From the literature of neonatology. *Psychoanalytic Quarterly,* 50, 290-295.

Dunlap, D. (1984). Brooklyn diocese agrees to homosexual measure. *New York Times,* p. 55.

Duyckaerts, F. (1970). *The sexual bond* (J. Kay, Trans.). New York: Delta Books. (Original work published 1964)

Eccles, J. (1977). *The understanding of the brain* (2nd ed.). New York: McGraw-Hill.

REFERENCES

Eccles, J., Ito, M., and Szentágothai, J. (1967). *The cerebellum as a neuronal machine.* Berlin-Heidelberg-New York: Springer Verlag.
Eckholm, E. (1984, September 18). New view of female primates assails stereotypes. *New York Times,* pp. C1, C3.
Edel, A., and Edel, M. (1959). *Anthropology and ethics.* Springfield, Illinois: C.C. Thomas.
Efron, A. (1968). Criticism and literature in the one-dimensional age. *Minnesota Review,* 8, 48-62.
Efron, A. (1973). Philosophy, criticism, and the body. (Paunch, #36-37, pp. 72-162.
Efron, A. (1975). Perspectivism and the nature of fiction: "Don Quixote" and Borges. *Thought,* 50, 148-175.
Efron, A. (1977). Freud's self-analysis and the nature of psychoanalytic criticism. *International Review of Psycho-Analysis,* 4, pp. 277-280.
Efron, A. (1980). The mind-body problem in Lawrence, Pepper and Reich. *The Journal of Mind and Behavior,* 1, 247-270.
Efron, A. (1981). The problem of Don Quixote's rage. *Denver Quarterly,* 16, 29-46.
Efron, A. (1982a). Bearded waiting women, lovely lethal piratemen: Sexual boundary shifts in Don Quixote Part II. *Cervantes: Bulletin of the Cervantes Society of America,* 2, 155-164.
Efron, A. (1982b). On some central issues in Quixote criticism: Society and the sexual body. *Cervantes: Bulletin of the Cervantes Society of America,* 2, 171-180.
Efron, A. (1982c). "Histoire d'O": Un approche Reichienne (G.H. Durand, Trans.). *l'Arc,* #83, pp. 43-49.
Ehrenreich, B. (1985, February 7). Is abortion really a moral dilemma? *New York Times,* p. C2.
Ehrlich, M. (1970). The role of body experience in therapy. *Psychoanalytic Review,* 57, 181-195.
Ehrlich, P., and Ehrlich, A. (1981). *Extinction: The causes and consequences of the disappearance of species.* New York: Ballantine Books.
Eissler, R., and Eissler, K. (1966). Heinz Hartmann: A biographical sketch. In R. Loewenstein, L. Newman, M. Schur, and A. Solnit (Eds.), *Psychoanalysis—A general psychology: Essays in honor of Heinz Hartmann* (pp. 3-42). New York: International Universities Press.
Eliot, G. (1979). *The mill on the floss.* Harmondsworth: Penguin Books. (Original work published 1860)
Elshtain, J. (1981). Against androgyny. *Telos,* #47, pp. 6-21.
Emde, R.N., Gaensbauer, T.J., and Harmon, R.J. (1976). *Emotional expression in infancy: A bio-behavioral study* (Psychological Issues Monograph No. 37). New York: International Universities Press.
Emde, R.N., and Robinson, J. (in press). The first two months: Recent research in developmental psychobiology and the changing view of the newborn. In L. Noshpitz and J. Call (Eds.), *Basic handbook of child psychiatry.* New York: Basic Books.
English, D. (1984, December). The Masson-Malcolm dispute. *Mother Jones,* p. 6.
Erikson, E. (1963). *Childhood and society* (2nd ed.). New York: W.W. Norton.
Erikson, E. (Ed.). (1978). *Adulthood.* New York: W.W. Norton Co.
Erikson, E. (1982). *The life cycle completed: A review.* New York: W.W. Norton.
Esman, A. (Ed.). (1983). *The psychiatric treatment of adolescents.* New York: International Universities Press.
Evans, D. (1983). *The lives of mentally retarded people.* Boulder, Colorado: Westview Press.
Eysenck, H.J., and Wilson, G.D. (1973). *The experimental study of Freudian theories.* London: Methuen.
Fairbairn, W. (1965). Synopsis of an object-relations theory of the personality. *International Journal of Psycho-Analysis,* 44, 224-225.
Fantz, R. (1958). Pattern vision in young infants. *Psychological Review,* 8, 43-47.
Fantz, R. (1961). The origin of form perception. *Scientific American,* 204, 66-72.
Farrell, B. (1983, September 9). The therapeutic alliance. *Times Literary Supplement,* p. 968.
Farson, R. (1974). *Birthrights.* New York-London: Collier; Collier Macmillan Publishers.
Feder, B. (1985, February 21). Contraception bill advances in Irish parliament. *New York Times,* p. A11.
Feigl, H. (1961). Mind-body: Not a pseudo-problem. In S. Hook (Ed.), *Dimensions of mind: A symposium* (pp. 33-44). New York: Collier Books.
Ferguson, A. (1984). Sex war: The debate between radical and libertarian feminists. *Signs: Journal of Women in Culture and Society,* 10, 106-112.

Finch, E. (1977, January). Sexuality and the disabled. *Canadian Nurse*, pp. 13-14.
Finkelhor, D. (1979). *Sexually victimized children*. New York-London: Free Press.
Finkelhor, D. (1980). Sexual socialization in America: High risk for sexual abuse. In J.-M. Samson (Ed.), *Childhood and sexuality: Proceedings of the International Symposium* (pp. 641-648). Montreal: Éditions Études Vivantes.
Finkelhor, D., and Yllo, K. (1983). Rape in marriage: A sociological view. In D. Finkelhor, R. Gelles, G. Hotaling, and M. Strauss (Eds.), *The dark side of families: Current family violence research* (pp. 119-130). Beverly Hills-London-New Delhi: Sage Publications.
Fischer, W. (1980). *The Soviet marriage market: Mate selection in Russia and the USSR*. New York: Praeger. (Studies of the Russian Institute, Columbia University)
Fisher, C. (1966). Dreaming and sexuality. In R. Loewenstein, L. Newman, M. Schur, and A. Solnit (Eds.), *Psychoanalysis—A general psychology: Essays in honor of Heinz Hartmann* (pp. 537-569). New York: International Universities Press.
Fisher, S., and Greenberg, P.R. (1977). *The scientific credibility of Freud's theories and therapy*. New York: Basic Books.
Fox, C., and Fox, B. (1971). A comparative study of coital physiology with special reference to the sexual climax. *Journal of Reproduction and Fertility*, 24, 319-336.
Fox, S.W. (1978). The origin and nature of protolife. In W. Heidcamp (Ed.), *The nature of life* (pp. 23-92). Baltimore: University Park Press.
Fox, S.W. (1980). The behavior of macromolecules and protocells. *Comparative Biochemistry and Physiology*, Part B, 67, 423-436.
Francoeur, R.T. (1982). *Becoming a sexual person*. New York: Wiley.
Francoeur, R.T. (1983). Religious reactions to alternative lifestyles. In E.D. Macklin and R.H. Rubin (Eds.), *Contemporary families and alternative lifestyles: Handbook on research and theory* (pp. 379-399). Beverly Hills-London-New Delhi: Sage Publications.
Francke, L. (1983). *Growing up divorced*. New York: Linden Press/Simon and Schuster.
Freedman, M. (1975, March). Homosexuals may be healthier than straights. *Psychology Today*, pp. 28-32.
Friedman, S., Bruno, L., and Vietze, P. (1974). Newborn habituation to visual stimuli: A sex difference in novelty detection. *Journal of Experimental Child Psychology*, 18, 242-251.
Freud, A. (1935). Psychoanalysis and the training of the young child (J. Demming, Trans.). *Psychoanalytic Quarterly*, 4, 15-24.
Freud, A. (1946). *The psycho-analytical treatment of children* (N. Procter-Gregg, Trans.). London: Imago Publishing Co. (Original work published 1926)
Freud, A. (1966). The ego and the mechanisms of defense (C. Baines Trans.). In A. Freud (Ed.), *The writings of Anna Freud*, Vol. 2. New York: International Universities Press. (Original work published 1936)
Freud, A. (1968). Psychoanalysis and education. In *The writings of Anna Freud, 1945-1956* (Vol. 4, pp. 317-326). New York: International Universities Press. (Original work published 1954)
Freud, A. (1974). Four lectures on child analysis. In *The writings of Anna Freud* (Vol. 1, pp. 1-69). New York: International Universities Press.
Freud, A. (1976). Changes in psychoanalytic practice and experience. *International Journal of Psycho-Analysis*, 57, 257-274.
Freud, S. (1953-1973). *The standard edition of the complete works of Sigmund Freud*, 24 vols. (J. Strachey, Ed. and Trans.). London: The Hogarth Press. [Cited below as S.E.]
Freud, S. (1896). Further remarks on the psycho-neuroses of defence. S.E., Vol. 3, pp. 159-187.
Freud, S. (1898). Sexuality in the aetiology of the neuroses. S.E., Vol. 3, pp. 261-285.
Freud, S. (1900). The interpretation of dreams. S.E., Vol. 4.
Freud, S. (1905a). Fragment of an analysis of a case of hysteria. S.E., Vol. 7, pp. 3-123.
Freud, S. (1905b). Three essays on the theory of sexuality. S.E., Vol. 7, pp. 125-207.
Freud, S. (1907). The sexual enlightenment of children. S.E., Vol. 9, pp. 129-140.
Freud, S. (1908). 'Civilized' sexual morality and modern nervous illness. S.E., Vol. 9, pp. 179-198.
Freud, S. (1909). Analysis of a phobia of a five-year-old boy. S.E., Vol. 10, pp. 3-151.
Freud, S. (1910a). The origin and development of psychoanalysis (H.W. Chase, Trans.). *American Journal of Psychology*, 21, 201-218.

REFERENCES

Freud, S. (1910b). *Über Psychoanalyse* [About psychoanalysis]. Leipzig and Vienna: Deuticke.
Freud, S. (1910c). Five lectures on psycho-analysis. S.E., Vol. 11, pp. 1-55.
Freud, S. (1910d). Leonardo da Vinci and a memory of his childhood. S.E., Vol. 11, pp. 59-137.
Freud, S. (1912). On the universal tendency to debasement in the sphere of love. S.E., Vol. 11, pp. 177-190).
Freud, S. (1914). On the history of the psycho-analytic movement. S.E., Vol. 14, pp. 1-66.
Freud, S. (1916-1917). Introductory lectures on psycho-analysis. S.E., Vol. 15-16.
Freud, S. (1920a). Beyond the pleasure principle. S.E., Vol. 18, pp. 1-64.
Freud, S. (1920b). The psychogenesis of homosexuality in a woman. S.E., Vol. 18, pp. 146-163.
Freud, S. (1921). Group psychology and the analysis of the ego. S.E., Vol. 18, pp. 65-143.
Freud, S. (1923). The ego and the id. S.E., Vol. 19, pp. 3-68.
Freud, S. (1924). The economic position of masochism. S.E., Vol. 19, pp. 157-172.
Freud, S. (1925a). An autobiographical study. S.E., Vol. 20, pp. 3-75.
Freud, S. (1925b). Negation. S.E., Vol. 19, pp. 234-242.
Freud, S. (1926a). Inhibitions, symptoms, and anxiety. S.E., Vol. 20, pp. 77-175.
Freud, S. (1926b). The question of lay analysis. S.E., Vol. 20, pp. 179-258.
Freud, S. (1930). Civilization and its discontents. S.E., Vol. 21, pp. 57-145.
Freud, S. (1933). New introductory lectures on psycho-analysis. S.E., Vol. 22.
Freud, S. (1940). An outline of psychoanalysis. S.E., Vol. 23, pp. 141-207.
Freud, S. (1951). Letter to an American mother. *American Journal of Psychiatry, 107,* 252. (Original work published 1935)
Freud, S. (1954). Project for a scientific psychology (E. Mosbacher and J. Strachey, Trans.). In M. Bonaparte, A. Freud, and E. Kris (Eds.), *The origins of psycho-analysis* (pp. 247-445). New York: Basic Books.
Freud, S. (1959). *Collected papers,* 5 vols. (J. Riviere, Trans.). New York: Basic Books.
Freud, S. (1971). Letter to C. Müller-Braunschweig (H. Stierlein, Trans.). *Psychiatry, 34,* 329.
Freud, S., and Jung, C.G. (1974). *The Freud-Jung letters: The correspondence between Sigmund Freud and C.G. Jung* (W. McGuire, Ed.; R. Manhein and R.F.C. Hull, Trans.). Princeton: Princeton University Press.
Frost, R. (1945a). *The masque of reason.* New York: Henry Holt and Co.
Frost, R. (1945b). *The poetry of Robert Frost* (E.C. Lathem, Ed.). New York: Holt, Rinehart and Winston, Publishers.
Frost, R. (1949). *Complete poems of Robert Frost.* New York: Henry Holt and Co.
Furstenberg, F., and Spanier, G. (1984). *Recycling the family: Remarriage after divorce.* Beverly Hills-London-New Delhi: Sage Publications.
Gaensbauer, T.J., and Hiatt, S. (1984). *The psychobiology of affective development.* New York: Cambridge University Press.
Gardner, H. (1983). *Frames of mind: The theory of multiple intelligences.* New York: Basic Books.
Gargiulo, G. (1978). Contribution to Kohut's *Restoration of the self:* A symposium. *Psychoanalytic Review, 65,* 616-617.
Gartrell, N.K. (1982). Hormones and homosesxuality. In W. Paul, J. Weinrich, J. Gonsiorek, and M. Hotvedt (Eds.), *Homosexuality: Social, psychological, and biological issues* (pp. 169-182). Beverly Hills-London-New Delhi: Sage Publications.
Gay, P. (1984). *The bourgeois experience: Victoria to Freud: The education of the senses* (Vol. 1). New York-Oxford: Oxford University Press.
Gesell, A. (1934). *An atlas of infant behavior,* Vol. 1. New Haven: Yale University Press.
Gesell, A. (1952). *Infant development.* London: Hamish Hamilton.
Gibbs, J. (1966). Conception of deviant behavior: The old and the new. *Pacific Sociological Review, 9,* 9-14.
Gibson, K. (1981). Comparative neuro-ontogeny: Its implications for the development of human intelligence. In G. Butterworth (Ed.), *Infancy and epistemology: An evaluation of Piaget's theory* (pp. 52-82). Brighton, Sussex: Harvester Press.
Gillett, J. (1979, October 27). Childbirth in Pithviers, France. *The Lancet,* pp. 894-896.
Giovacchini, P. (1977). A critique of Kohut's theory of narcissism. In S. Feinstein and P. Giovacchini (Eds.), *Adolescent Psychiatry* (Vol. 5, pp. 213-239). New York: Jason Aronson.

Girard, R. (1977). *Violence and the sacred* (P. Gregory, Trans.). Baltimore: Johns Hopkins University Press.
Glazier, L. (1975). Stills from a moving picture [Whole issue]. *Paunch*, #37.
Goldberg, A. (Ed.). (1983). *The future of psychoanalysis.* New York: International Universities Press.
Goldman, A.I. (1985, March 8). Priests gather to ponder their dwindling ranks. *New York Times*, p. B3.
Goldman, L. (1964). *The hidden God.* London: Routledge and Kegan Paul.
Goldman, J., and Goldman, J. (1982). *Children's sexual thinking.* Boston: Routledge and Kegan Paul.
Goldstein, H.A., and Segall, M.P. (Eds.). (1983). *Aggression in global perspective.* New York-Oxford-Toronto: Pergamon Press.
Goleman, D. (1984a, January 24). Psychoanalysis appears stung but little harmed. *New York Times*, pp. C1, C4.
Goleman, D. (1984b, March 13). Traumatic beginnings: Most children seem able to recover. *New York Times*, p. C1.
Goleman, D. (1984c, March 20). Human emotion under new scrutiny. *New York Times*, pp. C1, C8.
Goleman, D. (1984d, June 19). Order found in development of emotions. *New York Times*, p. C1.
Golombek, H., and Garfinkel, B. (Eds.). (1983). *The adolescent and mood disturbance.* New York: International Universities Press.
Gonsiorek, J. (1982). Results of psychological testing on homosexual populations. In W. Paul, J. Weinrich, J. Gonsiorek, and M. Hotvedt (Eds.), *Homosexuality: Social, psychological, and biological issues* (pp. 71-80). Beverly Hills-London-New Delhi: Sage Publications.
Goodman, W. (1984, November 16). New reproduction techniques redefine parenthood. *New York Times*, p. A21.
Gordon, C. (1966). *D.H. Lawrence as a literary critic.* New Haven: Yale University Press.
Gordon, C. (1983, December 2). The self inside us [Review of M.R. Khan, *Hidden Selves*]. *Times Literary Supplement*, p. 1351.
Gordon, S. (1981). Preteens are not latent, adolescence is not a disease. In L. Brown (Ed.), *Sex education in the eighties: The challenge of healthy sexual revolution* (pp. 83-99). New York-London: Plenum Press.
Gouldner, A. (1976). *The dialectic of ideology and technology.* New York: Seabury Press.
Gouldner, A. (1980). *The two Marxisms: Contradictions and anomalies in the development of theory.* New York: Seabury Press.
Gove, W., and Carpenter, G. (1982). Introduction. In W. Gove and G. Carpenter (Eds.), *The fundamental connection between nature and nurture: A review of the evidence* (pp. 1-15). Lexington, Massachusetts: Lexington Books/D.C. Heath.
Goy, R.W., and MacEwen, B.S. (1980). *Sexual differentiation of the brain.* Cambridge, Massachusetts: MIT Press.
Greeley, A.M., and Durkin, M.G. (1984). *How to save the Catholic church.* New York: Viking Press.
Greeley, A.M., and Durkin, M.G. (1985, March 17). Sexual love as a sacrament [Letter to the editor]. *New York Times*, p. 32.
Greenacre, P. (1952). *Trauma, growth and personality.* New York: International Universities Press.
Greenacre, P. (1960). Considerations regarding the parent infant relationship. *International Journal of Psycho-Analysis*, 41, 571-584.
Greenberg, J., and Mitchell, S. (1983). *Object relations in psychoanalytic theory.* Cambridge, Massachusetts-London: Harvard University Press.
Greenfield, J. (1974). *Wilhelm Reich vs. the U.S.A.* New York: W.W. Norton.
Grof, S. (1977). Perinatal roots of wars, totalitarianism, and revolutions: Observations from LSD research. *Journal of Psychohistory*, 4, 269-308.
Grosskopf, D. (1983a, July). Extramarital affairs. *Playgirl*, pp. 44-45, 108-110, 114.
Grosskopf, D. (1983b). *Sex and the married woman.* New York: Ritter/Geller Communications (Simon and Schuster, Distributor).
Grünbaum, A. (1983). *The foundations of psychoanalysis: A philosophical critique.* Berkeley-Los Angeles-London: University of California Press.

Guntrip, H. (1968). *Schizoid phenomena, object relations, and the self*. London: Hogarth Press.
Guntrip, H. (1973). *Psychoanalytic theory, therapy, and the self*. New York: Basic Books.
Guttentag, M., and Secord, P. (1983). *Too many women? The sex ratio question*. Beverly Hills-London-New Delhi: Sage Publications.
Hacker, K. (1983, October 9). Assessing 30 years of sex research. *Philadelphia Inquirer*, p. H1.
Hahn, S., and Paige, K. (1980). American birth practices: A critical review. In J.E. Parsons (Ed.), *The psychobiology of sex differences and sex roles* (pp. 145-175). Washington-New York-London: Hemisphere Publishing Co.
Haim, A. (1974). *Adolescent suicide* (A. Sheridan Smith, Trans.). New York: International Universities Press. (Original work published 1969)
Haith, M. (1980). *Rules that babies look by: The organization of newborn visual activity*. Hillsdale, New Jersey: Erlbaum.
Hale, N.G., Jr. (1971). *Freud and the Americans: The beginnings of psychoanalysis in the United States, 1876-1917*. New York: Oxford University Press.
Hall, G.S. (1904). *Adolescence*. New York: Appleton.
Hall, M.H. (1969). A conversation with Masters and Johnson. *Psychology Today*,3(2), 50-58.
Halper, E. (1984). Aristotle on knowledge and nature. *Review of Metaphysics, 37*, 811-835.
Halverson, H. (1938). Infant sucking and tensional behavior. *General Psychology, 53*, 365-430.
Halverson, H. (1940). Genital and sphincter behavior in the male infant. *Journal of Genetic Psychology, 43*, 95-136.
Hamburg, D. (1972). Forword to H. Katchadourian and D. Lunde, *Fundamentals of Human Sexuality* (pp. v-vi). New York: Holt, Rinehart and Winston.
Hamilton, V. (1982). *Narcissus and Oedipus: Children of psychoanalysis*. London: Routledge and Kegan Paul.
Hanna, T. (1970). *Bodies in revolt: A primer in somatic thinking*. New York: Dell Publishing Co.
Harley, M. (1983). On some problems of technique in the analysis of early childhood. In A. Esman (Ed.), *The psychiatric treatment of adolescents* (pp. 99-121). New York: International Universities Press.
Harry, J. (1983). Gay male and lesbian relationships. In E.D. Macklin and R.H. Rubin (Eds.), *Contemporary families and alternative lifestyles: Handbook in research and theory* (pp. 216-234). Beverly Hills-London-New York: Sage Publications.
Hazelwood, R., Dietz, R., and Burgess, A. (1984). *Autoerotic fatalities*. Lexington, Massachusetts: Lexington Books.
Hebb, D.O. (1959). Heredity and environment. *British Journal of Animal Behavior, 1*, 43-47.
Hebblethwaite, P. (1985). *Pope John XXIII: Shepherd of the modern world*. New York: Doubleday.
Heckerman, C. (Ed.). (1980). *The evolving female: Woman in psychosocial context*. New York: Human Sciences Press.
Heilbrun, C. (1973). *Toward a recognition of androgyny*. New York: Alfred A. Knopf.
Heller, P., and Bittner, G. (1983). *Eine Kinderanalyse bei Anna Freud (1929-1932)* [A child analysis by Anna Freud (1929-1932)]. Würzburg: Königshausen und Neumann.
Heller, P. (1984). [Presentation to the Group for Applied Psychoanalysis.] SUNY-Buffalo, October 12.
Hencken, J. (1982). Homosexuality and psychoanalysis: Toward a mutual understanding. In W. Paul, J. Weinrich, J. Gonsiorek, and M. Hotvedt (Eds.), *Homosexuality: Social, psychological and biological issues* (pp. 121-148). Beverly Hills-London-New Delhi: Sage Publications.
Herman, J. (1981). *Father-daughter incest*. Cambridge, Massachusetts: Harvard University Press.
Hite, S. (1977). *The Hite report*. New York: Dell Publishing Co.
Hofer, M. (1981). *The roots of human behavior*. San Francisco: W.W. Freeman.
Hoffer, W. (1945). Psychoanalytic education. *Psychoanalytic study of the child* (Vol 1, pp. 293-307). New York: International Universities Press.
Hoffer, W. (1981). *Early development and education of the child* (M. Brierley, Ed.). New York: Jason Aronson.
Hoffman, R., and Nead, J. (1983). General contextualism, ecological science and cognitive research. *The Journal of Mind and Behavior, 4*, 507-560.
Hofsten, C. von (1982). Eye-hand coordination in newborns. *Developmental Psychology, 18*, 450-461.
Hoge, W. (1983, May 23). Machismo murder case: Women bitter in Brazil. *New York Times*, p. A2.

Holland, N.N. (1975a). *Five readers reading*. New Haven: Yale University Press.
Holland, N.N. (1975b). Unity identity text self. *PMLA*, 90, 813-822.
Holland, N.N. (1978). Human identity. *Critical Inquiry*, 4, 451-469.
Holland, N.N. (1982). *Laughter*. Ithaca: Cornell University Press.
Holland, N.N. (1984). [Letter to the editor.] *Atlantic*, 253 (April), 6.
Holt, J. (1974). *Escape from childhood*. New York: E.P. Dutton.
Holt, R.R. (1965). A review of some of Freud's biological assumptions and their influence on his theories. In N.S. Greenfield and W.C. Lewis (Eds.), *Psychoanalysis and current biological thought* (pp. 93-124). Madison and Milwaukee: University of Wisconsin Press.
Holt, R.R. (1967). David Rapaport: A memoir. In R.R. Holt (Ed.), *Motives and thought: Psychoanalytic essays in honor of David Rapaport* (Psychological Issues Monographs No. 18-19, pp. 7-17). New York: International Universities Press.
Holt, R.R. (1984). Freud's impact upon modern morality and our world view. In A.L. Caplan and B. Jennings (Eds.), *Darwin, Marx, and Freud: Their influence on moral theory* (pp. 147-200). New York: Plenum Press.
Holt, R.R. (in press). Freud, the free will controversy, and prediction in personology. In R.A. Zucker, J. Aronoff, and A.I. Rabin (Eds.), *Personality and the prediction of behavior*. New York: Academic Press.
Homberger, E. [Erik Erikson] (1935). Psychoanalysis and the future of education. *Psychoanalytic Quarterly*, 4, 50-96. (Original work published 1930)
Hosken, F.P. (1979). *The Hosken report: Genital and sexual mutilation of females*. Lexington, Massachusetts: Women's International Network News.
Hotvedt, M., and Mandel, J. (1982). Children of lesbian mothers. In W. Paul, J. Weinrich, J. Gonsiorek, and M. Hotvedt (Eds.), *Homosexuality: Social, psychological, and biological issues* (pp. 275-285). Beverly Hills-London-New Delhi: Sage Publications.
Hoyenga, B., and Hoyenga, K. (1979). *The question of sex differences: Psychological, cultural, and biological issues*. Boston-Toronto: Little, Brown and Co.
Hunter, D. (1983). Hysteria, psychoanalysis, and feminism: The case of Anna O. *Feminist Studies*, 9, 464-488.
Hyman, R., Lewis, S., and Griffith, S. (1984). *The sexual rights of adolescents: Competence, vulnerability, and parental control*. New York: Columbia Unviersity Press.
Hyman, S. (1955). *The armed vision: A study in the methods of modern literary criticism*. New York: Vintage Books.
Imperato-McGinley, J. Peterson, R.E., Goutier, T., and Sturla, E. (1979). Androgens and the evolution of male-gender identity among male pseudo-hermaphorodites with 5α-reductase deficiency. *New England Journal of Medicine*, 300, 1233-1237.
Iran-Nejad, A., and Ortony, O. (1984). A biofunctional model of distributed mental content, mental structure, awareness and attention. *The Journal of Mind and Behavior*, 5, 171-210.
Isbell, V. (1985, December 5). Pill claims foolproof birth control. *Buffalo News* (UPI dispatch), p. 1.
Isikoff, M. (1983, May 19). She's Reagan's captain in campaign against sex. *Buffalo News*. (Originally in *Washington Post*)
Israël, L. (1980). *L'hystérique, le sexe et le médecin*. Paris: Masson.
Iranian law grants women the right to file for divorce. (1983, March 30). *New York Times*, Reuters dispatch.
Ito, M. (1984). *The cerebellum and neural control*. New York: Raven Press.
Itten, J. (1973). *The art of color: The subjective experience and objective rationale of color* (E. van Haagen, Trans.). New York: Van Nostrand Reinhold Co.
Izard, C.E. (1971). *The face of emotion*. New York: Appleton-Century-Crofts.
Izard, C.E. (1977). *Human emotions*. New York: Plenum.
Jackson, J., and Jackson, J. (1978). *Infant culture*. New York: Crowell.
Jacobson, E. (1964). *The self and the object world*. New York: International Universities Press.
Jacobson, G. (1983). *The multiple crises of marital separation and divorce*. New York-London: Grune and Stratton.
Jacoby, R. (1983). *The repression of psychoanalysis: Otto Fenichel and the political Freudians*. New York: Basic Books.
James, W. (1955). The will to believe. In A. Castell (Ed.), *Essays in pragmatism* (pp. 88-109). New York: Hafner Publishing Co. (Original work published 1896)

REFERENCES

Janus, S., and Bess, B. (1981). Latency: Fact or fiction? In L. Constantine and F. Martinson (Eds.), *Children and Sex: New findings, new perspectives* (pp. 75-82). Boston: Little, Brown.
Johnson, K.A. (1983). *Women, the family and peasant revolution in China.* Chicago: University of Chicago Press.
Johnson, W.R. (1980). Growing up with sexual language. In J.M. Samson (Ed.), *Childhood and sexuality: Proceedings of the international symposium* (pp. 94-96). Montreal: Éditions Études Vivantes.
Jones, E. (1935). Early female sexuality. *International Journal of Psycho-Analysis*, 16, 263-273.
Jones, E. (1955a). *The life and work of Sigmund Freud* (Vol. 2). New York: Basic Books.
Jones, E. (1955b). *The life and work of Sigmund Freud* (Vol. 3). New York: Basic Books.
Joseph, B. (Ed.). (1983). Melanie Klein centenary papers. *International Journal of Psycho-Analysis*, 64, 249-263.
Jourard, S. (1966). An exploratory study of body accessibility. *British Journal of Social and Clinical Psychology*, 8, 39-48.
Jourard, S. (1968). *Disclosing man to himself.* New York: Van Nostrand Reinhold Co.
Jung, C.G. (1968). *Analytical psychology: Its theory and practice.* New York: Vintage Books. (Original work published 1935)
Kagan, J. (1971). *Change and continuity in infancy.* New York: Wiley.
Kagan, J. (1976). Resilience and continuity in psychological development. In A. Clarke and D. Clarke (Eds.), *Early experience: Myth and evidence* (pp. 97-121). New York: Free Press.
Kagan, J. (1980). Perspective on continuity. In O. Brim, Jr., and J. Kagan (Eds.), *Constancy and change in human development* (pp. 26-74). Cambridge, Massachusetts: Harvard University Press.
Kagan, J. (1984). *The nature of the child.* New York: Basic Books.
Kahn, R. (1984). Taking charge of birth. *The Women's Review of Books*, 2(3), 15-16.
Kaplan, A. (Ed.). (1979). Psychological androgyny: Further considerations [Special issue]. *Psychology of Women Quarterly*, 3, 221-315. New York: Human Science Press. (Reprinted edition)
Kaplan, A. (1980). Human sex-hormone abnormalities viewed from an androgynous perspective: A reconsideration of the work of John Money. In J. Parsons (Ed.), *The psychobiology of sex differences and sex roles* (pp. 81-91). Washington-New York-London: Hemisphere Publishing Co., McGraw-Hill.
Kaplan, L. (1978). *Oneness and separateness: From infant to individual.* New York: Simon and Schuster.
Karacen, I., Goodenough, D.R., Shapiro, A., and Witkin, H.A. (1965). Some psychological and physiological correlates of penile erection during sleep. *Association for the Psychological Study of Sleep.* [As cited by Fisher, 1966, p. 568.]
Karacen, I., Goodenough, D.R., Shapiro, A., and Starker, S. (1966). Erection cycle during sleep in relation to anxiety. *Archives of General Psychiatry*, 15, 183-189.
Karasu, T., and Socarides, C. (Eds.). (1979). *On sexuality: Psychoanalytic observations.* New York: International Universities Press.
Katz, S. (1984, June 20). Stop the witch-hunt for child molesters. *New York Times*, p. A27.
Kaufmann, W. (1960). *From Shakespeare to existentialism.* New York: Anchor Books.
Kaye, K. (1982). *The mental and social life of babies: How parents create persons.* Chicago: University of Chicago Press.
Keane, N., and Breo, D. (1981). *The surrogate mother.* New York: Everest House.
Keleman, S. (1975). *Your body speaks its mind.* New York: Simon and Schuster.
Keleman, S. (1982). *In defense of heterosexuality.* Berkeley: Center Press.
Keller, S., and Buchanan, D. (1984, Spring). Sexuality and disability: An overview. *Rehabilitation Digest*, 15(1).
Kelley, K., and Byrne, D. (1983). Assessment of sexual responding: Arousal, affect, and behavior. In J. Cacioppo and R. Petty (Eds.), *Social psychophysiology: A sourcebook* (pp. 467-490). New York-London: The Guilford Press.
Kendrick, W. (1983, April 3). [Review of M. Sharaf, *Fury on earth: A biography of Wilhelm Reich*. *New York Times Book Review*, p. 1.
Kendrick, W. (1984, June). Not just another Oedipal drama: The unsinkable Sigmund Freud [Review of J. Masson, *The assault on truth: Freud's suppression of the seduction theory*]. *Voice Literary Supplement* #28, pp. 12-16.

Kennell, J., Trause, M.A., and Klaus, M. (1975). Evidence for a sensitive period in the human mother. In *Parent-infant interaction, CIBA Foundation Symposium 33*. Amsterdam: Elsevier Publishing Co.

Kerblay, B. (1983). *Modern Soviet society* (R. Swyer, Trans.). London: Methuen. (Original work published 1977)

Kernberg, O. (1974a). Barriers to falling and remaining in love. *Journal of the American Psychoanalytic Association, 22,* 486-511.

Kernberg, O. (1974b). Mature love: Prerequisites and characteristics. *Journal of the American Psychoanalytic Association, 22,* 743-768.

Kernberg, O. (1975). *Borderline conditions and pathological narcissism.* New York: Jason Aronson.

Kernberg, O. (1980a). Adolescent sexuality in the light of group processes. *Psychoanalytic Quarterly, 49,* 27-47.

Kernberg, O. (1980b). Love, the couple, and the group, in a psychoanalytic frame. *Psychoanalytic Quarterly, 49,* 78-108.

Kernberg, O. (1981). [Presentation to the Group for Applied Psychoanalysis.] SUNY-Buffalo, October 25.

Khan, M.M.R. (1981). [Review of F. Sulloway, *Freud, biologist of the mind.*] *International Review of Psycho-Analysis, 8,* 125.

Khan, M.M.R. (1982). [Review of M. Kanzer and J. Glenn, *Freud and his self-analysis.*] *International Review of Psycho-Analysis, 9,* 246-247.

Khatchadourian, H., and Lunde, D. (1972). *Fundamentals of human sexuality.* New York-Chicago-San Francisco: Holt, Rinehart and Winston.

Kinsey, A., Pomeroy, W., and Martin, C. (1948). *Sexual behavior in the human male.* Philadelphia: W.B. Saunders Co.

Kintgen, E.R., and Holland, N.N. (1984). Carlos reads a poem. *College English, 46,* 478-492.

Kirsch, J., and Rodman, J. (1982). Selection and sexuality: The Darwinian view of homosexuality. In W. Paul, J. Weinrich, J. Gonsiorek, and M. Hotvedt (Eds.), *Homosexuality: Social, psychological, and biological issues* (pp. 183-195). Beverly Hills-London-New Delhi: Sage Publications.

Kitzinger, S. (1983). *Women's experience of sex.* New York: Putnam.

Klauber, J. (1981). *Difficulties in the analytic encounter.* New York: Jason Aronson.

Klaus, M., Jerauld, R., Kreger, N., McAlpine, W., Steffa, M., and Kennell, J. (1972). Maternal attachment: Importance of the first postpartum days. *New England Journal of Medicine, 286,* 460-463.

Klaus, M., and Kennell, J. (1976). *Maternal-infant bonding.* St. Louis: C.V. Mosby Publishing Co.

Klaus, M., and Kennell, J. (1982). *Parent-infant bonding* (2nd ed.). St. Louis: C.V. Mosby Publishing Co.

Klein, F. (1981, May 14). Losing the way: Teen-age suicide toll points up the dangers of growing up rich. *Wall Street Journal,* pp. 1, 21.

Klein, G.S. (1967). Peremptory ideation. In R.R. Holt (Ed.), *Motives and thought: Psychoanalytic essays in honor of David Rapaport* (Psychological Issues Monographs No. 18-19, pp. 78-128). New York: International Universities Press.

Klein, G.S. (1976). Freud's two theories of sexuality. In G.S. Klein, *Psychoanalytic theory: An exploration of essentials* (pp. 72-120). New York: International Universities Press. (Original work published 1969)

Klein, Melanie (1932). *The psycho-analysis of children.* London: Hogarth Press.

Klein, Melanie (1948a). The psychological principles of infant analysis. In Melanie Klein, *Contributions to psycho-analysis, 1921-1945: Developments in child and adolescent psychology* (pp. 140-151). London: Hogarth Press. (Original work published 1926)

Klein, Melanie (1948b). The importance of symbol formation in the development of the ego. In Melanie Klein, *Contributions to psycho-analysis, 1921-1945: Developments in child and adolescent psychology* (pp. 236-250). London: Hogarth Press. (Original work published 1930)

Klein, Melanie (1948c). A contribution to the psychoanalysis of manic-depressive states. In Melanie Klein, *Contributions to psycho-analysis, 1921-1945: Developments in child and adolescent psychology* (pp. 282-310). London: Hogarth Press. (Original work published 1930)

Klein, Melanie (1975). *Narrative of a child analysis: The conduct of the psycho-analysis of children as seen in the treatment of a ten-year-old boy.* London: Hogarth Press.
Klein, Milton (1981a). Freud's seduction theory: Its implications for fantasy and memory in psychoanalytic theory. *Bulletin of the Menninger Clinic,* 45, 185-208.
Klein, Milton (1981b). On Mahler's autistic and symbiotic phases. *Psychoanalysis and Contemporary Thought,* 4, 69-105.
Klein, Milton (1984). The seduction theory controversy [Presentation to the Group for Applied Psychoanalysis]. SUNY-Buffalo, April 27.
Klein, M., and Tribich, D. (1979). On Freud's "Blindness." *Colloquium,* 2(2), 52-58.
Klein, M., and Tribich, D. (1981). Kernberg's object-relations theory: A critical evaluation. *International Journal of Psycho-Analysis,* 62, 27-43.
Klein, M., and Tribich, D. (1982). Blame the child: Freud's blindness to the damaging influence of parents' personalities. *New York Academy of Sciences,* 22(8), 14-20.
Kline, P. (1972). *Fact and fantasy in Freudian theory.* London: Methuen.
Kline, P. (1981). *Fact and fantasy in Freudian theory* (rev. ed.). London-New York: Methuen.
Kliot, D., and Silverstein, L. (1980). The Leboyer approach: A new concern for the psychological aspects of the childbirth experience. In B. Blum (Ed.), *Psychological aspects of pregnancy, birthing, and bonding* (pp. 280-293). New York: Human Sciences Press.
Kliot, D., and Silverstein, L. (1984). Changing maternal and newborn care: A study of the Leboyer approach to childbirth management. *New York State Journal of Medicine,* 84, 169-174.
Knight, I., and Herik, J. (1984, April 1). [Letter to the editor.] *New York Times Book Review,* p. 34.
Kohut, H. (1971). *The analysis of the self: A systematic approach to the psychoanalytic treatment of narcissistic personality disorders.* New York: International Universities Press.
Kohut, H. (1977). *The restoration of the self.* New York: International Universities Press.
Kohut, H. (1978). *The search for the self: Selected writings of Heinz Kohut, 1950-1978,* 2 vols. (P. Ornstein, Ed.). New York: International Universities Press.
Kohut, H. (1980). *The restoration of the self.* New York: International Universities Press.
Kohut, H. (1984). *How does psychoanalysis cure?* (A. Goldberg, Ed.). Chicago: University of Chicago Press.
Kolodny, R., Masters, W. Johnson, V., and Biggs, M. (1979). *Textbook of human sexuality for nurses.* Boston: Little, Brown and Co.
Korner, A. (1969). Neonatal startles, smiles, erection, and reflex sucks as related to state, sex, and individuality. *Child Development,* 40, 1039-1053.
Korner, A. (1977). Sex differences in newborns. In E. Oremland and J. Oremland (Eds.), *The sexual and gender development of young children: The role of the educator* (pp. 11-16). Cambridge, Massachusetts: Ballinger Publications.
Kovel, J. (1978). Things and words: Metapsychology and the historical point of view. *Psychoanalysis and Contemporary Thought,* 1, 21-88.
Kovel, J. (1981). *The age of desire: Case histories of a radical psychoanalyst.* New York: Pantheon.
Kragh, U., and Smith, G. (1970). *Percept-genetic analysis.* Lund: Gleerup.
Kris, E. (1952). *Psychoanalytic exploration in art.* New York: International Universities Press.
Kuhn, T.S. (1970). *The structure of scientific revolutions* (rev. ed.). Chicago: University of Chicago Press.
Lacan, J. (1975). *Le séminaire.* Text établi par Jacques-Alain Miller. Paris: Éditions du Seuil.
Lacan, J. (1977). *Écrits: A selection* (A. Sheridan, Trans.). New York: W.W. Norton; London: Tavistock.
Ladenbauer-Bellis, I.-M. (1980a). Bone and bio-energetics: Part 1. *Energy & Character: The Journal of Bioenergetic Research,* 11(2), 41-47.
Ladenbauer-Bellis, I.-M. (1980b). Bone and bio-energetics: Part 2. *Energy & Character: The Journal of Bioenergetic Research,* 11(3), 23-28.
Lamb, M., and Goldberg, W. (1982). The father-child relationship: A synthesis of biological, evolutionary and social perspectives. In L. Hoffman, R. Gandelman, and H. Schiffman (Eds.), *Parenting: Its causes and consequences* (pp. 55-73). Hillsdale, New Jersey: Erlbaum.
Lamb, M., and Hwang, C.-P. (1982). Maternal attachment and mother-neonate bonding: A critical review. In M. Lamb and A. Brown (Eds.), *Advances in Developmental Psychology* (Vol. 2, pp. 1-39). Hillsdale, New Jersey: Erlbaum.

Lang, J. (1984). Notes toward a psychology of the feminine self. In P. Stepansky and A. Goldberg (Eds.), *Kohut's legacy: Contributions to self psychology* (pp. 51-69). Hillsdale, New Jersey: Analytic Press/Erlbaum.

Langfeldt, T. (1980). Child sexuality: Development and problems. In J.M. Samson (Ed.), *Childhood and sexuality: Proceedings of the international symposium* (pp. 105-110). Montreal: Éditions Études Vivantes.

Langfeldt, T. (in press). Sexual development in children. In M. Cook and K. Howells (Eds.), *Adult sexual interest in children*. London: Academic Press.

Laplanche, J., and Pontalis, J.-B. (1973). *The language of psycho-analysis* (D. Nicholson-Smith, Trans.). New York: W.W. Norton. (Original work published 1967)

Laszlo, E. (1969). *Systems, structure, and experience: Toward a scientific theory of mind*. New York-London-Paris: Gordon and Breach, Science Publishers.

Laufer, M. (1983). Preventive intervention in adolescence. In A. Esman (Ed.), *The psychiatric treatment of adolescents* (pp. 89-116). New York: International Universities Press.

Lawrence, D.H. (1960). *Psychoanalysis and the unconscious: Fantasia of the unconscious*. New York: Viking Press. (Original work published 1922)

Lawrence, D.H. (1981). *The rainbow*. Harmondsworth: Penguin Books. (Original work published 1915)

Lawton, M. (1984). The varieties of wellbeing. In C.Z. Malatesta and C.E. Izard (Eds.), *Emotion in adult development* (pp. 67-84). Beverly Hills-London-New Delhi: Sage Publications.

Leboyer, F. (1975). *Birth without violence*. New York: Knopf.

Lederberg, J., Cavalli, L., and Lederberg, E. (1952). Sex compatibility in Escherichia Coli. *Genetics, 37*, 720-730.

Ledwitz-Rigby, F. (1980). Biochemical and neurophysiological influences on human sexual behavior. In J. Parsons (Ed.), *The psychobiology of sex differences and sex roles* (pp. 95-194). Washington-New York-London: Hemisphere Publishing Co., McGraw-Hill.

Legault, O. (1981). Psychoanalysis, aesthetic theory, and Picasso's 'Man with a sheep'. *Journal of the Philadelphia Association of Psychoanalysis, 3*, 1-24.

Lehrman, N. (Ed.). (1970). *Masters and Johnson explained*. New York: Playboy Press.

Leiderman, P.H. (1980). *Human mother to infant social bonding: Is there a sensitive phase?* Unpublished Manuscript.

Lemaire, A. (1977). *Jacques Lacan* (D. Macey, Trans.). Boston: Routledge and Kegan Paul.

Levinson, D., Darrow, C., Klein, E., Levinson, M., and McKee, B. (1978). *The seasons of a man's life*. New York: Ballantine Books.

Lewin, E., and Lyons, T. (1982). Everything in its place: The coexistence of lesbianism and motherhood. In W. Paul, J. Weinrich, J. Gonsiorek, and M. Hotvedt (Eds.), *Homosexuality: Social, psychological, and biological issues* (pp. 249-273). Beverly Hills-London-New Delhi: Sage Publications.

Lewis, M. (Ed.). (1983). *Origins of intelligence: Infancy and early childhood* (2nd ed.). New York-London: Plenum Press.

Lewis, R. (1976). Infancy and the head: The psychosomatic basis of premature ego development. *Energy & Character: The Journal of Bioenergetic Research, 7* (Sept.), 18-39.

Lewis, W.C. (1965). Coital movements from the first year of life. *International Journal of Psycho-Analysis, 46*, 372-374.

Lichtenberg, J. (1983a). *Psychoanalysis and infant research*. New York: International Universities Press.

Lichtenberg, J. (1983b). Is there a Weltanschauung to be developed from psychoanalysis? In A. Goldberg (Ed.), *The future of psychoanalysis: Essays in honor of Heinz Kohut* (pp. 203-238). New York: International Universities Press.

Lichtenberg, J., Bornstein, M., and Silver, D. (Eds.). (1984). *Empathy II*. Hillsdale, New Jersey: Analytic Press.

Lichtenberg, P. (1969). *Psychoanalysis: Radical and conservative*. New York: Springer Publishing Co.

Lichtenstein, H. (1961). Identity and sexuality: A study of their interrelationship in man. *Journal of the American Psychoanalytic Association, 9*, 179-260

Lichtenstein, H. (1977). *The dilemma of human identity*. New York: Jason Aronson.

Lieberson, J. (1983, October 13). [Reply to Rechy.] *New York Review of Books*, pp. 44-45.

REFERENCES

Lightfoot-Klein, H. (1984). Pharaonic circumcision of females in the Sudan. *Journal of Orgonomy*, 18, 44-57.
Linden, M. (1978). Breathing, gravity, and evolution. *Energy & Character: The Journal of Bioenergetic Research*, 9 (January), 63-71.
Lindon, J.A. (1966). Melanie Klein, 1882-1960: Her view of the unconscious. In F. Alexander, S. Eisenstein, and M. Grotjahn (Eds.), *Psycho-analytic pioneers* (pp. 360-372). New York: Basic Books.
Lindon, J.A. (1972). Melanie Klein's theory and technique: Her life and work. In A. Giovacchini (Ed.), *Tactics and techniques of psychoanalytic therapy* (pp. 33-61). New York: Science House.
Liss, J. (1976). Why touch? In D. Boadella (Ed.), *In the wake of Reich* (pp. 236-248). London: Coventure.
Loewenstein, S. (1984a). [Review of K. Obholzer, *The wolf-man.*] *Reviews of Psychoanalytic Books*, 3, 1-13.
Loewenstein, S. (1984b). [Review of A. Miller, *Prisoners of childhood, For your own good, and Du sollst nicht merken.*] *Review of Psychoanalytic Books*, 3, 319-332.
Lofgren, B. (1983, October 28). Swedes lead world couples in living outside marriage vows. *Buffalo News*.
Longino, H., and Doell, R. (1983). Body, bias, and behavior: A comparative analysis of reasoning in two areas of biological science. *Signs: Journal of Women in Culture and Society*, 9, 206-227.
Lowen, A. (1958). *The physical dynamics of character structure*. New York: Grune and Stratton.
Lowen, A. (1965). *Love and orgasm*. New York: Macmillan.
Lowen, A. (1967). *The betrayal of the body*. New York: Macmillan.
Lowen, A. (1970). *Pleasure: A creative approach to life*. New York: Coward-McCann, Inc.
Lowen, A. (1975). *Depression and the body*. New York: Coward, McCann and Geoghegan.
Lumsden, C.J., and Wilson, E.O. (1982). *Promethean fire: Reflections on the origins of mind*. Cambridge: Harvard University Press.
Lyons, R.D. (1983, October 4). Promiscuous sex believed declining in recent years. *New York Times*, pp. C1, C4.
MacGuigan, M. (1973). Is woman a question? *International Philosophical Quarterly*, 13, 485-505.
Mackin, T., S.J. (1984). *Divorce and remarriage*. Ramsey, New Jersey: Paulist Press.
Macklin, E.D. (1983). Nonmarital heterosexual cohabitation: An overview. In E.D. Macklin and R.H. Rubin (Eds.), *Contemporary families and alternative lifestyles: Handbook on research and theory* (pp. 49-74). Beverly Hills-London-New Delhi: Sage Publications.
Macklin, E.D., and Rubin, R.H. (Eds.). (1983). *Contemporary families and alternative lifestyles: Handbook on research and theory*. Beverly Hills-London-New Delhi: Sage Publications.
Madge, N. (Ed.). (1983). *Families at risk*. London: Heinemann.
Maguire, D.C. (1978). *The moral choice*. Garden City, New York: Doubleday.
Mahler, M. (1968). *On human symbiosis and the vicissitudes of individuation, Vol. I: Infantile psychosis*. New York: International Universities Press.
Mahler, M., Pine, F., and Bergman, A. (1975). *The psychological birth of the human infant*. New York: Basic Books.
Mahony, P. (1979). The budding international association of psychoanalysis and its discontents. *Psychoanalysis and Contemporary Thought*, 2, 551-591.
Mahony, P. (1982). *Freud as a writer*. New York: International Universities Press.
Malatesta, C.Z., and Izard, C.E. (Eds.). (1984). *Emotion in adult development*. Beverly Hills-London-New Delhi: Sage Publications.
Malcolm, J. (1982). *Psychoanalysis: The impossible profession*. New York: Vintage Books.
Malcolm, J. (1983, December 5). Annals of scholarship. *The New Yorker*, pp. 59-152.
Malcolm, J. (1984). *In the Freud archives*. New York: Knopf.
Marano, H. (1981). Biology is one key to the bonding of mothers and babies. *Smithsonian*, 11, 60-69.
Marcel, G. (1984a). Reply to Julian Marías. In P.A. Schilpp and L. Hahn (Eds.), *The philosophy of Gabriel Marcel* (pp. 570-572). La Salle, Illinois: Open Court.
Marcel, G. (1984b). Reply to Richard M. Zaner. In P.A. Schilpp and L. Hahn (Eds.), *The philosophy of Gabriel Marcel* (pp. 334-335). La Salle, Illinois: Open Court.
Marcuse, H. (1955). *Eros and civilization: A philosophical inquire into Freud*. Boston: Beacon Press.

Marías, J. (1971). *Metaphysical anthropology: The empirical structure of human life* (F. Lopez-Morillas, Trans.). University Park-London: Pennsylvania State University Press. (Original work published 1970)

Marías, J. (1980). *La mujer en el siglo xx.* Madrid: Alianza Editorial.

Marías, J. (1984). Love in Marcel and Ortega (J.I. Frondizi, Trans.). In P.A. Schilpp and L. Hahn (Eds.), *The philosophy of Gabriel Marcel* (pp. 553-569). La Salle, Illinois: Open Court.

Martindale, C. (1984). The pleasures of thought: A theory of cognitive hedonics. *The Journal of Mind and Behavior, 5,* 49-80.

Martinson, F. (1981a). Preadolescent sexuality: Latent or manifest? In L. Constantine and F. Martinson (Eds.), *Children and sex: New findings, new perspectives* (pp. 95-107). Boston: Little, Brown.

Martinson, F. (1981b). The sex education of young children. In L. Brown (Ed.), *Sex education in the eighties: The challenge of healthy sexual revolution* (pp. 51-82). New York: Plenum Press.

Masling, J., and Schwartz, M. (1979). A critique of research in psychoanalytic theory. *Genetic Psychology Monographs, 100,* 257-307.

Masson, J. (1984a). *The assault on truth: Freud's suppression of the seduction theory.* New York: Farrar, Straus and Giroux.

Masson, J. (1984b). [Replies to letters to the editor.] *Atlantic, 253* (April), 8-9.

Masson, J. (1984c, December). Persecution and expulsion of Jeffrey Masson as performed by members of the Freudian establishment and reported by Janet Malcolm. *Mother Jones,* pp. 34-37, 42-47.

Masson, J. (1984d, August 16). [Letter to the editor.] *New York Review of Books,* pp. 51-52.

Masters, W., and Johnson, V. (1963). The clitoris: An anatomic baseline for behavioral investigation. In G.W. Winokur (Ed.), *Determinants of human sexual behavior* (pp. 44-51). Springfield, Illinois: C.C. Thomas.

Masters, W., and Johnson, V. (1966). *Human sexual response.* Boston: Little, Brown and Co.

Matthews, G. (1982). Concerning childhood: 'Child animism'. *Nous, 16,* 24-37.

McCarthy, M. (1985, February 24). Attitudes shifting against abortion. *Buffalo News,* p. F5.

McGeer, P.L., and McGeer, E.G. (1980). Chemistry of mood and emotion. *Annual Review of Psychology, 31,* 273-307.

McWhirter, D., and Mattison, A. (1983). *The male couple: How relationships develop.* Englewood Cliffs, New Jersey: Prentice-Hall.

Meissner, W.W. (1983). Phenomenology of the self. In A. Goldberg (Ed.), *The future of psychoanalysis* (pp. 65-96). New York: International Universities Press.

Meltzoff, A. (1981). Imitation, intermodal co-ordination and representation in early infancy. In G. Butterworth (Ed.), *Infancy and epistemology: An evaluation of Piaget's theory* (pp. 85-114). Brighton, Sussex: Harvester Press.

Meltzoff, A., and Moore, M. (1977). Imitation of facial and manual gestures by human neonates. *Science, 198,* 75-78.

Merleau-Ponty, M. (1962). *Phenomenology of perception* (C. Smith, Trans.). London: Routledge and Kegan Paul; New York: Humanities Press. (Original work published 1945)

Mesnick, G., and Bane, M. (1980). *The nation's families: 1960-1980.* Boston: Auburn House Publishing Co.

Meyerowitz, P. (1982). *And a little child: Stories of anyone.* New York: rRp Publishers.

Michel, L. (1970). *The thing contained: Theory of the tragic.* Bloomington: Indiana University Press.

Midgley, M. (1978). *Beast and man: The roots of human nature.* Ithaca: Cornell Unviersity Press.

Miller, A. (1981a). *Prisoners of childhood: The drama of the gifted child.* New York: Basic Books.

Miller, A. (1981b). *Du sollst nicht merken: Variationen über das Paradies-Thema.* Frankfurt am Main: Suhrkamp Verlag.

Miller, A. (1983). *For your own good: Hidden cruelty in child-rearing and the roots of violence* (H. Hannum and H. Hannum, Trans.). New York: Farrar, Straus and Giroux. (Original work published 1980)

Miller, A. (1984). *Thou shalt not be aware: Society's betrayal of the child* (H. Hannum and H. Hannum, Trans.). New York: Farrar, Straus und Giroux.

Milner, M. (1969). *The hands of the living god: An account of a psychoanalytic treatment.* New York: International Universities Press.

Modgil, S. (1974). *Piagetian research: A handbook of recent studies*. Windsor: National Foundation for Educational Research.

Moley, V. (1983). Interactional treatment of eating disorders. *Journal of Strategic and Systemic Therapies*, 2(4), 10-28.

Money, J. (1977). The 'givens' from a different point of view: Lessons from intersexuality for a theory of gender identity. In E. Oremland and J. Oremland (Eds.), *The sexual and gender development of young children: The role of the educator* (pp. 27-33). Cambridge, Massachusetts: Ballinger.

Money, J. (1980). *Love and love sickness: The science of sex, gender difference and pair-bonding*. Baltimore: Johns Hopkins University Press.

Money, J., and Ehrhardt, A. (1974). *Man & woman: Boy & Girl*. New York: Mentor Books.

Montrelay, M. (1980). The story of Louise. In S. Schneiderman (Ed.), *Returning to Freud: Clinical psychoanalysis in the school of Lacan* (pp. 75-93). New Haven: Yale University Press.

More children found born out of wedlock. (1984, June, 5). *New York Times*, p. A17.

Morris, T. (1980). Bursting the foundations: A bibliographical primer on the criticism of cultures [whole issue]. *Paunch*, #55-56.

Morsbach, G., and Bunting, C. (1979). Maternal recognition of their neonate's cries. *Developmental Medicine and Child Neurology*, 21, 178-185.

Mosher, D. (1980). Three dimensions of depth of involvement in human sexual response. *Journal of Sex Research*, 16, 1-42.

Muensterberger, W., Boyer, L.B., and Grolnik, S.A. (Eds.). (1983). *The psychoanalytic study of society*, Vol. 10. Hillsdale, New Jersey: Analytic Press.

Muller, J., and Richardson, W. (1982). *Lacan and language: A reader's guide to ECRITS*. New York: International Universities Press.

Muller, P.F., Campbell, H.E., Graham, W.E., Brittain, H., Fitzgerald, J.A., Hogan, M.A., Muller, V.H., and Rittenhouse, A.M. (1971). Perinatal factors and their relationship to mental retardation and other parameters of development. *American Journal of Obstetrics and Gynecology*, 109, 1205-1210.

Munson, H. (Ed.). (1984). *The house of Si Abd Allah: The oral history of a Moroccan family* (H. Munson, Trans.). New Haven: Yale University Press.

Naroll, R. (1983). *The moral order: An introduction to the human situation*. Beverly Hills-London-New Delhi: Sage Publications.

National Public Radio: All things considered (1984, June 26). Presentation on teenage suicide in the U.S.

Neisser, U. (1967). *Cognitive psychology*. New York: Appleton-Century-Crofts.

Neisser, U. (1976). *Cognition and reality*. San Francisco: Freeman.

Nelson, B. (1983, October 11). Children who kill: Personality patterns identified in teen homocide. *New York Times*, pp. C1, C8.

Nelson, J. (1981). The impact of incest: Factors in self-evaluation. In L. Constantine and F. Martinson (Eds.), *Children and sex: New findings, new perspectives* (pp. 163-176). Boston: Little, Brown.

Nelson, N., Enkin, M. Saigal, S., Bennett, K., Milner, R., and Sackett, D. (1980). A randomized clinical trial of the Leboyer approach to childbirth. *New England Journal of Medicine*, 302, 655-660.

Newborns found able to imitate facial expressions. (1982, October 12). *New York Times*, p. C2.

New hurdles for unmarried couples. (1984, November 4). *New York Times*, p. 28.

Nitchie, G. (1978). *Human values in the poetry of Robert Frost: A study of a poet's convictions*. New York: Gordian Press.

Oakley, A. (1982). Obstetric practices—Cross-cultural comparisons. In P. Stratton (Ed.), *Psychobiology of the newborn* (pp. 297-313). New York: Wiley.

Oakley, A. (1984). *The captured womb: A history of the medical care of pregnant women*. Oxford: Basil Blackwell.

Obholzer, K. (1982). *The wolf man: Conversations with Freud's patient—sixty years later* (M. Shaw, Trans.). New York: Continuum.

Odent, M. (1976). *Bien naitre*. Paris: Éditions du Seuil.

Odent, M. (1979). *Genese de l'homme ecologique: L'instict retrouve*. Paris: Éditions de l'Epi.

Odent, M. (1980). Obstetric positions, consciousness, and maternity practice. *Energy & Character: The Journal of Bioenergetic Research*, 11(2), 9-14.

Odent, M. (1982). *Entering the world: The demedicalization of childbirth* (C. Hanch, Trans.). New York-London: Marion Boyers/Scribner Book Companies.
Odent, M. (1984a). *Entering the world: The demedicalization of childbirth* (C. Hanch, Trans.). New York: New American Library.
Odent, M. (1984b). *Birth reborn* (J. Levin and J. Pincus, Trans.). New York: Pantheon.
Offer, D., and Franzen, S. (1983). Mood development in normal adolescents. In H. Golombek and D. Garfinkel (Eds.), *The adolescent and mood disturbance* (pp. 23-24). New York: International Unviersities Press.
Offit, A.K. (1977). *The sexual self*. New York: Congdon and Weed.
Offit, A.K. (1981). *Night thoughts: Reflections of a sex therapist*. New York: Congdon and Lattès.
Offit, A.K. (1982, December 7). Sex in the morning. *Cosmopolitan*, pp. 78, 84.
Offit, A.K. (1983). *The sexual self* (rev. ed.). New York: Congdon and Weed. (Distributed by St. Martin's Press.)
Olds, S.W. (1983, May 24). Letters. *New York Times*.
Oliver, C., and Oliver, G. (1978). Gentle birth: Its safety and its effect on neonatal behavior. *Journal of Obstetrics, Gynecology, and Neonatal Nursing*, 5, 35-40.
Ornstein, P. (1978). Introduction. In H. Kohut (Ed.), *The search for the self: Selected writings, 1950-1978* (pp. 1-106). New York: International Universities Press.
Oshima, N. (1977). In the realm of the senses [Feature-length film].
Padel, J. (1975, July 18). Life without father [Review of M. Klein, *Narrative of a child analysis*]. *Times Literary Supplement*, pp. 798-799.
Palombo, S. (1978). *Dreaming and memory: A new information-processing model*. New York: Basic Books.
Papoušek, H., and Papoušek, M. (1982). Integration into the social world: Survey of research. In P. Stratton (Ed.), *Psychobiology of the human newborn* (pp. 367-390). New York: Wiley.
Parsons, J. (1982). Biology, experience, and sex-dimorphic behaviors. In W. Gove and G. Carpenter (Eds.), *The fundamental connection between nature and nurture: A review of the evidence* (pp. 137-170). Lexington, Massachusetts: Lextington Books/D.C. Heath.
Patton, C. (1984). Sex and sectarianism [Review of C. Vance (Ed.), *Pleasure and danger: Exploring women's sexuality*]. *Women's Review of Books*, 2 (December), 4-5.
Paul, W., Weinrich, J., Gonsiorek, J., and Hotvedt, M. (Eds.). (1982). *Homonsexuality: Social, psychological, and biological issues*. Beverly Hills-London-New Delhi: Sage Publications.
Peplau, L., and Amaro, H. (1982). Understanding lesbian relationships. In W. Paul, J. Weinrich, J. Gonsiorek, M. Hotvedt (Eds.), *Homosexuality: Social, psychological, and biological issues* (pp. 233-247). Beverly Hills-London-New Delhi: Sage Publications.
Pepper, S.C. (1942). *World hypotheses: A study in evidence*. Berkeley-Los Angeles: University of California Press.
Pepper, S.C. (1945). *The basis of criticism in the Arts*. Cambridge, Massachusetts: Harvard University Press.
Pepper, S.C. (1946). The descriptive definition. *Journal of Philosophy*, 43(2), 29-36.
Pepper, S.C. (1949). *Principles of art appreciation*. New York and Burlingame: Harcourt, Brace and World.
Pepper, S.C. (1958). *The sources of value*. Berkeley: University of California Press.
Pepper, S.C. (1967). *Concept and quality: A world hypothesis*. La Salle, Illinois: Open Court.
Pepper, S.C. (1969a). Survival value. *Journal of Value Inquiry*, 3, 180-186.
Pepper, S.C. (1969b). On a descriptive theory of values: Reply to Professor Margolis. *Zygon*, 4, 261-265.
Pepper, S.C. (1969c). On the uses of symbolism in sculpture and painting. *Philosophy East and West: A Quarterly of Asian and Comparative Thought*, 19, 265-278.
Pepper, S.C. (1970). Extentialism. In J. Bobik (Ed.), *The nature of philosophical inquiry* (pp. 189-211). Notre Dame, Indiana: Notre Dame University Press.
Pepper, S.C. (1971). A dynamic view of perception. *Philosophy and Phenomenological Research*, 32, 42-46.
Pepper, S.C. (1972). Systems philosophy as a world hypothesis. *Philosophy and Phenomenological Research*, 32, 548-553.
Pepper, S.C. (1982). Metaphor in philosophy. *The Journal of Mind and Behavior*, 3, 197-205. (Original work published 1972)

REFERENCES

Peterfreund, E. (1971). *Information, systems and psychoanalysis: An evolutionary biological approach to psychoanalytic theory* (Psychological Issues Monographs No. 25-26). New York: International Universities Press.
Peterfreund, E. (1978). Some critical comments on psychoanalytic conceptualizations of infancy. *International Journal of Psycho-Analysis*, 59, 427-441.
Peterfreund, E. (1980). On information and systems models for psychoanalysis. *International Review of Psycho-Analysis*, 7, 327-345.
Peterfreund, E. (1983). *The process of psychoanalytic therapy.* Hillsdale, New Jersey: Analytic Press.
Peters, M.F., and McAdoo, H.P. (1983). The present and future of alternative lifestyles in ethnic American cultures. In E.D. Macklin and R.H. Rubin (Eds.), *Contemporary families and alternative lifestyles: Handbook on research and theory* (pp. 288-307). Beverly Hills-London-New Delhi: Sage Publications.
Peterson, A. (1980). Biopsychosocial processes in the development of sex-related differences. In J.E. Parsons (Ed.), *The psychobiology of sex differences and sex roles* (pp. 31-55). Washington-New York-London: Hemisphere Publishing Corporation/McGraw Hill.
Phillips, S., King, S., and DuBois, L. (1978). Spontaneous activities of female versus male newborns. *Child Development*, 49, 590-597.
Piaget, J. (1952). *The origins of intelligence in the child.* London: Churchill.
Placzek, B. (Ed.). (1981). *Record of a friendship: The correspondence of Wilhelm Reich and A.S. Neill 1936-1958.* New York: Farrar, Straus and Giroux.
Poole, R. (1978). *The unknown Virginia Woolf.* Cambridge, England: Cambridge University Press.
Popper, K.R., and Eccles, J.C. (1977). *The self and its brain.* Berlin-New York-London: Springer International.
Postiglione, G., and Scimecca, J. (1983). The poverty of paradigmaticism: A symptom of the crisis in sociological explanation. *The Journal of Mind and Behavior*, 4, 179-190.
Prawer, S. (1983, July 29). The psyche in translation. *Times Literary Supplement*, p. 812.
Prescott, J.W. (1979). Deprivation of physical affection as a primary process in the development of physical violence: A comparative and cross-cultural perspective. In D. Gil (Ed.), *Child abuse and violence* (pp. 66-137). New York: AMS Press.
Price-Bonham, S., Wright, D.W., and Pittman, J.F. (1983). Divorce: A frequent 'alternative' in the 1970's. In E.D. Macklin and R.H. Rubin (Eds.), *Contemporary families and alternative lifestyles: Handbook on research and theory* (pp. 125-146). Beverly Hills-London-New Delhi: Sage Publications.
Pruyser, P. (1984). *The play of the imagination: Toward a psychoanalysis of culture.* New York: International Universities Press.
Public Broadcasting System. (1984, August 12). Crime of silence [Program on sexual abuse of children].
Ragland-Sullivan, E. (1979). Explicating Jacques Lacan: An overview. *Hartford Studies in Literature*, 11, 140-156.
Ragland-Sullivan, E. (1981). Lacan, language and literary criticism. *The Literary Review*, 24, 562-577.
Ragland-Sullivan, E. (in press). *Jacques Lacan and the philosophy of psychoanalysis.* Urbana: University of Illinois Press.
Ramzy, I. (1977). Editor's foreword to D.W. Winnicott, *The piggle*, pp. xi-xvi.
Rapaport, D. (1976). Pour une naissance sans violence: Resultats d'une premiere enquête. *Bulletin de Psychologie*, 29, 552-560.
Reck, A. (1968). *The new American philosophers: An exploration of thought since World War II.* Baton Rouge: Louisiana State University Press.
Reeves, J. (1958). *Body and mind in Western thought.* Harmondsworth: Penguin Books.
Reich, E. (1980). [Lecture on Bonding.] York University, Toronto, September 10.
Reich, W. (1933). *Massenpsychologie des Faschismus.* Copenhagen-Prague-Zurich: Verlag für Sexualpolitik.
Reich, W. (1934). *La crise sexuelle* [The sexual crises]. Paris: Éditions Sociales Internationales.
Reich, W. (1936). *Die Sexualität im Kulturkampf* [Sexuality in cultural combat]. Copenhagen: Sexpolverlag.

Reich, W. (1942). *The function of the orgasm* (T.P. Wolfe, Trans.). New York: Orgone Institute Press. (No German edition was published prior to this translation)
Reich, W. (1945). *The sexual revolution* (T.P. Wolfe, Trans.). New York: Orgone Institute Press.
Reich, W. (1968). *The function of the orgasm* (T.P. Wolfe, Trans.). New York: Farrar, Straus and Giroux. (Original work published 1942)
Reich, W. (1972). *Sex-Pol-Essays, 1929-1934* (L. Baxendall, Ed.). New York: Vintage/Random House.
Reich, W. (1975). Concerning the energy of drives. In W. Reich (P. Schultz, Trans.), *Early writings* (Vol. 1, pp. 143-157). Farrar, Straus and Giroux. (Original work published 1923)
Reich, W. (1983). *Children of the future: On the prevention of sexual pathology* (D. Jordan, I. Jordan, and B. Placzek, Trans.; M. Higgins and C. Raphael, Eds.). New York: Farrar, Straus and Giroux.
Researcher [S. Phillips] finds difference between male and female infant behaviors. (1978, April 17). *Behavior Today*, p. 3.
Restak, R. (1983, April 24). Is our culture in our genes? [Review of C. Lumsden and E.O. Wilson, *Promethean fire: Reflections on the origins of mind*]. *New York Times Book Review*, pp. 7, 22-23.
Ribble, M. (1943). *The rights of infants*. New York: Columbia University Press.
Ribble, M. (1956). *The personality of the young child*. London: Oxford University Press.
Ribble, M. (1965). *The rights of infants* (2nd ed.). New York: Columbia University Press.
Richardson, D. (in press). The metamorphosis of Faustian sensibility, 1630-1800. *Comparative Civilization Review*.
Riebel, J. (1980). Sexual abuse of children: A prevention strategy. In J.M. Samson (Ed.), *Childhood and sexuality: Proceedings of the international symposium* (pp. 688-693). Montreal: Éditions Études Vivantes.
Rieff, P. (1961). *Freud: The mind of the moralist*. Garden City, New York: Doubleday Anchor.
Ringler, N., Kennell, J., Jarvella, R., Navojosky, B., and Klaus, M. (1975). Mother-to-child speech at 2 years: Effects of early postnatal contact. *Journal of Pediatrics, 86*, 141-144.
Ringler, N., Trause, M., Klaus, M., and Kennell, J. (1978). The effects of extra postpartum contact and maternal speech patterns on children's IQ, speech, and language comprehension at five. *Child Development, 49*, 862-865.
Ritter, P. (1963). *Planning for man and motor*. Oxford: Pergamon Press.
Ritter, P. (1966). *Educreation: Education for creation, growth and change*. Oxford-London-New York-Toronto-Paris-Braunschweig: Pergamon Press.
Ritter, P., and Ritter, J. (1959). *The free family: A creative experiment in self-regulation for children*. London: Gollancz.
Ritter, P., and Ritter, J. (1976). *Free family & feedback*. Perth, Australia: Peer Institute.
Ritter, P., and Ritter, J. (1978). *A fascinating record: 25 years 1953-1978*. Perth, Australia: Peer Institute.
Roazen, P. (1976). *Erik H. Erikson: The power and limits of a vision*. New York: Free Press.
Robbins, M. (1980). Current controversy in object-relations theory as an outgrowth of a schism between Klein and Fairbairn. *International Journal of Psycho-Analysis, 61*, 477-492.
Robert, M. (1968). *The psychoanalytic revolution: Sigmund Freud's life and achievement* (K. Morgan, Trans.). New York: Avon Books.
Robertiello, R. (1979a). *A man in the making: Grandfathers, fathers, sons*. New York: Richard Marek Publishers.
Robertiello, R. (1979b). *Your own true love*. New York: Ballantine Books.
Rochlin, G. (1973). *Man's aggression: The defense of the self*. Boston: Gambit.
Rodman, H., Lewis, S., and Griffith, S. (1984). *The sexual rights of adolescents*. New York: Columbia University Press.
Rodman, S. (Ed.). (1951). *One hundred modern poems*. New York: New American Library.
Rogers, R. (1980). Psychoanalysis and cybernetic models of mentation. *Psychoanalysis and Contemporary Thought, 3*, 21-54.
Rogers, R. (1981). Textuality in dreams. *International Review of Psycho-Analysis, 8*, 433-447.
Roiphe, H., and Galenson, E. (1981). *Infantile origins of sexual identity*. New York: International Universities Press.
Rokeach, M. (1960). *The open and closed mind*. New York: Basic Books.

REFERENCES

Rorty, R. (1979). *Philosophy and the mirror of nature*. Princeton, New Jersey: Princeton University Press.
Rosenblatt, L. (1978). *The reader, the text, the poem*. Carbondale and Edwardsville, Illinois: Southern Illinois University Press.
Rosenfeld, H. (1981). Whither conversational synchrony? In K. Bloom (Ed.), *Prospective issues in infancy research* (pp. 71-97). Hillsdale, New Jersey: Erlbaum.
Rosenthal, R. (1966). *Experimenter effects in behavioral research*. New York: Appleton-Century-Crofts.
Rosenthal, R., and Rosnow, R. (1975). *The volunteer subject*. New York: Wiley/Interscience.
Rosenzweig, S. (1954). A transvaluation of psychotherapy: A reply to Hans Eysenck. *Journal of Abnormal and Social Psychology*, 49, 298-304.
Ross, D. (1971). *G. Stanley Hall: The psychologist as prophet*. Chicago: University of Chicago Press.
Ross, O. (1983, October 7). Lingering Mexican machismo keeps sexual revolution at bay. *Toronto Globe and Mail*, p. 12.
Rossi, A. (1977). A biosocial perspective on parenting. *Daedalus*, 106(2), 1-31.
Rossi, A. (1981). [Debate on N. Chodorow, *Reproduction of mothering*.] *Signs: Journal of Women in Culture and Society*, 6, 492-500.
Rossi, A. (1984). Gender and parenthood. *American Sociological Review*, 49, 1-19.
Rotkin, I.D. (1980). Epidemiologic clues to increased risk of prostatic cancer. In E. Spring-Mills and E.S.E. Hafez (Eds.), *Male accessory sex glands* (pp. 289-309). Elsevier: North-Holland Biomedical Press.
Russell, D. (1984). *Sexual exploitation: Rape, child sexual abuse, and sexual harassment*. Beverly Hills-London-New Delhi: Sage Publications.
Russell, E., and Howell, N. (1983). The prevalence of rape in the United States revisited. *Signs: Journal of Women in Culture and Society*, 8, 688-695.
Russell, M., Switz, G., and Thompson, K. (1980). Olfactory influences on the human menstrual cycle. *Pharmacology, Biochemistry and Behaviour*, 13, 737-738.
Rynne, X. (1985, March 24). Caretaker who launched a revolution [Review of P. Hebblethwaite, *Pope John XXIII: Shepherd of the modern world*.] *New York Times Book Review*, pp. 9-10.
Sabbah, F. (1984). *Woman in the Muslim unconsious* (M. Lakeland, Trans.). Elmsford, New York: Pergamon Press.
Salter, A. (1978). Birth without violence: A medical controversy. *Nursing Research*, 27, 84-88.
Samson, J.M. (Ed.). (1980). *Childhood and sexuality: Proceedings of the international symposium*. Montreal: Éditions Études Vivantes.
Sanders, W. (1980). *Rape and woman's identity*. Beverly Hills-London-New Delhi: Sage Publications.
Sayers, J. (1982). *Biological politics; feminist and anti-feminist perspectives*. London-New York: Tavistock Publications.
Schaal, B., Montagner, H., Hertling, E., Bolzoni, D., Moyse, A., and Quichon, R. (1980). Les stimulations olfactives dans le relations entre l'enfant et la mère [Olfactory stimulation in the infant-mother relation]. *Reproduction, Nutrition, Development*, 20, 843-858.
Schachtel, E.G. (1959). *Metamorphosis: On the development of affect, perception, attention and memory*. New York: Basic Books.
Schafer, R. (1976). *A new language for psychoanalysis*. New Haven: Yale University Press.
Schafer, R. (1980). Narration in the psychoanalytic dialogue. *Critical Inquiry*, 7, 29-53.
Schmeck, H.W., Jr. (1983, September 20). Scientists, commemorating DNA, discuss function of 'reverse twist'. *New York Times*, p. C7.
Schmeck, H.W., Jr. (1984, October 30). Bid to ban transfer of genes is rejected by panel. *New York Times*, pp. C1, C10.
Schneiderman, S. (Ed. and Trans.). (1980). *Returning to Freud: Clinical psychoanalysis in the school of Lacan*. New Haven: Yale University Press.
Schneiderman, S. (1982). To open. Lacan Study Notes (New York Lacan Study Group), 1(1), 1.
Schneiderman, S. (1983). *Jacques Lacan: The death of an intellectual hero*. Cambridge, Massachusetts: Harvard University Press.
Schrotenboer, K., and Subak-Sharpe, G. (1981). *Freedom from menstrual cramps*. New York: Pocket Books/Simon and Schuster.

Schumacher, E. (1985, April 25). Spanish parties agree to vote for law permitting some abortions. *New York Times*, p. 5.

Schur, M. (1966). Some additional 'day residues' of 'the specimen dream of psychoanalysis'. In R.M. Loewenstein, L. Newman, M. Schur, and A. Solnit (Eds.), *Psychoanalysis-a general psychology: Essays in honor of Heinz Hartmann* (pp. 45-85). New York: International Universities Press.

Schwartz, D., Weinstein, L., and Arkin, A. (1978). Qualitative states of sleep mentation. In A. Arkin, J. Antrobus, and S. Eldman (Eds.), *The mind in sleep: Psychology and physiology* (pp. 143-241). Hillsdale, New Jersey: Erlbaum.

Schwartz, G., and Merten, D., with Behan, F., and Rosenthal, A. (1980). *Love and commitment*. Beverly Hills-London-New Delhi: Sage Publications.

Schwartz, J. (1984). *The sexual politics of Jean-Jacques Rousseau*. Chicago: University of Chicago Press.

Schwartz, M., and Willbern, D. (1982). Literature and psychology. In J.-P. Baricelli and J. Gibaldi (Eds.), *Interrelations of literature* (pp. 205-224). New York: Modern Language Association of America.

Seaman, B. (1972). *Free and female*. New York: Coward-McCann and George Hegan.

Searle, J. (1982, April 29). The myth of the computer. *New York Review of Books*, pp. 3-6.

Sedgwick, P. (1983, September 9). Dramatic crossings [Review of E. Erikson, *The life cycle completed*.] *Times Literary Supplement*, p. 968.

The seduction theory controversy. (1984). [Plenary session of the Annual Conference of the Center for the Psychological Study of the Arts.] SUNY-Buffalo, May 12.

Segal, H. (1980). *Melanie Klein*. New York: Viking Press.

Seiler, H.P. (1982). New experiments in thermal orgonomy. *Journal of Orgonomy*, 16, 197-206.

Seligman, M.E.P. (1975). *Helplessness: On depression, development and death*. San Francisco: W.H. Freeman.

Sexual activity of women studied. (1985, February 16). *New York Times*, (AP dispatch) p. 8.

Sevely, J., and Bennett, J. (1978). Concerning female ejaculation and the female prostate. *Journal of Sex Research*, 14(1), 1-20.

Sgroi, S. (1975, May-June). Child sexual molestation: The last frontier in child abuse. *Children Today*, pp. 18-21, 44.

Shapiro, A., Cohen, H., DiBianco, P., and Rosen, G. (1968). Vaginal blood flow changes during sleep and sexual arousal. *Psychophysiology*, 4, 394 [Abstract].

Sharaf, M. (1973). Further remarks of Reich: 1950. *Journal of Orgonomy*, 7, 254-260.

Sharaf, M. (1976). Wilhelm Reich and the biosocial revolution. In D. Boadella (Ed.), *In the wake of Reich* (pp. 5-27). London: Coventure.

Sharaf, M. (1983). *Fury on earth: A biography of Wilhelm Reich*. New York: St. Martin's Press/Marek.

Sheleff, L.S. (1981). *Generations apart: Adult hostility to youth*. New York: McGraw-Hill Book Co.

Sidel, R. (1972). *Women and child care in China*. New York: Hill and Wang.

Siewert, D. (1971). The body in Marcel's metaphysics. *Thought*, 46, 389-405.

Silverman, L.H. (1971). An experimental technique for the study of unconscious conflict. *British Journal of Medical Psychology*, 44, 17-25.

Silverman, L.H., Lachman, F.M., and Milich, R.H. (1982). *The quest for oneness*. New York: International Universities Press.

Simon, W., and Gagnon, J. (1967). Homosexuality: The formulation of a sociological perspective. *Journal of Health and Social Behavior*, 8, 177-184.

Simons, M. (1984, December 27). Activism said to swell ranks of Latin Catholic priesthood. *New York Times*, p. A12.

Singer, I. (1973). *The goals of human sexuality*. New York: Schocken Books.

Skolnick, A. (1973). *The intimate enviornment: Exploring marriage and the family*. Boston: Little, Brown.

Sluckin, H., Sluckin, W., and Sluckin, A. (1982). Mother to infant "bonding." *Journal of Child Psychology and Psychiatry*, 23, 205-221.

Sluckin, L., Herbert, M., and Sluckin, A. (1984). *Maternal bonding*. Oxford: Basil Blackwell.

Small, M. (Ed.). (1984). *Female primates: Studies by women primatologists*. New York: Alan R. Liss, Inc.

REFERENCES

Smelser, N., and Erikson, E. (Eds.). (1980). *Themes of work and love in adulthood.* Cambridge, Massachusetts: Harvard University Press.
Smirnoff, V. (1971). *The scope of child analysis* (S. Corrin, Trans.). New York: International Universities Press. (Original work published 1966)
Smith, D. (1980). Birth and submergence. *Energy & Character: The Journal of Bioenergetic Research, 11*(1), 21-33.
Smith, H.F. (1984, July-August). Notes on the history of childhood. *Harvard Magazine* (Special Supplement), pp. 64A-64G.
Smith, J., and Kerrigan, W. (Eds.). (1983). *Interpreting Lacan* (Psychiatry and Humanities, Vol. 6). New Haven: Yale University Press.
Socarides, C. (1979). A unitary theory of sexual perversions. In T. Karasu and C. Socarides (Eds.), *On sexuality: Psychoanalytic observations* (pp. 161-188). New York: International Universities Press.
Socarides, C. (1984). [Review of R. Bayer, *Homosexuality and American psychiatry.*] *Review of Psychoanalytic Books, 2,* 87-96.
Solnit, A.J. (1972). Aggression: A view of theory building in psychoanalysis. *Journal of the American Psychoanalytic Association, 20,* 435-450.
Spector, J. (1972). *The aesthetics of Freud: A study in psychoanalysis and art.* London-New York: Penguin.
Spiegel, J.P., and Machotka, P. (1974). *Messages of the body.* New York: Macmillan.
Spitz, R. (1965). *The first year of life.* New York: International Universities Press.
Staples, R. (1982). *Black masculinity: The black male's role in American society.* San Francisco: Black Scholar Press.
Stechler, G., Bradford, S., and Levy, H. (1966). Attention in the newborn: Affect on motility and skin potential. *Science, 151,* 1247-1248.
Stechler, G., and Carpenter, G. (1967). A viewpoint on early affective development. In J. Hellmuth (Ed.), *Exceptional infant* (Vol. 1, pp. 163-189). New York: Brunner/Mazel.
Stechler, G., and Latz, E. (1966). Some observations on attention and arousal in the human infant. *Journal of American Academy of Child Psychiatry, 5,* 517-525.
Stein, P.J. (1983). Singlehood. In E.D. Macklin and R.H. Rubin (Eds.), *Contemporary families and alternative lifestyles: Handbook on research and theory* (pp. 27-47). Beverly Hills-London-New Delhi: Sage Publications.
Stepansky, P. (1977). *A history of aggression in Freud* (Psychological Issues Monograph No. 39). New York: International Universities Press.
Stepansky, P., and Goldberg, A. (Eds.). (1984). *Kohut's legacy: Contributions to self psychology.* Hillsdale, New Jersey: Analytic Press.
Stern, D. (1971). A micro-analysis of mother-infant interaction. *Journal of American Academy of Child Psychiatry, 10,* 501-517.
Stern, D. (1977). *The first relationship: Infant and mother.* Cambridge, Massachusetts: Harvard University Press.
Stern, M., with Stern, A. (1980). *Sex in the USSR* (M. Howson and C. Ryan, Trans.). New York: New York Times Co.
Stevens, W.K. (1983, April 22). Sexual repression in the land of the Kama Sutra. *New York Times,* p. A2.
Stokes, A. (1972). *The image in form: Selected writings* (R. Wollheim Ed.). New York: Harper and Row.
Stoller, R. (1968). *Sex and gender.* New York: Science House.
Stoller, R. (1975). *Perversion: The erotic form of hatred.* New York: Delta Books.
Stone, L. (1971). Reflections on the psychoanalytic concept of aggression. *Psychoanalytic Quarterly, 40,* 195-244.
Stone, L.J., Smith, H.T., and Murphy, L.B. (Eds.). (1973). *The competent infant: Research and commentary.* New York: Basic Books.
Storr, A. (1984, February 12). Did Freud have clay feet? *New York Times Book Review,* pp. 3, 35.
Stratton, P. (1982a). Rhythmic function in the newborn. In P. Stratton (Ed.), *Psychobiology of the human newborn* (pp. 119-145). Chichester-New York-Brisbane-Toronto-Singapore: John Wiley and Sons.
Stratton, P. (Ed.). (1982b). *Psychobiology of the human newborn.* Chichester-New York-Brisbane-Toronto-Singapore: John Wiley and Sons.

Suicide among students alarms Germans. (1978, December 9). *New York Times*, p. 43.
Sulloway, F. (1979). *Freud, biologist of the mind.* New York: Basic Books.
Suransky, V. (1982). *The erosion of childhood.* Chicago: University of Chicago Press.
Svejda, M., Campos, J., and Emde, R. (1980). Mother-infant "bonding": Failure to generalize. *Child Development, 51,* 775-779.
Symonds, C., Mendoza, M., and Harrell, W. (1981). Forbidden sexual behavior among kin: A study of self-selected respondents. In L. Constantine and F. Martinson (Eds.), *Children and sex: New findings, new perspectives* (pp. 151-162). Boston: Little, Brown.
Symons, D. (1979). *The evolution of human sexuality.* New York: Oxford University Press.
Szent-Györgi, A. (1957). *Bioenergetics.* New York: Academic Press.
Tavris, C. (1983, October 23). [Review of P. Blumstein and P. Schwartz, *American couples: Money, work, sex.*] *New York Times Books Review,* pp. 7, 31.
Tavris, C., and Sadd, S. (1977). *The Redbook report on female sexuality.* New York: Dell Publishing Co.
Taylor, C. (1977). Fragments toward a new chauvinism: The masculist manifesto. *Paunch,* #48-49, pp. 20-39.
Teens show big increase in anorexia. (1984, April 8). *Buffalo News* (UPI).
Textor, R.B. (1967). *A cross-cultural summary.* New Haven: HRAF Press.
Thelan, E., and Fisher, D. (1983). From spontaneous to instrumental behavior: Kinematic analysis of movement changes during very early learning. *Child Development, 54,* 129-140.
Theodor, J. (1970). The distinction between "self" and "not-self" in lower invertebrates. *Nature, 227,* 690-692.
Thomas, A., and Chess, S. (1977). *Temperament and development.* New York: Brunner/Mazel.
Thomas, A., and Chess, S. (1980). *The dynamics of psychological development.* New York: Brunner/Mazel.
Thomas, J. (1984, September 4). Other countries: Extensive facilites and controls. *New York Times,* p. B11.
Thomas, L. (1974). *The lives of a cell: Notes of a biology watcher.* Toronto-New York-London: Bantam Books.
Thomas, L. (1979). *The Medusa and the snail: More notes of a biology watcher.* New York: Viking Press.
Thompson, E.H., and Gongla, P.A. (1983). Single-parent families: In the mainstream of American society. In E.D. Macklin and R.H. Rubin (Eds.), *Contemporary families and alternative lifestyles: Handbook on research and theory* (pp. 97-124). Beverly Hills-London-New Delhi: Sage Publications.
Thompson, L., and Winnick, R. (1976). *Robert Frost: The later years, 1938-1963.* New York: Holt, Rinehart and Winston.
Tolman, E.C. (1932). *Purposive behavior in animals and men.* Berkeley and Los Angeles: University of California Press.
Tomkins, S. (1962). *Affect, imagery, consciousness,* Vol. 1. New York: Springer Publishing Co.
Tomkins, S. (1963). *Affect, imagery, consicousness,* Vol. 2. New York: Springer Publishing Co.
Tomkins, S. (1980). Affect as amplification: Some modifications in theory. In R. Plutchik and H. Kellerman (Eds.), *Emotion: Theory, research, experience* (Vol. 1, pp. 141-164). New York-London: Academic Press.
Tomkins, S. (1981a). The role of facial response in the experience of emotion: A reply to Thorangeaur and Ellsworth. *Journal of Personality and Social Psychology, 40,* 355-357.
Tomkins, S. (1981b). The quest for primary motives: Biography and autobiography of an idea. *Journal of Personality and Social Psychology, 41,* 306-329.
Toronto Psychoanalytic Society and Institute. (1984). [Brochure: Seventh annual self psychology conference, October 19-21.]
Tripp, C. (1975). *The homosexual matrix.* New York: McGraw-Hill Book Co.
Tsai, M., Feldman-Summers, S., and Edgar, M. (1981). Childhood molestation: Differential impacts on psychosexual functioning. In L. Constantine and F. Martinson (Eds.), *Children and sex: New findings, new perspectives* (pp. 201-216). Boston: Little, Brown.
Turchin, C. (1979). Working with bone. *Energy & Character: The Journal of Bioenergetic Research, 10*(2), 67-79.
Tuttman, S. (1978). Contribution to Kohut's *Restoration of the self:* A symposium. *Psychoanalytic Review, 65,* 624-629.

REFERENCES

Utts, H. (1984). Touch: The human connection for health and survival [Presentation for Conversations in the Cathedral]. St. Paul's Cathedral, Buffalo, February 16.
Vaillant, G. (1977). *Adaptation to life.* Boston: Little, Brown.
Vance, C. (Ed.). (1984). *Pleasure and danger: Exploring female sexuality.* Boston: Routledge and Kegan Paul.
Vance, C., and Snitow, A. (1984). Toward a conversation about sex in feminism: A modest proposal. *Signs: Journal of Women in Culture and Society, 10,* 126-135.
Vatican eases curbs on priests who marry. (1983, November 27). *New York Times* (Reuters dispatch).
Veevers, J.E. (1983). Voluntary Childlessness: A critical assessment of the research. In E.D. Macklin and R.H. Rubin (Eds.), *Contemporary families and alternative lifestyles: Handbook on research and theory* (pp. 75-96). Beverly Hills-London-New Delhi: Sage Publications.
Waddington, C. (1957). *The strategy of the genes.* London: Allen and Unwin.
Waldron, I. (1982). An analysis of causes of sex differences in mortality and morbidity. In W. Gove and G. Carpenter (Eds.), *The fundamental connection between nature and nurture: A review of the evidence* (pp. 69-116). Lexington, Massachusetts: Lexington Books/D.C. Heath.
Wallace, L. (1984). *Pleasure and frustration: A resynthesis of clinical and theoretical psychoanalysis.* New York: International Universities Press.
Wallon, H. (1925). *L'Enfant turbulent.* Paris: Alcan.
Watson, J.B. (1928). *Psychological care of infant and child.* New York: W.W. Norton.
Weinberg, G. (1972). *Society and the healthy homosexual.* New York: St. Martin's Press.
Weinberg, M., and Williams, C. (1975). *Male homosexuals: Their problems and adaptations.* New York-Baltimore: Penguin Books.
Weiner, H. (1980). Contemporary research on the mind-body problem. In R. Rieber (Ed.), *Body and mind: Past, present and future* (pp. 223-240). New York-London-Toronto-Sydney-San Francisco: Academic Press.
Weinrich, J. (1982a). Summary and conclusions. In W. Paul, J. Weinrich, J. Gonsiorek, and M. Hotvedt (Eds.), *Homosexuality: Social, psychological, and biological issues* (pp. 209-211). Beverly Hills-London-New Delhi: Sage Publications.
Weinrich, J. (1982b). Task force findings: Overview and prospects. In W. Paul, J. Weinrich, J. Gonsiorek, and M. Hotvedt (Eds.), *Homosexuality: Social, psychological, and biological issues* (pp. 377-382). Beverly Hills-London-New Delhi: Sage Publications.
Weis, D. (1983). 'Open' marriage and multilateral relationships: The emergence of nonexclusive models of marital relationships. In E.D. Macklin and R.H. Rubin (Eds.), *Contemporary families and alternative lifestyles: Handbook on research and theory* (pp. 195-214). Beverly Hills-London-New Delhi: Sage Publications.
Weiss, A. (1981). Merleau-Ponty's concept of the "flesh" as libido theory. *Sub-Stance, #30,* pp. 85-90.
Werry, J. (1968). Studies on the hyperactive child, IV: An empirical analysis of the minimal brain dysfunction syndrome. *Archives of General Psychiatry, 19,* 9-16.
Whipple, B., and Perry, J. (1981). Pelvic muscle strength of female ejaculators: Evidence in support of a new theory of female orgasm. *Journal of Sex Research, 17*(1), 22-39.
Whiting, B.B. (1963). *Six cultures: Studies of child rearing.* New York: Wiley.
Whiting, B.B., and Child, I.L. (1953). *Child training and personality.* New Haven: Yale University Press.
Whitman, R. (1984). [Review of E. Peterfreund, *The process of psychoanalytic therapy.*] *Review of Psychoanalytic Books, 3,* 381-383.
Wiener, H. (1980). Contemporary research and the mind-body problem. In R.W. Rieber (Ed.), *Body and mind: Past, present, and future* (pp. 223-240). New York-London—Toronto-Syndney-San Francisco: Academic Press.
Williams, F. (1983). Family therapy: Its role in adolescent psychiatry. In A. Esman (Ed.), *The psychiatric treatment of adolescents* (pp. 281-301). New York: International Universities Press.
Willbern, D. (1979). Freud and the interpenetration of dreams. *Diacritics, 9,* 98-110.
Wilson, E.O. (1975). *Sociobiology: A new synthesis.* Cambridge, Massachusetts: Harvard University Press.
Wilson, E.O. (1978). *On human nature.* Cambridge, Massachusetts: Harvard University Press.

Wilson, G.D., and Fulford, K.W. (1979). Sexual behaviour, personality and hormonal characteristics of heterosexual, homosexual and bisexual men. In M. Cook and G. Wilson (Eds.), *Love and attraction: An international conference* (pp. 387-393). Oxford-New York-Toronto-Sydney-Paris-Frankfurt: Pergamon Press.

Winnicott, D.W. (1957). *Through paediatrics to psycho-analysis: Collected papers*, Vol. 1. London: Hogarth Press.

Winnicott, D.W. (1960). The theory of the parent-infant relationship. *International Journal of Psycho-Analysis, 41*, 585-595.

Winnicott, D.W. (1964). *The child, the family, and the outside world.* Harmondsworth: Penguin Books.

Winnicott, D.W. (1965). *The maturational process and the facilitating environment: Collected papers*, Vol. 2. London: Hogarth Press.

Winnicott, D.W. (1971). *Playing and reality.* London: Tavistock Publications.

Winnicott, D.W. (1977). *The piggle: An account of the psychoanalytic treatment of a little girl* (I. Ramzy, Ed.). New York: International Universities Press.

Wolff, P.H. (1966). *The causes, control, and organization of behavior in the neonate* (Psychological Issues Mongraphs No. 17). New York: International Universities Press.

Wolff, P.H. (1968). The serial organization of sucking in the young infant. *Pediatrics, 42*, 943-956.

Wolkomir, R. (1983). Just babes in the woods. *National Wildlife, 21*(3), 50-59.

Wollheim, R. (1971). *Sigmund Freud.* New York: Viking Press.

Wolpert, L. (1983, March 4). The multiplication of the living. *Times Literary Supplement*, p. 216.

Woolf, V. (1927). *To the lighthouse.* London: Hogarth Press.

Wright, P., and Crow, R. (1982). Nutrition and feeding. In P. Stratton (Ed.), *Psychobiology of the human newborn* (pp. 339-364). New York: Wiley.

Yates, A. (1980). The effect of commonly accepted parenting practices on erotic development. In J.M. Samson (Ed.), *Childhood and sexuality: Proceedings of the international symposium* (pp. 367-372). Montreal: Éditions Études Vivantes.

Zaner, R. (1964). *The problem of embodiment: Some contributions to a phenomenology of the body.* The Hague: Martinus Nijhoff.

Zaner, R. (1967). The radical reality of the human body. *Humanities, 2*, 73-87.

Zaner, R. (1981). *The context of self: A phenomenological inquiry using medicine as a clue.* Athens, Ohio: Ohio University Press.

Zaner, R. (1984). The mystery of body-qua-mine. In P.A. Schlipp and L.E. Hahn (Eds.), *The philosophy of Gabriel Marcel* (pp. 313-333). LaSalle, Illinois: Open Court.

Zenoff, E., and Zients, A. (1979). Juvenile murderers: Should the punishment fit the crime? *International Journal of Law and Psychiatry, 2*, 533-553.

Zimmerman, B. (1984). The politics of transliteration: Lesbian personal narratives. *Signs: Journal of Women in Culture and Society, 9*, 663-682.

Zimring, F. (1984, August 5). Crime maybe going out of style in the U.S. *Buffalo News*, p. F3.

The Journal of Mind and Behavior

Editorial Board

Editor:
Raymond C. Russ, Ph.D.
Department of Psychology
University of Maine, Orono

Assistant Editor:
Richard D. Schenkman, M.D.
Neuropsychiatric Institute
University of California, Los Angeles

Associate Editor:
James Bense, M.A.
Department of English
University of California, Davis

Associate Editor:
Edward M. Covello
Pacific-Sierra Research Corporation
Los Angeles, California

Book Review Editor:
Steven E. Connelly, Ph.D.
Department of English
Indiana State University, Terre Haute

Managing Editor:
Ingeborg M. Biller, Soz.Päd.Grad.
The Institute of Mind and Behavior
New York City, New York

Liaison for Medical Affairs:
Elliot M. Frohman
California College of Medicine
University of California, Irvine

Assessing Editors

Lloyd Abrams, Ph.D.
Agnews State Hospital
San Jose, California

Charles I. Abramson
Department of Psychology
Boston University

John Antrobus, Ph.D.
Department of Psychology
The City College of New York

David Bakan, Ph.D.
Department of Psychology
York University

Allen B. Barbour, M.D.
School of Medicine
Stanford University

Thomas C. Cadwallader, Ph.D.
Department of Psychology
Indiana State University

Kenneth D. Carr, Ph.D.
Department of Psychiatry
NYU Medical School

Paul D. Cherulnik, Ph.D.
Department of Psychology
Susquehanna University

Phyllis Chesler, Ph.D.
The College of Staten Island, CUNY

Nancy Datan, Ph.D.
Department of Human Development
University of Wisconsin

Florence L. Denmark, Ph.D.
Department of Psychology
Hunter College

James Dietch, M.D.
California College of Medicine
University of California, Irvine

Leonard W. Doob, Ph.D.
Department of Psychology
Yale University

Arthur Efron, Ph.D.
Department of English
SUNY at Buffalo

Robert Epstein, Ph.D.
Cambridge Center for Behavioral Studies

Philip Jose Farmer
Peoria, Illinois

James Fastook, Ph.D.
Institute for Quaternary Studies
University of Maine

Eileen A. Gavin, Ph.D.
Department of Psychology
The College of St. Catherine

Kenneth J. Gergen, Ph.D.
Department of Psychology
Swarthmore College

Felicitas D. Goodman, Ph.D.
Cuyamungue Institute
Columbus, Ohio

Robert Haskell, Ph.D.
Psychology Department
University of New England

Robert R. Hoffman, Ph.D.
Department of Psychology
Adelphi University

Manfred J. Holler, Ph.D.
Department of Economics
University of Munich

Jean Houston, Ph.D.
The Foundation for Mind Research
Pomona, New York

John C. Lilly, M.D.
Human Software, Inc.
Malibu, California

Salvatore R. Maddi, Ph.D.
Department of Behavioral Sciences
University of Chicago

Maria Malikiosi, Ed.D.
National Centre of Social Research
Athens, Greece

W. Edward Mann, Ph.D.
Department of Sociology
York University

Colin Martindale, Ph.D.
Department of Psychology
University of Maine

C. Raymond Millimet, Ph.D.
Department of Psychology
University of Nebraska at Omaha

Hiroshi Motoyama, Ph.D.
The Institute for Religious Psychology
Tokyo, Japan

Thomas Natsoulas, Ph.D.
Department of Psychology
University of California, Davis

Jordan Paper, Ph.D.
Department of Humanities
York University

Gordon Patterson, Ph.D.
Department of Humanities
Florida Institute of Technology

Kenneth R. Pelletier, Ph.D.
California Health and Medical Foundation
Oakland, California

Stanley S. Pliskoff, Ph.D.
Department of Psychology
University of Maine

Gerard A. Postiglione, Ph.D.
School of Education
University of Hong Kong

A.D. Potthoff, Ph.D.
Department of Psychology
University of California, Los Angeles

Sonia Ragir, Ph.D.
Department of Sociology and Anthropology
The College of Staten Island, CUNY

Naomi Remen, M.D.
The Humanistic Psychology Institute
San Francisco

Steven Rosen, Ph.D.
Department of Psychology
The College of Staten Island, CUNY

Ralph L. Rosnow, Ph.D.
Department of Psychology
Temple University

J. Michael Russell, Ph.D.
Department of Philosophy
California State University, Fullerton

Joseph F. Rychlak, Ph.D.
Department of Psychology
Loyola University of Chicago

Seymour B. Sarason, Ph.D.
Department of Psychology
Yale University

Gertrude Schmeidler, Ph.D.
Department of Psychology
The City College of New York

Virginia S. Sexton, Ph.D.
Department of Psychology
St. John's University

Samuel I. Shapiro, Ph.D.
Department of Psychology
University of Hawaii

Imad Shouery, Ph.D.
Department of Philosophy
Indiana State University

Laurence Smith, Ph.D.
Department of Psychology
University of Maine

Steve Soldinger, M.D.
Neuropsychiatric Institute
University of California, Los Angeles

William F. Stone, Ph.D.
Department of Psychology
University of Maine

Thomas S. Szasz, M.D.
Department of Psychiatry
Upstate Medical Center, Syracuse

Dorothy Tennov, Ph.D.
Department of Psychology
University of Bridgeport

Silvan S. Tomkins, Ph.D.
Emeritus Professor of Psychology
Rutgers University

Tom Trueb
Department of Social Sciences
Logansport State Hospital

Sheila A. Womack, Ph.D.
The Institute of Mind and Behavior, NYC

Robert C. Ziller, Ph.D.
Department of Psychology
University of Florida

European Distributor: Verlag Holler München, Gnesener Strasse 1, 8000 München 81, F. R. Germany
Counsel: Marc L. Bailin, Esq., Jacobson and Bailin, 575 Madison Avenue, New York City, New York 10022
Business Editor: Leslie Gross; *Cartoonist:* Stu Copans, M.D.; *Artistic Production:* Lindsay Roy
Communications Consultant: Roy D. Krantz; *International Desk:* Dwight Hines, Ph.D.

CONTENTS OF BACK ISSUES

Volume 1, Number 1, Spring 1980

Self-Determination Theory: When Mind Mediates Behavior. *Edward L. Deci and Richard M. Ryan, University of Rochester.*
Developmental Value of Fear of Death. *Salvatore R. Maddi, University of Chicago.*
How To Think About Thinking: A Preliminary Map. *J. Michael Russell, California State University, Fullerton.*
Concepts of Free Will in Modern Pychological Science. *Joseph F. Rychlak, Purdue University.*
Psychiatry and the Diminished American Capacity for Justice. *Thomas S. Szasz, Upstate Medical Center.*
Stress, Aging and Retirement. *Hans Selye, International Institute of Stress.*
The Social Psychology of J.F. Brown: Radical Field Theory. *William F. Stone, University of Maine, and Lorenz J. Finison, Wellesley College.*
Days of Our Lives. *Nancy Datan, West Virginia University.*
Theory and Method and Their Basis in Psychological Investigation. *Raymond C. Russ, University of Maryland, European Division, and Richard D. Schenkman, Dartmouth Medical School.*

Volume 1, Number 2, Autumn 1980

Cognitive Differentiation and Interpersonal Discomfort: An Integration Theory Approach. *C. Raymond Millimet and Monica Brien, University of Nebraska.*
The False Promise of Falsification. *Joseph F. Rychlak, Purdue University.*
Zeitgeist: The Development of an Operational Definition. *Bronwen Hyman, University of Toronto, and A.H. Shephard, University of Manitoba.*
A Personal Introductory History of Ethology. *Konrad Lorenz, Austrian Academy of Science.*
Figureheads of Psychology: Intergenerational Relations in Paradigm-Breaking Families. *Dean Rodeheaver, West Virginia University.*
The Myth of Operationism. *Thomas H. Leahey, Virginia Commonwealth University.*
Human Freedom and the Science of Psychology. *Wayne K. Andrew, The University of Winnipeg.*
"Unspeakable Atrocities": The Psycho-Sexual Etiology of Female Genital Mutilation. *Tobe Levin, University of Maryland, European Division.*
The Mind-Body Problem in Lawrence, Pepper, and Reich. *Arthur Efron, State University of New York at Buffalo.*
Myth and Personality. *Salvatore R. Maddi, University of Chicago.*

Volume 2, Number 1, Spring 1981

Intelligence, IQ, Public Opinion and Scientific Psychology. *Alfred H. Shephard, University of Manitoba.*
Psychology's Reliance on Linear Time: A Reformulation. *Brent D. Slife, Purdue University.*
A Behavioral Approach to Eliminate Self-Mutilative Behavior in a Lesch-Nyhan Patient. *Hilary P. Buzas and Teodoro Ayllon, Georgia State University, and Robert Collins, Georgia Institute of Technology.*
Toward a Reformulation of Editorial Policy. *C. Raymond Millimet, University of Nebraska.*
Gergen's Reappraisal of Experimentation in Social Psychology: A Critique. *Paul Cherulnik, The College of Charleston.*
The Growth and Limits of Recipe Knowledge. *Leigh S. Shaffer, West Chester State College.*
Sensation Seeking as a Determinant of Interpersonal Attraction Toward Similar and Dissimilar Others. *Billy Thornton, Richard M. Ryckman, and Joel A. Gold, University of Maine.*

Volume 2, Number 2, Summer 1981

Metatheoretical Issues in Cognitive Science. *John A. Teske, The Pennsylvania State University, and Roy D. Pea, Clark University.*
Theory-Tales and Paradigms. *H.L. Nieburg, State University of New York, Binghamton.*
On Animal Analogies to Human Behavior and the Biological Bases of Value Systems. *R.E. Lubow, Tel Aviv University.*
States of Consciousness: A Study of Soundtracks. *Felicitas D. Goodman, Emeritus Professor of Anthropology and Linguistics, Denison University.*